ROCK AND ROLL ALWAYS FORGETS

ROCK AND ROLL ALWAYS FORGETS

A QUARTER CENTURY OF MUSIC CRITICISM

CHUCK EDDY

Foreword by Chuck Klosterman

DUKE UNIVERSITY PRESS   DURHAM AND LONDON   2011

© 2011 Duke University Press
Foreword © 2011 Chuck Klosterman
All rights reserved
Printed in the United States
of America on acid-free paper ∞
Designed by Amy Ruth Buchanan
Typeset in Chaparral Pro
by Achorn International.
Library of Congress Cataloging-
in-Publication Data appear on the
last printed page of this book.

For Lalena and Annika

CONTENTS

8. *SINGLES AGAIN AND AGAIN*

Chuck Eddy likes more music than just about any person I've ever known, but the music he likes most makes him impossible to understand. If you want to understand Chuck Eddy for real, you need to focus on the music he hates. And this is not because his taste is irrefutable or because there's some sort of larger truth imbedded within his vitriol—it's because the music Chuck Eddy hates shows how his mind works.

Take a look at this list: 1. Björk; 2. DJ Spooky; 3. Robyn Hitchcock; 4. Iron Maiden; 5. Jodeci; 6. Korn; 7. My Bloody Valentine; 8. Notorious B.I.G.; 9. Pantera; 10. Henry Rollins.

These are the artists Eddy submitted (at some point in the mid-to-late 1990s) as "The Worst Music Ever," a list published in Philadelphia's *City Paper*. In many ways, the list encapsulates the mathematical superstructure of Eddy's cerebellum: we have one band that every critic loves, two acts that every critic pretends to love, a dead man critics are obligated to appreciate, two metal acts that most people don't take seriously (but that Chuck takes seriously enough to hate), one band that people might expect Chuck to support, a singer-songwriter nobody thinks about, the common-sense recognition of an obvious buffoon, and Jodeci. I do not doubt that if someone asked Eddy to make that list today, at least seven of the selections would be different. In fact, they all might be different. But I am certain the underlying Eddy ethos would remain: "All thoughts about music are valid, but most thoughts about music are backwards." Not *all* thoughts about music, but *most* thoughts about music (and certainly those thoughts coming from all the people who are supposed to know better). And it's not just that these thoughts are flawed—it's that the people thinking them know that they're flawed. They know they're promoting (or attacking) artists for reasons that have almost nothing to do with the music itself. When Chuck hears a pop song, it's like he is the first person who has ever heard it; he's certainly aware of what the rest of the world already wants to believe, but those pre-existing perceptions are never convincing to him. If anything, they push him in the opposite direction. They galvanize his darkest suspicions. Chuck Eddy is his own man, and sometimes he's the only man.

I will never forget the day in 1992 my friend Rex purchased *Stairway to Hell* at a B. Dalton in Grand Forks, N.D. Rex walked into my dorm room and said, "You gotta read this fucking book, man. Some crazy guy has ranked the 500 greatest metal albums of all time, and four of them are by Kix. And you know how many are by Mötley Crüe? None!"

This was a lot of information to absorb.

First of all, I could not believe that there would ever be a book that would mention Kix, unless it was a book about cereal. I also could not believe that any book celebrating Kix would somehow not celebrate Mötley Crüe, a group that struck me as superior in every possible way. But more than anything, I simply could not believe that there was a book about heavy metal, and that this book cost money and existed in stores, and that the adult writing this book seemed to think about Faster Pussycat and Rush in the same way I thought about them in my parents' basement. I disagreed with at least half of the author's opinions and I hated the sans serif font, but the writing style obliterated my skull—it felt like some brilliant weirdo was talking directly at me, yet with no regard whatsoever for how much I enjoyed the conversation. To this day, I've never found a nonfiction book with more voice-per-square-inch than *Stairway to Hell*. It was so funny. It was so maddening. It made no sense. Jimi Hendrix was boring? White Lion was a blues band? Black Sabbath was a jazz band? Poison's second record was better than *Houses Of The Holy*? How could someone with a real job like Poison more than I did? How could someone overrate Poison? And why did this writer seem to mock all the bands he was classifying as important? Moreover, why did he keep mentioning artists who had absolutely no relationship to heavy metal, most notably disco diva Teena Marie (whose *Emerald City* was ranked in the Top 10)?

The answer, as it turns out, was sleeping in the introduction: Teena Marie, Eddy argued, would be "accepted with open arms by all headbangers in the perfect universe of my imagination (which exists in metal's life span because I do!)" It took me years to understand what that sentence truly meant, but it's the premise behind everything meaningful Eddy creates (regardless of the genre or the performer). Very often, a person reading Chuck Eddy's work will conclude, "Oh, come on. No person could ever think that." But the fact that they're actively reading those (seemingly unbelievable) thoughts proves that such thinking exists. More than any other critic, Chuck Eddy showed how the experience of listening to music was both intellectually limitless and acutely personal. There was no "correct" way to hear a song, and there were no fixed parameters on how that song could be described in print, and if that song made you reconsider abortion or the Oakland Raiders or your father's suicide, then that intellectual relationship mattered (because your engagement was real). I didn't want to write like Chuck Eddy, but I wanted to think like him.

For most of the '90s, I wondered who Chuck Eddy was. I knew he was from Detroit and that he'd served in the army, but that was the extent of my tangible knowledge. He was a literary monolith in the zine world, but I didn't really read zines; he'd write reviews for *Spin* and insist that a certain guitar player sounded like what would have happened if Billy Duffy had liked Tony Iommi more than Jimmy Page, and I would spend two days trying to figure out if that was a compliment. I found an *Entertainment Weekly* review online where he gave the Pet Shop Boys' *Discography* an A and Mötley Crüe's *Decade Of Decadence* an A-minus, which partially contradicted his first book and somehow made me feel better. He wrote an essay about the sociopolitical brilliance of Michael Jackson's *Dangerous* that seemed ridiculous for 18 years, until it suddenly became prescient. I read his second book, *The Accidental Evolution of Rock'n'Roll*, but I think it just confused me. I bought a Status Quo album. I saw his picture in a magazine's contributors' page and was surprised he wore a hat.

To me, Chuck Eddy was way more famous than most of the bands he wrote about. I wondered if he was as sarcastic in person as he was in print. I wondered if he was happy with his life. I wondered if he named his kid Linus because he liked *Peanuts*. I wondered if he thought Oasis was cool. I wondered about a lot of things, which is what you do when something changes your life.

Just before I published *Fargo Rock City* in 2001, I contacted Eddy by e-mail, theoretically to convince him to blurb the cover but really because I wanted him to know that I knew that I never would have written my book if I hadn't come across *Stairway to Hell* first. Throughout the decade that's followed, we've usually sent each other one or two e-mails a year, usually for some semi-work-related matter. And because we have the same first name, he always signs his emails "The Other Chuck." That's his signature, and I'm sure he types it casually and without thinking. To him, it has no meaning. But it always makes me uncomfortable, because it's so totally wrong. He is not the Other Chuck. I am the Other Chuck. Only Chuck Eddy can be Chuck. He was the first Chuck and the better Chuck. And that will never change, even after all the kids that Kix was made for are deader than the diplodocus.

Top of the list, I have to thank Ken Wissoker, for backing this project and giving me the flexibility to pull it off; my wife, Lalena Fisher, for putting up with me while I did so; Robert Christgau, who was hugely instrumental in my making this questionable career choice to begin with; and Chuck Klosterman, for writing a foreword that made me blush.

Phil Dellio, Frank Kogan, and Richard Riegel provided some invaluable advice on what pieces to include when I first started brainstorming—not to mention Xeroxes of old writing and correspondence I hadn't seen for several years.

Here are some, but by no means all, of the editors who first published these pieces, often polishing them in the process: Doug Simmons, Eric Weisbard, Rob Harvilla, and Christgau (again) at the *Village Voice*; Dave DiMartino, Bill Holdship, and John Kordosh at *Creem*; Milo Miles at the *Boston Phoenix*; John Payne at *L.A. Weekly*; Nathan Brackett at *Rolling Stone*; Greg Boyd and Bill Reynolds at *Eye Weekly*; Jack Thompson at *Swellsville*; Andrew Palmer at *Where's The Snake*; Jeff Pike at *Tapeworm*; Kogan (again) at *Why Music Sucks*; Dellio (again) at *Radio On;* William Bloody Swygart at *Singles Jukebox*. Several pieces I've included were specifically reprinted with permission from the *Village Voice* and from CREEM Media, Inc. (And I should probably also mention here that a few of the pieces have been altered, very slightly, from their original published form for purposes of clarity and accuracy. Pretty sure you don't have much use for old record label mailing addresses from 1984, for instance.)

I've been stealing opinions outright from Metal Mike Saunders, Scott Seward, and George Smith for decades now. My kids—William, Cordelia, Sherman, and Annika—have taught me more since 1985, 1989, 1991, and 2008 than I'll ever hope to teach them. And I'd be remiss if I didn't thank these folks as well, just for jump-starting my thinking process and working as intellectual foils and/or plus-ones over the years: Charles Aaron, Don Allred, Kevin John Bozelka, Tom Breihan, Jon Caramanica, Nick Catucci,

Ed Christman, Hillary Chute, Joshua Clover, Jonathan Cohen, Chris Cook, Don Forst, Michael Freedberg, Christian Hoard, Edd Hurt, Steve Kiviat, Martina Kominiarek, Michaelangelo Matos, Rob Michaels, David Cooper Moore, Amy Phillips, Ann Powers, Mike Rubin, Rob Sheffield, Sara Sherr, Richard C. Walls, Chris Weingarten, Bill Werde, Mikael Wood, Scott Woods.

If I left you out, it doesn't mean I'm not thankful—it probably just means the Alzheimer's is settling in.

Here's the first thing: none of this happened on purpose. I never intended to be a music critic—much less somebody who'd make some semblance of a living at it for more than a quarter century. It just happened. I could just as well have been a paleontologist.

But somewhere around 1972, when I was 11 or 12—not long before my dad died, which was a couple years after my mom died, so call it therapy if you're so inclined—I started reading the sports pages. Or maybe it was a couple years before that; my childhood timeline is all screwed up in my head, and I do have fuzzy memories of reading headlines about "Reds" in the *Cincinnati Enquirer*, I guess it would've been, and thinking the article would concern Pete Rose but finding out it concerned Russians instead. (Is that even possible?) Anyway, my family left Ohio in 1970; if '72 is right, I would've been reading the *Detroit Free Press*, same paper I wound up delivering to 50 or so subscribers in North Potomac Green subdivision every morning before sunrise for a couple years, often tromping through two feet of virgin Michigan snow. I also regularly devoured the *Sporting News* and *Baseball Digest*. And somewhere in there, I decided I wanted to be a sportswriter. Despite, or maybe because of, being really bad at sports.

So I started keeping a little diary about baseball (other sports were just time-killers between the World Series and spring training), filing notes every night in a green hard-covered date book, which wound up in the garbage somewhere along the way. And when I started at West Bloomfield High School in the autumn of 1974, I signed up right away to work on the school newspaper, the *Spectrum*. My first article was about baseball cards, and I talked about how the Topps 1969 Aurelio Rodriguez card erroneously pictured the Angels' batboy instead, which I called an honest mistake since they were both Mexicans—in retrospect, a somewhat racially insensitive assertion. Eventually, I wound up reporting lots of other sports stories, mostly on our school teams, the Lakers, who wore green and white. For a couple years, I was even the "manager" for the junior varsity baseball team, basically a glorified way of saying "scorekeeper." And "batboy."

I took part in other extracurricular activities as well, mostly as a way of escaping my increasingly traumatic homelife. In the 1978 edition of the school's annual yearbook, *Exodus*, here's what's listed after my name: "Debate 1, 4; J.V. Soccer 2, 3; Gong Show 3; J.V. Baseball 1, 2 (Manager); Powderpuff Cheerleader 3; NHS 3, 4; Spectrum 2, 3, 4 (Editor-in-Chief) 3, (Feature Editor) 4; Talent Show 3 (Emcee) 3; Theatre Week 3."

At the *Spectrum* (inevitably derided as *The Rectum*, as best-selling author and my former three-years-older-than-me schoolmate John Grogan points out in *The Longest Trip Home*, his 2008 follow-up memoir to *Marley & Me*) I wound up covering all sorts of other school issues and more wide-ranging current events as well, writing features and editorials, plus satires for the April Fool's edition; in one piece, I recommended that, since the school had a "smoking area" for students who smoked, and since smoking by minors was illegal in Michigan, there should logically be a drinking area for students who drank and a murdering area for students who murdered as well. In another editorial, part of a point/counterpoint page, I took the side in favor of clubbing baby harp seals. (Seminal influence: *National Lampoon*'s 1964 school yearbook parody.) Through high school, I wrote only one article about music. It talked about how teens who were improperly disruptive at a Nugent/Aerosmith/Foghat bill at the Pontiac Silverdome were unrepresentative of our generally well-behaved generation. Why I would have cared about that issue, I have no idea. I was probably just trying to piss other students off.

Which is surprising, of course, because once I started writing about music for a living, I *never* tried to piss anybody off. Or maybe I did—that's for you to decide. Anyway, speeding the story up (you'll find more details later in the book): I graduated high school in 1978; got an Army ROTC scholarship to attend college; went to University of Detroit for a year; worked a couple summers covering local sports, zoning commissions, school boards, sewer disputes, and police reports for Waterford-based suburban weekly paper, the *Spinal Column*; transferred as a sophomore to University of Missouri–Columbia where I wrote for the weekly *Maneater* and daily *Missourian*, won the school's annual feature writing award, got my bachelor's in journalism in 1982, and started writing lots of music reviews then voting in the *Village Voice's* annual Pazz & Jop critics' poll; got married; entered the army as a second lieutenant; was assigned to West Germany; worked as a platoon leader in the 8th Signal Battalion in Bad Kreuznach and then as a communications-electronics staff officer for the 1/59 Air Defense Artillery Battalion in Mainz where I also ran a security vault loaded with secret cold war codes and hardware; spent weeks at a time sleeping in a tent on hilltops in the woods not far from the East German border; had a son; started writing for the *Village Voice*; got promoted to first lieutenant then captain; was assigned to Fort Knox, Kentucky, where I worked as a communications officer for the Armor School; ended my term of service with an honorable discharge; assumed I'd go back to reporting about sewers and high school baseball but instead wound up writing freelance pieces for *Rolling Stone* and *Entertainment Weekly* and most everywhere else that covered music; moved back to Michigan and then to Philadelphia; wrote two books; had two more kids; got divorced; was told by the *Village Voice* that they didn't want to print my writing anymore, making me persona non grata for a few years; moved to New York a few years later when the *Village Voice* hired me as music editor; did my dream job for seven years; got laid off along with just about every other editor at the paper when Village Voice Media merged with the Phoenix-based New Times chain; freelanced for a summer; was hired as a senior editor at *Billboard*, a job I kept for a year and a half and excelled at but which fried my brain to the point of insomnia and one middle-of-the-night collapse requiring hospitalization despite enjoying drinking beer with lots of my coworkers; got married again; returned to freelancing; had another baby; moved to Austin; put this book together.

During all that time, as I expect this collection will make clear, my musical tastes never stayed in one place long. Frequently my ideas were years ahead of the apparent critical consensus; almost always, they ran against the grain, though probably not as much as I've been given credit and/or chastised for. As might be expected for somebody who started writing about music only a couple months after he'd started listening to it, my earliest tastes as a critic were easily swayed by reading other critics—especially Robert Christgau, who first brought me to the *Voice* and whom I eventually wound up editing there. But before long, out of compulsion or boredom or obstinacy or mischief or just plain being born a thinking human being, I was making a point of questioning both my own assumptions and those of my peers and mentors, of being invited to sit at the table for grown-up rock critics but then flipping the table over. Biting the hands that feed me and making them wish they'd never seen me, as my rarely acknowledged early inspiration Elvis Costello put it.

So my tastes evolved—never in anything approaching a straight line, never anything like exclusively, but roughly—from mainstream alt through underground metal through underground alt through mainstream metal through mainstream pop through mainstream country, with periodic investigative stop-offs at avant jazz, Mexican rock, Latin freestyle, German industrial, Southern soul, and several subspecies of hip-hop and post-disco dance music, electronic and otherwise. Only once—for a couple years in the early '90s, when I was in my early 30s, an age when rock critics in general often start dogpaddling until they sink or swim again—did I feel like I was treading water. And now, alive for a half century, somehow weathering increasingly bleak and unlikely to recover rock-writing doldrums wherein fewer and fewer paying publications have any interest in publishing criticism that isn't phoned in, I can honestly say that I'm as excited about listening to music as I've ever been. Austin is an amazing mythical land of awesome $1 vinyl bins and garage sales and record conventions, and now that CDs are speedily approaching their historical end zone and college students who've only ever downloaded MP3s are suddenly all buying used turntables again, piling up on old vinyl somehow doesn't feel so anachronistic anymore. So between falling for new music by Collin Raye, Už Jsme Doma, Traband, Scooter, Ke$ha, Jace Everett, Flynnville Train, Luther Lackey, Bigg Robb, and This Moment In Black History, I'm falling for old music by Benny, D.C. Larue, Good Rats, Christ Child, Charlie Rich, Hank Thompson, the Delmore Brothers, the Mystics, the Headboys, Head East, Millie Jackson, Pebbles, Joe Tex, Andrae Crouch and the Disciples, Maze featuring Frankie Beverly, Fatback Band, Steve Gibbons Band, Willie Alexander and the Boom Boom Band, Kevin Coyne, Chris Rea, Tonio K, Yesterday & Today, Riot, Pat Travers, and Axe. Few of whom you'll find mentioned anywhere else in this book. Though if any generous publisher out there needs a record guide to awesome dollar-bin LPs nobody's ever heard of, please give me a call.

All of which is to say the wheel keeps turning, and where it stops next nobody knows. But to return to a late-nineteenth-century figure of speech that Bill James and/or Ted Kennedy hadn't yet redefined when the sport got me into this mess, this is all inside baseball. You want to hear about music, not just me, right? This book has plenty of both.

If you've written as much as I have, for as long as I have, you're bound to get some things right by chance alone. But rock criticism is not a particularly predictive genre, and trying to guess where music will go five or 10 or 20 years down the line is generally a fool's game. Robert Christgau used to do pretty well now and then in his *Village Voice* Pazz & Jop poll essays—predicting "New Wave disco" at the end of the 1978 one and then watching M's "Pop Muzik" and Ian Dury's "Hit Me With Your Rhythm Stick" battle it out for top single in the poll a year later, for instance—but just as often he seemed to be foretelling a devastating collapse of Western culture that never quite showed up, not entirely anyway. My own crystal-ball work has generally proven even less successful than his. But I've had my moments.

In early 1986, in perhaps the shortest review ever to lead off the *Voice* music section up to that point, I reviewed Aerosmith's *Done With Mirrors*—a very good album pretty much everybody else ignored, since at that point they'd been considered drugged-out toppling-off-the-stage has-beens plying an extinct musical style for years—and I talked about growing up surrounded by the band's music in the '70s, and about how songs like "Walk This Way" and "Lord Of The Thighs" were sort of rap music before rap music existed, and maybe an enterprising DJ should segue one of them into the (not yet famous) Beastie Boys' "She's On It" single sometime. Doug Simmons, a Boston boy like Steve Tyler and Joe Perry himself and the *Voice*'s music editor at the time, thought I was just being provocative and messing with readers' heads, and told me so. Which maybe I was, but he was clearly short on copy to fill his pages that week, so the lines stayed in, and apparently future Beastie producer and Columbia Records exec Rick Rubin read them—or at least writers bound for greater news-magazine glory such as John Leland later reported that Rubin did. But either way, a couple weeks later, press releases were definitely issued saying Rubin's charges Run-D.M.C. would cover "Walk This Way" on their next album. The song became a Top 5 hit and a bigger video, with Tyler and Perry symbolically busting through a wall to lend the rappers a hand. Which both set in motion a couple decades' worth of rap-metal (yep— all my fault!) and relaunched the now-sober Aerosmith's career; starting with their next album, *Permanent Vacation* in 1987, they wound up bigger-selling (albeit smaller-rocking) stars than they'd ever been in their initial '70s heyday. They still owe me, and so do Liv Tyler and Alicia Silverstone.

And here's a story I didn't piece together until 20 years after the fact, over beers in Austin with critic Kevin John Bozelka in early 2009. Writing about Sonic Youth's album *Sister* in the *Voice* in 1987, I smart-assedly called it "*Afterburner* to *Evol*'s *Eliminator*"—which is to say, a half-hearted Xerox of their previous album. I'm pretty sure nobody had ever compared Sonic Youth to ZZ Top before that. Over the years, as it turned out, *Sister* wound up being by far my favorite Sonic Youth album—just a lot of concise catchy songs that didn't drag, I guess. But what I somehow never noticed until Bozelka mentioned it to me decades later is that, in 1988, Sonic Youth wound up ending their next LP—*Daydream Nation*, Bozelka's favorite album of all time and probably the critic-consensus SY choice but one that I never fully connected with and that precipitated me never caring about another note of their subsequent music—with a song called "Eliminator Jr." Coincidence? Your call. (For what it's worth, Thurston Moore also put out a fanzine called *Killer* in the '80s in which he called me "Fuck Eddy." And he and Kim named their 1994-born daughter Coco not long after I'd written about my own 1989-born daughter Coco in the *Voice*. Not that I'm actually taking credit for the latter.)

Anyway, neither the Aerosmith nor Sonic Youth reviews show up in this book—while perhaps prescient, they just really don't read all that good. But I am including my 1983 Top 10 album list printed with the Pazz & Jop poll, in which I was probably the first critic ever to vote for a Sonic Youth album (namely *Confusion Is Sex*), and unquestionably the first one whose ballot-containing-Sonic-Youth was ever actually published. Though I'd previously voted in the poll in 1981 ("That's The Joint"!) and 1982 (um, Pere Ubu's *Song Of The Bailing Man* I think—actually, I never kept copies of those ballots), I'm pretty sure Christgau had no idea who I was. But in 1983, I augmented my ballot with an 11-page manifesto complaining about the state of rock criticism, declaring that everything interesting in music was already over, and mourning my having missed the whole boat. He printed a big chunk of it (the "Over and Out" piece that follows this intro) and quoted me in the opening paragraph of his own essay ("Chuck Eddy, the West Bloomfield, Michigan freelancer"—actually I was a U.S. Army officer in West Germany by then, but I little-white-lied on my ballot to circumvent potential anti-military bigotry; technically, since I wasn't actually reviewing records anymore like I had been in college, I wasn't even eligible to vote). Christgau also mentioned that my ballot had inspired him to "share [his] essay with the voters"; though Pazz & Jop dated back to 1974 (or 1971—it's complicated), he'd never done that before. But from then on, for the next 23 years until he and I were fired from the *Voice*, he included voter comments in the Pazz & Jop section. He also asked me to start writing for the paper; the first review I got paid for, of Bad Religion's *Into The Unknown*, ran a month or so later and shows up in this book's alternative rock section. The rest is history, or a sorry excuse for it.

And the rest of this section should be self-explanatory. But in case you're wondering: Rap music did turn into something more than a passing fad. Rock music from Seattle did indeed get really big on MTV and elsewhere for a few years there, after Skin Yard founding member Jack Endino produced early records by bands like Nirvana and Soundgarden and the Screaming Trees, though for some dumb reason people decided to call the sound he helped invent "grunge" (a genre name I and any number of other critics had been applying to loud dirty rock for years) rather than "bigfoot-rock." The Flaming Lips, whom I'm pretty sure I was the first writer ever to profile for a national publication, got more and more famous as they got more and more boring. Radiohead became the universally acclaimed Most Important Rock Band On The Planet for reasons that never made much sense to me. Acid house and techno irrevocably changed music around the Western world, except in the United States, yet dropped off my radar after I chronicled them in January 1989. The interweb altered how artists promoted themselves and how kids learned about new bands and so on. New Kids On The Block broke up. And if you want to get technical, as of this writing, World War III still hasn't happened yet.

OVER AND OUT

Chuck Eddy: X *More Fun In The New World* (Elektra) 22; **Blasters** *Non Fiction* (Slash/Warner Bros.) 19; **Was (Not Was)** *Born To Laugh At Tornadoes* (Geffen) 11; **Richard Thompson** *Hand Of Kindness* (Hannibal) 9; **Sonic Youth** *Confusion Is Sex* (Neutral) 8; **Al Green** *I'll Rise Again* (Myrrh) 8; **Nile Rodgers** *Adventures In The Land Of The Good Groove* (Mirage) 7; **Rolling Stones** *Undercover* (Rolling Stones) 6; **Divinyls** *Desperate* (Chrysalis) 5; **ESG** *Come Away* (99) 5.

How the fuck can you revolutionize an industry which has accepted Pere Ubu and Essential Logic and the Angry Samoans and Teenage Jesus and the Birthday Party? You can't. Nothing scares anybody anymore, nothing surprises anybody anymore, there's no such thing as a real mindfuck because people's minds have already been fucked with over and over and over again. I never realized it until now, but the Sex Pistols were the worst thing that ever happened to rock'n'roll—they demanded anarchy, and they got it. Anarchy means you can do whatever you want, and that's what everybody since the Sex Pistols has done. This has given us a surplus of interesting music, but it's also given us a situation in which you can't tell the artists from the poseurs. Sly Stone and the Dolls were able to make revolutionary music because, back then, there were dictated limits on what you could or couldn't do, and they did what they "couldn't." Now there are no such limits—what if Sly and the Dolls had waited until 1983, and everything else (the Ramones, the Pistols, PiL, Prince, and all) between 1970 and now had happened without them? Would Greil Marcus still be able to write that "there is no vocal music in rock to match" *Riot*, or that "nothing short of the Sex Pistols' singles has touched it"? I doubt it.

And yet, the rock critics of the world are going to spend their time voting on which 1983 videos were the most fun to watch. And we're going to accept Prince, or Grandmaster Flash, or King Sunny Adé, or Flipper, or Big Country, or Bob Fucking Dylan, or (see my Top 10) X, and we're gonna push whatever we like as the bearer of the future of rock'n'roll, as if there is such a thing. I think this is kind of what Lester Bangs meant by the "be the first one on your block" attitude; unfortunately, he died before he could offer any kind of solution or alternative, except that we should listen to old John Lee Hooker records. I wish I had a solution, and God and Lester know I need one more than the Christgaus and Marcuses of this world do—I just turned 23 a month or so ago, and I only started to listen to music "seriously" in 1979, and I haven't seen a real rock'n'roll revolution yet, and I want a *There's A Riot Goin' On* or a New York Dolls or a Johnny Rotten so bad I could shit. But I'm not going to get one.

What I'll probably get is World War III, and then we'll start all over again, and if I'm lucky and if I cut down on my salt intake I might live to see Prehistoric Ring Shouts II when I'm an old old man. And ring shouts will lead to spirituals and field hollers, and the Delta Blues and Appalachian banjo music and Western Swing will happen in there somewhere, and then yet another Elvis, and maybe I'll be able to see the next New York Dolls or Sly Stone when I'm in heaven. Great hope for the future of rock'n'roll, right? I mean, I might not even make it to heaven. Fuck you, Johnny Rotten.

Village Voice, 28 February 1984

RHYMED FUNK HITS AREA

Jerry Hand isn't modest. Sometimes in midsentence, he'll begin tinkling the piano keys in front of him and break into a song about himself.

"I'm not Sugarman or Discotron, and this I'm sure you know . . ." chants the Columbia College music and business major who performs as rap disc jockey DJ Romancer. "But I'm DJ Romancer and I always steal the show/I've got the super action, dynamite attraction/Coming straight to you/Yes, I'm number one and I'm having fun/No, baby, not number two/You just open up your mind, and you check me out, and I'm sure, you'll all agree/That I'm the baddest dee-jay there ever was, and the baddest there'll ever be."

Hand's ego is a valuable commodity among rap disc jockeys. But there's more than mere self-confidence behind his boasts. The transplanted Queens, N.Y., native is the most accomplished rap singer in Columbia—he, of course, claims there's none better west of the Mississippi.

He even fares well against the big competition in New York, the birthplace of rap and still the genre's hotbed. Hand may not have won the "Great M.C. Showdown" in Harlem this past August, but he says he got the most applause.

That's quite a claim, considering the contest featured such acts as Kurtis Blow, Grandmaster Flash and the Furious Five, Funky Four Plus One, and DJ Hollywood. They may not be household names in mid-Missouri music circles, but in the rap world they're stars.

Most radio listeners are familiar with rap music, though few could define it. The rock group Blondie scored a major hit early this year with a rap song—but Hand is quick to point out that rap is much more than "Rapture."

Walter Anderson, the KOPN disc jockey who calls himself "the Sugarman" and hosts Columbia's only radio show featuring current soul music, explains that rap is merely rhymed couplets set to a syncopated funk rhythm. "It works almost like a cadence," he says.

The form dates back 30 years to black New York radio DJs who boasted about their prowess against a backdrop of the day's hits, Anderson says. At the same time, Jamaican disc jockeys developed a similar form called "toasting." Their delivery was slow and the words didn't always rhyme, but Hand says they set the pattern for today's rap.

Anderson and Hand agree that it wasn't until late 1979 that the majority of Americans—black, as well as white—even heard of rapping. In September of that year, a Harlem trio called the Sugarhill Gang released its first single, "Rapper's Delight."

"The Adventures Of Grandmaster Flash On The Wheels Of Steel," which was given an almost unprecedented, five-star rating this fall in *Rolling Stone*, represents an apex of sorts in the rap technique known as "cut mixing," Hand says. Cut mixing is a process in which bits and pieces of hits ("Good Times," "Rapture," Queen's "Another One Bites The Dust") are doctored, then spliced into one song.

Hand says "mixing" also refers to various ways rap disc jockeys alter the records they play. For example, a song might be phased out halfway through and another phased in. Or instrumental and vocal versions of the same song might be played concurrently, as the DJ alternates between two turntables. Or a single line from one record might be "injected" into another song.

When talking about his own mixes, Hand refers to qualities such as key and pitch and beats per minute. You can't just mix anything with anything, he explains.

But that doesn't mean a disc jockey can't experiment with sound, even going so far as to push a needle across a record. "Sometimes a disturbance to the ear is preferable," Hand says. "If you mix it right, you can get people dancing to just about anything."

At a typical rap show, he says, the disc jockey stands on a platform above the crowd, while the rappers (called "emcees") perform on a nightclub stage. When he works with his partner Bucky T., Hand is emcee. But he sometimes performs alone with a tape of his own mixes.

Some famous rappers sing their hits, but the best think up rhymes on the spot, says Hand. Impromptu rapping isn't as difficult as it sounds, he adds. "After a while, you can rhyme just about anything."

It can get a little monotonous after a while, Anderson admits. He says he has considered devoting an entire Saturday radio show to rap records. "But I couldn't take three hours of thump-thump-thump," he says.

The rap audience consists mainly of 13- to 18-year-old black "teenyboppers," Hand says. Many older people like the music as well, but they'd hesitate to attend a concert including only rap songs.

But that doesn't mean rap is a passing fad. "Everytime it looks like it's going to die, somebody comes up with something new," says Anderson.

When Hand first rapped in Columbia, way back in 1978, "Rapper's Delight" hadn't even hit yet, he says, and the rap sound wasn't familiar to most Missouri ears. He remembers that dancers came up to him and said, "I don't know what this is, but I like it."

If Hand decides to perform in Columbia again, his audience will at least be familiar with the rap form. Though his own tastes run closer to classical music and jazz, he sees relevance in what he's doing.

"You can tell rap is an art just by listening to it," he says. "It's so creative it's a shame."

Missourian, 1981

SKIN YARD: *SKIN YARD*

Sometime in the not-so-distant future (after all the music in question has turned into manure, no doubt) you're gonna switch on MTV and hear all this hype about how the not-so-distant future of hard rock lies in the Northwest. Last year, I purchased the debut album and follow-up single by the

Seattle band Green River, along with this compilation called *Deep Six* that had Green River plus lots of fellow Seattlites (the Melvins, Malfunkshun, Skin Yard, Soundgarden, U-men), and what I found was a locale festering with an inexhaustible number of vulgar avant-garage guitar-groups. And the place had even developed an identifiable sound of sorts—an approximate description might be Sabbath/Stooges-style sludge sifted through the animalistic AOR of Aerosmith and Angel City. With significant others such as Metal Church and the Wipers and Rancid Vat calling this remote region home, what we've got here is the making of muck-megalopolis on the level of Michigan '69. Not long ago, I figured Oregon and Washington housed only vegetarians and bearded women and Rajneesh-worshipers and neo-Nazi survivalist loonies, but it looks like bigfoot-rock has taken over.

Old-timers have probably already noted what's doubly cool about this phenomenon, namely that the Pacific Northwest is kinda sorta where hard rock was forged in the first place, initially with raw late '50s instrumental ensembles like the Wailers (of "Tall Cool One" fame), and later with mid-'60s protopunk jumbos such as the Kingsmen and the Sonics and Paul Revere & The Raiders, the last of whom wore funny suits on stage. Don't know if it's a reference to the old days, but on the back cover of Skin Yard's first album (the best record I've heard so far from the new Northwest explosion), the singer is on stage wearing what appears to be a funny mask! Skin Yard doesn't sound anything like Paul Revere's combo, though—they're a bit more arty, to say the least.

Which ain't to say these four gents don't flaunt their pretensions here and there. Ben McMillan (who also honks a mean skronk-jazz saxophone) is one of those unnatural ultra-proper vocalmen who phrase every single syllable just right (like maybe Peter Hammill or John Cale or Bono Vox, though I'm not sure those are the best examples). He's got a phony aristoBrit accent, and his morose monologues are mannered enough to gag a maggot-farm: "Somewhere, a son is sitting in a room alone, and his father comes in and gives him a gun and a book of rules entitled *This Is The Real World*." And Skin Yard's fracas can get a little dirgey or a little shapeless or a little indirect sometimes, too. But mostly it jolts in a big way; I can put up with baloney about slaying dragons when the headbang is as severe and as heterogeneous as it is here. I can't wait to hear Skin Yard's version of "Louie Louie," though.

Creem Metal, 1986

DRUG CRAZED TEENS: FLAMING LIPS

The Flaming Lips would probably not be the best spokesmen for our president's War on Drugs. This trio of Okies plays the trippiest bron-y-aur stomp yet to emerge from the lava-lamp pits of post-p-rock muck: 99th-floor-thick fuzz riffs, dead-sea-scroll basslines, cans slapped like a bustle in your hedgerow, all truckin' through static time 'n' space amidst recited yin-yang, such as: "When I walk with you, I feel weird/When I talk with you, I feel weird . . . All I know/Is my mind is blown/When I'm with you."

"It wasn't so much that we wanted to be psychedelic," says singer/guitarist Wayne Coyne. "We just wanted to play Led Zep–type stuff and then play echo and play weird." Countering the massive lysergic onslaught of last year's self-released debut *Flaming Lips* EP, the threesome deliberately downplays its six-oh reference points on its new *Hear It Is* album. Nowadays, Coyne denies the "psychedelic" tag entirely. "We're more what you would call acid rock. It's like biting your teeth together and going 'Shit!' That's drug music. Plasticland is like clothes music."

Coyne can't quantify to what extent hallucinogens actually shape the Flaming Lips sound. He's more or less a teetotaller when it comes to that stuff, he says, and though drumboy Richard English and bassboy Mike Ivins have been known to indulge, they avoid heavy dope use during band work. Coyne does admit, though, that his tastes were largely molded by his "totally-wigged-out-on-drugs" older brothers' record collections. The Flaming Lips do a 20-minute *Tommy* medley live. They also cover Zeppelin's "Communication Breakdown" back-to-back with Sonic Youth's "Death Valley '69."

In fact, *Hear It Is* seems to bear a fairly striking Sonic Youth structured-nihilist-clamor influence, especially in songs like: "She Is Death," "Jesus Shooting Heroin," and "Charlie Manson Blues." But Wayne says any resemblance is merely coincidental; he discusses "Jesus Shooting Heroin" as a study in good and evil and says the Manson tune is about how "everybody could be capable of wanting to thrash somebody just to see what it was like, which seemed like a real cool thing to examine." Besides, he says, Sonic Youth are "real wimps who can't get away from doing things that they know people are gonna like." He also says Henry Rollins "is getting fat," Pussy Galore "is, like, the worst band," and that the guy from Dr. Hook who wears the patch over his eye (who the Lips saw shooting pool in Nash-ville) "was drunk off his ass, and he's stupid."

Speaking of billiards, Coyne admits the light-socket-haired Flaming Lips aren't the best pink-sinkers, "but we play so we can look tough, and we don't let the balls go in the holes, and we scratch a lot, because that makes the game last longer. You get more for your quarter that way." If you don't yearn for mind-burnt meaning-of-life declamations from some-body with that kind of flawless logic, I'd venture you just ain't an inquiring mind.

Spin, December 1986

MUSIC THAT PASSES THE ACID TEST

In England, the strident squall of acid house has united a bevy of fickle fandom factions, taken charts and tabloids by storm, and become a hal-lucinogenic experience identified by a what-me-worry smiley face. Yet this is no cabaret, old chum. These impatient pulsations and unnerving combustions are an antisocial irritant, a negation, a soundtrack for falling through Western society's cracks at a time when the fall's easier than ever. At its nastiest, acid house is Staggerlee 1989, and its apparent pop poten-tial only makes the venom more intriguing.

"Chicago/The streets are mean/This ain't no joke/It'll make you choke," an enigmatic man named Mr. Lee shouts in "Pump Up Chicago," reviv-ing horn-section R&B as a grating computer groove space jam. He divides the urban desolation into sectors of fire, takes on London and NYC in al-ternate versions. You picture a six-foot ex-linebacker who claims he's the parking-lot attendant, and you give him 10 bucks so he won't heist your tapedeck.

Recurrent stutter-syncopation peers back at Run-D.M.C.'s "It's like That," Public Image's "Poptones," and Sly Stone's "Thank You for Talkin' to Me Africa," summoning a stark, deadening stasis where evil's always waiting to strike, to catch you off-guard just as the digital distortion de-tours. No quarter's given to retro-notions of sophistication or class, even to the respectable just-say-no and don't-drop-out niceties that castrate so much recent rap. The audience isn't comforted; often, it gets what it doesn't want.

"Art Of Acid," Mr. Lee's cut on *Acid Trax Volume 2*, runs a heart murmur from Art Of Noise's '83 crossover "Beat Box" through the salad shooter, and stomps on it. Bargain basement down to its plain white sleeve, the compilation is raw, unyielding outta-my-way music. Hula's "Hot Hands" devours you with electronic loops, then turns swirls into peachfuzz, returning to its original motif just as your speakers start spitting. His "70th And King Drive" does more of the same, sneakier and more hesitant, with timbales for counter-rhythm. In "Box Energy," DJ Pierre squeezes out a fingers-on-chalkboard boom-chucka at some tortuous frequency that keeps climbing in pitch, setting tooth enamel on edge. I'm reminded of those new Black & Decker commercials in which you win a prize if you guess which power tool is making a particular kerrang.

In avant-garde rock, attempts at noise disruption are so old hat they no longer disrupt, but in dancing-in-the-streets genres, they're a shock. R&B has relied on applied science, more on rhythm and less on blues, ever since soul became disco in early '70s (if not since T-Bone Walker plugged in his six-string in the '30s), but the barrage that emerged from Chicago in 1987 (initially with Phuture's "Acid Tracks") obliterated song and sense with machines: Lacking volcanic climaxes or overbearing divas, acid house was at first radically more knotted and desolate than house proper, but by now the forms have been blurred into a continuum. Brit DJs mixed in Mediterranean modulations for something they call "Balearic beat," Prince and the Pet Shop Boys picked up the ball and ran the wrong way, art-schoolers reduced ingenuity into a self-important hoax. By the time the majors catch on, there might be nothing left.

Which is not at all true today. Phuture's latest experiment, "We Are the Phuture"/"Slam!"/"Spank-Spank," is background music that refuses to stay in the background, arrogant laser-zooms thickening into a dark, viscous gel as skeletal kickdrums push through wormholes that grind their conflicting gears against each other. (Think of Sun Ra's cosmos-explorations, and William Burroughs's assertion that you could kick off a riot with a couple tape recorders.) On the A-side, this monotonal roar vows to "own your body and soul"; on the busier B-side, gymnastic oildrum-like beats alley-oop between Phuture's legs, around his back two times, through the hoop, into a conga line. No notes or melody, really, but if you're expecting this to be "cold," you might get burned.

Unless the singles are as proud as Phuture's, which few are, it's probably smartest to observe the evolving-idiom rule of thumb and investigate acid on anthologies. A pile of them have reached these shores (if only a few hundred at a time) through import channels. (Once again, limey ears-to-the-ground hear a new Yank sound and sell it back.)

In good acid house, slices of echo interlock like an elastic puzzle, and no matter how relentlessly the bass-drum four beat clashes with the blue-light boogie-woogie additives, they don't dissolve into mere hissing hypnotics. The voices can flow disengaged from the rhythm, lag way behind, ascend with Sylvester-style intensity or descend through vocoders and octave multiplers, but mainly we've got to know these are breathing, yearning, loathing, midnight-rambling human beings, not Gobots or Transformers. It's a tough trick, but the six acts on *In The Key Of E* (Desire, import), a dense dance hall of a collection comparable to Jamaica's dreadest dub, pull it off.

Adonis's three contributions are layered blocks of clutter that stay celestial, with ecstatic heaven-and-earth sighs rising above and eerie mullahs winding through, "hurting for the lack of love." Fingers Inc. antagonizes green-world pastorality with an incessant bassline and a harsh but horny parson rasping Biblical quotes. Both Bam Bam and Count Bass-E conjure the surreal grits-and-grind feel of Westbound-era Funkadelic's most indulgent throwdowns, sloppy suede singing opposing orchestral strings, disorienting stop-and-surge guitars, battalions of drum slaps, and sax work that harks back to the chitlin circuit. Bam Bam's "Where's Your Child" is scariest: Atop the slowest, sparest throb, gongs clank, babies scream, and this deep, electronically slowed vocal—half satyr, half Satan—groans "No one likes to be left alone/Especially when they don't know right from wrong." He starts laughing and cackling, but nothing's funny.

"Where's Your Child" could be an anthem in Detroit, where the crack a trade guns down black teens as a matter of course. But the seemingly war-torn town's warehouses have already spawned their own, even more transistorized, acid branch; it's called. "Detroit techno" in the disco biz, "Robocop pop" by me. Some, like Blake Baxter's full-throttle pillow fight "When We Used to Play," point toward Ted Riley's melodic stable of chart-topping Nerf-funk new-jacks; such is the case with Inner City's "Big Fun," an upbeat-yet-disconcerting quasi-tribal shuffle with a flighty doo-wop whimper disappearing behind a curtain of steely bass and stately piano. "Big Fun" sold big in Britain and, thanks to its big-label support, could break out here.

But the inner-city blues that most make me wanna holler come from fellow Motowner Derrick May, a/k/a Rhythim is Rhythim, whose angri-fying Spanglish-percussed turntable symphony "Strings Of Life" jumbles brittle keys of ivory with hair-trigger agility and a deceptive logic that sug-gest the daunting note patterns of Cecil Taylor. If elegance this angular can make it in supposedly lowbrow clubland, just wait till May realizes his stated goal and starts scoring movies. You'll see me waiting in line, nervous but smiling.

Boston Phoenix, 20 January 1989

NEW KIDS IN THE '90S: A DECADE IN THE LIFE

1990. March: Donnie Wahlberg is quoted in the *New York Times* as say-ing, "Every white person in America should read *The Autobiography of Mal-colm X*." The FBI immediately initiates a highly controversial Wahlberg file. **June:** Columbia releases *Step By Step*, which includes a good Beatles pas-tiche, a good Stylistics imitation, and one good rap. **September:** A fifth al-bum is released, untitled save for five pagan runes said to signify "the cute one" (Joey), "the smart one" (Donnie), "the banana-nosed one" (Danny), "the preppy one" (Jon), and "the preppy one's brother who often catches the flu" (Jordan). Amid false rumors of black magic, shark-meat orgies, and a particularly vicious assertion that NKOTB actually stands for New Kids on the Throne of Beelzebub, *NODOZ* (as the album is often referred to by the press) quickly becomes the best-selling LP in the history of the record industry.

1991. January: *NODOZ* places 41st in *Village Voice* Pazz & Jop critics' poll. Several well-meaning voters boycott because NKOTB once recorded "White Christmas." **July:** Directed by Spike Lee and featuring an all-black cast except for the New Kids, the blaxploitation spoof *Hard Day's Nike* opens to near-unanimous critical and popular acclaim. Though the movie receives no best picture nominations, Redd Foxx is awarded a best sup-porting actor Oscar for his portrayal of Donnie's adopted grandfather.

1992. October: New Kids make what will be their final concert appearance. Donnie meets Naoko Yamano, who sings and plays guitar for the Japanese bubble-punk band Shonen Knife. **December:** Media Age of Afrocentrism, White Milk, and Safe Sex in the Streets begins.

1993. May: New Kids release *Robert Mapplethorpe's Lonely Art Schtup Banned*, an agitprop kiddie-rap opera dedicated to the tax funding of dirty pictures. Comparisons to Bertolt Brecht abound, as do violins. "We are bigger than 'Piss Christ,'" Joey declares. Nobody argues. **August:** Citing creative differences, NKOTB fires Maurice Starr and changes its name to the more adult People in Your Neighborhood. *Sesame Street* sues for copyright infringement, to no avail.

1994. May: Donnie weds Naoko, who seeks sixth New Kid status. **June:** People in Your Neighborhood records roots CD in order to regain fleeting *esprit de corps*; *People In Your Neighborhood* (The Black Album) is released instead but stalls at No. 78 on the charts. **July:** Donnie forms Plastic Bono Band with Naoko; releases include "Give Peas A Chance," "Pride In The Name Of Lunch," "Baby's Heartbeat—It's A Lovebeat," and *Like Two Virgins* (produced by Madonna).

1995. February: Joey releases a self-indulgent solo LP of silly love songs; in the press kit, he calls Donnie a "pretentious creep." **April:** Joey quits the band. **May:** The roots CD (now called *Dorchester Calling*) is released. **June:** Joey sues to dissolve PIYN.

1996. Greil Marcus publishes *I Want You Back: Images of Situationist Struggle and Turn-of-the-Century Art Movements in Kiddie-Rap Music*, likening "I'll Be Loving You Forever" to select novels by Henry James and Nathaniel Hawthorne. Albert Goldman publishes *One Bad Apple: How Donnie Wahlberg Spoiled the Whole Bunch*. Dave Marsh publishes *Hangin' Tough*, about the tribulations of growing up blue-collar in the Reagan years.

1996–2000. New Kids pursue solo careers: Joey gets the biggest hits; Donnie gets the best reviews. Danny buys the Red Sox and moves the team to Bangladesh. The Knights marry the Judds.

Request, **September 1990**

RADIOHEAD: *THE BENDS*

This is one of those follow-up albums (like the last Spin Doctors one and, I fear, the next Counting Crows, the Offspring, and Blur records) that I always hope will sound like ten imitations of the one or two great hits of the band's not-so-great previous commercial-breakthrough LP, but instead just proves the band is afraid to be pigeonholed into the only style it's very good at.

Radiohead's breakthrough hit was "Creep," which at first I dismissed as a wussy David Bowie cabaret ballad with corny Jesus and Mary Chain lawnmower guitar snags stuck in there. But eventually I fell in love because I'm a creep and a weirdo who wonders what the hell I'm doing here myself, plus the lawnmowers really did snag me, and the falsetto part was heaven. Radiohead singing "I want you to notice when I'm not around" was even better than creepy weirdo Michael Jackson singing "You won't be laughing girl when I'm not around" in "Give In To Me" (my *second*-favorite song of 1993), and both lines felt like suicide.

The Bends is never "Creep"-like enough, but "My Iron Lung" (a late Beatles pastiche with surprise noise) and "Just" (which seems to swipe powerchords from "Smells Like Nirvana" by Weird Al Yankovic) come close. There's more nice guitar gush (e.g. the sub-Tom-Scholz anthemic stairclimb of "Black Star"), but the rest of the album mostly reminds me of Suede trying to rock like Sparks but coming out like U2, or (more often) that hissy little pissant in Smashing Pumpkins passive-aggressively inspiring me to clobber him with my copy of *The Grand Illusion* by Styx. Too much nodded-out nonsense mumble, not enough concrete emotion.

Spin, 1995

WALKING INTO SPIDERWEBS: THE ULTIMATE BAND LIST

Back in my word processor days, only a year ago, I assumed the whole computer thing was a pernicious divisive plot, significant mainly in how it separated folks who had modems from folks who didn't. But now that I'm an e-mail and online junkie, I'm eating my prejudices. The Ultimate Band List at its best strikes me as a *social* tool, a cool new way to connect with other people. Locate the elaborate Web page dedicated to French disco chantoozy Mylene Farmer, and you get passionate stories of Internet pen pals from all over Europe convening to swap imports, attend a concert together, then catch a sad bus ride home: "The other passengers (normal tourists who don't know nothing about Mylene) were talking about Versailles, Paris by night . . . and I increased the volume on my Walkman."

Reduced to endlessly anal collector-geek cataloguing of B-side fetishes, such obsessiveness can feel neurotic. But it can also feel hilarious. A letter called, no kidding, "Camel Long May They Continue" has some nut detailing his Camel collection and how many times he's seen said obscure '70s prog group live, proving his loyal devotion to the ridiculous. If he were truly solipsistic, he wouldn't be sharing his hobby with us. I get off on the surprise in fans' voices upon learning that they're not *alone*. "Wow, technology is great!" writes a Tiffany fan. But he's still not quite satisfied: "Why doesn't she email a little message to say 'hello'? Maybe there are too many Tiffany stalkers out there (hint, hint . . . thanks a lot)."

Okay, maybe that one's a little creepy. But stars are, by definition, objects of desire. "Feast your eyes on the glory that is Timothy B.!!! :-)." (Schmit, that is; three delectable head shots.) An article entitled "why girls love Girls Against Boys" conducts a survey: "Scott has one of the most notable necks in rock and roll. . . . He looks like a slick Italian hood-kid and a prince." Gina G, not unlike Atari Teenage Riot, had a Web page even before having an album to sell. The Gina G Experience lets you choose between "Samples: Forgotten what she sounds like?" and "Images: After all, she is very pretty." Click the latter, you get the Gina G Picture Postcard Gallery: "Gina looking sultry," "Gina looking cheesy," "Gina showing a bit of body." (Oooh, ahh, *just* a little bit, sad to say.)

The ultimate Ultimate Band List objective is to prove you've had actual contact with the band: "I met Local H TWICE!!!" Your handwritten note from Bananarama, even your dream where the Fall's Mark E. Smith beats up his Tibetan drummer—anything's fair game. Webpagers yearn to connect with their fantasy figures as real people, then impart inside info: "Ricky dresses the weirdest to me, and I'm weird so I love it . . . carries his arrows around in a fox pouch that hangs over his shoulder. How tits is that?" (From Black Oak Arkansas page, reprinted from *Circus* magazine in 1975—hey, I'm not saying the Internet *invented* this kind of fantalk. How tits would that be?) Almost everybody on Failure's website brags about getting high with the band backstage: "Greg seemed very intelligent using words i had to look up when I got home." (A shame Greg's not in Bad Religion, whose site actually has its own dictionary: "Herein lies most of the big words found in the lyrics of every Bad Religion song." Sounds like a parody, but it's not: *aberration, absolve, abstain, accolade* . . .)

Slick press-releasey sites laid down by record companies are never as fun as fans' own creations, which can be self-effacing about their amateurism ("I couldn't figure out the lineup changes, and if I could, I probably couldn't fit it in a decent sentence," Martin Mathis confesses on his page on Australian hard rock gods Angel City) and shameless in their enthusiasm. Turn to the Pat Benatar Addict Support Page, and a box flashes before your screen: "WARNING: Dangerously low Benatar levels detected! Installing BenaWare for proper enjoyment. One moment." Then you get to "name that Benatune"!

I love all the blatant editorial hyperbole. "This page is dedicated to perhaps the most prescient band ever . . . Well, did video kill the radio star, or what?" (which introduces the confusingly titled "Not Complete Discography of the Buggles," full of cryptic compliments like "It's used strange rhythm skilfully"). The Jane Child page consists of reams of e-notes, all swearing the Canadian singer was ahead of her time. "Do you find it slightly amusing that *everyone* has a nose ring, now?" one asks. Another: "It is so obvious that the success of Alanis Morissette, Joan Osborne, PJ Harvey, and Ruby is relevant to Jane Child's alternative style." Most rock critics would be scared to suggest such comparisons, or to devise, as somebody somehow found time to, a meticulously calibrated 10-point rating system dissecting every last tune poodle-metallers Britny Fox ever recorded: "Let's face it 'Stevie' is a *boy's* name, not a girl's name. Even though the song could be awesome, I just can't get over that name thing." (Good thing he's not reviewing Fleetwood Mac.)

Tiffany's site has a file called "In the Trash" into which "people who really need to get a life" can submit "nasty, hostile or obscene comments." The *only* comment posted so far on Nada Surf's bulletin board snipes: "Is this the band with the idiotic cheerleaders and jocks in a video? Man, that was gay." And now that their hit "Stuck On You" has been swallowed by the "braindead mainstream," all the midnight tokers on Failure's page are worried about "screeching girls" and "alternative sluts," not to mention TV star Margaret Cho's crush on the lead singer. If we're lucky, it'll explode into a full-blown culture war.

There's a sense of involvement here, an excitement, a commitment to how people really talk. In the fleeting space of cyber, nobody cares much for punctuation or spelling. Grammatical errors and run-on phrases make UBL writing gyrate like some hyperactive new dance step. The Web being worldwide, there's no lack of English-as-foreign-language twistedness about Boney M, say, or Einstürzende Neubauten—"Very first website in French about this sound makers out of Germany." *Anybody* can be a critic here, and there's something equally democratic in how the list itself reduces every musical act from local bar bands hyping homemade hackery to

Johann Sebastian Bach to the same level, one line item each. Cypress Hill, for some reason, are filed under "W." Maybe they picked their UBL spot the same day they ordered that classical orchestra for Homerpalooza.

Village Voice, 25 March 1997

TALKING WORLD WAR III BLUES

After squinting from my Park Slope rooftop as the smoke blew into Brooklyn last Tuesday, sneezing through the ashes dusting cars even that far south, staring choked-up and bleary-eyed at the atrocity exhibition on CNN for most of the afternoon and night, wondering if my family and friends back in the heartland would connect to all this more if it hadn't happened in a city they mainly know from disaster movies, I found myself relieved again that the army no longer lists my onetime Signal Corps Captainhood on their reserve rolls. In the 24 hours following the destruction, a line about mushroom clouds from the grief-ridden song "Shattered Within" by ambient Finnish metal band Amorphis kept repeating inside my head, and the only music that made any sense when I put it on was other desolate enveloping doomsday metal like Neurosis and My Dying Bride, funereally moaned and codeine-tempoed and devoid of shape or reason—just blank nuclear-winter mood, no personality to get in the way since there was too much to think about already. And I didn't play it loud.

Wednesday morning, the eerily paper-strewn and sparsely populated Armageddon blocks between the Prince Street subway stop and Astor Place reminded me for the first time ever of Detroit, in the wee hours after Devil's Night maybe. In my e-mailbox: a long letter from Iranian-born former *Voice* intern Sanaz Mozafarian, about her hearing that Arab Americans were already being harassed in public, about cars near Wall Street with "Revenge Is the Only Answer" scrawled into the soot on their hoods, about how trying to reach the financial district's ground zero from her midtown morning dance class after Tuesday's explosions had reminded Sanaz of braving Seattle's "no protest zone" in December of 1999. Spinning in the background was a newly arrived *Best Of Randy Newman* CD I put on just to drown out whatever, and the song that goes "They don't respect us, so let's surprise 'em, let's drop the big one and pulverize 'em" gave me shivers.

Back in oddly sunny Brooklyn later that day, friends and I walked up to Methodist Hospital to offer blood donations, and on the way back stopped at a five-dollar rack, where we found a tank top with the twin towers on the front, surrounded by fireworks and the word "Celebrate!" (On Saturday, I walked by the same store, and "We Are The World" was blaring through its doors.) Wednesday night I had a beer with *Blender* fact checker Gabe Soria, who said he'd turned to Al Green's *I'm Still In Love With You* the night before to reassure himself there was still something good and beautiful and unassailable in the world. I wished I had a taste for spiritual redemption myself.

And though once in a while as the week wore on my internal soundtrack would reach for "Rivers Of Babylon"—damn right we remember Zion—more often, especially while devouring the *Times*, I was hearing the Clash's "Washington Bullets" (the only song I know featuring Afghan rebels), Breaking Circus's "Knife In The Marathon" (the only song I know featuring Middle Eastern terrorists brandishing sharp objects), Baader Meinhof's "Meet Me At The Airport" ("waste them without mercy"), Emily XYZ's "Who Shot Sadat" (thanks to Osama bin Laden's ties to the Egyptian Islamic Jihad), Brooks & Dunn's "Only In America" (both the hardest-rocking and most blatantly flag-waving hit on any radio format this summer, now guaranteed to become a national anthem), the Butthole Surfers' "Jet Fighter" (anti-war-against-Allah song of the year), and the Cure's sadly inevitable "Killing An Arab" (which maybe Ted Nugent will finally cover). None of them explained a thing. But you never ask questions when God's on your side.

Village Voice, **18 September 2001**

Though I owned a handful of LPs and maybe another handful of 45s when I graduated high school in 1978—considerably fewer than the typical member of my graduating class, I'm guessing—I didn't in any sense become a conscious music *fan* until the second semester of my freshman year at University of Detroit, living in Holden Hall and hanging out with a bunch of Sigma Pis apparently too budget-strapped to afford their own frat house. They asked me to pledge, but I turned them down, just as I'd later turn down the black fraternity bros at University of Missouri who got wind of my funky white boy Motor City square-biz music tastes—those black frats are hardcore, and an Alpha or Omega branded on my arm sounded *scary*. I wouldn't have survived pledge week.

But I'm getting ahead of myself. When I started paying attention to music, my preferred radio stations were Detroit AORs WWWW and WRIF and WABX, and my music was New Fucking Wave. Not the androgynous MTV synthesizer-duo kind yet; the skinny-tie-and-powerpop guitar-band kind. As I recall, the first five albums I bought in 1979 were, in some order or other, the Fabulous Poodles' *Mirror Stars*, Boomtown Rats' *A Tonic For The Troops*, Elvis Costello's *Armed Forces*, Elvis Costello's *This Year's Model*, and Elvis Costello's *My Aim Is True*. (So, uh, guess who my favorite artist was? Strangely, by the time I started getting paid to review records, I'd pretty much given up on the erstwhile Declan Patrick McManus. Last album I *bought* by him was his crummy *Goodbye Cruel World* in 1984; the only time I ever wrote about him was an *All This Useless Beauty* brief hacked out for short-lived "CD-Rom magazine" *Launch* in 1996.)

Anyway, New Wave was my music! I even regularly went out pogoing and rock-lobster-ing on Monday New Wave Nights at a bowling alley turned disco in West Bloomfield, once on an actual *date* in a rusted-out used car with a girl who, according to Google, is now some kind of events director at the highfalutin private school Cranbrook. (See Eminem piece later for more Cranbrook information.) First album I actually reviewed was Joe Jackson's *Look Sharp*, for the student paper at Oakland Community College whilst taking a shorthand class to sharpen my journalism/interview/note-taking skills that summer. Never used shorthand again in my life, but did review other albums—next one was the superior American version of *The Clash* for Mizzou's *Maneater* that fall; in that one, I talked about how, though I loved New Wave, I thought most punk rock wasn't musical enough.

Problem was, seeing how (as David Lee Roth once pointed out) all rock critics look like Elvis Costello, New Wave was pretty much what *everybody* wrote about. And, at least in the early and mid-'80s, almost nobody wrote about metal—at least not for non-genre-specialist publications in the States. And even though in high school I was scared most Aerosmith and Kiss fans would beat me up, and though I distinctly remember being spooked the first time I heard Black Sabbath on my transistor late at night, in suburban Detroit in the late '70s one did grow up surrounded with such stuff. So I felt it in my bones and knew its power, and loud rock quickly became my fallback niche as a critic.

As the '80s progressed, when I listened to and went out to see and wrote about the alternative rock that New Wave eventually evolved into, I was naturally drawn to the noisier, more testosterone-flaunting stuff, much of which was being released on small labels like SST in the west and Homestead in the east and Touch and Go in the middle and which would eventually in turn evolve into blockbuster Seattle multiplatinum. Flipper, Feedtime, Greenhouse Of Terror, Couch Flambeau, Squirrel Bait, Breaking Circus, Scratch Acid, the Janitors, Celibate Rifles—hardcore bands growing their hair out and rediscovering guitar solos, pretty much. Basically, I gravitated toward the same music Kurt Cobain did, but more of it, and I got to it first. I'd bet money he even read some of my reviews. But then I got cynical about its shtick and figured out Tiffany was more interesting than Mudhoney—seeing those guys live in Ann Arbor in 1989, I decided all that Seattle crap sounded the same and would never amount to anything. A couple years before, when I was contributing a pigfuck-heavy underground metal column called *Selectric Funeral* to *Creem Metal*, Subpop founder Bruce Pavitt would mail me Green River test pressings with a note attached saying the band was eager to hear what I thought of them, and I was getting self-released White Zombie 45s in my mail direct from Rob Straker, too. But come early 1991, by which time such earnest upstart true believers as Simon Reynolds and Joe Carducci had famously formulated treatises outlining an increasingly insular indie-rock aesthetic, I'd long given up on all that institutionalized fury, and I sold most of the vinyl in question for a pittance. Should've learned my lesson from baseball cards, but nope. If I'd held out a few months, maybe I'd be all set for retirement by now. Hey, never said I was a financial genius.

Or any other kind of genius, for that matter. No, dipshit '86 self, Urge Overkill weren't really "white-supremacist homophobic" (just Erica Kane fans, it turned out), and punk rock wasn't really "invented in the Midwest" any more than anywhere else. But hey, we're all allowed to be chauvinistic about something, right? And maybe my impending skepticism toward indie-label rock—especially after Nirvana and White Zombie et al. took the loud stuff mainstream and "indie" came to mean the piddly, emaciated, arhythmic, vocally blank, seemingly gonad-free quietude exemplified by Pavement and Sebadoh and their ilk, which I couldn't hear hardly at all— was owed in part to the fact that New Wave's descendants are really my type of people. I'm a white guy with a college degree, basically an intellectual with bohemian tendencies no matter how much I try to hide it; when I moved to New York at the end of the '90s to edit the *Voice* after my divorce, I saw obscure bands in small clubs all the time—still vastly prefer those to arenas, especially if there's a barstool open and Stella on tap. And when I got married again, it was to somebody who sang and played guitar for a (really good) band called the Color Guard that frequently played in those clubs—and who'd once been the studio assistant to avant visual artist and Björk babydaddy Matthew Barney—not to somebody in a country or hip-hop or metal group. We met each other in 2001, at a Lower East Side lesbian dive known as Meow Mix, when I was on stage attempting to help the mostly female local pop-rock band Lava Baby cover a Gary Glitter/ Joan Jett song. Eight years later, we'd moved to proudly "weird" Austin, live indie-rock capital of the world.

Anyway, it's often difficult to separate the social from the musical; probably one reason that, say, Liz Phair's *Exile In Guyville* hit me as shallow and irritating in the early '90s is that I *wasn't* a single guy out on the town at the time. And now I'm not one again. I will say, though, that my timing was superb: by the late '90s, garage-rock, New Wave (!), and even pigfuck revivals were helping things turn back around again. And in the '00s, any number of indie-bred bands—the Hold Steady, White Stripes, Red Swan, Red Planet, FM Knives, Drive-By Truckers, Sirens, Donnas, Dropkick Murphys, Drunk Horse, Black Lips, New Bloods, Notwist, Oneida, Electric

Six, Kultur Shock, Gogol Bordello, Gore Gore Girls—continued to make pretty darn good rock'n'roll when inspired to do so.

Still, compared to hip-hop, compared to R&B, compared to teen pop, compared to goofball Eurocheese hits, compared to country (though maybe not compared to the lunkheaded and constipated post-post-post-grunge and emo/screamo dreariness that started entrenching itself as the rock mainstream), indie seemed only easier to ignore as time passed, especially since the genre's web-bound gatekeepers more often than not ignored or scoffed at bands that actually managed to show flashes of life. By decade's end, as more and more of the music insipidly succumbed to introversion and infantilism, my selective blinders had removed me so fully from the milieu in question that I could scarcely imagine how anybody else might still consider it the cutting edge of anything—I mean, have you *heard* Grizzly Bear or Animal Collective? Gag me. Yet despite all that—and thanks mostly to a coincidence of history where the genre's compliant target audience corresponded perfectly with the demographic most amenable to new technology—indie was dominating critics' polls like never before as the '00s wound down. So it's not like the music, or its supporters, ever went away. One popular explanation was that the genre was "finally coming to terms with dance music"—as if people hadn't been saying that about New Wave and its offspring for 30 years. Another, oddly, was that it was turning more prog—same thing I wrote about Bad Religion's soon permanently disowned synthesizer sellout album in 1984. But maybe, to have known that, you had to be there.

BOMBAST IN THE BLOOD: BAD RELIGION

Since my generation has always equated supersonic bombast with rock'n'roll, and since that equation has always been one of the things which has made me more than a little ashamed of my generation, it bewilders me no end that the album I've listened to more than any other in recent months is so supersonically bombastic. Maybe like Bad Religion, whose punk-to-pomp move on *Into The Unknown* is what has me so captivated, I'm just discovering my roots.

Some roots, huh? But let's face it—to us white males who came of age in the suburban Midwest in the mid-to-late '70s, and to I bet a lot of females and urbaners and ruralers and Easterners and Southerners as well, "Bohemian Rhapsody" and "Dust In The Wind" and that ELP song the radio used to play a lot are truer folk music than Loretta Lynn or the Wild Tchoupitoulas will ever be. Inasmuch as the people I grew up with are of the same species and therefore as in need of musical ritual as your average Creole or Bantu, "Stairway To Heaven" was (for a while, anyway) our "Cai-manera," our "Iko Iko," our "Cotton-Eyed Joe."

Which isn't to say it didn't suck. But to suggest that it had nothing going for it except AOR brainwashing techniques is to deny the reasoning capabilities of my entire high school senior class, many of whom scored higher on their SATs than I did. There had to be some intangible which attracted all of those unsuspecting hordes. Bad Religion—an L.A. punk band whose 1982 debut *How Could Hell Be Any Worse* was rightfully lumped with Christian Death, 45 Grave, et al. into the ephemeral "horror rock" sub-sub-genre—has found that intangible.

What they've discovered is simple, really; nothing that arena-watchers haven't known for years: everybody loves an anthem. Just about all of the songs on *Into The Unknown* build to these incredible, mighty climaxes, fully awash with track upon track of piano and organ and synthesizer and acoustic and electric guitar. Sounds Wagnerian or phallic or corny to you, I know, and it is; it's all those things. But it's also inspirational as all get-out. And I bet if I were 16, and I heard this stuff on the radio, I'd be even more enraptured than I already am.

BAD RELIGION LOVE ANTHEMS, JUST NOT ENOUGH TO KEEP THEM IN PRINT.
(PHOTO: GARY LEONARD)

Drawing on the anthemic nature of '70s AOR is nothing new, I know; great songs from "Born To Run" to "Love Will Tear Us Apart" to Glenn Branca's "The Ascension" do it, and so do supposed '60s-revival groove bands like the Neats and the Dream Syndicate and the Smiths. But while I can't imagine, say, "Do The Things" or "What Difference Does It Make" following "Roundabout" on Detroit's WABX or WWWW eight years ago, I think Bad Religion's "It's Only Over When . . ." would fit right in.

Bad Religion's been compared to the stubbornly "psychedelic" three-chord organ-groove band Hawkwind, but frankly, I don't think they're that exotic. They're more like Styx or Kansas; like the American art-schlock bands, they write teen-angst anthems for the post-Tang generation. What sets them apart from the pomp-rock mainstream is their tendency toward irony as well as their allegiance to the hook aesthetic; conceptually, at least, *Into The Unknown*'s real antecedents are records like Led Zep's *Houses Of The Holy,* B.Ö.C.'s *Agents Of Fortune,* and Cheap Trick's *Heaven Tonight,* albums which attempted to explode AOR from within via self-parody and an awareness of pre-AOR rock'n'roll. Bad Religion strips everything that made pomp-rock the excrement it was: its "Dust In The Wind" nihilism, its "Cold As Ice" misogyny, its *Welcome Back My Friends To The Show That Never Ends* pomposity. And what's left over still sounds like pomp-rock.

Bad Religion's songs are mostly just little parables about bad things old people do and about how young people can and should keep from becoming bad like the old people. Typical is "Chasing The Wild Goose," which sounds like Todd Rundgren. A man walks out on the good life after 20 years, and a woman kills herself when marriage proves not all it's cracked up to be. Both "Wild Goose" and the next song, "Billy Gnosis," are dedicated to Kurt Vonnegut; in the latter, a regular guy kills his wife, blows up his car, loses his mind to drugs and worms, and just generally goes bonkers to a tune lifted outright from Steve Miller's "Take The Money And Run."

The idea, I guess, is that stuff is pretty absurd once you've stopped striving for it and just settled down and accepted it; that Wampeters, Foma, and Granfalloons who aren't busy being born are busy dying; that, in the words of the guitarist Brett Gurewitz, life is pointless in the presence of prize. Seems like a pretty good teen-angst idea, as teen-angst ideas have been going lately, so it's not surprising that the two completely acoustic songs Bad Religion contributed to Mystic Records' *Sound of Hollywood* compilation also deal with the futility of modern existence. In the ethereal, keyboard-driven "Waiting For The Fire," young people tend "to the rigors of their daily chores" and "social mores" although immersed in what I guess is nuclear anxiety, while in the more upbeat, folk-rockish "Every Day" a guy tells us, "Don't be deceived by my wife/I'm stuck here all the time, it's a lonely life." The characters haven't yet broken free from their lives, which is perhaps why the influences are prebombast, Buffalo Springfield and early Jeff Airplane.

Most of *Into The Unknown*'s songs are by singer/pianist/organist/synthesist Greg Graffin, whose tunes break down pretty easily into your life's-terrible-if-you're-young-but-not-terrible-enough-to-do-that numbers and your grown-ups-really-fucked-up-the-ecology numbers. Songs of the former ilk open and close the record; "It's Only Over When . . ." and ". . . You Give Up" are as inspirational in their own way as—no shit—great Al Green or Mighty Clouds or Swan Silvertones. When you haven't a friend in the world, and you turn to light and all you get is darkness, and you're lost in space, and your life's in the garbage can, it's only over when you give up. The Lord will make a way, somehow. No, Graffin doesn't exactly say that, but the hope he displays in these songs (and in his ballad, "Million Days") suggests that his sort of humanism isn't that bad a religion after all. If I knew a kid who was considering suicide, I'd play him these songs, and he'd decide to start a band instead. That's what rock'n'roll's for, right?

And if it's also for changing the world, Greg Graffin knows it as well as anybody. I don't particularly care for harp seals myself, but I can't remember the last time I heard a song about an endangered species. (Can't figure out exactly which one—I'm hoping Tasmanian wolf and betting pronghorn antelope.) And "Time And Disregard," which clocks in at 6:50 of Zep-to-Tull acoustic-to-electric grandiloquence, would be annoying if it wasn't so damn catchy: when Graffin, after telling us how he used to wander around in the wilderness like some hippie gypsy, shouts "Tomorrow the trucks come," I swear I get goose pimples. And I realize that that's probably what happens to some people my age when they hear "Stairway To Heaven" or "Aqualung." As much as I hate to admit it, bombast is apparently in my blood.

Village Voice, 3 July 1984

CONSCIENCE OF SOME CONSERVATIVES: THE RAMONES

If I'd cared about music back in '76 instead of worrying about whether I'd get a varsity letter for my debate team experience, I probably wouldn't be able to claim that *Too Tough To Die* is the first Ramones album that's ever really mattered to me. Like, considering that the music which did turn my ears in my pre-music years (Chuck Berry, "Ballroom Blitz," "Macho Man") was a lot different from most of the junk I'd heard on the radio and my brother's stereo, it's likely that if someone had played *Ramones* for me I might have begun to give a shit about rock'n'roll before I hit college. And maybe if I'd been younger and less jaded when I first heard the band, I never would have decided that pretending you're young and not jaded yet is a shtick that gets old too fast and is impossible to recover from. And I'm not even gonna get into the terrible things that could have happened if the kid who carried around a copy of Barry Goldwater's *Conscience of a Conservative* to rebel against what he took for the mindless liberal complacency of his classmates had realized that the most hep rock'n'roll band in the universe was four nonhippies who wanted it to be the '50s all over again and who employed the American eagle and even more fascist symbols—I mean, I ended up accepting the ROTC scholarship as it was; if I'd listened to the Ramones, I probably would have *liked* it. And who knows where that would have left me now.

As it is, now I'm doing the tax-funded blitzkrieg bop just south of Frankfurt as a First Looey in the Army Signal Corps, supposedly protecting y'all from the red hordes, but really just hoping the luftballons don't go up before that day in May of '86 when my military career becomes history. And though I find some solace when I think of LKJ making his own history or Hüsker Dü turning on the news or the Imposter petitioning for peace in our time, rarely does agit-pop hit me the way the Ramones do with the political stuff on their current album, mainly because rarely does political pop address such gut-level emotions—like, "I don't understand what drives di Eagle and di Bear, and frankly I don't really give a shit, just please let me live to see another summer, goddammit." Which is about the only kind of politics you could expect from a down-to-earth-type crew like the Ramones. And on *Too Tough To Die* they dish it out with a vengeance, taking dead aim at the "Russian and American war machine" and saying the Soviets piss them off as much as their own government does (something some liberals may wish they hadn't mentioned) and getting down on their knees to pray for peace in not one song but two. Add the stuff about bag ladies and racial discrimination and murder in the streets and the minimum wage and you've got yourself, in a sense, a whole new Ramones, and I believe every word they say. Not that you can't talk out the side of your neck re bag ladies and war machines. But I don't think the Ramones are bullshitting—they really sound like guys who've suddenly realized that the world ain't such a cartoon after all. There's a big difference between a song that chides the KKK for abducting your girlfriend and one that tells how seeing a poor old woman on the street can make you wonder how much your own pleasures are worth. Or between one that says you remember your East Berlin girlfriend every time you eat vegetables and one that describes how unemployment leads 16-year-olds into crime, drugs, and military service. The Ramones have written a lot of fairy tales in their time, but their new album is about real life.

What I really think *Too Tough To Die* is about is how to maintain some sort of sense of humor or sanity or perspective or whatever you wanna call it after you grow up and start to learn that life isn't all it's cracked up to be. "It's a sick world/Sick sick sick," they scream in one song. Only they don't take the usual rock'n'roll cop-out and tell us they wanna die before they get old, or it's better to burn out than fade away, which sounds cool but does result in quite a few Jimis and Janises and Sids. My favorite song on the LP is "I'm Not Afraid Of Life," a Stooges/Doors keyb-driven dirge in which the Ramones ask whether it's really a crime to get old and state flat out that they "don't wanna die at an early age," adding that though nuclear war could be just the thing to help us die young and stay pretty, that doesn't mean we should sit around and pray for purple rain. And from there they go straight into the title track, where they use a macho weight-lifter to mock the rock virility-worship; on the Day After, it's not gonna matter how young and pretty you are, or how much you can bench-press; nobody's too tough to die. The gist is that the hulk in that song, and the rich little Miss America in the soap-operatic "Daytime Dilemma," like the bag ladies and dope dealers and basic trainees on the rest of the album, are gonna have to face some grim realities after Four More Years: the "death destruction bombs galore" in "Planet Earth 1988."

Heavy stuff. Way fucking heavier than anything the Ramones had given us in the previous eight years and eight albums. But it's not just words that make this one special. Ever since 1977's *Leave Home*, the Ramones had been struggling to build on their original minimalist values and still some-how stay true to those values; starting with 1980's Phil Spector-produced *End Of The Century*, they succumbed to the straw-grasping of a group that realizes it's shot its wad—though 1981's *Pleasant Dreams* and 1983's *Sub-terranean Jungle* were hailed as comebacks by some, they still sound to me like good product and not much more. *Too Tough To Die* is the first album produced by ex-drummer Tommy Ramone (a/k/a T. Erdelyi) since Spector got to the band. Ranting like there's no tomorrow and drawing on every-body from Arthur Baker to Flipper, they seem to have finally found their new niche—as a mainstream rock group, of all things.

I trace the LP's sound back to the Iggy-groove of *Road to Ruin*'s "I Just Want To Have Something To Do." That song's maximum rock'n'roll crunch progressed through *End of the Century*'s "I'm Affected" and *Pleas-ant Dreams*'s "We Want The Airwaves" as a sort of Black Sabbath punk rock and started to become more dominant on last year's *Subterranean Jungle*, making appearances in the crudely metallic "What'd Ya Do," in the AOR-mystic (as in Yes or Bad Religion) "Highest Trails Above," and in the band's garage-psychedelic version of the Chambers Brothers' "Time Has Come Today," already covered by those ultimate Ozzy Osbourne fans, the Angry Samoans. Inspired, apparently, by the metal textures of hardcore bands such as Suicidal Tendencies and the Samoans and Hüsker Dü, the Ramones have let the grunge take over on the new album, and I swear it sounds like the kind of rock'n'roll I'd make if I ever started a band, mutating into an Alice Cooper/Dolls vamp in "Mama's Boy," Hüsker Dü/early B.Ö.C. rave-ups in "Danger Zone" and "Humankind," Descendents-to-Flipper-tempo schizophrenia in "Endless Vacation," Ventures-meet–Van Halen doodling in "Durango 95," and early-Minutemen speedrock in "Wart Hog." In 1984, only Hüsker Dü's *Zen Arcade* has made more noise with more purpose.

Dee Dee seems to be the mastermind behind most of the metal stuff, and his stuttering borderline-fluent David-Johansen-doing-Lux-Interior-doing-Elmer-Fudd guest vocals give the whole album a certain post-hardcore credence. By comparison, Joey sounds like he's enunciating, and his material is used mainly for comic relief; he gets at least partial author-ship credit for three of the four cuts I'd call toned-down. Each side ends with a Joey-penned "fun" number: side one's Busta Jones–produced and Jerry Harrison–keyed "Chasing The Night" is a DOR-thing somewhat reminis-cent of the "Dancing In The Dark" 12-inch. Side two's "No Go" is more Sat-urday night escapism, a rockabilly tune with a hook that sounds swiped from Aerosmith's version of "Train Kept A-Rollin'." Dee Dee's "Howling At The Moon (Sha-La-La)," produced by Eurythmic Dave Stewart, is banana-boat rock about trafficking dope; Joey's aforementioned "Daytime Dilemma" is AOR-pop with Beatlesque harmonies and lyrics about a good girl gone bad. Beyond that, though, it's all grungy rammalamma, search-and-destroy-time at the zen arcade: the Ramones still want the airwaves, but at long last they've realized that they have a better shot at AOR than CHR. Stick 'em between Ratt and Joan Jett, Mr. Programmer—the kids won't know what hit 'em. And maybe it'll teach 'em somethin' if they're not careful.

Village Voice, 20 November 1984

PUNK'S FIRST FAMILY GROW OLD TOGETHER:
THE RAMONES

The April 1977 issue of 16 magazine had teen icons the Bay City Rollers on the cover. But inside, in her "Music Makers" column—amid textual analy-sis of the Sylvers and David Soul—a writer named Mandy answered the question "What is Punk Rock?"

This was no doubt the first time many young Americans had heard this curious phrase. "Punk Rock is a term being applied to lots of differ-ent groups!" wrote Mandy. "Most Punk Rock groups have one thing in common—a good, loud, exciting hard rock sound, and a tendency to keep songs fairly short." Actually, that's *two* things they have in common. Regardless, nobody has explained it better since.

Two months earlier Mandy had gushed over "I Wanna Be Your Boyfriend," the new Ramones single, calling it "super romantic and sexy." "I Wanna Be Your Boyfriend," like another Ramones song called "Now I Wanna Sniff Some Glue," was in the grand tradition of "I wanna" records, dating back through the Stooges' "I Wanna Be Your Dog" to the Beatles' "I Want To Hold Your Hand." Like other punk bands, the Ramones presented themselves as a return to what had once made rock'n'roll great, before it became soggy and serious and slick and stagnant. Punk set out to revive what it saw as simplicity, chaos, danger, irony, fun. So, throughout the mid-'70s, at such New York venues as the Mercer Arts Center and Max's Kansas City and CBGB, bar bands and art bands full of dropouts and prep-school misfits and failed poets from Forest Hills and Rhode Island and Detroit ruled the roost, often glorifying being down and out, a condition that more than a few such scenesters consciously selected. They wore unusual haircuts and jumped up and down a lot. Most of these groups—the Mumps, Tuff Darts, Psychotic Frogs, Laughing Dogs—aren't even footnotes anymore.

In 1976 the Ramones, one of the best and most famous of these New York bands, toured England and instigated an explosion. The Sex Pistols—vermin that had found their artistic calling while killing time at a respected bondage-and-rubber outlet called Sex, owned by a Situationist huckster named Malcolm McLaren—had played their first show in November 1975; a year later, their singer snarling as though he were burning himself at the stake, they issued "Anarchy In The UK," their first single. Within months it seemed every other disgruntled resident of the United Kingdom under the age of 20 had joined a band and released a punk single of his or her own. (The *her* was important—like no rock before, punk inspired women to develop their own voices.)

The New York bands had sung with their tongues in their cheeks, but in the U.K., punk was played as if far more were at stake than the future of rock'n'roll—the future of their nation, perhaps, or the human race. England, then, was where most of the enduring punk recordings—the early Pistols singles, the first Clash album, the Vibrators' *Pure Mania*, the Adverts' *Crossing The Red Sea*, X-ray Spex's "Oh Bondage Up Yours!"—came from.

In 1977 people thought this stuff might take over the world, or at least the Top 40. In England, at least for a while, it did. Back in the United

States of America, it didn't even come close. But in both countries bands playing original material appeared in every borough, suburb, and hamlet, having learned from the Ramones and Pistols that "anyone could do it" (which turned out to be a bald-faced lie, but what the heck).

Every town had its own punk-rock club; in 1982, *Volume: International Discography of the New Wave* listed more than 16,000 records by more than 7,500 bands on 3,000 labels, as well as 1,300 fanzines. Eventually, the music split into scores of factions, encompassing everything from Marxist avant-funk to revivalist rockabilly to power pop and techno-disco. But one congregation of stubborn souls insisted on remaining true to punk as it was played in 1977, and in 1990 the Ramones are still among them.

"There's some of us here today that still fuckin' *remembuh rock'n'roll radio*," shouts Joey Ramone from the concrete stage, lamenting the passing of the Animals and Murray the K, beating a horse that's been dead for decades. With the rest of his band, Joey is wrapping up the Cincinnati installment of Escape From New York, a summer package tour also starring Debbie Harry, Tom Tom Club, and Jerry Harrison (the last two units billing themselves collectively as Shrunken Heads), graduates all of the Bowery punk milieu of the mid-'70s.

Joey, still a string bean, exudes a warped charisma none of the thousand punk frontmen he inspired can touch. But it's 1990, and it's really hard to care. Behind him, bedecked with that classic Ramones emblem—an American eagle clutching a baseball bat in one talon and an apple-tree branch in the other—is a canvas sheet painted to look like a brick wall. The canvas could represent the urban hell from which this band supposedly sprang, or the Phil Spector Wall of Sound they electrocuted into a wall of noise, or the wall whose collapse they celebrated in their beloved Germany last year. Or what it may represent is the wall that's held the Ramones at square one, the wall that's kept them, and so very much of the music they fathered and grandfathered, safe.

To Joey's left is C.J. Ramone, a bassist who these days moves around more than any of his proud pinhead siblings; onstage he is the new king of the Ramones' leg-spread stance. C.J. wasn't born till 1965, so he's too young to remember rock'n'roll radio. Instead, he grew up on the Ramones and the Dead Kennedys and Metallica; he knew only one other punk rocker at his high school. When Dee Dee Ramone defected to rap, C.J. figured he'd never attend a Ramones show again, but then the band hired him to take Dee Dee's place. C.J. was AWOL from the marines at the time. Joey says

C.J. had the right attitude, but guitarist Johnny Ramone says he makes the band look young. That was a priority.

As he finishes breakfast at a Bob Evans restaurant in Lafayette, Indiana, C.J. realizes this is the hometown of another early Ramones fan by the name of Axl Rose. Which figures—with his torsoful of tattoos, C.J. is the only Ramone who'd look right in Guns N' Roses. Later that day, in Cincinnati, Robin Frantz, the seven-year-old son of Chris Frantz and Tina Weymouth of Tom Tom Club and Talking Heads, is running around wearing a Guns N' Roses T-shirt. Robin says he likes G N' R "the same" as Tom Tom Club; says most heavy metal is just good for pumping your fist but "Welcome To The Jungle" is good for dancing; says Donatello is his favorite Teenage Mutant Ninja Turtle "'cause he can hit things from far away"; says he doesn't have a favorite Tom Tom or T-Heads song, but his favorite G N' R tune is "Sweet Child O' Mine"; and says his mom doesn't like G N' R, because "Axl's voice goes too high." Tina Weymouth says she thinks Axl is cute and tells me she's "sick of boring pseudo-intellectuals like David Byrne."

Escape From New York is *not*, the principals will assure you, a nostalgia tour, but when ? and the Mysterians played Bookie's Club 870 in Detroit in 1980, *that* was certainly nostalgia, and ? was a punk before CBGB punks were punks, and "96 Tears" came out in 1966, and *Ramones* came out in 1976, and 14 years is 14 years, right? Johnny, clad in the band's best shag and a U.S. Army Special Forces T-shirt, insists the Ramones aren't relics, because "we never stopped putting out records, and when I watch us on videotapes from five or ten years ago, I find out we're better now than we were then."

And they've got a point—to a point. Though there are a few well-bred waistline casualties who look as if they had closed up the office early for the day, the Cincy crowd isn't mostly old New Wavers out for memories; it's kids out for kicks, scrubbed suburban brats in Smiths and 7 Seconds and Faster Pussycat T-shirts. The teenybopper girls in Cure and Depeche Mode T's are way more lively than the rad boys in Misfits and Danzig T's, but every last member of the crowd is involved, screaming at lung tops while standing on seat tops.

The Ramones have a very loyal audience, and all the way back to "Sheena Is A Punk Rocker," Joey's songs have suggested that he loves his disciples as much as they love him. "They know that we care about them," he says. Their audience has evolved over the years, from post-Warhol art students in the early days to gobbing mohawk-wearers of yore to postmetal high-school students today, but all along it's been a self-classified community of misfits—"Gabba gabba we accept you we accept you one of us," goes that Ramones anthem "Pinhead."

An obvious comparison is to the Grateful Dead (an analogy C.J. likes, though Johnny can't stomach it), with Joey as the punk Jerry Garcia. Could be. The extent to which these original punks are still children of the '60s at heart—greasers and hippies—is surprising. Tina Weymouth uses the word *Zen* a lot; the Ramones stay tuned to the oldies stations. Still, it's easy to understand why teenage newcomers keep joining the Ramones army—take the guns-on-automatic part, the five or six straight crash-bangs, at the end of their set. In concert the Ramones play the "hits," like "I Wanna Be Sedated," because that's what the fans scream for. They play them like seasoned pros; the problem is, standing against seasoned profes-sionalism is what once made this a great band.

And an important one, too, obviously. British punk can be read as a reaction to the dole queue and impending Thatcherism, but inasmuch as Ameripunk meant anything, it meant putting a generation of old farts out to pasture. At least that's what it meant if you're to believe most of the zillion words that have been written about it since—that the music had grown overblown and impersonal and corporate and soft, that the stars were all either blow-dried bores or black-tied jet-setters sniffing powder in the back seats of limos, blah blah blah. Punks defined themselves, or were defined, as the opposition; the New Wave audience identified itself as an "alternative." Drummer Marky Ramone, all Brooklyn biceps beneath his *War of the Worlds* shirt, says how "in those days there were a lot of stuffy people who took rock way too seriously." So punk rock, starting with the Ramones, changed the rules. It redefined "success."

What does this formulation ignore? First, punk rock didn't just "hap-pen." In New York, at least, it was a direct offshoot of glitter rock as typi-fied by the New York Dolls, who were inspired by the British glitter of David Bowie, who was inspired in turn by New York's Velvet Underground, which also largely inspired mid-'70s Cleveland bands like Rocket From the Tombs and the Electric Eels, both of which also drew on late-'60s Detroit bands like the Stooges and MC5, which were inspired by the Stones and the Doors . . . and so on.

Yet in the early '70s, while Joey Ramone was biding time at Slade and Black Sabbath shows and not finding them impersonal in any way he can remember, Marky Ramone was still Marc Bell, drumming for a street-level speed-metal band named Dust. And as late as 1975 and 1976, AC/DC's *High Voltage* and Aerosmith's *Toys In The Attic* and Ted Nugent's "Free For All" were uniting punk volumes with punk tempos with punk attitudes with better-than-punk rhythm sections. And unlike the bands the Gotham media were falling in love with at the time, these bands were selling records—to high-school kids, of all people!

So was punk rock really new? Who knows! The Ramones combined old stuff, mainly power chords and bubblegum-surfboard harmonies, but they did it in a brand-new way. "Our music was structured like nothing else was ever structured before it," says Johnny. "Ballroom Blitz," by the Sweet, had gone Top 5 the year before the suspiciously similar "Blitzkrieg Bop" hit the racks, but the Sweet never had the Ramones' singleness of purpose. In Ramones rock, there was no respite, no letup; the slightest change—a hand clap, a falsetto, an echo, a three-second Farfisa or a twenty-second guitar solo—felt cataclysmic.

And nobody else had ever celebrated the fuck-up-at-life disease the way the Ramones did—nobody ever sang anything like "Sitting here in Queens/Eating refried beans/We're in all the magazines/Gulping down Thorazines" before. "We always had this trademark," Joey says. "I just figured it was some kind of chemical imbalance." They gave a voice to the junk-food anomie of postaffluent American adolescence—like Chuck Berry or *MAD* magazine, only sicker.

The Ramones still don't understand how this linked them with Blondie and Talking Heads and Television and Patti Smith. "I never thought we had anything in common with those bands," says Joey. "We were the only hard-rock group there." But Tina Weymouth claims that all the bands were making music that hadn't been made before, that "the Ramones were an art band too, in their own way." To be that "spontaneous" in 1976, to record your album in a week for $6,400, to adopt a common last name and common leather-jacket-and-ripped-jeans uniform, to create such cartoonish personas—to do all these things required a degree of meticulous thought unheard of in the land of AC/DC and Nugent and even Kiss. "What set the Ramones apart from all the hardcore bands that came later was their discipline," says Weymouth. They chose to be primitive.

And, boy, did the idea ever catch on. "I bet the Ramones influenced more bands than anybody else on the scene today," says C.J. Between speed metal and the Sex Pistols and hardcore and the whole idea of do-it-yourself, which spawned the whole idea of local scenes, which spawned the whole idea of postpunk independent labels, C.J. may be right. Consider, too, all the onetime punk rockers who wound up as stars, invariably playing something other than punk rock—Billy Idol, the Beastie Boys, Belinda Carlisle, Neneh Cherry, Debbie Harry, Joan Jett, various members of Guns N' Roses. And then think of the Ramones T-shirts you'll find on the chests of guys in Def Leppard and Poison; then the Megadeth and Skid Row covers of the Pistols—sometimes it seems heavy metal simply absorbed punk outright.

But that hasn't stopped the Ramones from rolling. They're now into their fifth van in umpteen years (it's a Chevy with transmission problems). Their twelfth album, *Brain Drain*, released in 1989, has a song about not fighting on Christmas, a Freddy Cannon cover, some leaden playing, some heartfelt crap, even some bubble-headed rock poetry in "Punishment Fits The Crime." Like every Ramones recording after their uncharacteristically scary "Bonzo Goes To Bitburg," in 1985, *Brain Drain* is impossible to get excited about. Maybe they should try house music or something. As Johnny says, "In this ever-changing world the Ramones stay the same." (Or as their tour manager, Monte Melnick, puts it, "The song Ramones the same.") Only the Ramones don't see it as a problem.

"We try to maintain what the Ramones are known for—hard, fast, crazy music," says Joey. Unfortunately, in 1990, hard, fast, crazy, three-chord, two-minute alienation feels like old hat. Johnny says he plans to retire after twenty years, which means 1994, since this combo dates to 1974. Until then, he says, "we just have to keep doing what we do well, even though there's no way we're gonna shake the world like we did with that first record." Sounds a bit like he's surrendering, doesn't it?

Instead of learning from Bon Jovi or New Kids on the Block, the way they once learned from the Ohio Express and the Trashmen, all the Ramones can do now is dismiss today's teenyboppers as kids who "don't know anything about real music and who just get suckered in by the radio" (according to Johnny) or who "buy records just because they like how the band looks" (according to C.J.). These nice guys are missing the boat, missing the joke, missing what's fun, pretending the world has stopped turning. Discussing the contradictions inherent in Ramones-on-CD, Marky says: "You can't fight progress." These days punk rock is trying its damnedest to do just that.

Rolling Stone, 20 September 1990

HOWLS FROM THE HEARTLAND:
THE UNTAMED MIDWEST

As every domehead schoolkid knows, punk rock was invented neither in New York by the Ramones nor in London by the Sex Pistols. It was invented in the Midwest—first in Detroit by the MC5, Iggy Pop, and Alice Cooper, later in Cleveland by Pere Ubu, the Pagans, and the Electric Eels, and eventually everybody else got the idea. Mid-America has always been conducive to innovative, violent music. And why not: If rock'n'roll, among other things, is a statement of the realization that the American dream is a lie, who can better express it than those most completely brainwashed by that dream? Middle-American white boys, offspring of the middle-management rat race and gobblers of industrial waste, are born consumers who eventually have to contend with real life. They either fall into the humdrum footsteps of their fathers or try to get out, which isn't always easy. Punk rock in the heartland has never meant art or revolution or fashion so much as it's meant escape from boredom, in the most traditional rock'n'roll sense—even obviously avant-garde acts like the early Pere Ubu and MX-80 Sound weren't designed to be radical concepts like the Ramones and Pistols were; Ubu and MX-80 considered themselves heavy metal bands. That they came out sounding so strange was more a result of their isolation than their pretension.

Oftentimes the midwestern preoccupation with escape has manifested itself literally, by musicians relocating to the coasts to make it big. Even in fertile early-'70s Detroit, Alice Cooper wasn't noticed until he moved west; more recently, slight media attention to Cleveland/Akron in the late '70s sent bands scurrying to New York, and effectively helped deplete that scene. Nowadays, with the luxury condos coming to your neighborhood making such relocation an unaffordable proposition, with the most chickenshit-conservative radio programmers and major labels in rock history making mass success next-to-impossible, and with smart indies like Detroit's Touch and Go close to home, good bands tend to stay put. Where, needless to say, they don't get famous. Critics in New York and Boston and Los Angeles don't hear them, and since most midwestern aficionados and entrepreneurs tend to mimic their coastal peers, good stuff is ignored even in its own backyard—the best shows often go unlisted in entertainment

DIE KREUZEN PLAYED ART-ROCK FROM HELL—OR AT LEAST MILWAUKEE.
(PHOTO: RON FORD)

weeklies, only safe locals (yuppie-billy Bodeans, lite-metal Adrenalin) get airplay, and so on. Ultimately, the untamed bands have about as much chance on the *College Music Journal* charts as they do in *Billboard*.

All of which, in the long run, just makes them better. Today's midwestern bands, even more isolated than their predecessors, are forced to rely on their own language, not on whatever's chic in the capitals of style. Speaking generally, two primary influences have emerged: First, the '70s album-oriented hard rock these kids grew up with, rejected when they discovered "New Wave," and re-adopted when they found it meant more to them than hardcorps clichés. And second, the first wave of British post-punk avant-garde, which many suburbanites are aware of because it touched down when they still had money to burn on import records, and which makes sense to them both because it was the least fashion-conscious Anglowave era and because it too was rooted somewhat in '70s heavy metal and art-rock. Of the two midwestern bands that have managed to make a major critical and minor commercial dent in the past year, the Replacements initially drew on Alice Cooper and Kiss, Hüsker Dü on the Fall and Wire, and both had mostly abandoned these influences by the time their modest ships came in. But from where that pair came there are scores of other fine bands.

Some of them, of course, have important flaws: Chicago's **Blatant Dissent**'s early-Wire-gone-hardcore on *Is There A Fear,* Indianapolis's **Math Bats**' early-Cure-gone-bombastic on *Bat Day,* Detroit's **Seduce**'s early-Sweet-gone-speedmetal on *Seduce,* Minnesota's **Halo of Flies**' psychedelic blues on "DDT Fin 13/PCP," and Ohio's **Sister Ray**'s Detroit-grunge-cum-early-Floyd on "Yellow With Black Lace" all sound fairly cool the first time out, but don't surround even one interesting lyric (save maybe the Bats' Margaret Mead reference in "Samoa") or notable attitudinal quirk. Meanwhile, Madison's **Tar Babies** combine stiff white-boy feedback-"funk" à la Red Hot Chili Peppers with "alienated" white-boy sloganeering à la Henry Rollins and come out like yer average spoiled-brat psychopaths-manqué on *Respect Your Nightmares.*

Cleveland axe-clamor heir apparents **Death Of Samantha** show off their dissonant-but-fluid Rocket From The Tombs–style guitar interplay on *Strungout On Jargon,* but John Petkovic whines like a Violent Femme and strings jargon together like an art-school dropout running out of nonexistent ideas—Death of Sam's in-the-can *Weighing Culture on the Counter* EP has the foursome resorting to cheap sound-effect gimmicks and a hyperbolized version of "Werewolves of London" even Linda Ronstadt couldn't top. Minneapolis Replacements-Hüskers hybrid **Soul Asylum** put on a frenetic live show that includes an amazing "Mercedes Benz"/"Play That Funky Music White Boy"/"Free For All" medley. But they sound way more ambitious than the teenage garage-metal "alternative music"-hype-of-'86 ought to on their Bob Mould–overproduced *Made To Be Broken.* And while the anthems of industrial-wasteland dislocation on Chicago's gridlocksteppingly melodic **Naked Raygun**'s *All Rise* cohere better than those on their previous EP-cut comp *Throb Throb,* they're so humorless in their chastisement of backstabbing bastards and bleeding-heart liberals and bandwagon-jumping poseurs that I have to question their authenticity—I mean, shouldn't good cynics be able to laugh at themselves, too?

Detroit's **Angry Red Planet**, who hawk the same B.Ö.C./Buzzcocks/Mission Of Burma dynamic as Naked Raygun on the four-song, seven-inch *Gawkers Paradise* EP, are more my idea of fun: About time somebody wrote a song about curling; if sliding a 44-pound stone down the ice and whacking it with a broom ain't a rock'n'roll subject, nothing is. Otherwise, *Gawkers Paradise* works as a damn concise moral statement—"Mediocrity" is about the world falling apart not in one big boom but piece by piece and it's our own fault; "Sun Goes Down" about maybe we'd be better off if the big one fell anyway; "On The Waterfront" about how riding the crest would be nice, "But now I got better things to worry and fret about/Like getting the lead out." Inner-directed hardcore anger ain't yet a dime-a-dozen commodity. But then, it's not always necessary: Single-of-'86, hands down, is "Tangled Up," by transplanted-to-Michigan northern Ohioans, the **Necros**, and its catchline goes "There's a noose around my neck that strangles every day/Tangled up in a web of lies, mistakes I never made." The idea is that suffering for other people's fuck-ups is pretty frustrating, and not just if you're a white Anglo-Saxon mid-American male, though that's got a lot to do with it when you're talking affirmative action or whatever. Sound, therefore, is riff-wars like how Ted Nugent used to jam before he fell for all that *Miami Vice* glitter, but even more monstrous. This 45 is Midwest-WASP teen music taken to its logical conclusion. Punk rock for real punks, like the burnout in the Iron Maiden shirt in Ann Arbor who told me he thought "Tangled Up" kicked ass from here to kingdom come.

Milwaukee's **Die Kreuzen** draw on mid-'70s radio metal too, though less literally than the Necros: Dan Kubinski wails straight from the tonsils, gagging on hard consonants, stretching vowels in the manner of Aerosmith's Steve Tyler doing that "Ah'm baaaaackk in the saddle" thing, but the vowels stretch until they snap, and you can only decipher occasional snatches of words. His rhythm section takes Aerosmith's heavy metal hip-hop and accelerates it beyond recognition, but so convincingly that Run-D.M.C.'s Profile label reportedly offered Die Kreuzen a deal (which the band rejected) a few months back. *Die Kreuzen,* the band's late-'84 debut, has proved as single-minded (though not unvaried) a testament to the power of pure ultra-thrash as hardcore has produced; the quartet's new *October File* is more like art-rock from Hell. Kubinski sounds like he's tearing the rubber casing off live wires with his teeth, then all of a sudden some lovely "Layla"-esque guitar line comes out of the abyss, then it all degenerates into sonic quicksand and you're sinking, but soon you're racing against the speed of sound, and then the off-kilter beat undulates like a spastic elevator or drummer Erick Tunison's sticks pop like miniature firecrackers, then Herman Egeness's pickax comes in and slashes your throat, and next thing you know Kubinski's screeching and drooling about "tunes running through my head . . . downstairs and out the front door" or "There's a place in Memphis/I was born there." Die Kreuzen's a hyperactive crew, but darn tight; slide-rule precise and minimalist at any given nano-second, but all over the fucking place before you know it. Scary as mortal sin, and beyond artificial concepts like "meaning."

TAKE PITY, FOR KILLDOZER ARE ORPHANS. (PHOTO: EYDIE WAHLBERG)

Killdozer, three suburban Minneapolites united at the University of Wisconsin at Madison, are more straightforward, in a way—at least their lyrics make sense. On *Snakeboy*, their second album, songs like "River," "Live Your Life Like You Don't Exist," "Revelations," and "Big Song Of Love" serve as existential queries into the meaning of love and death, good and evil, injustice and power and suffering and heroism and spatulas. Michael Gerald howls his blues in a feral, blistering tone almost fit to match Beefheart or the Wolf; the Telecaster and skins of Hobson brothers Bill and Dan combine with Gerald's bass into a terribly dense and rhythmic conflagration, comparable only to what Flipper might be like if they'd emerged from the Mississippi Delta, sludge and heart of gold intact. Or maybe Killdozer is the Birthday Party as wisecracking midwestern college guys—Gerald's personae on *Snakeboy* include a little boy turning a happy day with mom and dad into a backwoods nightmare in "Going To The Beach," a blue bluesman bragging that "They make us big in the state of Texas" in "King Of Sex," a middle-aged loser mourning the deaths of his retarded baby daughter in "Gone To Heaven" and his oedipally attached mother in "57," and a lustful cad seducing a bedpan-ridden elderly woman in "Don't Cry," and yearning for brown sugar in an oozingly heavy rendition of Neil Young's "Cinnamon Girl." Then there's "Burning House": "While the family slept I took daddy's axe and cut off their heads/I'm the only one living in this house who is not now dead/Take pity sir, for now I am an orphan." Live in Detroit recently, Killdozer closed with a gender-bent reading of Jessi Colter's "I'm Not Lisa." Is this an identity crisis, or what?

Even more extreme than *Snakeboy*, but certainly worth recommending: *Boy Dirt Car—F/I,* which gives an album side apiece to an industrial-strength Die Kreuzen spinoff, **Boy Dirt Car**, and some Wisconsin avant-rockers partial to Blue Cheer and Amon Düül; **F/I**'s *On Off* cassette, where the Wisconsin avant-rockers get to stretch out and manage to hold my attention anyway; the **Laughing Hyenas**' "Stain"/"Hell's Kitchen"/"Playground" demo tape, what the Swans might sound like if they liked the Stooges as much as Byron Coley pretends they do; and, regrettably, **Urge Overkill**'s *Strange, I . . .* EP, just what we *don't* need after Big Black—more white-hot, white-supremacist homophobic funk-punk from Chicago. At your peril, you can dismiss every one of these recordings as noise; you'd be right, basically, though you'd be saying more about your own limitations than the bands'.

But the most startling music to come out of the Midwest this year is noisy only in the sense that rock'n'roll has always been noisy. The self-released, self-titled debut album by suburban Chicago trio **Green** is pure pop for jaded people, great clean-cut songs about girls and records that turn pop music's overdue funeral into a rip-it-up, rock-around-the-clock wake. Not since Green's Illini predecessors, the Shoes, debuted with *Black Vinyl Shoes* in the pre-Knack dog-daze of 1978 has a powerpop album sounded this complete, and to my ears Green cuts even those Zion boys. They work from a bouncy white-r&b realm inevitably reminiscent of the early Beatles, tempered by a Searchers/Records folk edge on some songs and a Sweet/Cheap Trick metallic one on others; Jeff Lescher sings in a cigarette-rasp even rougher than Paul Westerberg or the young Rod Stewart, weirdly robust in a music this teenybop, but John Diamond's more-Julian-than-John background "aah-oooh"s are as naively silly as classic disco-era Bee Gees. And best of all, there's none of that Winston-Salem-Athens studio majik to justify Green as High Art. Overall effect is sorta like the Osmonds in their too-brief hard-rock period (circa "Yo-Yo"), but funnier: "Not Going Down (Anymore)" is an anti-cunnilingus double-entendre worthy of the Jesus and Mary Chain; "Hurt You" is an s&m double-entendre worthy of rough boys ZZ Top; "Big In Japan" (embellished with Deep Purple guitar crunch) is rock criticism worthy of Nick Lowe. And darned if I can figure what to compare to the breathtakingly wimpy "Curry Your Favor," with its hilarious mock-archaic "If I do curry you, I'll curry any old time you want me to" hookline. But this isn't parody; *Green*'s courting and cheating and never-falling-in-love-again and girl-next-door-grows-up songs convince me these young adults are as sensitive as they pretend to be. And "Gotta Get a Record Out" and "I Play the Records" and "Big In Japan" convince me they love rock'n'roll as well. If Green came from New York or Los Angeles or London, they'd have made the cover of *Tiger Beat* their own by now, and maybe they'd have their own TV series. But if they came from New York or Los Angeles or London, no way would they sound as good as they do. That's my point.

Village Voice, 29 July 1986

AN INDIE RISES ABOVE: SST RECORDS

My drug of choice is Mountain Dew, and I'd teetotal no less on a desert island, but if I were stranded and had to choose the one record label that could keep sending me new wax, I've got no doubt that (accusations of marijuanified and/or peyotefied company aesthetic to the contrary) I'd pick SST. Couple years ago, back when the guys at POB 1 Lawndale CA 90260 were taking over the world with their Black Flags and Minutemens and Hüsker Düs and Meat Puppets, SST would've been a real popular rock-write desert island selection. But near as I can tell, the current party line is that the label has degenerated into heavy metal and hippie wank, forfeiting whatever integrity it once had; a few months back in this very publication, A&M-affiliated Twin Tone was proclaimed "the most vital American indie" by a critic who a year earlier had suggested that SST had "blown its wad."

Well, that's total hogwash, and not just because the new Mekons album reeks and Twin Tone/Coyote's never put out an interesting record, either. SST is the only reasonably productive rock Amerindie left that makes individual expression its primary priority, the only reasonably selective one that doesn't limit itself to "rock" "bands" playing "rock" "songs" (like the not terrible but increasingly disappointing Homestead and Touch and Go do). Therefore it's the only one not inextricably tied to an existent (college radio or HC or HM) audience, and the only one that still consistently provides the culture shock and respite from convention all this indie garbage claims it does. To my ears, the label's better now than it's ever been.

Which is saying a mouthful. Founded on borrowed money in 1978 so Black Flag could put out their "Nervous Breakdown" single (which nobody else would touch), named for Flag fretburner Greg Ginn's electronics business, SST's always been one of the rawest, most radical, and most controversial fellowships out there. Even more than most indies, it's had to rely on play-everyday club tours with band members at the van wheel, finicky press coverage, and record-sales-at-shows to get its product on the streets; from the start, distribution and promotion were learned the grassroots way—from scratch, by trial and error. And unlike so much of its competition, it's never come close to selling its soul to RCA or MCA or Capitol or Columbia. But by 1984 it was funding acclaimed double-albums (*Zen Arcade* and *Double Nickels On The Dime*), and all along it's put out classic records that have fallen through the cracks—Würm's *Feast*, Saccharine Trust's *Worldbroken*, Gone's *Gone II But Never Too Gone*.

But when the road killed D. Boon in late '85, label death knells started, and the bells got louder when Flag broke up and the Hüskers graduated to Warners; one of the biggest acts SST signed since that time, Bad Brains, has already moved on to Island. Throughout the last year or so, though, SST's been working an idea that reminds me that ESP-Disk must've been really amazing in the '60s with Albert Ayler, the Godz, the Fugs, and Patty Waters; has to do with climbing out farther and farther on a limb, usually for the sake of riff-interactive (sometimes improvised and often wordless but hardly ever "art") music with a beat you can dance to. *Not* mainly for a propped-up, politic-wise agenda or a sicko, death-defying hate-trip, but just to fucking do it, 'cause it's an effective and honest way of communicating (and entertaining) person-to-person. Forget the consensus, forget what you "know," just play what's on your mind, son.

Needless to say, principles like this can lead to a lot of smelly manure from people who aren't as naïve and/or clever as they think they are, and I guess what drives most would-be supporters off the SST bus is that you've gotta wade knee-deep through the manure to find the treasures. Myself, I kind of enjoy wading: Only two of SST's 40-some releases this year have really killed me, but every one I hear is another piece in the puzzle, and all but the very worst ones (take Blast's *My War* tributes and shove 'em) deserve credit for fortitude and singular vision, however trivial. My pro-grunge prejudices let me excuse D.C.3's parched lack of jocularity and St. Vitus's unduly civilized lack of overblown dementia (like howls and shit), but what satisfaction I get out of these crews is meager enough for me to understand why you might dismiss 'em. And I know Television devotees who'll proclaim Slovenly's new *Riposte* God's gift to ringing guitar inter-play, and while I'm pleased that it's got more angular beats than their last album, ringing guitar interplay's just never impressed me much, and I'll never really take the combo seriously until their angst-affected gripe-sniveler burns whatever thesaurus is feeding him all those hokey show-off phrases about "corporate compatriots" and "sober disenchantment" and "horrid disbelief." A lot of this ramalam is unfocused and self-consciously peculiar, and only a fraction of it stands up to close scrutiny. But you've gotta admit that it's cool that any of it gets vinylized at all.

Case in point: Plenty of punk rock groups lately would be plenty more believable if their ego-pumping vocalizers would just keep their damn traps shut, and SST's the firm that's working hardest to rectify said situation. The instrumental launchpads are psych-era "jam"-illogic both intentional (ESP, Plastic Ono, Mothers, and maybe some Kraut-kraft) and accidental (Blue Cheer and Sab), plus presmarm jazz/art-rock; best instro-hope lies with Blind Idiot God, three Missouri 19-to-21-year-olds whose debut disc starts with Stravinsky and soars through five more slices of dynamic amp-attack crescendo-rock (pigfuck without the useless "fuck"s) and into three rumbling dubs. What I can't figure is why B.I.G. don't mix up the echo and distortion, why they don't put the advanced rhythm *behind* the advanced guitars. Only Idiot God grooves that really move are "More Time" (a Meters cover!) and "Dark & Bright," which open side two with second-line stutter under loads of leaping phallic feedback. If Pussy Galore can get head pats for grating to that corpselike 1965 forcebeat *they* use, seems to me some-body oughta up the ante.

For now, SST's most solid current no-singing disc comes not from unknown young Turks, but from an old fart who's worked with Richard Thompson, Bill Laswell, and Ronnie Montrose. *Devil In The Drain* is mainly just Henry Kaiser on elephant-flatulence guitar, dialoging in harmolody with the tribalist drum, bass, and horn effects he samples out of his syn-clavier. Fractured solos, symphonic weirdness, handsaw friction, bluesy note-picking, twangy, high-pitched xylophonic Vietnamese parlor-room minimalism, gurgling and rattling and wailing all happening at the same time, this record has it all—there's even a slashful-to-placid thunder-duet with MX-80 Sound Fender-deity Bruce Anderson, and the words in the one song with words (the title track) come from a top-notch children's book. Which is about all you could ask for, unless you ask for Crazy Backwards Alphabet's *Crazy Backwards Alphabet*, on which Kaiser also plays. The al-bum's got loose *Trout Mask*-ish Delta-free-(Western)-swing syncopation-switches every couple seconds; best adjective for it is "difficult" (but not not-fun), the kind of made-to-order abstraction open-minded, old Euro-rock partisans will pee their pantaloons over in *Musician* magazine. You know: mucho slide, metallic Ayler cover, facetious (because sung in Russian) ZZ Top cover, tastefully intelligent, grown-up sense of humor guarding against any threat of visceral overload or genuine personality. I like it (especially the edgy eight-minute "Dropped D"), but I don't listen much.

When you get down to it, the only actual SST must-owns of late are Dinosaur's *You're Living All Over Me* and Screaming Trees' *Even If And Especially When*, both sophomore LPs but SST debuts, and both (oddly enough) songful slabs of toetap savagery that wouldn't sound that out-of-place on campus airwaves. Transplanted-to-N.Y.-Bostonians, Dinosaur sound how you want Hüsker Dü to sound, which ain't to say they sound like Hüsker Dü—more like Neil and Crazy Horse, but with a wilder percussive bent and guitars that weigh a ton. (Their most Zeppish tune's called "Sludge-fest," and live they stack Marshalls.) J. Mascis is a lonely boy, mumbling in a raw, cracked, pained-but-unfeigned drawl about waiting for someone on a corner: "Got the guts now, to meet your eyes/These guts are killin', but I can't stop now/gotta connect with you girl, or forget how," then scythe-swaths of his masculinist string-spuzz seep in, and holy fucking shit. The guitars nap and wake up hungry, the melodies are full and folkish, the vocals more like shadows than monuments, the feelings complicated and laid-bare and sensitive and expecting the worst. But there's no self-pity, and though nothing sounds thought-out, nothing sounds sloppy, and the back of the record jacket has flowers and smiles. Dinosaur knows a wise and wooly beauty that makes their ugliness ring true.

So do Screaming Trees. Really wasn't expecting much from their new issue, seeing how their first one (*Clairvoyance*) hit me as by-the-book acid-retrogression, but *Even If And Especially When* hits me like the most-gear acid-retrogression on the books. And since these four oddballs hail from three hours outside Seattle, and since I bet it's real tough to locate copies of the Seeds' *Web Of Sound*, the Amboy Dukes' *Call Of The Wild*, and Love's *False Start* out there on the farm, mayhaps it ain't retrogression at all. Around tucked-tight, dirty-ass, balls-out, brass-knuckle power-crunch with corrugated bass hooks and two conflicting guitars spurting freaky in-yer-face wah-wah that cancels out the geeky Farfisa that sometimes even sounds all right, a gravel-voiced guy unravels into catchy choruses mysteries about minds racing at midnight and about how he wants to explode his town without a sound, Gregorian background hum excavating deep windswept craters of confusion that somehow seem disconsolate without seeming doomed—you'll analyze Screaming Trees as groovesters with nothing "meaningful" to say, but their humongous open-expanse chunks are eloquent enough to help me face the day, so you're wrong.

Imminent or just out on SST: Honky half-funk from the Tar Babies, Guernsey-punk from Blood On the Saddle, nirvana-directed picture-postcard ethnofusion from Glen Phillips, goatee-type art-damage from Elliot Sharp, an arkestra led by Violent Femme Brian Ritchie that we're supposed to believe will resemble Sun Ra, and a new Leaving Trains LP called *Fuck*. You can wager I'll make fun of some of this stuff, but don't ask me how or why most of it fits into the SST "plan," 'cause I haven't the slightest. Some say the label's floundering, throwing darts at the wall blind, but these are generally the same dunces who figure Robyn Hitchcock and Alex Chilton have bigger brains than David Lee Roth. Me, I've long given up on this whole "semi-popular" facade, but I think SST's just determined to make certain unheard music gets heard no matter what, and from their fecundity alone it's obvious they're succeeding. Coming from an organization that not too long ago did its business from phone booths, I'd say that's an accomplishment worth commending.

Village Voice, 22 September 1987

SLIME IS MONEY (BASTARD)

Pigfucker, *n*. **1.** Pejorative used to label participants in any of several strains of obstinately uncommercial, abstract yet noncerebral, post-hardcore art-rock, characterized by peculiarly structured intentional dissonance (typically loud, often unconventionally tuned electric guitars), mechanical and/or funkless rhythms, subtle textural shifts, violent lyrics addressing taboo subjects, and a general quest for assumed "extremes." **2.** Fan or apologist of this subgenre.

[coined as music term by Robert Christgau in the *Village Voice*, 3 March 1987; from *pig* and *fucker*, compounded in 1967 by Hunter S. Thompson to describe Hubert H. Humphrey.]

Pigfuckersymp that I am, I spend an inordinate amount of time listening to music that's ugly for no particularly cogent reason, like this band called

Wiseblood that I'll get to in a couple paragraphs. First on the agenda is the inordinate time I spend in the john with *Forced Exposure*, a proudly decadent rockmag put out about thrice a year by Jimmy Johnson and Byron Coley. It's a fat publication, slicker and more professional every time out, and it's fast becoming the standard by which one's pigfuck credentials are judged. If your own are floundering, you can revive 'em in a minute by stopping by See Hear, the fanzine specialty shop where *Forced Exposure* easily outsells all comers, even *Spin*.

Anyway, *FE*'s editors give plenty of coverage to spastic rhythms and horrible noises, and since I'm neurotically partial to both (especially when combined), at first I thought the zine was pretty terrific. Now I'm not so sure: lately, it strikes me as staid, stodgy, tightassed. It tries to confront underground swindles (like *Maximum RocknRoll* and R.E.M. and the Dead Milkmen, say), but if anything, when dealing with less clearly bankrupt postures, it's not skeptical enough—seems vinyl marginalia earn decent write-ups, only to be filed for eternity in well-publicized "collections." For all their neo-beatnik lingo and gonzo grammatical disfigurement, Johnson and Coley come off as lukewarm and business-as-usual as your standard daily-news rockscribes—except as it serves as a status symbol, music doesn't seem to excite them much. It's just another commodity to be catalogued.

In his superlative "Poolside Pep Talk" column in Boston's regrettably short-lived *Take It* punk paper in 1980, Coley opined that "We don't need no more elitism in this world." A stellar notion for sure, except that the primary point of his current journal would appear to be in establishing its superiority over the ignorant multitudes. Its genre-narrowcasting is inexcusable but maybe inevitable; fanzines chronicle specific subcultures, after all (though that never stopped *New York Rocker* from branching out). What's more infuriating is *FE*'s glaring cliquishness—too much space is devoted to the sleazily self-aggrandizing ruminations of Lydia Lunch, Chris Desjardins, Tesco Vee, and Steve Albini (all of whom, it should be noted, frequently release records whose pretensions invariably go unchastised by *FE*'s purported cynics). Vee's brattiness can be entertaining in a trivial way, Albini's outrage can be convincing if you're not paying close attention, and I suppose one could argue that Lunch's and Desjardins's bohemian blathering is "poetic," but none of it's half as disturbing as it wants to be. And it all adds up to two-bit clichés: homophobia, racism, misogyny, and perversion feigned (or suggested) by reasonably privileged and educated young white adults.

It's an easy mask to put on—I've done it myself. And in small defiant doses, it can even be effective at knocking complacent liberal scum off their high horses. But in *Forced Exposure,* where Albini celebrates kiddie porn expressly as a means of shocking the unshockable, then pretends he *accidentally* stepped over "some kind of imaginary bad voodoo line" laid down arbitrarily by "lefty humanist fuckers," the game amounts to a frat-haze rite where you're forced to suspend your instinctual squeamishness at pederasty or cannibalism or whatever to prove your cool or your manhood. *FE* is mean-spirited and cranky, but it's not so much outrageous as "about" being outrageous. In a subculture that's subsisted on dangerous irony ever since the Ramones first nodded to the Nazis, the stance certainly ain't "new" or "original": not unlike *Maximum RocknRoll's* rote yippie socialism, it's just a crutch that allows writers not to say a damn thing. *FE* often contains useful articles by guest contributors who forgo the hepper-than-thou attitudinalizing, but mostly the rag's as snooze-inducing as watching some geek crap on stage, and so hypocritical it's meaningless.

Some pundits dismiss the music *Forced Exposure* embraces for the same reasons I dismiss *Forced Exposure,* and once in a while that makes sense: Big Stick and Pussy Galore know one good joke apiece, Live Skull are too dirgey, Das Damen too groovy, Crime and the City Solution too lethargic, and they're all drenched in this campy dread/death/degradation. But less rudimentary pigfuckers make some of the most adventurous and brutally visceral rock available nowadays, and it's willful to reject them on lyrical insubstantiality alone. For lots of 'em, as with most art punks since Wire, vocals are simply one more component of the total dynamic—words are just sounds. Discounting puritanical questions of moral propriety, the best excuse I've heard for not listening to this nihilist racket is that it doesn't swing, which for a lot of it is right on the mark. But show me a funk or rap disc with fiercer, more pliable polyrhythms than the Swans' "The Screw" or Einstürzende Neubauten's "Yü Gung" and I'll show you a release date before 1985.

Dancebeats are in fact the most praiseworthy attribute of Wiseblood's six-song *Dirt Dish* album, a collaboration between former Swans skinsman Roli Mosiman and Scraping Foetus Off The Wheel one-clod-demolition-derby Jim Thirlwell. As Foetus, Thirlwell concocts an eccentric amalgamation of industrial gadget-pop, hi-NRG electronics, blues minstrelsy, country-swing, and whatnot, all underlying a stream-of-punplay songwrite vision that *FE* calls genius but I call obvious and overdone: "supercalifragilisticsadomasochism," my butt! Wiseblood is more conventional, and less sloppy—the pair's frantic 1985 debut single, "Motorslug," simulates drag-race exhilaration as expertly as Kraftwerk's "Autobahn" simulates interstate highway tedium.

On *Dirt Dish*, Thirlwell's kerosene-charred mushmouth glorifies anal rape and Satanism as Mosiman's chiseled Fairlight-bleats and massive two-fisted real-drum pounding chuck Rick-Rubinesque bricks at your glasses and play Pac-Man with your brain cells. Most potent cut by far is "Stumbo," about a dinosaur who shoves over buildings, naps in volcanoes, and roves "the countryside behind the wheel of a mammoth Chevy '55." The opus begins absurdly slow, with this lizard king waking up in a swamp amidst croaking frogs; the reptile starts grunting and groaning and lowing, and by the end he's stomping out the human race. The non-LP 12-inch version, where metal-riff cue sticks rattle beats that catapult off each other like cosmic billiard balls, is the coolest single I've heard this year, and so hilarious I originally figured the dominance and submission on the rest of *Dirt Dish* were just as tongue-in-cheek. Seeing Wiseblood live proved me wrong.

A guy with a microphone and a guy with a synthesizer ain't no rock'n'roll show anyhow, and the crowd full of death-worship creeps didn't help, but what really pissed me off about Wiseblood's recent Detroit gig was the way Thirlwell pranced and sneered and unzipped his jeans and kept grabbing his groin like Jim Morrison's narcissistic exhibitionism was worth emulating—might as well have been Billy Idol up there. Now the Doors quotes on my Wiseblood records don't seem so clever, and garbage like "I'm a beaver cleaver/And there's plenty of beavage and plenty of cleavage around here" sounds like true idiot-babble. This asswipe's as full of himself as Sweet Baby Morrisey, and like M. Gira and Henry Rollins he's erroneously convinced his insipid spiel is important, so he makes himself heard; at least Sonic Youth (as comic as David Lee Roth in my book) are smart enough not to take their own bullshit seriously.

Yeah, I need radically abrasive noise that challenges me, and if it's irresponsible or insurrectionary, better still. But ego plus gumption don't equal talent, and pigfuckers who insist on regurgitating sham morbid/misanthropic theatrics had better clobber me with aural ideas more inventive than mere disco and drone. There's way too much genuinely stimulating stuff out there to settle for phony sociopaths too lazy to think for themselves.

Village Voice, 24 March 1987

BIG BLACK GIVE YOU A HEADACHE

This past summer, Chicago's hate-punk trio Big Black put out a supposedly audacious four-track EP called *Headache*. The audacious part was that the original limited-edition collectors-only sleeve featured morgue photos of the blood-laced heads of two men killed in an auto accident. The title track featured the gang's usual volcanic guitar combustions and beatbox pulsations, seasoned with the adenoidal screams of Big Black mouth and punkzine contributor Steve Albini, who squealed bile like "Who says you're mine, you little monster?" Reading the liner notes, which is often the only way to figure out what Big Black numbers are about, I discovered that the line came from a tune about a doctor who repeatedly drops his deformed newborn baby on the noggin, until the kid dies. Especially once I'd noted that the rest of the EP consisted of ditties about a homicidal toolworker, a hitman, and a bad dude who was nevertheless a good cop and of course wasn't "a colored man," my response was the only response that this done-to-death shock shtick warrants anymore: "Get outta my face, asshole." Or in other words: "Ho Hum."

Once upon a time, the idea of Big Black made sense, or at least it seemed to. The EP debut, *Lungs* (1983), was mainly just bone-thin Albini and his bone-thin Roland electrode-machine bleats recorded on a four-track, and the narrator's teeth-clenched intensity and the sound's doomy amateurism slapped you like Brut. "The only good policeman is a dead one, the only good laws aren't enforced," Albini wailed. "I've never hung a darkie but I've fed one, I've never seen an Indian on a horse/And I live like this 'cuz I like it, and I've seen too much to pretend/You can't ignore the beauty of the things that you love, like you can't stand the hatred and the lies." Albini wrote in the fanzine *Forced Exposure* that he needed "big ass vicious noise . . . whipping through me like a fucking jolt," and his own noise grew bigger and blacker on '84's *Bulldozer* EP (compiled with *Lungs* last year on Homestead's *Hammer Party* album), more brutal and impenetrable still on '85's *Racer X* EP, two guitars abrading against each other like steak knives (or tanks) and filling up every last hole with packed-tight bear grease, beatbox pounding out a hammerlike disco-referent march that forced James Brown's "Big Payback" into a bulletproof straitjacket, and the vocalist at a self-abuse peak: "Your foot in my face/Is what keeps me alive" ("Sleep").

BIG BLACK, STEWING IN THEIR OWN GUILT.

Albini was obviously a brainy, candid kid; he speculated about the ubiquity of evil, about the power people lust to exert over others, about the pain and agony and even death we're willing to subject ourselves to out of fear, or for the sake of money or entertainment or sexual gratification. ("Cables," the best song on *Bulldozer*, had some voyeurs getting their rocks off watching cows get clubbed to death in a slaughterhouse.) And everything Albini churned out, both as a songwriter and a journalist, suggested a deliberate effort to make you hate him, which at first seemed a valid aim, since upsetting social norms is one of those imperatives rock's forgotten how to carry out. Music's supposed to make you feel something, which at this late jaded stage means it's first got to make you uncomfortable. Big Black disrupted shaky ethical preconceptions, forced you to deal with what you didn't want to deal with, made you stew in your guilt.

And though they were subtle and even cynical about it, they maintained rock'n'roll ideals amid the carrion and carnage—after all, if you've gotta make nihilist clamor that mourns modern moral decay you might as well have fun doing it. Through voiceovers, mike-feedback, self-depreciating album notes, multitudinous guitar effects, all sorts of weirdo "instruments" (steel girders, M-1 carbines, mortar shells), and a couple of songs about race-car drivers, they even displayed something like a sense of humor. (Recent press-promotion packages have been loaded up with foreign-language articles, a hilarious dada-type fuck-you move.) The violence in their sound mirrored the violence in their lyrics, but they were rarely as pretentiously arty as most of their shardcore/pigfrig/you-name-it contemporaries—they never managed to swing (at best they'd just bunch all their gunk up and jerk the "rhythm" with a vengeance), but they sure could kick.

Big Black broke up a few months ago so Albini's fellow guitarist Santiago Durango, could attend law school, and I haven't cared much about the crew since their '86 *Atomizer* (which united Durango/Albini with bassist Dave Riley to solidify the core lineup). At first I thought *Atomizer* blew away the EPs—the din was more ferocious than ever, Motörhead-meets-Suicide, all these strings grinding up uranium and squeezing out the juice, everything catching fire at once, offhand beats or brassy snatches of melodic clang making whole songs change direction, words about pyromania and pederasty and perversions I didn't know existed. But with subsequent listens it became clear that the louder kerboom and in-depth library-research were just a substitute for the fresh thrills of anger venting the band had started with—like Elvis Costello around the time of *Armed Forces* (a comparison Albini will despise), Big Black were down to refining their craft, going through deeper and darker but futile and inconsequential motions. Rampant world hate and spastic postskronk cacophany were racing neck and neck toward the rest home for bankrupt indie-rock clichés, and by the year's end *Atomizer* was neither radical nor scary nor exciting.

"When bands take their public approval and recognition as a measure of success, then the quality, inventiveness, and inspiration of their music become wee significant," Albini wrote in a fanrag called *Matter* in 1984. "There's that choice again: do what you know you can do without exerting any effort, or try swimming away from the ship and risk the sharks." Albini was discussing bands who "sell out," but he had the situation half-wrong, because for a troupe like Big Black, being afraid to "sell out" can be the same as being afraid to "risk the sharks": springwater-pure "integrity" that makes you cling to an imaginary or moribund "edge" can be as self-defeating as dollar signs in your eyes. Big Black's failure, as confirmed on *Headache* (cover sticker, "Not as good as *Atomizer,* so don't get your hopes up, cheese!") and most of the new *Songs About Fucking,* has been a lack of courage, an unwillingness to counter the repulsiveness and loathing and corruption and moral void that come so easily to them with whatever love or happiness or virtue has kept them from exploding silver bullets through their thick skulls, relieving themselves of wickedness and sordidness once and for all. Any music that settles for such a skewed fraction of what life and human interaction can deliver is just a cartoon, and a deceitful one at that.

Albini's apologists claim he's no sensationalist, just a normal guy matter-of-factly telling stories, usually true ones, from which we're allowed to draw our own moral judgments. But his desire to horrify is right there in his choice of topics, and what helps make his subjects shocking is that they're so removed from his audience's (and his own) day-to-day existence. If Northwestern University journalism grad Albini's not an unreconstructed racist, which I'm certain he's not, then his use of phrases like "little cartoon nips" and "criminal communist coons" is willfully ironic, just like all the Mickey Spillane icepicks-to-the-gonads macho personas he canonizes in his trucker/gangster/soldier/fascist songs. And a number like *Atomizer*'s "Jordan, Minnesota," especially when you know it's about a claque of child molesters not from its lyrics but from what you've read in Albini's commentary, especially when it shines no insight or feeling on the tragedy it exploits, especially when it ends with Albini screeching "Suck me! Suck me!"—a number like that is just an art-punk equivalent of "Ripley's Believe It or Not" or *The Weekly World News*. I guess I'm supposed to take the tune as a metaphor for more mundane degradations, but that's hard when the song's liner notes are more frightening, moving, and thought-provoking than the song itself.

Once or twice—with the U.S. chauvinist overseas in "The Ugly American," maybe the 1920s mulatto jazz pianist in "Passing Complexion"— Albini exhibits some smidgen of empathy for his characters. But the only time he's moved beyond transparent poses, the only time he's depicted himself as more than a one-dimensional junior curmudgeon, is in the December 1985 diary he contributed to the Summer 1986 issue of *Forced Exposure*. Writing off the cuff, not concerning himself with what we'll think or even what we'll be able to make sense out of, he talks about love dying, the uselessness of his job, friends getting arrested, cultivating an ulcer, coming home at night unlaid, fearing death, wishing he were still 15 and innocent and back in Montana. In the process, he lets himself look not just mean but also wimpy, vulnerable, stupid, boring, caring, nervous around the opposite sex, obsessive. Just like the rest of us, I guess, except the rest of us don't have the nerve to put the stuff on paper and pass it around to people we've never met. Which means Albini's blessed with the gift of honesty, and that gift is all the more reason he shouldn't let his music turn into a fraudulent parody of what it once was.

Well, I've chastised the guy enough, and I oughta point out now that he's working on it. Along with *Headache* this summer, Big Black released a single on which they respectfully bludgeoned Wire's tensile "Heartbeat." Except as evidence of the trio's improved dynamic/melodic finesse, the 45's no big deal (shitty B-side filler and all), but I like the humbled way Albini croons the first lines: "I feel old, I feel cold." Big Black's latest (and probably last) single is a bigger surprise: the sleeve of "He's a Whore"/"The Model" has the trio duded up as Cheap Trick and Kraftwerk, with once-proud homophobe Albini looking the daintiest and friskiest and most mascara'd of the bunch. Inside is the most playful music Big Black have ever turned out, two seedy cover tunes where roguish gents fantasize about taking lovely women home. The rendition of Cheap Trick's "He's a Whore" is even self-referential, in a way, because who but craven whores would revert to something this "commercial," right? With that tinny synth, those jangly guitars curling around and then blanketing each other, Durango and Riley chirping Rick Nielsen's subterranean Beatle quote ("anytime at all") behind Albini's lewd growl, it's close enough to a sellout to satisfy my cravings, though the ax sound is a little flat. And Big Black's still-robotic fleshing-out of Kraftwerk's joyfully contrived ode to a cover girl's contrivances, with their guitars slashing both ways across the mechanical tune, is even funnier. Just what we need: a two-sided concept 45 about the artificiality of lust.

Songs About Fucking is a fucking hodgepodge, and most of it's trash done better before: two tracks too dense to decipher (though once again the liner info helps); a few cuts that mix together sex and sadism (one with surfoid riffs, another with Sam Kinison yelps); Big Black's third hitman song ("Kasimir S. Pulaski Day," on the heels of "Ready Men" and "Shotgun"); a Wagner-disco instrumental outro called "Bombastic Intro" that I'll admittedly take over the bombastic intro that ends Aerosmith's new album. Then there's "The Model" itself, and I really enjoy "Kitty Empire," a lighthearted, perhaps partly autobiographical ditty about a guy who plays strange music and has lots of cats and jumps around naked in the weeds once in a while, causing his neighbors to freak out. The story brings the devious behavior of a would-be epic like "Jordan, Minnesota" down to a more manageable level, and Albini yowling "I piss on everything you value" over construction-work crunge hits me like a statement of purpose.

But on the three most vital cuts. Albini bares more of himself than he ever has, more than he's ever deemed proper before, maybe more than he wants to; he ends up sounding scared, sensitive, and most of all alone. "Bad Penny" could be about an unfaithful squeeze, but its spare and nasal drone clues you that it's Albini's version of John Lydon's "Public Image," a denial of past transgressions and a rebuke of the audience that's turned the singer into the kind of idol he's always held in contempt: "Oughta know what a liar I am/Oughta know me by now/Don't curse me for my nature/Don't bless me . . . should've known you couldn't trust me." "Pavement Saw" is graceful, almost anthemic, building its granulations from *Chairs Missing* Wire toward *New Day Rising* Hüsker Dü, but the oddest thing, especially given Albini's continued denouncement of the genre, is that it's a love song: "I feel so stupid 'cuz I feel so stupid without her/She smokes herself to death, it makes me sick/She's so pretty that I don't give a shit." He gets her pregnant, and she's keeping the baby.

Finally Albini, who's small and who's been billed as a "messiah" in more than one punkzine, ends his Big Black singing career with "Tiny, King of the Jews," a slow, understated dirge that takes us back to *Lungs*, or to the first Joy Division album. Guitars swoop in parabolas over him and his Roland; his voice, mixed way-the-hell back, sounds more tired than angry. "Man's gotta hate someone/I've just go to/And when I'm through with myself/I start on you." The sleeve notes claim that suicide's not punishment enough. It's self-serving, but the song cuts deep enough to draw blood; Albini feels sorry for himself, and you end up feeling embarrassed for him even after the pointless venom and derision he's sprayed the last few years. Not that I'm looking forward to his soon-to-come Pussy Galore collaboration or anything (the LP he produced for 'em can't stand up to its Manhattan hype), but I'm starting to think again that I kinda *like* the poor jerk. So credit Big Black with pulling off an unexpected rock-and-roll coup, and then let's put this particular pigfrigger to rest once and for all, okay?

Boston Phoenix, 9 October 1987

NIRVANA: "ALL APOLOGIES"

Wanna know how big a jerk *I* am sometimes? After Kurt Cobain came out of his barbiturate-and-champagne coma in March, I wrote letters to two or three people joking that maybe his bandmates should increase the dosage next time. His intense new age sincerity in Nirvana's acoustic "All Apologies" video convinced me he was getting ready to move in with Sting (and Nirvana don't even have as good a rhythm section as the Police did, and now I hear Kurt's widow had been "getting into Zen Buddhism"!). My favorite person in the band was always the tall dimpled guy who looks like Andy Kaufman (who looks like my son Linus's friend Stephen), so maybe Nirvana would be better off without Kurt. His guitar might be missed, but what the heck.

I'd seen him on MTV going on about how great it was that the Beatles could progress from "I Want To Hold Your Hand" to *Sgt. Pepper's* (how great it was that they sank from rock'n'roll to pompous mush in other words), and Kurt was hoping Nirvana could do something similar. (I heard the news today oh boy about a lucky man who made the grade. He blew his mind out in an attic or somewhere, I forget. The lyric sheet's so hard to find, what are the words, oh never mind.) A few years ago, Mike Saunders told me that if Lou Reed had shot himself after *White Light/White Heat*, there'd be a whole lot fewer crummy Lou Reed albums on the shelves. But I never expected some fool would actually go *do* it.

Then again, it makes sense. Kurt Cobain came out of a subculture that puts a premium on stupid integrity, he was embraced by rock critics who put a premium on stupid integrity, and he didn't want to disappoint them. I even identify with him in a way: I'm in charge of the baby bottles in our house; my dad was a manic-depressive who hung himself when I was 13; I have an ulcer, and when I was prescribed Tylenol II after my wisdom teeth were removed last year, the codeine calmed my tummyaches. But when I think about how dull rock criticism is these days, and how it inevitably got even more sanctimonious in the wake of Cobain's death, and even how sanctimonious this sentence sounds, I still get depressed, and my stomach burns. (Too bad no editors had sense enough to hire Weird Al Yankovic to write the obituary, since Weird Al's the only person who wrote anything interesting about the poor schmuck while he was *alive*.)

The night after Cobain died, I heard him sing a song called "In The Pines" on MTV *Unplugged*, and the very next morning we went to a flea market in Lehaska (which Linus thinks is "Alaska"), and we heard two old guys sitting inside a store singing the exact same song, which I guess is about a husband-murder or something. It seemed somewhat distantly familiar, but I couldn't place where I might've heard it before. I checked my copies of Hank Williams's *40 Greatest Hits* and Lead Belly's *Last Sessions*, and I couldn't find it on either record. So maybe *I* wrote it.

Well anyway, I suppose one reason I'm so hard on Cobain is because I think people who remind me of myself should make better music than he did. Anybody who believes Nirvana were an innovative band never heard very many bad '80s Midwestern noise-rock records. Depeche Mode have prettier droning melodies, and I've never understood why so many people always said Nirvana had a great drummer—outside of "Teen Spirit," he was just *average*, completely stiff compared to the guy on the first Guns N' Roses album. Lee Brilleaux, singer from '70s British pub band Dr. Feelgood, died of cancer (as in "I want to eat your cancer") the day Cobain's body was found, and his band was as "influential" as Nirvana—without them, British punks would have had no clubs to play in, and Nirvana would be crooning Firefall songs.

Weird thing is, I was actually starting to *like* Nirvana; I was coming real close to buying back the copy of *In Utero* I sold. I always had trouble telling *Nevermind*'s post-"Teen Spirit" singles apart, and they always seemed like incoherent-poetry bullshit (though of course now they "move" me in some sick voyeuristic masochistic way, now that I know all those "I'm not gonna crack"s were about feeling sorry for yourself, like Joy Division or somebody). When I first heard *In Utero*, it dragged like an awful pile of half-dead gunk, and I wished "Tourette's" was about Jim "Poop" Eisenreich of the Phillies, but it was really just lots of swear words, an idea Warrant beat Nirvana to on *Cherry Pie*. (Or maybe "Tourette's" could've been about Watley Goode in the funniest line of Mary Gaitskill's *Two Girls, Fat and Thin*: "a clinically diagnosed schizophrenic who had to take special brain medicine and would sometimes go nuts anyway and suddenly start yelling things like 'Penis!' and 'Vagina!' in public. Justine was very impressed; it was the first time she'd met a mother as glamorous as her own.")

Still, in the long run, both *In Utero* singles had cool guitar parts and memorable words. In "All Apologies," that "I wish I was like you, easily amused" line sounded more "sarcastic" (though not better) to me than anything in the supposedly sarcastic "Teen Spirit." Reminded me of this fanzine jerk named Torky who used to whine about my writing being nothing but trivial pursuits, and it reminded me that underground rock fans are easily amused by retarded garbage. So sometimes I'm Cobain, and sometimes he's Torky with hey-wait-a-new-complaint about me, just like Aerosmith used to chew me out for "talking about things that nobody cares" back in high school. And sometimes Kurt Cobain is just another overrated celebrity I never cared much about when he was alive, so why should I care now? Anyway, refusing to be easily amused is a badge of honor, like refusing to sell out. So is the title of "All Apologies," at least if you hear it wrong: "What else can I be? Oligopolies." But it wasn't oligopolies that killed Kurt Cobain. It was integrity. (A lie, I know, but it sounded nifty on paper.) And like Lester Bangs didn't say about Elvis, I can guarantee you one thing: we will never disagree again on anything like we disagreed on "Smells Like Teen Spirit." (7.0)

Radio On, 1994

WRONG IS RIGHT: MARILYN MANSON

The day before Halloween, Marilyn-Manson-the-band's audience at Philadelphia's Electric Factory wore too much black makeup, but they didn't scare me—mostly they seemed to be upper-middle-class Catholic school-teens from the burbs (the girls generally younger than the boys), clad in T-shirts with "The Lord Is Your Shepherd"-type proverbs on the back, no more threatening than if they'd headed out to catch a slasher flick for their dose of pre-sexual catharsis instead. I went as the plus-one of a friend who was reviewing the gig for a local paper, and we were way in the back where we couldn't see too well, so I agreed to squeeze my way toward the ornately decorated stage to note what supposedly Satanist omnisexual Marilyn-Manson-the-man (27-year-old Brian Warner to his nurse mom and furniture-salesman dad) was wearing (turned out to be a kinkyish beige hospital back brace and tattoos). Despite the sardine-packed denseness, pushing through was way too easy—this handclapping horde was too domesticated to *mosh*, even.

Compared to other musically useless industrial-metal hypes I've seen live in the past year (Stabbing Westward, Gravity Kills, and especially Nine Inch Nails, who barely even moved), Manson put on quite a show. They made the stage look like a church during high Mass (Station-of-the-Cross stained glass depicting Lucifer battling archangels); they set up pulpits and threw Bibles. The singer's facial hygiene repulsed me like fellow Alice Cooper–mimic Dee Snider of Twisted Sister a decade ago, but though his vocals' sickly industrial-whisper/deathmetal-barf switchoffs turned predictable quick, at least the drums pounded okay. Manson's ugliness never got nearly as campy as the fully transvestited Impotent Sea Snakes, whom I'd seen open for industrial-glitter hypes Psychotica a week before as part of an alleged glam-revival club tour, and who brought out whip-cracking, almost-naked third-gender dominatrixes and submissives holding signs proclaiming "Worship the Devil!," not to mention a life-size cutout of Marilyn Monroe to be sawed in half. (I swear Rush used the same cutout when I caught them in an arena concert a week later; oddly, Marilyn Manson is just about the only band I've seen this fall that *doesn't* rely on Marilyn Monroe pictures!)

All week long, at parties and over my phone, people were wondering if Marilyn Manson really slices himself up onstage, really sucks Nine Inch Nails members' members in front of his dad, really sacrifices dead babies and picks his nose with dildos made from neck bones. This pesky guy who sodded my lawn and bugs me for classic-rock promo CDs every week, who even purchased a Slayer one from me once, turned pale at the mere mention of Manson, swearing the singer was "evil." My pal Barb, who kickboxes, wears a wolf tattoo, saw Alice Cooper live this summer, and works as a publicist for Manson's opening band, New York Loose, insisted to me that Manson music is *different* from earlier shock-rock attempts somehow, that kids really might be in mortal danger this time. M.M.'s new *Antichrist Superstar*, meanwhile, penetrated *Billboard*'s chart at No.3, behind Celine Dion and Kenny G. It's like Alice's hugeness back when *I* was in Catholic school; the only comparably popular blasphemy in between came from Alice's Detroit homegirl Madonna. All of which proves that M.M.'s silly publicity stunts *work*.

Manson plays a fucked-up creep who wants to fuck you, fuck with you, tell you "fuck you." His lyrics tend toward your usual dorky decadence slogans: "Abortions in my eye," "I am the god of fuck," "Time for cake and sodomy," "I wasn't born with enough middle fingers." But cynics who call him humorless aren't paying attention. Interview snippets I heard on the radio the day after his show had wisecracks worthy of Mötley Crüe if not David Lee Roth, like when he said that fans who want to hang out with him "better make sure they've had their veterinary shots first," nyuk nyuk.

DID MARILYN MANSON TAKE UP GOLFING YET? (PHOTO: MARILYN MANSON)

In magazine profiles he's always dropping Nietzsche's and (*Satanic Bible* scholar/Led Zep influence) Anton LaVey's names side by side with Dr. Seuss's and Willy Wonka's. He's even a fairly coherent aesthetician: "I don't care if something's good or bad or if it's Christian or anti-Christian—I want something that's *strong*, something that believes in itself." Reminds me of Black Sabbath in 1970: mix up some horror-movie bullshit with Jesus bullshit, and folks naturally assume that you host decapitation rituals in your catacombs. "Now it's almost that anti-organized-religion stances are such a cliché that I'm almost ready to be pro-religion," Manson told *RIP*. "What people don't understand is, with even the most politically correct bands out there right now, it's all a gimmick, it's all a lie."

I'm not sure if his pubescent minions think he's a put-on, and I'm not sure it matters (did Alice's?), but don't discount the possibility—Manson's first two albums presented themselves basically as *pranks*. Their 1994 debut, *Portrait Of An American Family*, had Mr.-Bill-on-*Saturday-Night-Live* claymation parents and kids, plus Beatle figurines and Matchbox cars on the cover, and inside the band looked more glam than Goth, with the lead pervert wearing rainbow-fruit-striped socks and slouched in a shopping cart. On 1995's *Smells Like Children*, the group painted themselves up in sicko drag à la Alice-Cooper-the-band on *Pretties For You*. Song titles were

Mad magazine material ("May Cause Discoloration Of The Urine Or Feces," "Scabs, Guns And Peanut Butter," "Dancing With The One-Legged"); same goes for instrument credits ("Reverend Marilyn Manson: Spitting, Self-Mutilation, Chickens"; "Madonna Wayne Gacy: Sound Deformation, Poop Games").

What's lacking is Cooper's genius for hooks and vernacular. Mostly, Manson's early music watered down pre-1972 Coop through far less stomachable later horror hacks like Sisters of Mercy, Danzig, White Zombie, and W.A.S.P. (who of course were fucking like beasts years before Trent Reznor fucked like an animal). Once or twice, the voices would fall into some tasty fast high hoarse wicked-witch rapping (see also Psychotica's best song, "Starfucker Love"—Manson does the trick again in "Angel With The Scabbed Wings" on the new album); more often, mannered ominoso-bloat vocals and cumbersome sludge riffs were noise-distorted into a big muffled mess. *Smells Like Children* had remixes, aural porn, unpluggeds, interview tapes, phone calls about heart medicine, and a blatant rip-off of Einstürzende Neubauten's sturm-und-bang "Yü Gung" rhythm in "Kiddie Grinder." Plus covers of Screamin' Jay Hawkins (because he invented shock rock in the '50s by emerging from coffins), Patti Smith (because she said "nigger" and wanted to be outside of society), and Eurythmics (because M.M. figured they could make "Sweet Dreams"' already-ironic abuse-or-be-abused dichotomy more "intense" by making the music slower, a typically deluded '90s anti-pop fallacy that's embarrassed everybody from Rosanne Cash covering "Wouldn't It Be Loverly" to Afghan Whigs covering "If I Only Had a Heart").

To be fair, it did take even Alice Cooper a couple of LPs of tuneless ineptitude before he/they finally clicked with *Love It To Death*. And though *Antichrist Superstar* is hardly on that level (in fact, old codger Alice himself has made better albums in the '90s), it is a major leap forward in terms of playability: slicker, less shticky slop, more multifaceted and less obvious-on-the-surface, more skippity rhythms. It appears to be a concept album about a rock star, but I've still never made it through *The Wall*, so who cares; what's more important is that "Wormboy" is easily the band's catchiest track ever, a new wavey robopop concoction equal to David Bowie's *Scary Monsters*, or Depeche Mode or Devo at their funkiest (even though for some dumb reason its music stops dead for 30 seconds in the middle). "Antichrist Superstar" has hockey-glam hey-hey-hey crowd shouts over boingy beats reminiscent of Trio's 1982 German hit "Bum Bum"; "The Reflecting God" opens by parodying Smashing Pumpkins ("your world is an ashtray"); "Tourniquet"'s melody flirts with Alice's epic asylum-escape joke "Ballad of Dwight Fry"; "1996" flaunts a punning pinch (though not nearly enough) of the Stooges' "1969" (the year Mr. Manson was born). And whereas a year ago Manson was admitting to *Spin*, "I don't think there's anything sexy for girls to attach themselves to," now he's doubling his demographic by drooling plenty of borderline-pretty cabaret-serenade panty-soakers full of hushy come-ons like "I'm on my way down, I'd like to take you with me" and "You are the one I want and what I want is so unreal." Watch out, kids: before you know it your hero will be rewriting "Only Women Bleed," guesting on game shows, and bragging about his golf handicap.

L.A. Weekly, 13 December 1996

LIVE: TOWER THEATER, PHILADELPHIA, 18 FEBRUARY 1997

All the most-embarrassing-to-watch dancers in the '90s are bald: Sinéad O'Connor, Michael Stipe, Peter Garrett of Midnight Oil, and now Live's Ed Kowalczyk. In Illadelph on the opening night of Live's *Secret Samadhi* tour, Right Said Ed did both the hula and the "Shiny Happy People" hop, facing drummer Chad Gracey so he could shake his little tushy for the camera. Thanks to Kowalczyk's fancy hipwork and his somber sensitivity, these murmurers are managing to reel in the female constituency their desexed-Zep role models Rush never connected with. Call it "Importance of Being Earnest Rock," or maybe "Monk Rock": Kowalczyk's ruby-red guru robe could have been swiped from O'Connor's closet, and the Tower Theater's cathedral-like inner architecture was an apt metaphor for Live's militant bloody-Sunday grandeur. With U2 currently pretending to be cheesy, Live fills a major void, consecrating serious young adults with the integrity they crave. The set list even included songs titled "Ghost" and "Spirit."

Some hall-monitor type kept shushing me, so maybe the band should make everybody kneel in silence for certain hymns, like in church. Bassist Patrick Dahlheimer looked like a Renaissance painter, but the crowd— well-groomed post-teens on leave from frats, the Ivy League, and tech-school—was anything but arty. Live had a home-team advantage: They're dorks from York, not far from Amish Paradise. Maybe *that's* the unnamed nation their elusive anthems are about.

Backdropped by a video screen depicting interlocked industrial gears, Kowalczyk howled an oddly oedipal new ditty called "Freaks," something about your mom sleeping with you after picking you up in downtown Philly with a Henry Miller novel in your back pocket. He uncorked an array of 1997-vintage whines, although it was easy to confuse "Century" (in which "puke stinks like bee-ur" and "everybody's hee-ur") with "Rattle-snake" (which concerns "skinning dee-ur"). Later he covered Psychedelic Furs' "Love My Way," and flopped around like a scarecrow during the climactic "I Alone."

Kowalczyk's voice is way too low-registered to soar like he wants, but Chad Taylor's guitars reached high, approximating Arabic scales and Irish Spring jigs reminiscent of Scotch pre-grungesters Big Country. Gracey's quasi-polyrhythmic drumbeats suggested "world music," over which Kowalczyk recited vowels in Sinead O'Connor's old sheik shriek. You could tell when the group was trying to be funky, because strobes would switch on and Kowalczyk would erupt into mantras like "give it up, give it up, give it up." Totally cornball, but you can't fault the guy—I'd sell my drama, too, if people would buy it.

Spin, May 1997

CITY OF DREAMS: ROCK IN MEXICO

Mexico City is the biggest and allegedly most air-polluted city in the world, with freeways more traffic-jammed than L.A., but as soon as I got there my hay-fevered sinuses mysteriously dried up. And to my non-burning eyes there appeared a crossroads for culture from around the world: Spanish, Arabic, Afro-American, Aztec, Caribbean, Long Islandian (Debbie Gibson on my hotel radio), *mucho* French architecture, and this is where all the Volkswagen Beetles went when they died. They all seem to be owned by cabbies who stay tuned to the local techno station.

"All the popular music in Mexico was *always* a fusion," says Pacho, drummer for lengthily-named rock band Maldita Vecindad Y Los Hijos Del 5° Patio. Pacho is an intellectual who wrote his book *Rock Mexicano* on a borrowed typewriter, surrounding words like "Iggy Pop" and "Cheb Khaled" with Marshall Berman quotes and Mexican fanzine clippings and lots of Spanish stuff I don't understand. "Each generation in Mexico has their own way to make American music their own," Pacho theorizes—jazz turned into mambos, polkas into norteño, and now rock into "*rockero.*" The way James Brown screams reminds Pacho of mambo master Perez Prado, and Algerian rai reminds him of certain traditional Mexican melodies. Maldita and other Mex-rock bands make those melodies *stomp*, and like their artier cousins Caifanes the group has members who moonlight in mariachi combos on Garibaldi Square.

At Garibaldi, you can be serenaded by 100 mariachi sextets all playing at the same time. And even if the singer's packing a pistol, peddlers will step in front of him and try to sell you tequila or roses or blankets. Music in Mexico is a big part of *life*. "Each concert is like a big celebration, a space of freedom for two and a half hours," Maldita singer Roco (no last name for these guys) tells me. When rock was banned in Mexico for years, bands shared space with artists and human rights demonstrators in abandoned warehouses, like early Detroit techno musicians or the criminals in *Reservoir Dogs*. There's still no real concert circuit; it's more like barnstorming whistle-stops into towns where rock's still a rumor. Sometimes Maldita play outback saloons where the opening act is a cockfight.

"HERE PEOPLE LAUGH about death," Caifanes drummer Alfonso Andre told me way past midnight after an incredible Mexico City show last spring. The Day of the Dead is a major holiday here, and wherever you go you can buy tiny skeletons and sugar cubes shaped like skulls. High above Caifanes' audience the mythical grinning-skeleton character Death bounced back and forth on a playground swing. The stage was framed by six huge pastel-colored crucifixes leaning on each other, plus a perimeter of church candles, which for some reason were never lit. I kept looking for altar boys.

The night before, I'd visited the Metropolitan Cathedral in the city's Zocolo Square, only to learn that the Catholic masses I was raised on are really some pre-Christian pagan ritual in disguise. The church was built on Aztec pyramid ruins, relics of which are still visible around the edges. The Aztecs used to display bones of unlucky enemy soldiers on the pyramid steps, and in front of the Cathedral you run into a prehistoric crucifix fashioned from two logs, surrounded by four skulls. Caifanes eat up this stuff—one of their song titles translates as "Ash Wednesday," and they load up their CD covers and videos with skeletons and crosses and heathen icons. I think they just might be the best Goth-rock band since the Yardbirds.

Caifanes' shows kick off at a death-march tempo, but quickly become a metal hoedown. Self-confessed fans of four-eyed prog rock from King Crimson to Weather Report to XTC, they're capable of Latin counter-rhythm but prefer guitar friction and synthesizer symphonics. Their 1992 Adrian Belew–produced *El Silencio* album starts with "Metamorfeame," a punk rocker whose beat pounds at a breakneck pace that reminds me of Led Zep's "Communication Breakdown." The record flows through cotton-candy high notes, rumbling ocean rhythms with upsurges that bellow like sea elephants, Salvation Army funeral-wake honking, stuttery little chamber-group guitar figures. Acoustic blues build toward belted-out jubilation, Police-like rhythm dexterities and electro-handclapped darkness shift into slashing and scraping wah-wah parts, flamenco-strummed cumbias evolve into catacomb music over timbale percussion.

Caifanes consists of two guys with their heads in the clouds, two with their feet on the ground, and one grouch who's just doing his job, dammit. The grouch is Sabo Romo, squat and unshaven with frilly sleeves and a lime-green bass and no qualms about smooching singer Saul Hernandez backstage (so maybe he's just grouchy to *interviewers*). The sensible guys are square-faced keyboardist and saxist Diego Herrara (who puffs cigarettes while playing à la Bun E. Carlos) and triangle-faced drummer Alfonso Andre (who could pass for European-American and wears shirts with skulls). But the flighty New Age–brained guys are my two favorites. In fact, Alejandro Marcovich might be the only guitarist I've ever seen live whose solos didn't go on long enough. He's got ragdoll hair and wears paisley tights and work-boots and looks like he has to squeeze his head into his Slade-style top hat, and his tone is bluesless because, starting at age nine, he only played Argentine (where he's from) folk music. He attributes his technique to his sense of humor (he's fond of Pope jokes), and says to this day he doesn't know how to play properly and gets intimidated whenever he picks up a copy of *Guitar Player*—few of whose cover boys have ever come up with anything as ravishing as his solo in "El Communicador."

SAUL HERNANDEZ IS CAIFANES' pretty boy. He used to grow his hair to-wards the sky like The Cure's Robert Smith (who deaf people say he sings like), but he says the real inspiration was an old Mexican pachuco comedian named Tin Tan. Now Saul lets his tresses flutter down toward his leopardskin coat and Mayan skull leggings. When his hips are in motion he's a ringer for a young Robert Plant, whom he *might* sing like if Plant had grown up absorbing romantic bolero croons off his sister's José José records like Saul did. Saul's mom died when he was 15, and he recalls that pretty soon after that he started devoting his time to guerrilla adventures in street gangs with older friends. Now he's always gliding into Algerian rai falsetto *"aaaah"* notes that are absolutely melodramatic without sounding stilted.

Alejandro offers the opinion that Caifanes' entire approach to playing is "perverse." It's as if they reached rock by accident, by a path nobody knew was there. When they tried traditional music, Alfonso swears, they pulled it off but played badly. Yet in 1987, they rewrote the Mex-rock record book by selling half a million copies of their great single "La Negressa Tomassa," a partly parodic electrified cumbia version of a traditional Cuban salsa. Cumbia fans who heard the hit on the radio figured Caifanes were a cumbia band, so they went to their shows, only to start throwing tomatoes. But Caifanes still encore with the tune, and even in Philadephia (where the group drew the piddliest crowd of its mostly sold-out U.S. club tour) middle-aged Latinos get up and do fancy ballroom dances to it.

The 25,000-seater Sports Palace, where I saw Caifanes in Mexico City, is shaped, appropriately enough, like a gigantic armadillo. The band hired additional rent-a-saxes for the show, letting them join Diego for squawky non-R&B solos that brought to mind Andy Mackay in old Roxy Music. But mostly this was the closest I'll ever come to seeing Led Zeppelin in 1971— that's how virtuosic and monumental and outrageous the music was, how at any given moment there was just so *much* singing and guitaring and rhythm going on. Except this wasn't a Zep audience, and nor were these the brutal barrio punks that Caifanes claim are their main constituency; instead, they were middle-class teen-screamers who knew every last word, flicking Bics to the beat and (if they were shy girls who arrived in pairs) holding each other's hands on the way out so they wouldn't get lost. A few who'd saved up $50 for front row seats climbed onstage, maybe on a dare from friends; bouncers tried to throw them off, but Saul saved them and pulled a girl from the throng to dance with, Springsteen-style, during "La Negra Tomasa." In the English-speaking world you don't get crowds this unjaded and devoted and excited any more.

BASICALLY, MEXICO *invented* rock'n'roll, at least in the sense that dapper zoot-suited cha-cha-dancing street toughs known as pachucos originated

Elvis's ducktail in the '40s. But through the '60s, Mexican rock'n'roll proper consisted almost entirely of bar bands with names like Los Hooligans and Los Crazy Boys doing Spanish versions of songs by Elvis, who was allegedly slanderous toward Mexicans on occasion.

Then in 1971 500,000 Mexican young people gathered for two days at a giant Woodstock imitation of sorts in Avandaro, not far outside Mexico City. Roco of Maldita says the most dangerous thing any of the revellers did was to sit naked on the hoods of cars, but the Mexican government knew a threat when they saw one (three years earlier, in 1968, they'd sent in the army to massacre a few hundred student protesters). So rock was banned, or pushed underground at least, for the next 15 years. Shows by U.S. and U.K. acts were tiny and unaffordable when they happened at all, and the only Mexicans who came close to thriving were El Tri, a manly power-blues trio that never graduated from small clubs.

In 1985, in the middle of the country's worst economic depression for 75 years, an 8.1 Richter scale earthquake shook Mexico City inside out, killing 4,200. Eight years later, some parts still haven't recovered. But in 1986, pretentious dance bands from Spain (Radio Futura) and Argentina (Soda Stereo) drew sizeable crowds into Guadalajara, having a somewhat similar effect to the Ramones touring England in 1976, and also altering government and media preconceptions about the economic fate of Spanish-language rock. A troupe of comedians called Botellita De Jerez came up with a spicy roots-based concoction they named "Guacarock," Caifanes scored with their cumbia tribute, and record companies took to sending out search parties for bands fluent in the now-trendy native tongue.

TO FOBIA, AIMING for mohawked barrio teenagers by yelling "Viva Mexico" in concert and recording punk cumbias would just be an easy way out, what goateed drummer Gabriel Kuri calls "forcing dignity." Fobia's members have no discernible accents, peach-colored skin, and recorded their excellent new album, *Leche*, in New York.

The group's music stirs all sorts of Led Zep poundage and samba-classical crescendos and Lipps Inc. keyboard tweaks into blatantly bouncy and effetely impassioned dance-rock tunes. 1992's *Mundo Feliz* sold 70,000 copies, and its title means "Happy World," which keyboard guy Inaki Vasquez explains is the name of a cheesy old Mexico City amusement park where you'd be greeted at the gate by "big flowers going like this" (he opens and shuts his mouth real wide a few times). Fobia like circuses and kiddie music—especially Cepillin, a "silly, sad clown" who used to translate songs like Pat Boone's "Speedy Gonzalez" (!) on Mexican kids' TV, and Cri-Cri, a 1930s Isaac Asimov lookalike who created a string-orchestrated special-effect micro-universe of ugly dogs and cowboy mice and cricket narrators that many Mexicans swear was purloined by Walt Disney back when the two used to smoke peyote together in Veracruz.

"Mexico is a very hermetic culture," says Paco Huidobro, one of Fobia's two long-haired hippie types. "Historically, Mexicans worry too much about their Mexicanness." So his band went ahead and recorded (unreleased) English versions of a few *Mundo Feliz* tracks behind their label's back. Fobia can envision being promoted condescendingly in the U.S. as a "weird animal" like Shonen Knife from Japan. But Inaki admits, "I'd rather be a weird animal than be like a typical *charito*."

He may not have a choice. Last year's U.S. Caifanes/Maldita Vecindad tour was sponsored by Cuervo Tequila, and Maldita's earlier invites to the States mainly resulted from their famous fan Perry (Jane's Addiction/Porno for Pyros) Farrell's obsession with Mexican witch-doctor magic. U.S. Latin radio stations and record companies generally ignore Mexican rock bands, preferring to promote "adult" dance-pop and salsa singers who get nominated for *Billboard*'s Lo Nuestro Awards. Which isn't always horrible seeing as how Paulina Rubio and Gloria Trevi rock harder than most Anglo guitar bands around nowadays anyway—but it means Fobia still won't reach much of the expanding U.S. Hispanic population, which was 15 million in 1980 and is slated to be twice that by the year 2000.

BACK IN MEXICO, all the blonde pretty fair-skinned women seem to wind up reading the news on Televisa, the country's inescapable TV network and all-encompassing media conglomerate. Record producers help the station assemble a few replaceable clean-cut boys or girls into bubblegum groups called Menudo or (more recently) Magneto, who the rock bands naturally dismiss as "totally manufactured" or "Americanized." A silly criticism— compared to mariachi bands, Mexican rock *itself* is an Americanization. Still, as Fobia's Gabriel points out when we're discussing Nirvana's shtick in their "In Bloom" video, "It really *is The Ed Sullivan Show* down here." And rock is suddenly so popular that Televisa has no choice but to invite Fobia and Maldita and Caifanes, the way Ed used to invite the Stones and the Doors. Fobia did kung fu moves all through one song, but got invited back anyway. Saul of Caifanes says, "Teenagers are living something that didn't *exist* when I was a teenager."

"For us, this specific moment is a real charge," Maldita spokesman Pacho agrees. "We're *using* the media." Which means sneaking quick shots of dog turds on the road or homeless earthquake victims encamped in front of Harvard economist El Presidente Carlos Salinas De Gortari's house into videos, and thereby onto a network that pretends ugliness doesn't exist. "On Televisa, all the people look happy, but it's a real sad situation," Pacho broods. "There exists two Mexicos—the imaginary culture, the good parts that get shown on Televisa, and the culture that exists in the street—the *real* culture." Naturally he never explains how suburban kids buying Magneto records are less than "real," but what the heck, Pacho sees the government trying to control every aspect of life. "It's a system of corruption. They take you to the police car, then take your money."

Maldita supposedly sing about women's rights, Indian rights, and condoms. Their name roughly translates as "Damned Neighbourhood And The Sons Of The Lowest Caste On The Economic Totem Pole," but what they are is a hyperactive six-piece who turn world rhythms (reggae, Tex-Mex, rap, calypso, South African guitars, all manner of chanted call-and-response) into jump rock. They do what early '80s British Two Tone bands did with ska and what the Pogues (on their first LP or two) did with Irish jigs. Their 1989 debut album only sold 25,000, but their 1991 follow-up *El Circo* climbed to 500,000, the most for any Mexican rock album ever. And since *Billboard* estimates that two-thirds of cassettes sold in Mexico are bootleg pirates, a truer figure might be closer to one and a half million.

On stage they seem clownish but mostly unemotional. They take their shirts off right away after the concert starts, the singer high-dives with his legs spread, and they march in step and stomp around and act like jumping beans and soak their hair with sweat and do all these corny whole-world-in-my-hands hippie movements.

The Maldita numbers that work best live are the fastest ("Pachuco"), slowest ("Solin," "Kumbala"), and most Afro-Caribbean ("Papa De Perro," "Male"). *On El Circo* they cover "Querida," a norteño hit by Mexican star Juan Gabriel; it starts lovely, then turns into a fast polka with honked horns through about four false endings. And "Solin" has desert-movie guitar and undulating Arabian night vocals, and it rocks the way world beat boosters pretend rai king Cheb Khaled rocks.

"We're not introducing these sounds to become ethnomusicologists," emphasizes Pacho, quick to distinguish Maldita from, say, Los Lobos, who are scoffed at in Mexico as a nostalgia band, or David Byrne and Paul Simon, who reduce foreign sounds into museum artefacts. Today's Mexican rock bands come as naturally to Caribbean syncopations as Bo Diddley or '60s garage rock or '70s disco did. They don't wear beats as proof of eclecticism. More to the point, none of the ethnic folklore peddled by labels like Earthworks or Shanachie sounds this *alive*. I hear this as 'rock,' not 'World Music.' And lately it's pretty near the only rock I can imagine caring about.

The Wire, 1994

CHUMBAWAMBA AT THE PISS FACTORY

So when was the last time *any* drinking song became so huge a pop hit? I don't mean songs *about* drinking ("Gin And Juice," say); I mean songs expressly created *for* drinking—Will Glahe's 1939 chart topper "Beer Barrel Polka," maybe? In "Tubthumping" by Chumbawamba you can still hear steins being clanked together. The bleary-eyed video is set in a backwater British karaoke pub, men and women wandering in and out of the loo. There's this phat ale-bellied gang shout; oppressors are trying to keep some bloke down, but the harder they come the harder they fall, one and all: "I get knocked DOWN, but I get UP AGAIN, you're never gonna keep me DOWN." It's Weeble Rock!

Boots my arse but good, like Slade or oi! music. Same soused-lout, slurred accent. Then a prim womanfolkie warbles "Danny Boy" and "Don't Cry For Me Next Door Neighbor" (sorry *Evita*) and sweeter still about "pissing the night away," equal parts yearn and urine. (One of George Carlin's seven words you can't say on the telly, and apparently Chumbawamba's favorite—their previous album had a catchy rant about "I wouldn't piss on you if you were a fire" plus a Brit hit called "Homophobia," where piss and beer mixed with blood gushing from a kicked-in head.) The only other 1997 hit with so much energy was the Spice Girls' "Wannabe"; only one so unclassifiable to any known musical genre was OMC's "How Bizarre," with which "Tubthumping" shares brass charts, New Wave beat, distaff backup, flatly exuberant foreign rapping, and a knack for tossing whatever's warm into a pop hybrid so new and natural and uplifting that it doesn't sound like a hybrid at all.

A tubthumper is a soapbox speaker like Emma Goldman, Chumbawamba explain in the most extensively theory-heavy band-created web-

ALE-BELLIED AGITPROP WEEBLE-ROCKERS CHUMBAWAMBA.
(PHOTO: CASEY ORR)

site I've ever seen. They list major chains (HMV, Tower, Virgin) you should shoplift their album from, they compose essays praising Black Panther plane hijackers, they even collect their most scathing (and maybe accurate) reviews: "The band who are to irony what Dr. Stephen Hawking is to pole vaulting." They've railed about free education, dock strikes, poll taxes, Nicaragua, apartheid, trickle-down economics; they have ridiculous song titles on the order of "Fight the Alton Bill!" and "Smash Clause 28!" And they sure do get stifled a bloody awful lot—for uncleared samples (their never released 1992 album *Jesus H. Christ*), for uncleared quotes (ones from Orwell, Aristotle, Chomsky, Mae West, and anonymous 1968 graffiti artists left out of *Tubthumper*'s booklet), for piss-poor timing (alcohol song yanked off BBC when Princess Di died). Which sadly only gives them more self-righteous grandstand leverage, more permission for empty tag line slogans.

I doubt their propaganda overkill has jarred many contemporaries out of complacency: usually, I have trouble figuring out the words. But I respect them for pissing off pinko punks (ones who slash tour-bus tires in Poland!) by abandoning straight-edge dogma and selling out to mass culture, despite a history of sampling Poly Styrene (and Lenny Bruce) and covering Wire and collaborating with extremists the Ex and Crass. A nine-person anarchist collective (seven in the band since the start, five sharing vocal duties) A&Rd into the United States on the basis of VH1 VP of programming Lee Chesnut's hearing their hit song on a British "tip sheet" sampler, they're all in their thirties, though they look older. Their online discography opens with quotes from "Rebellious Jukebox" by the Fall. It's hard to imagine more unlikely new pop stars. Chumbawamba still come off like protégés of Leeds's most venerable punk institution, the Mekons, whose Jon Langford was their mate back in squatting days. Like the Mekons, they know a spoonful of wit and sex and drink helps the doomsaying go down. Even their name is fun to say. And "One By One" on the new CD, a white wisp of darkness and doubt about labor unions and Pontius Pilate over holy pipe organs, is easily the prettiest Mekons song of 1997 not recorded by Cornershop.

The very Leeds trick of interspersing charmingly amateurish Mekons two-step with forced Gang of Four art-funk made up for the fact that their 1986 Live Aid–sledgehammering debut was called *Pictures Of Starving Children Sell Records*. By 1988, they were pomping up singular time signatures and crooning angelic Yes harmonies at polka-ska tempos, thus countering all their unbearably sore-thumb thespian skits subverting Armour Hot Dog commercials. Next came a Fairport Convention–comely collection of *English Rebel Songs: 1381–1914*: insurgent madrigals about cutty wrens, noble diggers, the gentry, barley wheels, the scaffold high, and the exorbitant price of malt. By 1992, folkish structures were admixing with up-to-date disco-floor aesthetics. Determined not to preach to the converted, *Tubthumper* has Latin breaks, garage riffs, sophisticated crescendos, trip-hop lounge moods, and fast gurgling jungle electronics, all somehow congealing with Cockney recitations about "bollocks" and brain extraction dialogue into a dozen discreetly melodic pop songs. In the irritatingly titled maritime metaphor "The Good Ship Lifestyle," massed working-girl harmonies, unschooled but alive and more rainy than icy, surge their Titanic turbulently past ports of call, through the tides of fate. "Steer a course, a course for nowhere"—the Mekons called it floating off the edge of the world, but I bet they never expected a top 40 audience would go down with the ship.

Village Voice, 29 October 1997

MR. AND MRS. USED TO BE: THE WHITE STRIPES
FIND A LITTLE PLACE TO FIGHT 'EM OFF

Success has made a failure of our home. Loretta Lynn said that; Elvis Costello covered it once. (Sometime later, somebody changed the words to "the mo money we come across, the mo problems we see.") Costello also covered "I Just Don't Know What To Do With Myself" once. As do, on their new *Elephant* album, the White Stripes—who like Loretta Lynn so much they dedicated their previous album to her and are bringing her to Hammerstein Ballroom this Saturday.

The White Stripes open *Elephant* with a really paranoid song—paranoid about groupies, or imitators, or sycophants. Or somebody. "I'm gonna fight 'em off. . . . They're gonna rip it off." Slow chords, blues notes, muffled voice eventually climbing in pitch. Ominous sound, tense and bothered. Sloweddown Little Richard in the chorus. Words about how a seven-nation army, which is to say a nation of millions, couldn't hold Jack White back. He wants to escape from fame, run away to Wichita. (Same state as Loretta's beloved Topeka, where one is a-toddlin', one is a-crawlin', and one's on the way.) A corny old travails-of-stardom song. It's the radio single right now, and it doesn't say what the seven nations are. Which seems rather sneaky, given the War With No Allies.

Anyway, now that the White Stripes are in a bigger room, they might not know what to do, and they might have to think of how they got started, sitting in their little room. So in "Seven Nation Army," and later in "The Hardest Button To Button," they deal with it. The latter's a boogie, a very antisocial one. And a marriage-rocker to boot—everything the White Stripes do best. "Now we're a family/And we're alright now/We got money and a little place to fight now." The room gets bigger. "It was 1981/We named him Baby/He had a toothache/He started crying/It sounded like an earthquake."

It's gotta start right in your own backyard. Dion DiMucci said that, in a song about losing his kids and wife to drink and drugs. And the White Stripes, Detroit domestics that they deep-down are, sing about backyards a *lot*. "The Hardest Button To Button" and "Little Acorns," which follows it on *Elephant*, are more vacant-lot ecology, more dead leaves and dirty ground to help us look at all the bugs we found. But when the acorn song opens with a moral fable about a squirrel saving up nuts for winter, I'm thinking it's about the Stripes preparing for *their* future. Which they should.

Besides being an out-of-left-field smash (which thus suggests that Clear Channel's warmongering assholes might not be as monolithic as doomsayers say) and birthing some of history's shortest AOR hits, 2001's *White Blood Cells* was thematically of a piece, distinguished by Mr. and Mrs. Used to Be's best songwriting ever, much of it conceivably autobiographical. Which is to say it was, in some ways, a classic D-I-V-O-R-C-E LP in the Fleetwood Mac/X/Human Switchboard/Richard and Linda Thompson/ Womack and Womack tradition.

You get married in a big cathedral by a priest and if I'm the man you love the most you can say "I do" at least, but it's getting harder to find a gentleman to stimulate devotion. I read it all as Jack being more committed to the union forever and Meg not being able to help how a woman feels when the tingle becomes a chill. But art can lie, of course.

For instance: more and more, I'm convinced Jack is basically a one-man band. Meg, as wonderful a person as she seems to be, is an entirely replaceable drummer—musically, at least, if not conceptually. On *Elephant*, she fills in space competently enough when the guitar stops, but otherwise I forget she's even there. Though then again, I've never understood why people make a big deal about Dave Grohl or Janet Weiss (neither of whom can swing a 16th note to save their lives), so maybe my standards are too high. But there are definitely garage-revival bands out there who dance like White Stripes don't—a half-dozen minimum in Detroit alone, and that's not even counting Jack's pals Electric Six covering Roxy Music's "Street Life" at the Bowery Ballroom last week. Better yet, play any six *Elephant* songs next to the half-dozen that end ZZ Top's *Mescalero*, which hits the stores this week, and tell me which band's got the funk. (Hint: the one with the bass player.) All of which, may I remind you, matters, since garage rock is about how nobody can do the shing-a-ling like I do as much as it's about how sometimes good guys don't wear white. Thing is, Meg *looks* so cool. And it's *beyond* cool that my 13-year-old drummer daughter Cordelia wears pigtails like her sometimes and has the White Stripes' photo framed in her room. But especially given how much White Stripes sound more like Led Zeppelin than like anybody else, Meg's got no brontosaur Bonham stomp at all. And not much propulsive Moe Tucker pulse, either. And when her voice sneaks out of a couple *Elephant* tracks, it's even blanker than her drums and her facial expressions. Somehow, across the board, she's figured out how to come off *charmingly* blank, which is to her credit. But mostly what her musical anonymity proves is that Jack White is one heckuva rhythm guitarist. And singer, too. In "Little Acorns," he gives us a huge downbound guitar stutter, and vocal hiccups like if Herman's Hermits covered "D'yer Mak'er." He's got this high, glammy vibrato, almost comical—intentionally tweedledee frilly and fey. (And has anybody noticed his increasing visual resemblance to Michael Jackson? OK, never mind.) So maybe "Black Math" on *Elephant* is a black mass, lisped. Unless it's math-rock gone blues. Killer divebomb fuzztone repetition, faster and faster, deeper and deeper, more and more pissed; Jack's learned over the course of four albums how to be heavy without being sluggish. He's developed this unusual knack for getting an extremely grimy slide sound into an extremely pretty pop song, for letting thick gangliations coalesce into melody, for taking cool explorations within a totally tight framework, for making his six-string ring like Salvation Army horns. He stated his aesthetic philosophy early on: "Crumble crumble/The bag is brown/Rip up the paper/To hear a sound/ Pick up the pieces/Off the ground." His guitar style comes out of Jeff Beck, Roger McGuinn, Tom Verlaine, Neil Young, Angus Young. So whippersnappers who compare his band to Violent Femmes make no more sense than ones who say he's Jon Spencer.

Like all great garage-rock bands, White Stripes are omnivorous in their cover versions: Blind Willie Johnson, Bob Dylan ("One More Cup Of Coffee," a couple years before Robert Plant covered it—on an Upper Peninsula road trip last summer, my kids got sick of me playing *both* versions in the car), Dolly Parton, the Kinks, the Premiers' "Farmer John," the Flamin' Groovies' "Teenage Head," Captain Beefheart's "Ashtray Heart," Robert Johnson via the Stones, now Dionne Warwick. On *Elephant*, "Hypnotize" might be my favorite song just 'cause it's the best dance track, not to mention a blatant Xerox of some famously distorted '60s proto-punk pebble if not nugget, though damned if I can figure out which one. And like any good garage album, *Elephant* has more than its fair share of it-ain't-me-you're-looking-for-babe-don't-hang-around-'cause-two's-a-crowd flare-ups: "The Air Near My Fingers," whose riff is pure "Wild Thing"/"More Than A Feeling"/"Smells Like Teen Spirit"; the even meaner "There's No Home For You Here," Jack in his verbosely faux-proper Ray Davies mode: "I'm only waiting for the proper time to tell you that it's impossible to get along with you." Massed, churchy chorus; muffled, maybe backward hook hinting at psychedelia like any antsy suburban hoodlums circa 1966.

WHITE STRIPES JUST DON'T KNOW WHAT TO DO WITH
THEMSELVES. (PHOTO: PATRICK PANTANO)

Waking up for breakfast, taking pictures, throwing garbage, breaking bottles, lighting matches: mental refuse of a pointless relationship.

By now, you got your white stripes on black zebras, your black stripes
on white zebras, your black and white stripes on invisible zebras, and your
invisible stripes on black and white zebras, and how can you tell the difference? Which is to say it just might be pointless to make qualitative distinctions between White Stripes albums—their 1999 debut, where Jack
was still a bit too obsessed with the *Anthology Of American Folk Music*, and
from back when he hadn't quite figured out yet how to make his blues pop
enough, is barely a notch below the later three, which are all too close to
call. Like all those *TRL* teens, I assume *White Blood Cells* will always be my
first pick because it's the first one I ever heard. But all the hardcore garage
hipsters I know who heard *De Stijl* first prefer that one. And in the long run
Elephant may be no different.

Certain facets are missed on the new one, though. The second side (on
the vinyl version, sent to critics back in February to thwart downloads,
which didn't work) is the dullest sequence they've put together since tracks
five through 11 on their debut. There's nothing as dark as the 300 people
living out in West Virginia who ended *White Blood Cells* (and who always
made me think of "The Ballad Of Hollis Brown"), and nothing as beautiful
as the jousting-faire folk-rock of "Dead Leaves And The Dirty Ground" or

"The Same Boy You've Always Known," and no stompin'-our-feet-on-the-wooden-boards barn-dance beats worthy of "Hotel Yorba." Could use more Dock Boggs country-blues dirt, too, about how your Southern can is mine in the mornin' and when I find you mama you'll feel my hand (and maybe lose your heart on the burning sand) and if I catch you in the heart of town gonna make you moan like a graveyard hound. I mean, Jack's sounding increasingly precious in interviews, spouting confused aesthetic theories that he'd stated more succinctly way back when he named *De Stijl* after an art movement built on straight lines and primary colors. And now he's babbling about the return of the gentleman and sweetheart like he's Beck's little Delta brother. But fact is, some of his sexiest songs have never been gentlemanly at all—and what most saves *Elephant* from drowning in impending professionalism isn't good manners, it's hostile boogies like "Ball And Biscuit": very deliberate, all evil boll-weevil eight-bar George Thorogood have-love-will-travel backdoorman jellyroll prowess, with ripping Crazy Horse headbangs thrusting deep inside. "Let's have a bawwwl, girl, and take our sweet little time about it." Read about him in the paper, or just ask your girlfriends, 'cause they already know. Not as heavy a heffalump stampede as Mastodon or Mammoth Volume, maybe, but at least as heavy as Black Keys.

So while *Elephant* may not be the subspecies of pachyderm that never forgets, it's at least the kind where you'll be as clueless as all those blind guys from India if you only concentrate on its tusks or tail. And if it's got a big trunk, let me search it. Side two really does worry me, too. To wit: (1) "I Just Don't Know What To Do With Myself," never one of Bacharach-David's (or Warwick's) best songs. Once presaged Elvis Costello's own eternal descent into meaningless good taste. (2) "In The Cold, Cold Night." Sung cold and detached, by Meg. Sounds merely spare and retro—not a big stretch from what's wrong with Adult Alternative Radio. You could imagine it on a Nick Hornby soundtrack; that's how "pure" it is. (3) "I Want To Be The Boy To Warm Your Mother's Heart." Ornate, dainty little chamber-room figure eights. Yet another forlorn bid for the Aimee/Norah/*O Brother* crowd, which I hope White Stripes get (though if Beck's mellow record didn't even get *him* there, good luck). Sitting in her backyard (see?!) for hours, and Mama baked a cake. A couple albums ago, Jack broke rules just so a cute classmate would notice him; now he's inclined to finish high school (and turn cartwheels) for the same reason. He wants to be the kind of guy who tries to win you over. (4) "You've Got Her In Your Pocket." Not as good a boy-to-boy advice song as "Don't Mug Yourself" by the Streets.

Again, slow and atmospheric and trying hard to be romantic, not in an especially coherent way. Jack is fine writing about commitment issues, but even when he hits his generally convincing high register here, he never quite engages.

He can be a real stick-in-the-mud, you know? At least when it's convenient for him. But then again, his conservative bent—his smelling a rat around little brats who disrespect their parents, his memories of elementary school as a warm safe place where as a child he'd hide, his know-nothing complaints about hip-hop being harmful to children and other living things—is frequently quite commendable, even comparable to the aggressively reactionary whiteness of punks back during disco. He can be a real sweetheart, too, as you might've noticed—in his old back-to-school songs, for instance, or that one where he told his little apple blossom to put her troubles in a little pile. And he's so straightforward, so unpoetic and vernacular in his language, and that's absolutely rare now. *Elephant*'s finale is a jovially warmhearted, self-deprecating thing called "Well It's True That We Love One Another," where Holly Golightly of Brit post-pub cult heroines Thee Headcoatees calls him by his true name (shades of his fellow Detroit sometime-prude Marshall Mathers, who also knows that white blood sells): "I love Jack White like a little brother." Stuff about phone numbers written in the back of Bibles, and Meg sounding even more blank and bored up against Holly, which only makes it cuter when she confesses how Jack really bugs her. The song's jolly-good-cup-o'-tea coda is the sweetest way a Top 10 album has ended in, like, forever. And when Jack requests some English lovin', Holly says if she does that she'll have one in the oven. I'm expected, she's expecting. One's on the way.

Village Voice, 15 April 2003

3

Well, okay—I already wrote a book about this stuff. It's called *Stairway to Hell: The 500 Best Heavy Metal Albums in the Universe*, and it came out in 1991 and then in an updated edition in 1998. You can probably find it cheap on Amazon, so I'll do my best not to be redundant here. Basically, when I started writing about music, heavy metal needed defending; class biases of rock critics being what they are, it still does to a certain extent. But now plenty of younger critics out there write about nothing but, which frees me up to pay only as much attention as I feel up to. Lately, I feel up to less and less.

   Basically though, I've been off-again/on-again since *Stairway* came out. Got rid of almost every album in the book when I finished it the first time, figuring I'd had my fill of noisy guitars for a while. So when I put together the updated version, way too many of the 100 '90s releases I added were just new reissues of stuff from the '70s and '80s, and too many other ones were just passingly loud-guitared alternative rock records that stretched the heavy metal definition to its breaking point at a time when alt-rock was usurping the metal moves I'd been reared on. Which meant I missed a lot of interesting '90s music that had slipped past my intermittent focus— which wasn't difficult, since heavy metal's definition never stops changing. Give or take Black Sabbath, almost nothing that was called heavy metal in the '70s, and barely half of what was called heavy metal in the '80s, is considered heavy metal anymore; by now, Nashville country sounds more like Bon Jovi or Cinderella than heavy metal does. Naturally this leads to lots of entertaining arguments, especially when one stubbornly insists on sticking to the original definition as I've tended to, or even on doing what I did in *Stairway* and claiming "metal" should include any music from any time in history that would've been called metal had it come out at any time in metal's lifespan, even if it wasn't considered metal at the time of its actual release. Which is to say that, if *Stairway* were to be updated again, I'd almost feel obligated by my own cranky precedent to include a Jason Aldean album or two.

Frankly, though, I'm getting pretty tired of that routine (and country-chart-topping AC/DC-cum–Bad Company power chords or no, Aldean's not really even all that good). I'm content now to leave metal's definition to the metalheads. To whom, starting around the time of Iron Maiden and then especially with Metallica and Slayer and their myriad "extreme" spawn, metal meant music largely devoid of the blues and swing that defined metal in the '70s (or "hard rock" at least—same difference then). As mid-'80s thrash turned into early '90s death metal and black metal and grindcore, the music just sounded more and more gratuitously ugly to me, innovating (or pretending to) in almost indiscernible increments, within a more and more prescribed perimeter. By the late '90s and early '00s, though, goth-oriented "dark metal" bands like the Gathering and Tiamat had turned in another direction, incorporating morose beauty learned from Kate Bush and Swans and Enigma and Joy Division. That woke me up a little, as did stoner rockers like Monster Magnet (featuring former members of Shrapnel, whose 1984 EP is reviewed herein) reviving old Sir Lord Baltimore grooves, and metalgazers like Isis thickening My Bloody Valentine ambience into more meaty Muzak, and prog revisionists like Opeth doing something similar with complicated Stonehenge time signatures from days of yore. But most of those moves turned codified and predictable within a few years, as well.

Now, maybe inevitably, metal is taken seriously as actual music—it gets analyzed in avant-garde magazines like the *Wire*, and in the *New York Times* it's reviewed by the same guy who covers jazz. But for me, at least, while I still occasionally hear extremely extreme folk-metal, doom-metal, Viking metal, space-metal, snow-metal, and whatnot-metal albums that *sound* cool—Fentanyl's 2006 *Feeble Existence* and Necrodemon's 2007 *Ice Fields Of Hyperion* were doozies, I swear—the sheer quantity of marginally decent stuff ultimately all muddles together. And when it comes to memorable songs per se, the genre seems to offer a disconcerting lack of truly discrete ones to latch on to. Also, it's really hard to make wisecracks about lyrics the singer won't let you hear.

The joke of it all, of course, is that I notice this stuff at all anymore, since I basically became The Metal Go-To Guy for magazines like *Rolling Stone* and *Entertainment Weekly* entirely by accident—I identified a void, and jumped in, and when they assigned me a new Scorpions album and

I'd never actually listened to a Scorpions album before in my life, I usually kept my mouth shut. Poverty is the mother of invention: one big reason *Stairway To Hell* wasn't the definitive and complete metal encyclopedia Harmony Books originally asked for was that I didn't actually own any Iron Maiden or Judas Priest albums (I now have the latter's 1977 *Sin After Sin* on CD; it's pretty good), and since I couldn't afford to buy them all, it made more sense for me to plow through my shelves and pick out 500 LPS that an alien unfamiliar with subcultural clothing styles might conceivably consider heavy metal in some alternate universe. I still get asked now and then to write, say, a "history of hair metal" focusing on groupies and co- caine, but that tabloid crap's never interested me—I've never read a page of Mötley Crüe's *The Dirt* bio, and have no plans to. I'm more interested in where hair metal came from (small-town Pennsylvania and Indiana and Maryland) and where it wound up (Nashville) than whatever sins were committed at the Whisky A Go Go in between.

That said, what follows are a few samples of my metal writing that didn't wind up in that other book. I even talk at length to some people from well- known bands, at least three of which (Def Leppard, AC/DC, Led Zeppelin) are really just "rock" by now; Def Lep, for their part, have been fortunate enough to collaborate on Country Music Television with Taylor Swift, the premier singer-songwriter of her generation. I also converse with Metal- lica, who I fully expect won't count as metal anymore by the time you read this. Which is kind of amusing, right?

FIVE GREAT BEATS-PER-MINUTE

Of course it's a minor pleasure, and none of it means shit, I know, but slightly above-average heavy metal played by slightly above-average heavy metal bands still manages on occasion to get where I want to go. Def Leppard may not be Hüsker Dü or Proletariat, but they sure beat the hell out of REO Speedwagon, whom eight college roommates in as many college semesters forced me to put up with, back in the days when MOR-with-guitars-instead-of-strings passed for the hard stuff. Things have improved these last three years, but not by that much; every time a rock critic tries to lure me toward the Smiths' MOR-with-guitars, or the Thompson Twins' MOR-with-synthesizers, or Linda Ronstadt's MOR-with-strings, or for that matter King Sunny Adé's MOR-with-guitars-and-talking-drums, I say fuck this shit, and I turn on the radio, and I hope Def Lep's "Rock of Ages" or Van Halen's "Panama" comes on and puts some sense back into my impressionable young mind.

Anyway, outside of Van Halen, who are so good they don't even count anymore, the best heavy metal song I've heard on the radio this year is "Round and Round," by Ratt. It's reasonably fast; and it's got an MC5-ish first line ("Out on the street/That's where we'll meet") that gets your attention right away, and a simple repeating riff that serves (and works) as the hook, and no real guitar showboating to speak of, and best of all, a beat; you could dance to it if you had to. Plus, with its funny Milton-Berle-and-a-platter-full-of-rats video, "Round and Round" actually improves on MTV. And I've heard worse albums (for example, *Goodbye Cruel World* and *This Is What You Want, This Is What You Get*) than Ratt's major-label debut, *Out Of The Cellar*: the L.A. five-piece does get self-indulgent once in a while, but it never messes with keyboards or strings or any of that sissy stuff, and a couple cuts ("I'm Insane," "She Wants My Money") approach Ramones/Motörhead velocity and intensity. The band's 1983 Liam Sternberg-produced and independently released EP was even better; its highlight was a version of "Walkin' The Dog" that beat Aerosmith's, and it had a couple more fast-as-punk metal numbers. If Stephen Pearcy gets over his

SHRAPNEL: *SHRAPNEL* (ELEKTRA/ASYLUM, 1984)

tendency to scream when he ought not (like, when the tape's running) Ratt could conceivably put out a real good greatest-hits package some day.

Like Ratt, Powertrip comes from California, and like Ratt's EP (and a lot of other HM records, now that the genre has its own grassroots fanzine network), Powertrip's first album is on an independent label, Public Records. But Powertrip is notable mainly because its lead singer is former Angry Samoan Jeff Dahl, a rather ugly young man who told *Creem*'s Richard Fantina last year that Powertrip is attempting to forge a punk-HM alloy they call "speed metal." While the band's hybrid never approaches the wonderful Amboy Troggs-cum-Ozzy Stooge dry rot the Samoans shovel out on their two EPS, the foursome does manage to deliver enough good songs—the Buzzcocky "Lab Animal," about some girl who goes to jail or something; the Black Flagrant "No Place," in which Dahl hits his head against the wall; "Flight of the B.B.'s," an instrumental which beats the Sidewinders and I guess ELP at the Rimsky-Korsakov game; and the almost-AOR "Caught In The Act," which might or might not be about jerking off—to suggest that they may be onto something. I wish their material was hookier, they ought to get rid of those stupid fake British accents, and they lack a discernible raison d'être, as they say in Halifax, but I don't think I'd complain if they ever came onto the radio.

I wouldn't change the station on Shrapnel, either. I saw these New

Yorkers open for a reunited ? and the Mysterians at Bookie's Club 870 in Detroit about three years ago, and I liked them a lot; they had a cartoon-patriotic, cartoon-militaristic stance which brought to mind the MC5 and early Ramones, and their sound was noisy enough to be metal and fast enough to be punk. But their new debut EP aims for commercial respectability; it sounds a lot like what we used to call powerpop, only with more pompous keyboards and louder guitars, sort of like a mutant hybrid of the Shoes, the Dictators, and Foreigner. Gross, I know, but I like it—especially during "Master Of My Destiny," a hard pop number with handclaps and Human Beinz quotes and lyrics about self-determination, during the metallic cover of Gary Glitter's "Didn't Know I Loved You (Till I Saw You Rock-n-Roll)," and during the psychedelic-DOR "Nations," which was produced by former P-Fur Vince Ely and sounds like it.

This is a pretty strange way for a heavy metal band to sound, I guess, but not quite as strange as how Armored Saint sounds for the first eight seconds of one of the three songs on their debut EP on Metal Blade Records. For the other 11 minutes and 34 seconds, Armored Saint sounds like your typical horrid eighth-generation "let's pretend we worship devils" sludge merchants; their roots seem to go no deeper than those of Iron Maiden or Judas Priest or whoever else is making the rounds in chains and leather these days. I mean, dig these groovy lyrics: "My fear is gone/Battled and conquered, now I'm up front/To sail through the dawn"—that's almost better than Spinal Tap, and Spinal Tap never did anything as smart as when Armored Saint thanks "Jay's Liquor" on their record sleeve. Which'd be the most distinctive thing about Armored Saint if the first eight seconds of "False Alarm" didn't make them sound as if they'd spent the last four years of their lives listening to "Albatross" by PIL.

For all I know, they did, and that Jah Wobbly bassline is just a clue to let on that the rest of their EP is a farce, in which case it's a great one. But if nobody in Armored Saint ever even heard of *Metal Box*, I'm impressed anyway—I'm reminded of the people who, after hearing E.S.G. for the first time a couple of years back, wondered how these teenage black girls could ever get "that sound" without having ever heard PIL, as if teenage black girls are somehow inherently less creative than your average Briton. And I'm reminded as well that a lot of my favorite rock'n'roll, if not most of it, has been made by people who had no idea what the current trends were—ignorance keeps people honest, I guess.

So even though I now mostly use Hüsker Dü and "Rock Box" for what I once mostly used heavy metal for, and even though I doubt I'll return much to the new records by Ratt and Powertrip and Armored Saint and maybe even Shrapnel, that doesn't mean they don't speak to me. I hear bands of their ilk as the true independent voices, untainted by Pazz & Jop polls, making rock'n'roll because it makes them feel good. Or making rock'n'roll because they figure it'll help them get rich or get famous or get laid, which amounts to the same thing. I listen to them for the same reason some critics listen to King Sunny Adé or the S.O.S. Band or the Neville Brothers—to assure themselves that rock can still exist without pretensions—not just technical ones, but conceptual ones as well—and that rock is still strong enough without those pretensions to produce an abundance of major and minor pleasures. With heavy metal, sometimes those pleasures come just because somebody like Twisted Sister or Quiet Riot has finally brought the songs and sounds of a great ignored band like Slade to the masses, or because a rich bitch like Eddie Van Halen has recorded a song that sounds just like Iggy and the Stooges, or because Motörhead has once again lulled me into a stupid happy cathartic nirvana, or just because any one of the new heavy bands has played a song that's "five silly beats-per-minute faster," as Robert Christgau somehow calculated last year that a lot of them are. Silly or no, those five beats-per-minute make me feel great, or at least make me forget why I don't, and oftentimes that's all I ask of rock'n'roll.

Village Voice, 25 September 1984

SEDUCE: *SEDUCE*

An art that nobody seems much willing to apply anymore is that of combining the undeniable power of the hard-rock heavy riff with the undeniable (though you'll no doubt deny it) power of the pop-rock catchy hook. Which may sound at first like a waste of time. But when you think about it, makes a lot of sense, because when you get down to it, heavy metal (like bubble-gum) is really just a kiddie music anyway, no matter how often its pseudo-macho practitioners pretend otherwise. (And now that kids reach puberty when they're still wearing diapers—I mean, I read in the paper the other day about this 14-year-old girl and her 12-year-old companion who were gonna have a baby and get married—it's about time we stopped claiming a distinction between "childhood" and "adolescence," don'cha think?) Thing is, this bubble-metal I'm talking about useta be a pretty popular sport, back when the Sweet was cranking out junk like "Blockbuster" and "Fox On The Run" and "Wig Wam Bam," and when Kiss, Slade, Alice, the Runaways, and those people were doing their thang. But then everybody grew up and got boring. A while back it looked like Cheap Trick was gonna pick up the ballroom blitz and run with it, and when I first heard "Round And Round" I figured Ratt would cut some fine cheese, but they both decided to wimp out and buy blow-dryers instead. Nowadays there's Redd Kross (into Zep and the Brady Bunch, no less!), who only punk-rockers know about, and that's it. (Yeah, I'm well aware that sushi-eaters like Quiet Riot and Krokus and Snötley Crüe try to cover all those early-'70s hard-pop hits. And I suppose Amy Grant does a kick-ass live version of "Hot Rails To Hell," right?) What I really wanna know is what teenybop-speedmetal is gonna sound like.

Which brings us to Seduce, who, stupid name (unless it's a pun on "The Deuce," off *Kiss*, in which case it's pretty rad) to the contrary, may not play speedmetal per se, but do manage to bazookafy some equally cool Motörhead-style ultragrunge on their stupidly-named debut album *Seduce*. How much of this is intentional I'm not sure (never am with good hard rock bands, come to think of it): They ain't exactly pretty boys, but their jewelry and frills (and is that *lipstick??*) do strike closer to Crüe/Riot than to Metallica/Motörhead, there's a bad dose of ho-hum he-man derring-do in their lyrics, and liner info indicates session musicians made a lot of the noise. But Mark Andrews's bass and David Black's guitar are positively hep Flying V's, and they've got some interesting song titles ("Chopping Block," "Madcap"), and (this is all that really matters, anyway) they sho'nuff can shake my rafters. *Seduce* may not be the heaviest metal album I've heard this year, but it sure is the catchiest. And it's heavy enough.

Or most of it is, anyhow—side one blows away side two. The LP opens with "Viper's Bite," launched by axe explosions devolving into compact '65-Who fuzztone lines surrounding a herky-jerky Stooges-Motörhead rhythm and the record's only vaguely memorable lyric ("I'm gonna set myself on fire"), all leading up to a fantastic race-to-the-finish coda. Then "Love To Hate," which starts like *Desolation Boulevard*. Sweet and has an OK Metallica-like tempo change halfway through; "Streets," all three-chord overdrive until Black's solo at the end; and "Face To Face," with a heavy blues beginning and Andrews both dueting with himself and managing a screechy Geddy Lee Roth falsetto. All these songs hook themselves around Andrews's echoey vocal or Black's crud riffs, and despite trite rape-and-kill poetics (typical lines: "the strong will survive," "the world is cold and mean," "what you see is what you get"), they all work. The second side starts OK, with the circular-riff stomper "Chopping Block." But then we get an obligatory fist-in-the-air metal-unity rallying cry, an obligatory "sensitive" ballad, and some obligatory guitar pud pounding.

Seduce may be on the right track most of the time, but they'll never make their niche as the bubble metal champeens of the Molly Ringwald era until they stop pretending to hunt heads or bang heads or give head, and start acting like the mid-class mid-American twerps they probably are. I mean, Cheap Trick had the right idea when they sang about mom and dad rolling numbers and rock'n'rolling and rolling on the couch to the kid's Kiss records. And Sweet useta do songs about their bisexual girlfriends and Alexander Graham Bell and stuff. Bet Seduce could come up with a great one about Sammy Hagar and the traveling salesman if they tried hard enough.

Creem Metal, 1986

AGNOSTIC FRONT, BEYOND POSSESSION, DR. KNOW, HELSTAR, RAW POWER

About time all we crickers at this publication faced the facts, ain't it? You, young inquisitive mind of a reader, have doubtlessly grown weary of repeatedly hearing manly *Metal* scribes complain that your fave-rave heavy metal band looks like a bunch of pansies, haven't you? So, always placing your feelings as my foremost cricking priority, I've intentionally gathered a whole gaggle of practitioners of said genre who appear to be nothing of the sort—judging from the photographs at my disposal, there's not a rouge or mascara utensil amongst them. (Well, to tell you the truth, a couple of the guys in Helstar do seem to be wearing earrings, but they're, like, the kind of earrings *pirates* or somebody would wear, and one of the guys in the band also has on these white studded boots that I expect maybe a pirate would wear so as not to get his feet soggy whilst raping and pillaging the seven seas, and everybody knows what tough guys pirates are, so just because Helstar seem to have, you know, a "thing" for buccaneers doesn't seem like any reason to chastise them, does it?) Anyway, by purposefully selecting five death-metal crews that dress like they refuse to encourage the dropping of soap during communal band showers after gigs, I feel I can better direct my reviewing talents toward aspects of bandmanship that more concern the readership, and hence can I be more of a consumer-assistance service and give the reader the most for his ever-more-precious heavy-metal-magazine dollar. And, when you get down to it, that's why we're all here, right? I mean, is it not in actuality our sheer *love* of this music that unites us? Though, to be sure, if the reader really cared about music as much as he says he does, what he'd be listening to these days would be Faust's *So Far,* Miles's *Jack Johnson,* the new Died Pretty and Fall and Sorry and Gone albums, and maybe the Ex double-single and Janitors EP and Laughing Hyenas demo, plus more than likely just about anything ever written by Jimmy Webb. If that is in fact what you have stacked next to your hi-fi at this moment, forgive me. If it's not, I'm sure it won't bother you that I really don't plan to talk much about music in what follows.

First up in my pile is Agnostic Front, who (according to the way-informative press release we critics always get free with our free records) are a hardcore band from New York who decided they'd get richer if they started pretending to be a heavy metal band from New York. The cover of their album has a big garish cartoon that makes no sense to me, probably because these guys are so smart that their jokes go right over my head, but of course I'm only guessing. Anyway, the cartoon has a big bat-creature with red suspenders (Why? To hold his pants up, stupid) looking down on some fat guy eating lots of tiny people with a fork and some young man with a strip of hair in the middle of his head (an Indian, I guess) and a gun pointing into his ear. Also, there's an American flag in the background and lots of Easter-Island-type totem-pole-things with their mouths open. Like I said, I don't get it. But the picture of the band has one of 'em wearing one of those "Kill 'Em All—Let God Sort 'Em Out" airborne T-shirts like Greil Marcus discussed in his last *Artforum* article about the Mekons and that little toy soldier game he bought, so I'd venture that Agnostic Front is looking for Greil's approval, and whatever he writes is too complicated for me anyway, so maybe the cartoon is a reference to *Moby Dick* or *Tom Saw-yer* or something. About the only other distinction I can garner about this band, many of whom have Italian surnames and suggest that the dreaded pasta-core is here at last, is that they once performed some action that caused noted communist punk-rock magazine *Maximum Rock 'n' Roll* to call them Nazis, a charge the band denies. What's weird is that, when you listen to their record, Agnostic Front sure sounds like the sort of thing you'd always figured *MRR* would find extremely groovy. I mean, maybe these guys embellish with some guitar-solo-ish nonentity now and then to keep their sound "current," and maybe they're really *not* singing about how much "war sucks" (damned if I can tell, actually—I'll take their word for it), but otherwise this is just by-the-numbers HC crapola. You can always tell these hardcore-turning-metal bands are just spinning their wheels by how their "music" always speeds up every time they feel like "singing." Agnostic Front reminds me a lot of the Crumbsuckers, to tell you the truth.

On the other hand, the first thing that came to mind when I initially peered at Beyond Possession's album cover was how I always forget the difference between "stalagmites" and "stalactites." Lemme see . . . stalactites "stick tight" to the ceiling of a cave, while stalagmites "mite" be the ones that come out of the floor. Which means that the thing on the front of *Is Beyond Possession* "mite" be a stalagmite shaped like how I always figured a Jabberwocky would look. (Oh these literary references by heavy metal bands just pour forth, don't they?). Another swell thing about Beyond Possession's album is that the only band picture that came with it seems to be a negative, and thus prevents full analysis by metal-crits. But even from this deceptive photo, my well-trained eyes can still manage to detect that one BP member looks like Iggy Pop, that another one likes wearing Slayer T-shirts, and that a third one has a skull for a head. Besides the skull-guy, all of their heads seem to be in the right place. The vinyl confirms this suspicion: real short songs, but enough hyperkinetic riff/chord/tempo changes in each one of 'em to suggest that these guys are definitely not playing with a full deck, all at full in-your-face aggression-level and with horrible and deadly screech-type vocalwork. Slayer's the operable comparison, obviously, but the fragmentary nature of these tracks actually has more in common with unjustly-forgotten D.C. artcrew Void. A real cool time, for sure.

This Island Earth, by Beyond Possession's labelmates Dr. Know, is yet more evidence to support my (heretofore underdocumented) hypothesis that the magnates at Metal Blade/Death Records are pretty obviously aiming at the geology majors this month—I mean, first we get stalagmites (I think), and now we get cumulus clouds! (Or, well, maybe not cumulus clouds exactly, but whatever kind of clouds turn all black and make all that thunder and lightning stuff happen.) But the album title would seem to be more sitcom than science book, and one of the guys in the band (there's three of 'em) does seem to be some weird cross between Ricardo Montalban and Herve Villechaize in the facial features department. Of further note is that Dr. Know has the same name as the Bad Brains' guitar player, and that the band lists that particular thrashfunk outfit among the "persons and things" they "would like to personally thank." Also listed: the Necros (hurray!), Jello Biafra (boo!), *Maximum Rock 'n' Roll* (double-boo!), "Los Gumbys" (dunno what that is, but it *sounds* neat), and "the San Diego Party Hens" (I thought they were gonna say Padres.) Finally, the band's bio says that Dr. Know "formed in the jungles near Saigon in the sweltering summer of 1968 during the height of the Tet Offensive," and that "Dr. Know has survived many climate changes." Good—hope they don't mind the cold shoulder I'm about to give their album. Naw, just kidding, dudes—the *last* thing I need is Agent Orange sprayed all over my living room. *This Island Earth* is actually fairly chunky noise: early-Clash/Slade/ oi gang-choruses, early-Motörhead/Mentors hard-and-fast-but-not-too-fast mung-rock tempos, chock-a-block barroom-piano production, words that mention Dodger Stadium and Chrysler (I told you Ricardo was in on this) and Jarvik-7 artificial hearts and Pandora's box, vocals that verge on metalloid histrionics, but don't quite get there. Right-smart spume for a bunch of baby-killers.

I already covered Helstar's Blackbeard costumes, and about the only interesting item on their LP jacket is the sticker that claims they "are on the cutting edge of something very big" and "are not running with the rest of the pack." I take it this does not refer to the earrings. Their press release says they come from Houston, do lots of fund-raisers and charity benefits, and get compared to Iron Maiden a lot. This is gonna sound stupid, but I really don't think I've ever *heard* Iron Maiden. So I'll probably figure these guys are true originals, right? No way—not unless high-pitch operatics that suggest the singer had a catastrophic accident once, synthesizer hog-wash, mysticisms about "the wicked one," and grunge-free sluggishness are your idea of "the cutting edge." Yo-ho-ho and a bottle of dumb, as far as I'm concerned.

Which brings us to Raw Power, who you can tell right off are OK joes because they're named after a Stooges album, and who you find out real quick put Agnostic Front's idea of pasta-core to shame—I mean, these guys are actually *from* Italy. The gentleman who plays one guitar even calls himself Giuseppe, easily the best HM monicker I've heard since Voivod axeman Piggy came to my attention. On the back of the album, the other guitarist (Silvio) is wearing a red-polka dot-on-black tank top and a blue leather jacket. If this combo ain't got its poop together, nobody does. Good signs from the hardcore-zine clippings in the press kit, too: Lotsa "the lyrics may seem a bit violent"'s and "metal band . . . guitar wanking"'s from the punk-rock wimps. Real problem, of course, is just the opposite. If anything, the axe-ing is not quite crazed enough. This ain't a bore, in other words, but it does seem to lack something in the power category; the shifts that try to shock the nervous system aren't exactly obvious, but they don't tear your thoughtcenter to shreds like Void or early Die Kreuzen or early Meat Puppets (or Beyond Possession) do. Sung-rants are indecipherable more due to accent than due to speed, which is nice for a change, and the taped snatches (phone porn, for example) preclude tedium. I've heard lots worse.

I get off on grading this junk, so here goes: On a scale of 10, Beyond Possession comes out at six, Dr. Know and Raw Power at four, Agnostic Front at negative two, and Helstar at negative three. If I scored on a curve, the passable ones would do better. But curves are for nice guys, right? Ya gotta be tough if ya wanna survive in the world of heavy metal.

Creem Metal, 1986

TOP 40 THAT RADIO WON'T TOUCH: METALLICA

You can't call Metallica a garage band anymore. A garage band needs a garage, and Metallica drum-banger Lars Ulrich and axeman/screamer James Hetfield sold theirs when they left Frisco's East Bay to tour football stadiums with Ozzy Osbourne this past spring. Makes sense—like Lars says, leave a pad vulnerable when everybody and their teenage skate-punk brother knows you're gonna be back east and down south and north to Canada and then over to Europe and the Orient through early '87, and you're kinda askin' for the place to get trashed. You're liable to end up as homeless as James and Lars are right now.

But let's call Metallica a garage band anyway. Because being a garage band means being loud and aggressive and greasy and grimy and doing whatever the hell you feel like with your instruments. It means cutting the crap, leaving the makeup and pantyhose at home with lil' sis and the smoke-bombs and Mr. Wizard routine with the kid bro. It means playing your large intestine out for your audience because you feel like shit and you wanna let them know it, and making them bang their heads not just because they dig your clamor, but because they feel like shit too. It means you're really just one of them, not some jetset multi-trillionaire or Marvel Comics superhero. Metallica does all this so well they've got a top 30 album on their hands. And you don't get too many garage bands in the top 30 these days. Not to mention in football stadiums.

Metallica is selling records by the ton, but with next-to-zero radio play. Ulrich says Elektra, the band's label, has identified only four or five Album-Oriented-Rock stations nationwide, plus some kinda radical Top 40 outlet in Houston, which are airing Metallica's new *Master Of Puppets* album.

"We're probably a bit too extreme for those conservative rock stations," Ulrich guesses. That's putting it nicely. AOR now aims its sights at an up-scale, college-educated mid-to-late-'20s demographic that's square enough to believe that "(Name The City)'s Only Untamed Rock And Roll Station" is taking big risks when it plays Dire Straits compact disc tracks along with the hit singles.

The model Metallica fan is more like a 17-year-old kid who doesn't do so hot in high school, wonders whether he oughta sign up in Uncle Ron's Army to escape his hometown, and has about as much use for Dire Straits as he has for Wayne Newton. With no image to market on MTV, with no hip pseudo-intellectual cachet to get them onto college radio, and special-izing in eight-minute epics that fit nobody's format anymore, Metallica is left to fend for themselves like no major label act in years. "It's almost like us against the whole fucking world," Ulrich says, and damned if the world ain't losing the battle.

For the four guys in Metallica, the victory has been a long time coming. In 1980, Denmark-born Ulrich immigrated to suburban Los Angeles with his parents, not to play heavy metal, but to play tennis. Only when his court plans bit the dust did he settle on music. "But I was never into sitting by myself for four years doing triple paradiddles," he says. "I just wanted to play in a band." Inspired by Motörhead's amphetamine crunch and by the more refined extended-anthem approach of obscure Anglo-metal band Diamond Head, Ulrich teamed up with James Hetfield "just to play some fucking energetic shit—no image, just music." In an L.A. hard rock scene anchored by the mascaraed and blow-dried glitter-pop of Ratt, Quiet Riot, and Mötley Crüe, the early Metallica no-frills attitude didn't win much of a following. But San Francisco fans proved more responsive, and eventu-ally the band relocated there, first recruiting Trauma's Cliff Burton as their bassist, and later replacing half of their axe duo with Kirk Hammett. "We were looking for a more melodic guitar player, one who could do the fast shit, but could also do the subdued shit," Ulrich explains. Hammett proved proficient at both, and within months, Metallica was recording their first album. At 19 to 21 years of age, they were still kids. (Nowadays, 24-year-old

Burton is the group's old man, Ulrich and Hetfield are 23, and Hammett is all of 22.)

All the songs on *Kill 'Em All* (Megaforce, 1983) were written before Burton and Hammett joined the band. They are Metallica's shortest and simplest songs, and they lack the punch of later material. Although the debut album's velocity drew comparisons to Motörhead, the abrupt tempo changes and obtuse lyrics belie that careless claim—only the closing "Metal Militia" has Motörhead-worthy horsepower. But by the time Metallica next entered the studio, Ulrich says, "we realized that there's a lot more ways you can be heavy than just by playing fast." The band also figured out that it's more honest, not to mention more challenging, to write songs about real life than ones about phantom lords, vengeful gods, and leather steeds. The second Metallica album displayed considerable growth.

Ride The Lightning (Megaforce, 1984) opens with one of Burton's transcendent and dainty Gregorian basslines, which descends through the nine circles of Hell into "Fight Fire With Fire," a horrifying depiction of nuclear war. Other highlights include the cascading title track, which addresses capital punishment from the point of view of the guy in the chair. "For Whom The Bell Tolls," the most effective heavy metal death march since the demise of Led Zeppelin, and the humongous "Fade To Black," as inspirational a hunk of suicidal teen-angst bombast as this decade has produced. Hetfield begins the song by bellowing, "Life it seems to fade away/Drifting further every day/Getting lost within myself." On Metallica's debut, he had sounded like he was trying to be Beelzebub; here, he sounds like the confused suburban kid he probably is. Deservedly, *Ride The Lightning* set indie sales records. Several major labels approached the band, and Elektra won the bidding war.

Not that Metallica signed with Elektra for the money. Basically, Ulrich says, the label promised to leave the band alone—they said they'd let Metallica make its music the way the band wanted to make it. "I don't think there's a major label band that gets as much freedom as we do," he says. A gamble from Elektra's standpoint, maybe, but the approach has obviously worked. *Master Of Puppets*, the band's big-league debut, sold some 250,000 copies in its first week on the shelves, and more than doubled that figure within the following two months. The album is doing so well that Elektra has actually started bragging about its lack of airplay in magazine ads. It's too soon to tell, but the LP's success may be alerting record companies and radio stations to an audience they've been forgetting to exploit. "A lot of people are starting to pick up on the way we're going about the whole thing," Ulrich says. "They see we're a bit different than the rest of the heavy metal bullshit."

True enough. Heavy metal is more deeply embedded in inane self-parody than any other pop genre. There were hundreds of real Spinal Taps before the fake one made its movie. Bands like Judas Priest, Iron Maiden, and Mötley Crüe parade on stage in chains and leather or lace and lipstick, feign dangerousness, play a neutered sort of "hard" rock, sing trite songs about conquering women and shouting at the devil, rake in millions, and generally just scavenge off an audience they couldn't care less about. "It's so safe, so sterile," Ulrich says. "Some bands are made of four businessmen united around the cause of making money instead of making music." Even the few decent heavy metal acts—AC/DC and Motörhead, say, and some of the newer "speedmetal" bands—get trapped by their own vigorous formulas; they may not fake it, but they don't fuck too much with it, either. "The whole thing today, especially in heavy metal, is you're so locked in," Ulrich says. "Nobody's trying to do anything really different."

Nobody, that is, except Metallica. *Master Of Puppets* takes off from where *Ride The Lightning* left off, straight-ahead songs about real stuff, with enough noise to wake the dead and enough variety to not put them back to sleep. It's pure forward motion, like a speeding locomotive with broken brakes, but it's done with so much finesse that you get the idea the train is on a tightrope. It could fall off at any moment, but it never does. Ulrich and Burton lay down backbeats that swing hard enough to break a rhino's back, and Hammett and Hetfield charge from the bush like farm-boy infantrymen scared shitless to be in a jungle swamp, guitars set on automatic, laying waste to whatever's stupid enough to wander across their line of fire. Hetfield booms out his majestic anthems with more confidence than ever, and Burton's baroque bass licks add mere seconds of solace, only to disappear into uncontrollable walls of fatally toxic crud.

Lyrically, the new album centers itself around four tracks about people horrified by the cages in which they're boxed—drugs in the title cut, religion in "Leper Messiah," war in "Disposable Heroes," family in "Welcome Home (Sanitarium)." The LP title sums up the idea, and the record jacket portrays a graveyard as a marionette's stage, with a steel helmet and military dogtags flung over two of the cross-shaped headstones. Ulrich explains, "We write about shit that's interesting to us. One of those things, over the last year, has been people being manipulated subconsciously— when you think you're free, and you think you're leading your own life, but someone's really controlling you." Like Rush's Geddy Lee, an avid Ayn

Rand reader who Ulrich says has become one of Metallica's biggest fans, this band is obsessed by the survival of the individual in a world where individualism has become a facade.

Metallica's songs sound like they're based on real experiences. Which isn't to say they're written from some realist, adult, politically-perfect Springsteen/Mellencamp folk-rock perspective: the band uses the quasi-archaic metaphors which have become the bane of heavy metal and art-rock ever since Cream first passed down the tales of brave Ulysses and Zep first encountered Valhalla's Druids. But to dismiss Metallica's lyrics as mystic or cosmic would be foolish; it'd be like saying funk raps about partying 'til the crack of dawn are "meaningless." This is the language Metallica has inherited. None of the band's members lives in an insane asylum, but that doesn't make "Welcome Home (Sanitarium)" a lie. It's simply about being locked up, say in your room by your parents. And it's hilarious, because it conveys exactly what goes on in a kid's head when that sort of thing happens; he convinces himself he's crazy, he wonders why mom and dad "think it saves us from our hell," he fantasizes violence. Like Ulrich says, "I don't think you need to have been in a sanitarium to appreciate those lyrics."

Unless an Ozzy Osbourne concert constitutes a sanitarium, as some might argue it does, Metallica's current tour is certainly proving Ulrich's point. Metallica's drummer says the band's opening slot works like "a 55-minute slap in the face" for the Osbourne audience. In cities like Detroit, Chicago, and New York, Ulrich says, much of the audience is already familiar with Metallica's music, and some fans tell him they've paid the $16 gate fee just to see his band. But smaller towns are tougher. "In the B markets, people don't really know what we're all about. But after 45 or 50 minutes we can tell we've won them over." Ulrich denies the suggestion that listening to Metallica might convince the regally-attired elder statesman Ozzy that it's about time he settled down at home with his kids. "The tour actually works quite well for both of us," he says. "We generate a lot of natural excitement, and that gets people up for Ozzy's show." And fans who come to hear Ozzy go home liking Metallica.

The double-bill also encourages comparisons between Metallica and Ozzy's early Black Sabbath. Like the Sabs circa 1970–71, Metallica is experimenting with ways to embellish and refine a pure, chaotic, loud and fast rock sound while still retaining that sound's power; where Metallica is influenced by Motörhead, Sabbath was influenced by the Stooges. "I tend to think we're even more extreme than early Sabbath," Ulrich says. Maybe so.

By remembering that heavy metal was originally a teenage music, Metallica has managed to restore strength and vision to a rock genre which has been effectively dead for a decade or more. "People have a tendency to take themselves too seriously; they forget what this thing was about to begin with," Ulrich says. "We're giving heavy metal a good kick in the ass."

Which is one of the things punk rock was once supposed to do. Since the real McCoy never conquered the record charts, it never happened. But go to a Black Flag gig this summer and you'll hear between-set tapes of "After Forever," off Black Sabbath's 1971 *Master Of Reality* album. If it's an all-ages show, you'll see adolescent boys wearing Metallica jackets. Read *Billboard*, and you'll find out about off-duty Airborne soldiers at Fort Bragg, North Carolina, splitting their album cash between metal LPS by Metallica, Venom, and Slayer and hardcore punk stuff by the Dead Kennedys, GBH, and Black Flag. Metallica has been credited with uniting hardcore and heavy metal factions; if nothing else, they provide ultrafast punk tempos with an unprecedented popular base. Ulrich denies any conscious attempt to fuse metal and hardcore, but he admits that his band does listen to some of the more riff-oriented punk bands—Hetfield is often photographed sporting Misfits or Charged GBH T-shirts, and Ulrich says he likes Discharge. But he points out that Metallica's members also enjoy Deep Purple and Thin Lizzy and R.E.M. and the Byrds and Roxy Music and Elvis Costello and Sade and lots of other music, and that doesn't mean they're influenced by any of it. "Obviously, with our music nowadays, we're just trying to create our own shit," he says.

Fair enough. Because when you get down to it, Metallica doesn't sound like Motörhead or Sabbath or GBH or Byrds or anybody else, except for Metallica. But that doesn't mean the band's hardcore connection is insignificant. Metallica likes Charged GBH, and Metallica's fans like Charged GBH, and outside of the subculture that spawned Metallica and their fans, Charged GBH is an unknown entity—just another Stooges-influenced latter-day British band you never heard of. What Metallica's fans see in Metallica, no doubt, is themselves—kids with way-long hair and ripped jeans and old T-shirts, kids who feel trapped by their world but are trying their damnedest in it anyway, kids who need fast noisy rock music not because it inspires rape fantasies or puts them in touch with the devil, but because it makes them forget how much life otherwise sucks and reminds them they're not alone. "They can identify with us," Ulrich says. "They know that when they come up and talk to us it's like talking to a bunch of their friends."

Fuck if that's not what rock'n'roll's all about. With the superstar syndromes, both the '70s heavy metal one punk reacted against and the '80s MTV one punk helped produce, rock'n'roll seems to have forgotten that. But Metallica hasn't. Not to belabor the comparison, because there are some very important differences, but Metallica are in many ways reminiscent of the MC5—a loud, fast, experimental, political-but-not-ideological garage band, born of a white urban teen subculture, who put out their first Elektra album before the Metallica guys entered kindergarten. The MC5 didn't get much radio play, but they fared okay on the charts. And they didn't change the world, but they helped inspire punk rock, which sure made things interesting for a year or three before it got co-opted by the mainstream. If we're lucky, Metallica might inspire something similar. We need it now like we never have.

B.A.M., 20 June 1986

WELCOME HOME (SANITARIUM):
METALLICA SEEK PSYCHIATRIC HELP

Last fall, a hilarious 3,000-word review of Metallica's unlistenable *St. Anger* by some guy named Colin Tappe circulated over the Internet. He claimed he doesn't really care about the band since his motto was always "Those who can't Slayer, Metallica," but what the heck: "Maybe it's just me, but when you *buy a fucking Metallica album*, you're supposed to be able to hear the *fucking guitars*!!! . . . Like, ain't these cats something like a half a fucking century old a piece? And they're still wrestling with thesauruses to voice their 'pain'? Christ, I hope if I ever get to this state of living off fumes of nostalgia for my youth my retrogressive trip won't be so fucking *square* sounding as these assholes. . . . This (again) fucking Metallica album contains—are y'all ready—not one god damned motherfucking guitar solo." You get the idea.

Anyway, now there's a movie out about how Metallica made the album! And it got stellar grades at Sundance, no less, from people who couldn't distinguish "Whiplash" from "The Unforgiven" in a blindfold test. The supposed hook is the allegedly unprecedented way *Some Kind Of Monster*—a chronicle of the band's psychoanalytically assisted recording misadventures, directed by Bruce Sinofsky and Joe Berlinger, previously semi-famous for murder documentaries and *Blair Witch 2*—reveals these scary headbangers as, deep down, sensitive souls. Which is kinda true; once broken-childhood-surviving singer James Hetfield finally goes through rehab and starts insisting on working only four hours a day so he can make his daughter's ballet lessons, you feel sorry for the dork. But then you remember how crappy Aerosmith got after they knocked the monkey off *their* backs. Not to mention that Metallica haven't made a decent album of original songs for 16 years.

And you remember that "therapy rock" has been the dullest cliché on earth ever since Nirvana inspired emo, and that the whole idea that we're supposed to care about rock stars as *people* (as opposed to, say, makers of songs and riffs) is ridiculous, and that rare-vinyl-collecting tennis-prodigy geek turned Basquiat-collecting drummer Lars Ulrich and Buddhism-spoutingly mild-mannered half-Filipino hippie guitarist Kirk Hammett had never seemed remotely threatening in the first place, and that Lars's Napster-baiting period absolutely justified Metallica's recent legacy as the most hated band by their own fans in rock history, and that this group has been obsessed with suicidal tendencies and sanitariums and sundry other mental health issues ever since their beautiful "Fade To Black" in 1984, and it clicks: this flick is almost all old news. You'd be better off buying that new *Slade in Flame* DVD—and better rocked too, since (beyond one flashback to impossibly nimble original bassist Cliff Burton and his 1986 bus-accident death) *Monster*'s soundtrack somehow manages to entirely ignore the Renaissance-goth gorgeousness that once made Metallica distinctive. All that said, the mere way these eternal has-beens still take their art so seriously somehow makes them *more* endearing. Which might even be the point.

Rock critics show up in the very first scene (a cinema first?), but the film gives no acknowledgment that *St. Anger* got horrible reviews. In fact, from an opening blurb calling them the top touring band of the '90s through a concluding one where the album tops charts all over the world, *Monster* is mostly just a two-and-a-half-hour puff piece about how "important" Metallica are and, worse, how much "integrity" they have. ("We've proven that you can make aggressive music without negative energy," gawd.) The first 45 minutes drag; things pick up once old-married-couple control freaks Lars and James start acting like they're gonna beat each other's brains out.

James is pleasingly paranoid once he's on the wagon; earlier and more vodka-marinated, after bragging about shooting a constipated bear in

Russia, he returns to the studio and *sings* like a constipated bear, and no-body notices! Lars deserves bonus points for being shorter than his wife, and his remark that the band's "in a bit of a shit sandwich" wins the most-blatant-*Spinal Tap*-reference award. But he's not nearly as lovable as his ancient Danish dad, Torben—a bucktoothed, troll-bearded ex-Wimbledon third-rounder, jazz muso, painter, poet, filmmaker, and arts journalist who looks exactly like the wizard-of-the-rings mountain man inside Led Zep's *Zoso* gatefold. He's also the only person brave enough to tell Metal-lica their music sucks.

Psychobabbling $40,000-a-month shrink Phil Towle occupies the David St. Hubbins's girlfriend role; he never quite draws Zodiac-sign portraits of band members, but his implicit suggestion that they try being Kraut-rockers in "meditative mode" would've made him a more useful producer than biz-sucking slimeball Bob Rock. Another dumb personnel decision occurs during new-bassist auditions: Metallica pass over impressive un-known Elena Repetto and perfectly doom-toned Unida/Kyuss stoner Scott Reeder for Suicidal Tendencies klutz Robert Trujillo, apparently for his rap-metal cred. Pretty amusing, though, when Trujillo, stuck in a room with all these lonely men discussing "feelings," suddenly realizes he joined a new age band. And pretty tragic when Kirk Hammett, clearly the movie's good guy despite badly needing assertiveness training, argues for guitar solos, to no avail.

Village Voice, 29 June 2004

MENTORS: *UP THE DOSE*

I guess the big Catch 22 with reviewing this road-apple of a record is you've got to slag the living stink out of it without making any concessions to Tipper Gore and her cast of goons, seeing as how it's the politically cor-rect critic's duty to castigate sexist and/or homophobic exploitation at all levels—but it's also the politically correct critic's job to keep Amerika safe for Dead Kennedys and Frank Zappa and W.A.S.P. albums and so on, though don't ask me why. (Actually, yeah, I know doggone well why, 'cause people have a right to be stupid, blah blah blah, and listen to whatever they want, blah blah, and if you ban W.A.S.P. records it means McCarthyism is right around the corner, and the record industry is doin' a just-spiffy job censoring all the questionable junk no matter how worthless anyway, so who needs gov't intervention? Jeez, I'm hip to all that, even call myself a libertarian sometimes, so get off my *back*, OK?)

These Mentors dudes are the guys who got all that free publicity because some researcher hired by the PMRC found out that they said some boulder-brained thing about "anal vapors" on their last album, *You Axed For It*. As for the researcher job, I'm puttin' in my resume next week, because it sounds like even less work than bein' a rock critic, and I know all kindsa cool lines that'd make all those Washington Wives' beehives buzz bigtime. As for the Mentors, their new album (first and last one I will ever hear) fulfills my worst expectations: These boys ain't offensive; they're just boring. Somehow you knew that was coming, I bet.

OK, so I do find 'em pretty gross, *obscene* even. To that end, I guess you could say that they've "succeeded," and I'm a yellow-bellied liberal wimp and everything. Thing is, that's got nothing to do with why I hate this album so much. I *like* rock'n'roll that repulses me, and lots of my faves—AC/DC, Nuge (circa '74), Angry Samoans, the Left, Electric Eels, and so on—express ideas and/or attitudes that to me range somewhere between unsavory and intolerable. As I wish all the jerks who gave Los Lobos's recent Eurodisco sell-out a good review because it had "nice words" would realize, PROPER POLITICS HAS NOTHING TO DO WITH DECENT ROCK MUSIC. It doesn't *matter*. What does have to do with decent rock music is whether the band *rocks*, and Los Lobos don't (anymore), and neither do the Mentors. Only distinctive thing about 'em is that El Duce bangs the cans pretty hard (as if his fists were sides of beef, but faster, as it were). But not only can't El Duce sing; he can't even *growl*. And I could steal Motörhead and old-Nuge riffs better than Sickie Wifebeater, and I DON'T EVEN KNOW HOW TO PLAY GUITAR!! And I don't remember if there was a bass on this album. Mostly, the band plays like old ladies. *Fat* old ladies.

Those who live their sickening fantasies vicariously will want to know about the lyrics, but I'm not gonna quote any, 'cause they're all retarded; I'll just say there's no anal vapors this time. Themes are as follows: adultery is fun (hey, no country or soul singers ever beat 'em to *that* one), spouse-abuse is fun, menstruation is yucky, if you've got power maybe women will go to bed with you, if you've got money maybe women will go to bed with you, if you give them enough drugs maybe women will go to bed with you. All perfectly valid song topics, I suppose, except if this dry-humpin' trio really *believe* what they're singing, they're stupid, and if they don't, but they think they're funny anyway, they're *twice* as stupid—to me, they sound as fake as Alf is alien. I do want to point out two of their songs to the PMRC, though: "Heterosexuals Have The Right To Rock" says men with makeup are the most likely ones to have AIDS, and "S.F.C.C." says a woman's place is in the home. The way I see it, the Radical Right ought to be using the Mentors for *spokesmen*. Did I mention that they wear hoods?

Creem Metal, 1987

ROBERT PLANT, TECHNOBILLY

A few months back, Robert Plant walked into Atlantic Records' London offices and played "Scream," by Ralph Nielsen & The Chancellors. Now, I dunno if you've ever heard "Scream," but it's on Crypt Records' *Back From The Grave, Vol. 2* garage compilation, and trust me when I say it rages nastily— five adolescent Jersey Link Wray fans in shiny suits waxed it on Route 1 not far from Princeton in the summer of '62. Here's how Tim Warren described it in the catzine *Kicks* a while back: "Imagine the Burnettes' 'Train Kept A Rollin' 45 played at 78 rpm with frantic, non-stop, burnin' guitar breaks and a voice yellin', 'C'mon and scream, yeah yeah yeah' over and over; a scream howlin' throughout the 1:56 the song goes for—I counted 63 of 'em—that's more than one scream every two seconds!" Plant told the Atlantic honchos that this was gonna be his new record. "All I got was a look of disbelief," he recalls, "like I'd gone out of my mind."

Robert Plant turns 40 this August. He's divorced, has a couple kids, and hasn't played much tennis lately. He enjoys reading Kurt Vonnegut and Thomas McGuane because "they're so funny you wake up smiling, and how can you beat that?" Also, he used to sing (like guitar feedback or a scatting Martian, depending on who you ask) for Led Zeppelin. And between his Zep career and his (now four-and-a-half-LP) solo career, he's amassed a body of work which, in terms of wide-rangingly prolific weirdness and newfangled innovation, is unmatched by anybody of comparable commercial standing (and anybody of *any* commercial standing, except for George Clinton and maybe Captain Beefheart) in the annals of rock'n'roll. Lester Bangs once dismissed him as an "emaciated fop," which just goes to show that sometimes that fatso didn't know what the hell he was talking about.

Plant's new album, *Now And Zen*, has a song called "Tall Cool One," which quotes Charlie Feathers and Gene Vincent and which shares its title with a late '50s instrumental hit by Seattle's Wailers, who (seeing how they predated the unruly Northwest scene that begat the Sonics, Kingsmen, Paul Revere & the Raiders, etc.) could perhaps be considered the first hard rock band ever.

"'Tall Cool One' is like tipping my hat to the original song, and that whole Ralph Nielsen kind of approach. The sentiment in that song, like where it goes, 'I'm so tall and you're so cute/Let's play wild like the wildcats do,' that's what the Wailers tune always reminded me of. Also, the original always reminded me of 'Move It,' the B-side of 'Pipeline' by the Chantays," Robert explains. "I think I retain the attitude that got me into rock'n'roll in the first place—I haven't fallen for the way rock has deteriorated over the years, the way it's become so corporate again, just like in the early '60s, this situation where David Coverdale's mainly concerned with how he wears his sunglasses or whatever."

Plant agrees it'd be impossible, in a modern hi-tech studio, to get that gloriously horrible sound-quality you hear in "Scream," or the Wailers' "Tall Cool One." So I ask him if the horrible sound isn't a big part of what makes that music so *powerful* now. "Yeah, it makes it more romantic for us—it adds to the mystery of listening. But I'm too much a technocrat not to use what's available to me. Or a technobilly—*that's* what I am, a technobilly! My 'Tall Cool One' has, I think, the same intention as the original, but done in a contemporarily descriptive way."

"I'm trying to do something that's not been done before, even at the risk of not making that extra buck. There's so much I want to get in there on my records—it's hard to get in everything that I'd like to. And it *hurts* trying to do it that way. I mean, about the only encouragement I get, except from the band while we're working on the songs, comes from the record company. And it's like, they'll come up to me and say, 'Robert, why don't you use this song, it's got your name all over it.' And meanwhile, I'll be raving about Let's Active one minute and the Swans the next. I want to cut through radio with a hot knife, this idea where they say, 'We're only gonna play stuff guaranteed on being a hit,' I wanna stretch it out some. People like Tom Verlaine and Hüsker Dü are making quite important music now, and people aren't hearing it because it never gets played."

Yeah, well, there's no accounting for taste (the guy's talked up Visage and Alf Moyet in the past, and he told me that he really likes "the early

Del Fuegos when they were on Czech Records" and that "apart from a few Goth bands here in England, things really are looking quite sad again"), but you gotta admit it's cool that *some* superduperstar's keeping a finger or two on the pulse of the under(wear)ground, even if the Swans and Let's Active should've stuck with their day jobs, and even though the Hüskers have been churning out silly sea-chanteys of late. At least he ain't fallin' for Live Skull or Megadeth, like some college program directors I know. I told him he oughta get the Swans to open his American tour (I mean, forget the music—think of the sociological implications), and he said it sounded like a good idea (though I dunno if M. Gira would go for it).

Anyway. *Pictures At Eleven*, Robert Plant's first solo album, heavily inspired (sez *Hammer Of The Gods*) by Egyptian classical crooner Om Kalthoum, came out in '82. *The Principle Of Moments*, probably inspired at least in part by Ennio Morricone, came out in '83. The *Honeydrippers/Volume One* EP, a cheap nostalgia move featuring Jimmy Page and Jeff Beck and lots of moldy oldies, came out in '84. *Shaken 'N' Stirred*, Plant's best solo LP and some of the most structurally outlandish commercially successful white rock this decade (blows Lou Reed out of the water, believe me), came out in '85. The second side had nods to the Human Beinz and the Police, plus a creepy hit single (about shedding Zeppelin, perhaps) that went, "the air clears, I can breathe again"; the first side was mainly abstract soundscapes with bizarro changes, stutters, skids, and added-and-subtracted-tracks. The most expressionist cut was "Too Loud," and had Plant released a 12-inch hip-hop version of it in the South Bronx, I expect it would've sold like Filas. The only sounds I can imagine comparing it to are Afrika Bambaataa's "Looking For The Perfect Beat" and certain Mark Stewart and the Maffia obscurities (but with all the funk drained out, not necessarily a great thing). Mostly, it's like Plant was making some kind of music that doesn't have a name yet.

Can't quite say that about *Now And Zen*, which completely disappointed me at first, though now I think of it as Zep-as-an-MTV-era pop group—sort of the animal you'd get if you crossed *In Through The Out Door* (Zep's last) with *Panorama* (the Cars' strangest). Robert's backed by a whole new band ('cept for Page's appearance on a couple tracks, the importance of which should be clear later). It is his most rockingly Zeplike solo LP, and his most "accessible," as they say; it will probably also be his most successful, sales-wise. There's three mid-tempo-ish AOR-type rockers, two post-Police '80s-style prog-pop things, one sub-Zep off-kilter fusion-hop, and four high-velocity ravers, which are simultaneously the album's farthest-out, gimmicky, and (initially, at least) intriguing cuts. I'm impressed, but (like all of Plant's post-Zep work, especially compared to Zep) the LP still strikes me as emotionally restrained—too cold, too clever, too calculated. Too '80s, I guess. This is *Robert Plant*, and fans are gonna buy his records and radio's gonna play 'em no matter what, so he might as well *scream*, right?

Not that I'm accusing the man of anything unscrupulous, y'understand. "I haven't really, ever in my career, thought about what would make money and what wouldn't," he says, and I believe him. (The "calculation" I'm talking about has to do with "art," not cash.) "For now, I wanna get into something you can really put your arms around, something that kicks ass. *Shaken 'N' Stirred* is a record I'm very proud of, but you gotta remember that you and I love music—we pay attention to details. But I want people to still have a handle on what I'm doing. I mean, my daughter is so happy that I'm finally making songs she can sing along to!"

Three cuts on *Now And Zen* have what I deem to be doo-wop referents, so I pose the obvious query. "Well, I listened to the Jive Five a while back," Robert replies, "but I haven't heard much since then." And I also asked him if (unlike me) he could imagine kids dancing to "Dance On Your Own," which has teen-type lyrics about lusting over a girl on your block: "Well, I guess I can imagine Puerto Ricans in uptown New York dancing to it. Ahmet Ertegun took me to this club out on 79th and Nowhere, and there weren't fat guys doing the executive trot; there were just all these incredibly sexy young people looking so cool, and they're who inspired the song. It's also sort of a sequel to 'Doo Doo A Doo Doo,' on the last album." Now how come I didn't figure all that stuff out on my own, I wonder?

Mainly, as maybe you've deduced by now, *Now And Zen* is Robert Plant's attempt to make a Led Zep album in 1988. "I think this music is how Zeppelin would have sounded, had Zep been in a slightly different situation at the time," he says. "It isn't Led Zeppelin, but it is contemporary, young, virile music." I ask if he really believes *Now And Zen* is as young and virile-sounding as Zep, or if that's just something he's trying to convince himself of. It was an unfair question, probably: Plant's never embarrassed himself in the self-parodic Jagger/Ozzy/Yes/Floyd oldster-trying-to-act-coltlike sense. And I'm just 27, and *I* ain't as young and virile as Led Zeppelin, and I never have been, and neither have you. Rightfully, Robert seems rather annoyed: "It is what I say it is."

As "Tall Cool One" concludes, Plant samples in vocal and guitar segments from "Black Dog," "Whole Lotta Love," "When The Levee Breaks," and (most hilariously, given the Beastie Boys' use of the same riff in "She's Crafty" last year) "The Ocean." He's been dazed and confused for so long, like he's wanted to disassociate himself from that entire period in his life, refusing to perform Zep-tunes live and all, that this comes as something of a surprise. "I've denied it for so long, but then I thought to myself that, if Def Jam can do it, so can I—maybe Rick Rubin will sue me for it," he chuckles. "I think it's time to eat a few of my words. Maybe I seemed like I was ashamed of that music—I guess I figured that if I made enough noise, just continuing on my own, people'd stop asking me about the past. But I was always grinning inside, really. I mean, people tell me those old records still sound pretty great. So this time when I tour, we'll be playing 'Custard Pie' or 'Misty Mountain Hop' or whatever—we'll be playing the songs *I* like—at least at the end of 'Tall Cool One.'"

So, sad to say, it's not like he'll be encoring with "Stairway To Heaven": "No way will I do that bloody wedding song! It was nice for it to have been so popular—I mean, it *was* a consolidation of love and peace and utopian feelings and everything. But I really wish 'Kashmir' would have become what 'Stairway' did. Though I guess you can't really march up the aisle to the words in that one, can you?"

No, I can't. But then I grew up in the '70s, so I never *listen* to the words, and anyhow, it's time for a soapbox break. Lots of people, mainly the kind who write about music, have always hated Led Zeppelin. Heck if I can figure out why—guess it has something to do with their stomping all over a counterculture that was pretty silly to begin with (a counterculture which, not incidentally, gave birth to "rock criticism"), but I always thought that's what made 'em *good*. They weren't "political," and they made hippies feel like old-timers. Or maybe not. Here's part of a letter my fellow *Creem*-crit, Richard Riegel, sent to me last year: "I hate Zeppelin even *more* than Lester ever did, and I'll continue to attack their pernicious influence as long as I can draw critical breath. . . . A lot of us really got involved in the blues the English bands had taught us in the '60s, and like the way the Animals taught it, we thought the blues should get more bluesy and more *black* all the time. And Zeppelin come along and not only steal the blues musicians blind, but erect this superblooze skyscraper that's as *white* as possible."

Well, alright. The Four Zeps may well not have been the most perfectly upstanding young people—they took credit for music they didn't write, and they apparently did disgusting things with sharks and black magic. Their shows were supposedly "impersonal" fascist indoctrination sessions, or something like that. (Think I read that one in *Rolling Stone* once.) And they did do a bunch of boring boogie numbers on their (ridiculously over-rated) first two albums. But usually, they *improved* on the blues—try playing *their* "When The Levee Breaks" back-to-back with Memphis Minnie's! Purist regurgitation is the easy way out; Zep acted white because they *were* white—honesty counts for somethin', don't it? And so do humongous, avant-grunge hooks that letcha know you're alive, and so does that *sound*, the splendiferous Mesozoic immediacy of which I'm pretty certain nobody's ever gonna equal: Greil Marcus once wrote that *Zoso* "meant to storm Heaven," and if it didn't pull it off, it came closer than any other music (before or since) ever has. As for siring an atrocious amount of fraudulent imitators, so did the Velvet Underground. And so did Lester Bangs.

What makes Bangs's take on Led Zeppelin especially absurd, given his aesthetic criteria, is that they may well be the only band in history that truly expressed the full range of human emotion in a sonic context. *They did not hold anything back.* Jimmy Page once claimed that this music was meant to be a return to the direct emotion of early rock'n'roll, after years of Beatles/Dylan-type detached intellectualization. Think about it: "It's been a long time since 'The Book Of Love.'" Sez the singer, "We just thought rock'n'roll needed to be taken on again. So we had all these little rock'n'roll nuances, like in 'Boogie With Stu' (Zep's pre-Lobos tribute to Ritchie Valens!) or 'it's been a long time since I walked in the moonlight.' And I was finally in a really successful band, and we felt it was time for actually kicking ass. It wasn't an intellectual thing, 'cause we didn't have time for that—we just wanted to let it all come flooding out. It was a very animal thing, a hellishly powerful thing, what we were doing."

"This was such a deep and meaningful time, and everybody was smoking too much marijuana, and they could only see us making this intense and dramatic music, like Wagner or somebody, and nobody could see the fun in it," Plant continues. "I mean, Zeppelin was all sorts of things—some of it was dance music, some of it was music for folk clubs, some of it was music to play in hippie book-shops." And there was rockabilly ("Hot Dog"), skronk experimentation ("Whole Lotta Love"), reggae ("D'yer Mak'er," and if you don't hear humor in that title, you better read it again), and all-the-way wound-up punk-rock ("Communication Breakdown," with a riff the Sex Pistols *slowed down* when they recorded "God Save The Queen"!).

Finally, it'd take more space than I've got to explain why, but one thing that flew right over everybody's heads is that perhaps Zep's most important contributions were *rhythmic*: "Good Times Bad Times," "Whole Lotta Love," "Heartbreaker," "Immigrant Song," "Out On The Tiles," and so on throw down some warped kind of heavy Euclidean *funk*. Which is to say that maybe Zep weren't quite as "white" as Richard Riegel thinks they were.

In the last year or so, people have finally started to get the point—in the wake of Beasties/Cult/Soundgarden/Scratch Acid/Golden Palominos/Hose/Flaming Lips (not to mention U2's "Bullet The Blue Sky"), it seems about half of the world's "post-punk" population spent '87 trying to master *Houses Of The Holy* and *Physical Graffiti* licks. Plant says he wouldn't consider hiring Rick Rubin to produce a Robert Plant album, though: "I haven't heard him do anything *good* yet. I guess you could make a case for the work he's done with the Cult, though I don't know if that's the producer or the band you're hearing on there. And besides, Zeppelin did it better." And then there's the case of one Johnny Rotten, whose Sex Pistols were supposedly (among other things) a revolt against every excess Zeppelin stood for, despite that "Communication Breakdown" connection. "I have no comprehension as to what the hell happened, whether he ran out of ideas, or what," Plant perplexes. "All I know is all of a sudden one day John Lydon calls me up and asks for the lyrics to 'Kashmir.'" Public Image Ltd., who haven't released a decent album since Reagan was elected president, ended up using the tune as a set-opener. "I actually *met* Lydon about two months ago, and he seemed like a very nice chap—he's just a real manipulator of the media, that's all," Plant observes. "I told him he really could have accomplished a lot, but he blew it."

Needless to say, the present is not Robert Plant's favorite rock'n'roll era. Here's what is: "About 1959 or '58, when people were locking into the whole culture of it, around the time of 'One Hand Loose' by Charlie Feathers. What came after often missed the point of it. But I like anything that hasn't got too much self-consciousness in it—I had an intention of doing 'Love Me' by the Phantom and actually, when we were recording the album, I *did* record a version of this song 'Don't Look Back,' by the Remains." He says the Remains cover could end up as a non-LP B-side. "And also, I've recorded an instrumental for some invisible surfing movie." Whatever that means.

"White, Clean And Neat," the last cut on *Now And Zen*, starts out, "Thirteenth day of August, 1954/I was five years old"; the words talk about Johnnie Ray, whose "Cry" in '51 was (ironically?) one of the first major

R&B hits by a white man. "It's about how, at this time, Debbie Reynolds, Eddie Fisher, and people like that were offering this completely new way of living, where everything's clean, where you'd never fart while you were screwing. Pat Boone was playing whitened versions of Little Richard songs. In Cleveland, you had the Moondog, and he was playing this black rock'n'roll, and in America you also had local radio in Memphis and New Orleans or wherever. But in England, we were getting this watered-down version of rockabilly from Tommy Steele and Frankie Laine, a very faraway version of this guy Elvis. I was growing up submerged in this whole socialized Valium experience. But then we started hearing Bill Haley and Gene Vincent, and suddenly the whole situation changed. Problem is, before you know it, you've got the next generation of Pat Boones."

So I ask whether David Coverdale is the newest generation's Pat Boone. "Well, he's old enough to have been influenced by the same music that influenced me, but I guess it didn't sink in, somehow," critiques Plant. "Incidentally, he says he talks to me all the time, but I haven't spoken to him in about three years. He could be the next Glen Campbell, I guess. His makeup's real good, though. One thing he's *not* is Howlin' Wolf." I ask Robert if *he* was Howlin' Wolf, kinda taking him aback, it seems, but he says no. What we decided is that Plant sounds like somebody who's listened to Howlin' Wolf (or Muddy Waters or somebody—you get the idea), and Coverdale sounds like somebody who's listened to guys who've listened to guys who've listened to Howlin' Wolf. Same with Ian Astbury. And neither the Cult nor Whitesnake sound like Led Zeppelin so much as they sound like guys who want to sound like Led Zeppelin. They're kind of an idea: "Led Zeppelin." In quotes.

A few months ago, I wrote a *Village Voice* article entitled "Whitesnake Can Eat Puke." I received a letter from some guy who had "been a guitarist/ musician for more than 12 years," so if anybody oughta know he oughta, and here's what he said: "Whitesnake happens to be the best rock band to come around since Zeppelin. Both their album and live line-ups are composed of musicians who happen to be among the best in rock today, and they form a chemistry not to many bands can achieve. You probably were never talented enough to pick up an instrument, so now that you have the privledge of writing to the public, you're getting your revenge on society regardless of what the charts and record sales tell you." He's right, of course. But as Robert Plant says, "David Geffen's probably real pleased with himself about that one, but just wait and see what happens to Whitesnake when Zeppelin gets back together." WOW!! A scoop!!?? So, like, when's *that* gonna happen, Bob? "I don't know," he laughs. "Not for another year or so, at least."

Creem, May 1988

DEF LEPPARD'S MAGIC AND LOSS

When somebody who means a lot to you dies, you'll mourn them, but you're also allowed to be mad at them for being gone—maybe even hate them for it. Sometimes you can't help it. When I was 13, three years after my mom died and the morning after I went to my only pro hockey game ever, my dad hung himself, permanently ridding himself of whatever demons alcohol and a dead-end job at R.L. Polk had added to his already manic depressive chemistry.

So I never got to talk to him about all those philosophy books sitting on the bookshelves he'd built. I don't remember much from those days, but I remember one time, a few months earlier, when he fell off the wagon and bought my siblings and me hamsters and a Habitrail and then later that night told my older brother to hit him a few times because someday he'd wish he had. And I remember my new mom, who up to that point had just been a stepmother I suppose but now was stuck on her own with five kids too smart for their own damn good, cursing my dad out loud for weeks after he was in the ground.

The new Def Leppard album, *Adrenalized*, their fifth in 12 years, has a ghostly song where it sounds to me like Joe Elliott's cursing somebody out loud for being gone. It's called "White Lightning," and though this band has recorded many excellent songs, this is probably their best. It starts with a long instrumental part, sounding almost industrial or musique concrète or like a stained-glass window, like certain Gothic post-ABBA French techno-blues records hit me. Then the guitars turn into a sort of wobbly power-ballad, like one of their less memorable earlier hits: "Women," I think. Then Joe Elliott starts reciting about living a fucked life in a fucked place, foreign territory for him: "No promises, no guarantees, when you come down here you're already on your knees." He's talking to a guy who "can't say no," who dances with danger with rivers of tears in his eyes. Joe asks whether he's ready for the nightmare. Harmonies start curving up into these Beatlesy little Arabesques, and Elliott gets downright critical: "No one will ever hear you scream or shout . . . You'd rather laugh about it." It's not preachy, far from it. But this is like "Welcome To The Jungle," or Kix's "Cold Chills," in the way it admits to the excitement of opening Pandora's box but doesn't shy away from the evil you'll encounter. Or, more important, from how that evil will scare you.

I'm talking to Joe and to guitarist Phil Collen in Collen's Hollywood apartment. There's a copy of *Cosmopolitan* on the end table; I suppose it belongs to Phil's wife, a vegetarian just like him and his two-year-old son. ("It's a moral thing," he says. "I can't eat a dead body.") Phil says he hasn't had a drink in years; Joe (who arrived late) says he downs the occasional whiskey, but that's it. Joe also tells me I heard one of the lines in "White Lightning" wrong—claims it's "you *can't even* laugh about it," not so critical maybe. But I'm still getting the gist of the song (which Phil and Joe agree is the album's best) right (or maybe Joe just *sang* it wrong, some kinda subconscious Freudian thing—their last album *was* called *Hysteria*, after all). Anyway, we all know who the song's addressed to; if you knew the story of Def Leppard, you'd know, too (though if you didn't, it wouldn't make the song any less powerful).

In January of 1991, a few years after telling *People* magazine "this is the most exciting part of my life, I don't want to miss it," Steve Clark succumbed to a lethal combination of alcohol, morphine, valium, and codeine, some of which were chemicals he was taking to kill the pain in his back. When I found out I was going to interview Def Leppard, I originally intended to let the guitarist's death slide, partly because it seemed like none of my business and partly because I wasn't that interested, not as interested as I was in, say, the obvious similarities between "Rocket" on *Hysteria* and Boney M's "Mission To Venus" (both astronaut-disco songs with Gary Glitter drums; Collen and Elliott insist they've never heard the latter). But "White Lightning" kinda left me no choice in the matter.

Joe and Phil say of course they were grief-stricken when Steve died, but also, in a way pissed—pissed because, just like my mom, how do you pick up and move on? But they don't blame him. He was trying to turn around, they assure me. Attending AA meetings and all. But outside of playing guitar, he didn't have much else in his life, unless doing crossword puzzles counts. His death was no suicide, but according to Phil Collen, he was still a sad, lonely guy: "When he got bummed out, he got low, really low." Yet "he could be great fun," Joe says. "On tour he was fine, his life was fine, but as soon as we'd come off tour and he's not recording guitar parts, he has all this spare time he didn't know how to deal with."

Rock music has way too many death cults already, and it'd be really dumb to turn Steve Clark into one—before he died, no matter how much you love the chunky riffs in "Rock of Ages" or the hypnotic concentricities in "Hysteria," you probably didn't know his name. I know I didn't. But I want people to know there are real people behind this music, and talking about Steve Clark and "White Lightning" is one way. This band is pretty faceless; they don't exactly make spectacles of themselves.

Joe Elliott plays golf (I forgot to ask him how his handicap compares to Huey's or Iggy's or Alice's), collects Seventies glam rock videos, and roots for Sheffield United, who play soccer, which in case you never heard of it before is a sport where fans start riots in the stands. But Def Leppard don't. Robert Christgau, foolishly giving the great *Hysteria* a must-to-avoid in 1987: "I have trouble perceiving these guys as human beings under ideal circumstances." Certain little girls who write bassist Rick Savage lots of love letters would disagree, of course, but by now those letters probably go to Nirvana's Kurt Cobain, and the high-schoolers in the math classes my younger sister teaches in Oakland call Def Lep "out-of-date." I mean, *Hysteria* came out *five years ago*! All most people know about Def Leppard is that they've got the hardest luck in showbiz—before *Pyromania*, they fired guitarist Pete Willis for being a drunk asshole in a way Steve Clark never was. (Joe: "He had a small man's complex. He was 5'2", but after a couple beers he thought he was nine feet tall, and he would've tried to take on Mike Tyson"; Collen, from a cult mascara-rock band called Girl, replaced him.) Before *Hysteria*, on the eve of 1985, drummer Rick Allen lost his left arm in a traffic accident. (He started using a custom-made machine with lots of foot pedals, though Elliott tells me *Hysteria*'s drum-machine-heavy groove had more to do with technological advances.) Then before *Adrenalized*, Clark died. I mean, hey, selling 10 million copies of your albums is wonderful. But this is a hell of a way to go about it!

Yet like I said, you don't have to know Def Leppard's bios to appreciate their music. *Adrenalized* is dedicated to Clark, and "White Lightning" was written for him, but Elliott says it could just as well be directed to C. C. Deville, or Janis Joplin, or the older brother of whoever's listening. "It's a song about somebody's personal hell. We never mention Steve's name, though some fans might remember how he wore all white a lot, and used a white guitar, and on stage with his blond hair he looked like white lightning." Joe says, "The Babies had a 'White Lightning' song about cocaine. Ours could be about drinking or drugs, but also violence, or gambling, any kind of addiction. And the nightmare you'll face in this life, or maybe in an afterlife." (It occurs to me now that the song could also be about Freddie Mercury—Elliott and Collen were Queen fans growing up, and it shows in their music. I assume they met him, maybe were pals; I didn't think to ask.) And really, "White Lightning" might not seem so perfect to me if the balance of Lep's music weren't so happy.

Oddly enough, but good for us consumers, most of the rest of *Adrenalized* is the zestiest, fizziest music they've made. The first three songs, at least on the pre-release/pre-final-mixdown tape I heard in the Mercury Records office in January, are silly youthful uptempo post-T.-Rex dance music, in your face, bam bam bam. Like "Pour Some Sugar On Me" or "Armageddon It" last time, only more so. "Let's Get Rock," the first single, is my favorite—thick crunch more ZZ-boogie-like than this group usually gives us (a side effect of having a rhythm guy for your only surviving guitarist, Collen admits), big drums like 1985 Run-D.M.C., and Elliott comes in leading this speedy three-chord call-and-response that's archetypal like "Yakety Yak" filtered through "Surrender" or "Parents Just Don't Understand": "Mow the lawn! Take out the trash!" Joe calls himself an "average ordinary everyday kid," and before you know it he's in the car with a girl who likes all kinds of music as long as there's no guitars. She switches the radio to classical, and you hear violins, and eventually Lep's fat riffs begin to ring as lovely as violins themselves. It smells more like teen spirit than "Smells Like Teen Spirit."

Joe starts to get nervous whenever I call Lep's fast stuff dance music: "If by dance music you mean 'Honky Tonk Women,' I guess it is. I mean, you could dance to it. But when I think of dance music I think of New Order or, you know, 'Disco Inferno' by Taveres . . ." Calm down, Joe! "Disco Inferno" was by the Trammps, who used to be Wilson Pickett's backup band, and if you ask me it rocks *harder* than "Honky Tonk Women," which I like just fine. And while a couple Leppard songs remind me of the Stones (well, two: "You Got Me Runnin'" and "Excitable"), the latter of those two reminds me of *disco* Stones, of those Puerto Rican girls just dyin' to meetchoo in "Miss You." (Actually, Elliott says, "Excitable" was inspired by "State Of Shock," the Jacksons' 1984 power lunch with Mick Jagger.) And usually Lep's not *bluesful* enough to be the Stones—they're more like Sweet's "Ballroom Blitz," or Gary Glitter's "Rock And Roll Part Two," which were disco before disco had a name. "Rocket" was about going to a club and dancing to glam rock, and those dancers on Virgin Records' glam-rock videotape (sampled liberally in Lep's awesome "Rocket" video) look pretty disco to me. ("Yeah—*embarrassing*, aren't they?," Elliott asks. Compared to what, Metallica fans?) And Phil Oakey of Human League has said that *Hysteria* was basically a Human League record with a producer clever enough to make it sound heavy metal—in fact, *Hysteria* is also what Oakey named his 1984 Giorgio Moroder collaboration!

Well, it turns out that Joe Elliott is friends with Phil Oakey. "And it might not sound that way now, but when it came out 'Don't You Want Me' sounded pretty weird—the Human League were the first band except for maybe Kraftwerk to use so many synthesizers and make it sound like pop music." (An exaggeration—like, what about Silver Convention? Or Donna Summer's band?) "Anyway, when I first heard that record, it was the first time I ever really wanted to find out who the *producer* was. I found out it was Martin Rushent." Personally, *I* wanted to know who the female singer was. But that was 1981; by the time Leppard linked back up with their producer, Mutt Lange, they were determined to learn to use the recording studio as an instrument, a truly radical thing for a hard rock band to attempt. "We wanted *Pyromania* to be the *Sgt. Pepper's* of heavy metal," Joe remembers; what they came up with was a record better than *Sgt. Pepper's*.

"We have something stupid on there between every song, like somebody saying 'turn that down,' or the crowd at the start of 'Stagefright,' or Vietnam in 'Die Hard the Hunter.'" The most famous tidbit, the part at the beginning of "Rock Of Ages" where Lange mutters "ünten glieben glauben globen," is now being sampled for a rap record. Elliott says the words are complete nonsense, made up on the spot. Though lots of fans are apparently convinced it's German for "running through the forest silently!"

"The main thing is the singing, the song," Joe theorizes. "We build everything around that, because that's what most people will remember. In music, at least in the English-speaking part of the world, that's what people relate to." The bass and drums are the last instruments to hit the tape, and Rick Allen records to the same Linn Drum everybody else in the band does, and maybe that's got something to do with why the beat in Leppard songs is so much more pronounced—more disco, yeah, but also more *rock'n'roll*—than in 98 percent of the guitar-rock songs you'll hear these days. "The problem with most drummers and guitar players is they don't know when to stop," Phil Collen chides. "Our philosophy is, you eliminate any part that interferes with the spirit of the sound." Fun stuff, however, can stay in.

So both *Pyromania* and 1981's *High 'N' Dry* (vinyl versions anyhow) end with near-infinite semi-closed-groove tapeloops, the type that art bands like Ciccone Youth are so fond of; Elliott calls the one in *Pyromania*'s "Billy's Got A Gun" "the march of the wooden zombies." And *Hysteria* tracks like "Rocket" and "Gods Of War" bombard you nonstop with stolen Ronald Reagan speeches, backwards snatches of other tracks, dub parts, sound effects, sampled Burundi beats, you name it. "A lot of it was just studio wanking-off, putting stuff through a sampler or echo machine or slowing it down like 200 times," Elliott explains. "And some of it was just mistakes we decided to leave in, and a lot of it was Mutt—I remember leaving the studio and 'Rocket' being a three-minute-long song, then coming back and he'd stretched it to eight." So he agrees with Phil Oakey, in a way—"We use technology the way the Human League did; the only thing that limits you is your imagination." The difference, Collen suggests, is that Def Leppard still want to be a rock band. Maybe what *Hysteria* really was, then, was a metal record with a producer clever enough to make it feel like weird disco, and a band brave and smart enough to let him have his way.

"We want to stay sounding current," Phil Collen says. "We're really conscious of not wanting to wind up as a dinosaur band. So we don't have tunnel vision like lots of rock bands, we're not stuck in their rut; live, it's different, but when we're making records we use samplers, whatever else is out there. If we hear something we like on a Madonna record, like those little rhythm things that go back and forth in 'Vogue,' we'll try and do the same thing. A lot of bands are scared to do that."

The offensive thing, of course, is that the scared ones wear their scaredness as a badge, as if mediocrity gives them integrity. And at the same time, being Def Leppard presents a kind of catch-22. Because they don't wear their *eclecticism* on their sleeve either, because they do nothing that might advertise them as being "avant-garde" or "alternative," they'll never get the critic-poll/award-show acclaim of, say, a Faith No More, even though there's really no "innovation" on FNM's *The Real Thing* (which Joe Elliott likes, by the way) that Leppard hadn't already tossed off, on *Hysteria* or earlier, with prettier singing, less pompous lyrics, a less stilted beat. "You'll never see us on '120 Minutes' like the Chili Peppers," Elliott points out, and that stinks, because Leppard aren't only funkier, they're *stranger*: more "new wave," if you will. (A disco critic I know says they remind him of the Police.) "Not only that," Joe says, and I agree: "We have better haircuts!"

Why don't intelligentsia-type tastemakers realize Def Leppard are God's gift to rock'n'roll? "Because we have *hits*," Joe guesses. "I mean, we're not stupid—we *know* hits are the Antichrist." Well, not if you're Prince or Guns N' Roses or Madonna they're not, but Joe still has a point. Like Madonna says, the big thing that makes Elvis Costello "alternative" is the fact that he's not *popular*. ("I guess it's supposed to be music that makes you think, as an alternative to music that doesn't," she told *Interview*, I assume with the proper couple tons of sarcasm in her voice.) Elliott's not bitter—none of the band is—because "the people who make a difference to us love us— the *kids*." I bet they love the haircuts, for one thing: Elliott's is perched way up high, above his grey tracksuit like husks sticking out of a corn silo (he's real tall, see).

When he first walked into the room, from the back, I assumed Joe was Collen's wife. Which would've made for quite a couple, because Collen is this teensy little guy with his *own* mussed-up patch of yellow head-hedge vegetation. He was wearing tattered jeans, and about seven gold circular earrings in his right ear. His apartment was very clean and he seemed real shy and polite, especially compared to Elliott, who came off a tad cynical about me being there. Phil even moved his guitar so I wouldn't sit on it—I mean, what else can you ask of a multi-millionaire?

We talked a lot about music. Phil likes Kate Bush, Joe likes Mott the Hoople and Mariah Carey ("Nobody's reached high notes like that since Minnie Riperton!"), Joe reveals that the Sex Pistols took longer to record *Never Mind The Bollocks* than Lep took to make *Pyromania*, but he still thinks they were a great rock band. About Generation X he's not so sure—they'd grown up listening to the same glam as him, but they were punk where Lep was metal because they didn't know how to play their instruments and Lep did. (I tried to argue, then stopped.) Joe was well aware of punk, owned lots of the records, when Leppard made a punk-like move by debuting with their own homemade 7-inch EP (on Bludgeon Riffola Records, and a big U.K. hit) in 1979, but what really gave them the idea to do so was the fact that a different Sheffield metal band had already done something similar. So some joker at *Sounds* linked Lep with the burgeoning font of dorkitude he referred to as "the New Wave of Heavy Metal" (Saxon, Samson, Iron Maiden, etc.), and everybody since then assumed the connection was true. It wasn't. "We had nothing to do with those bands," Joe snickers. "They were like the beginning of black metal, and we dressed like *girls*. Whenever we read the stuff it was like this to us": He crosses his fingers in front of his face, like the crucifix you'd thrust at a vampire.

"I was a weird kid," he says about his younger life. "When I was nine all my friends were about 15. So I'd buy 'Sugar, Sugar' [which "Pour Some Sugar on Me" is based on] as a single, but I'd also buy *Tarkus*, and King Crimson and Jethro Tull. If it was a rock band like Status Quo, I bought the album; if it was a pop band like the Sweet or Slade, I bought the singles. I even bought 'Crazy Horses' by the Osmonds, that was great. But I had to carry it home in a brown paper bag, like the first time you buy condoms." How did he determine that Slade were a "pop" band, I wonder. "Because they were larger than life, they had like 20 number-one hits. And their albums always had lots of filler." (Compared to Status Quo or ELP??! You mean, those creeps had *non*-filler somewhere?) Fortunately, Leppard wound up more like Slade; they even put on vintage Slade boot-dancer threads for an all-glitter-classics-covers one-off charity gig last December. On the other hand, Elliott wrongly dismisses "Little Willie," "Poppa Joe," and "Wig Wam Bam," three of Sweet's best songs, as embarrassments ("Brian Connolly didn't even sing on 'em!"). Yet when confronted with the stupid claim from some Anthrax ignoramus that *Def Lep* sold out after their second album, he points out that Scott Ian was backstage during Lep's last tour whining that he wishes he was in a band *like* Def Leppard.

Who, I might add, are currently hunting for a guitarist to replace Steve Clark—the show must go on, as Freddie Mercury's record label might say. Potential resumé-senders must meet a number of qualifications, none of which have anything to do with being able to play Steve Vai under the table, Elliot says. First off, they've gotta be British at least by birth (even though none of the tax-exiled Leps have been Brit *residents* since back before they had Union Jacks in their videos). Second, they've gotta be about the same age, around 30—the Leppards ranged from 15 to 19 when they made their first record, and they're not about to hire a whipper-snapper now who'll make 'em look like greybeards by comparison. Third, they've gotta at least be *fairly* good on guitar. And most of all, they've gotta be nice guys. "Guitar playing, that's minority stuff only guitar players are interested in," Elliott says. "What's more important to me is that, when I mention a certain episode of *Fawlty Towers*, the guy will know which one I'm talking about. If he can't, there's no way he'll fit in with this band."

Creem, 1992

AC/DC'S AGED CURRENCIES

"In the beginning," Bon Scott began, "back in 1955, man didn't know that a rock'n'roll show, all that jive." His screaming grammar in "Let There Be Rock" didn't compute, as he recreated history to suit his whims, even rolling over Chuck Berry's "Roll Over Beethoven."

"The white man had the stops (or 'shorts' maybe?), the red man had the blues (he must mean '50s feedback-blues grandpa Link Wray, pure Cherokee; or '30s Delta blues founder Charley Patton, a half-breed with straight brown hair). No one knew what they was gonna do, but Tchaikovsky had the news. He said, 'Let there be light,' and there was light. 'Let there be sound,' and there was sound, 'Let there be drums,' and there was drums. 'Let there be guitar,' *woooaaagh* there was guitar. 'Let there be *rock* . . .'"

Sixteen years before Bon and AC/DC bounced out of Australia with "Let There Be Rock" in 1977, another happy-go-lucky fivesome, namely Los Angeles R&B clowns the Coasters, had suggested a creation scenario similar to AC/DC's only reversed. "In the beginning," a biblical voice intones between hallowed church notes, "There was nothing *but* rock. Then somebody invented the wheel, and things just began to roll." Lead comedian Carl Gardner describes saxes swinging like axes, "honkin' like a *fuck* down in a Harlem loft"—a simile Bon Scott could appreciate. (AC/DC and the Coasters both lusted after go-go strippers—in "Soul Stripper" and "Little Egypt.") "That Is Rock & Roll" the song title informs, but the music doesn't *sound* like rock'n'roll; it's too rural. There's a banjo, and more than any other '50s rock song, this one sounds like Louis Armstrong–bellowed Dixieland jazz, or like something medicine-show graduate Will Shade and his Memphis Jug Band might've played at ball games or fish fries not far from Beale Street, acting drunk and buck-dancing on roller skates to entertain white cityslickers in the '20s. You can imagine AC/DC writing the Memphis Jug Band's 1930 hit "Everybody's Talking About Sadie Green"— "When she dances she don't move her head, but moves everything else instead."

AC/DC'S great guitarist Angus Young looks like Rumpelstiltskin—a troll, shorter than me (and I'm 5'5") and skinnier, too, with way-too-long-and-scraggly middle-aged guy split-ended hair tied in a ponytail, and old jeans and a striped little-boy's T-shirt like Kurt Cobain wore sometimes.

"I heard this old record called 'Bye Bye,' made in 1928," Angus says, sitting in a record label conference room in New York. "And the singer, he'd been recorded in front of a store, and I'm thinking 'Shit, that's fucking *Bon!*'"—referring, of course, to late AC/DC vocalist Bon Scott—"It had the same feeling in the voice." Angus says that when Bon was still in AC/DC, Angus and his brother Malcolm would do stuff like try to make their guitars sound like the clarinets in old Louis Armstrong songs. "It's A Long Way To The Top" had Bon playing bagpipes, and "Can I Sit Next To You," "Show Business," and "There's Gonna Be Some Rockin'" used a Dixieland barrelhouse piano beat almost unique in hard rock (unless the Coasters count).

"Just before I came here I had on my player Elmore James," Angus says, "and he's singing 'Whose Muddy Shoes.' I laughed for two days every time I thought of it—'Whose muddy shoes are they?' My wife's lookin' at me like, "What's *he* on, and why is he laughin' so strongly?' Because, I see the connection—and there's a lot of humor in it. When Muddy Waters sang 'My Woman Left Home With a Busdriver To Florida,' I'm *laughing*."

"If you mention Chuck Berry to Angus," says AC/DC vocalist Brian Johnson, a great big, merry, *hardy* man, "you've hit the number-one right on the head as far as he's concerned. Muddy Waters was his idol when he was a kid, but whenever you mention Chuck Berry his eyes light up. He's always said that Berry was the ultimate performer. If you look at his lyrics, as far as I'm concerned, he's Shakespeare. In fact, to me, he's *bigger* than Shakespeare. I'm a big idol of Chuck Berry actually."

(I think he got that backwards.)

"We used to say that all the time—'Think Chuck,' you know, 'What would Chuck write?' Sometimes we'd sweat blood to get it."

Just like AC/DC, Chuck based an unmistakable-for-anybody-else sound around vernacular wordplay and simple guitar riff rhythms so all his songs sounded exactly the same—until you listened close.

Angus did not, however, lift his duckwalk from Chuck Berry.

"Actually, I got it from my nephew," he says, "'cause he used to always dance along to rock & roll tunes, y'know. He was little then, and the way he done it . . . I was looking at him, the way he moved. And he'd never seen Chuck, so he just had his little strut.

"When you're in a bar, you play Chuck Berry songs, rock & roll songs," Angus says. "I mean, not the same *as* . . . but the way that we played— your *interpretation*. I think the biggest compliment we ever got was, a guy came up and asked, 'Was that Chuck Berry's "School Days" you were playing?' We said 'Yeah,' and he said, 'That was the *worst* version I ever heard!'"

The Billboard Book of Top 40 Albums by Joel Whitburn calls AC/DC "a hard rock band formed in Sydney, Australia in 1974." In the early days, Angus says, they played "pubs, clubs—probably the same as here, what do you call them, *bars*—a lot of that. When we started out, music was music and everything was still locked together. We were a band that could go out and play rock & roll music and, uh, sort of . . . maybe louder than some of them. If there was an audience, we played—from bars to car parks to weddings. It was like, you done your bit . . . and then you always get the clone element."

Rose Tattoo and Angel City (whose early '80s albums *Assault And Battery* and *Face To Face,* respectively, blow away anything AC/DC has made since '77 if you ask me, but never mind) stole AC/DC's primal blues-stomp verbosity and turned it into an Oz genre of sorts.

"I think they certainly took bits of us," Angus recollects. "I know that (AC/DC drummer) Phil (Rudd) had actually played with the singer in Rose Tattoo, and they fired him, so they didn't even know good talent. But the other band you mentioned, they were a *jug* band when they played with us, and we done a little tour of South Australia, and they were just playin' things like the Big Bopper, 'Chantilly Lace.' And then they saw what we had going, and they figured maybe that was the way they should go."

I asked whether AC/DC had often played Australian redneck bars, dodging bullets from cowboy gunfights. Angus scowls. "No! That's stupid. That's like saying there's kangaroos hopping down Main Street. Of course, Sydney is a big city, too. And Melbourne's a big city. It ain't the wild west, y'know."

Angus says the first school uniforms he wore on stage—ball cap, tie, short pants, suit coat, book bag—were his own from school. "I think I was just about 17. That was the end of '73—I was the youngest at the time. The other guys were a bit older. I had left school by then—I was out of school by 15. The uniform was lying around growing moss." The school he left behind "was just a state school, public-funded, state money—just a working class school. The rule was you come to school wearing the uniform. They figured they were getting around discrimination. But that's all shit, because we all knew who was rich and who was poor. You can tell by whose parents have a say in the school's running and whose don't."

Angus and Malcolm were actually born in Glasgow, Scotland, and basically their parents kept them there just long enough to develop thick accents (Angus's is high and nasal like a cartoon weasel). Then, Angus says, Daddy Young moved his brood to Sydney "to work, really. He was a spray painter. He immigrated. They had a program for ten pounds and he took them up on it."

Brian Johnson, a Scotsman himself, explains that "those were the days of the big exodus from England for new lands—Canada, Australia, you know, in hopes of a better future for your kids." Says Angus, "I was eight years old and Malc was ten, I think."

An older Young brother, George, got into rock'n'roll first, with a band called the Easybeats. "Very big band," Angus recalls. "They were like the Beatles of Australia."

"George must be now, I think a year older than Brian, about 48, 49?" Angus estimates. "He might be younger, 'cause I've got many others—six brothers—some tell you their age voluntarily and others you gotta sort of pry it out of 'em." By the time AC/DC formed, Angus says, the Easybeats "had long gone. I think their last thing was in '69. But George was doing stuff in the studio and more and more people were coming in, 'You gotta check out your kid brother's band!' And he came and saw us and was knocked out." So George and fellow Easybeat Harry Vanda wound up producing AC/DC's first records.

Angus credits his big brothers with introducing him to music. "They had different tastes, but there was a lot of '50s stuff, and a lot of blues stuff. A lot of blues music sort of went across the Atlantic in the Clapton era. With my brothers, these were their idols. I had other brothers that liked Little Richard stuff, and the oldest brother took me to see Louis Armstrong. . . . When you're young, that's what sets you on the path where your taste lies."

"I love the blue *note*," Angus says. "But to me you don't have to play straight à la 12 bars to say that's a blues song." Get him talking about connections between Al Jolson and George Gershwin, and he just goes on and on: "'Birth Of The Blues,' in the middle section, it's prominent, the exact same as I think one of the Jolson songs, and Gershwin, there's the element, of, you know—he took it a step *further*. I'm not saying he didn't, but there's the *influence* there, and you hear it in the old, *dadadadada-dum! dadn'da* . . ."

It sounds like he's scatting a horn solo. I have no idea what he's trying to say, but I smile.

" . . . and that's 'Birth Of The Blues,' but if you hear the Jolson, I think it's one of the ones where he's singing about his mama as a little boy, it's the exact way, it's 'uh-duh-duh-duh-dannngh *bom! bom!* dub'n mamal' in a little baby voice."

This is right out of *Spinal Tap*, I swear.

AC/DC really likes to *scat* in interviews: "That was a guitar, oh yeah, we've never used keyboards—the *diddle-iddle-iddle-iddle-iddle-iddle-iddle*, that was all Angus," Brian says (replying to my query about how, in "For Those About To Rock," in 1981, AC/DC latched onto Pete Townshend's minimalist rainbow-in-curved-air keyboard-repetition loopings from *Who's Next* as an excuse to sound electronic but not seem too terribly "disco" about it. In case you're keeping score, Foreigner, Sweet, Manfred Mann, Loverboy, Girlschool, Kix, Van Halen, and Cinderella have all made similarly Who-do doodles on occasion).

When I go on to compliment Brian's rap-like use of his vocal as a rhythm instrument, the screamer's pleased. "I'm not a proper singer," he thickly rasps in his backslapping prole brogue. "I'm not a tuneful balladeer. I'm lucky enough that the boys picked me, 'cos me voice was, I guess, more like an instrument than a voice. I'm a lucky bugger, and I don't know fooking why, and you start thinking: 'I hope it's gonna last.' We've always laughed about me not having a voice of all—more like a primal fooking scream, y'know? It's not always as easy as it was, let's put it that way, when you're in your 20s. I was not a child wonder at singing, but when I listen to the old Geordie stuff I hear this little choirboy-high voice (he makes *la-la* opera notes.) It was *hard*, but it was so *clean* and *pure*. I mean, I hadn't smoked any cigarettes hardly then."

"You know, that was the glam-rock period; they weren't too bad," Brian says of his old band Geordie. "It was like Slade, it was exactly that kind of stuff, y'know, which was fun—with banal fooking trite lyrics. We were popular. People knew of us and we sold records all over Europe. We never did get one out in the States—a lot of English bands didn't, you know."

Bon Scott even saw them once.

"He said I wasn't too bad. He said a couple positive things about me, so I guess the boys remembered," says Brian. The AC/DC singer-to-be wasn't a major AC/DC fan himself at the time, but "I'd heard of them, and we did one of their songs in the set, 'Whole Lotta Rosie.' But I hadn't heard the album. And I saw them on British television, on *Rock Goes To College*. The program used to go to a different college every week and put a band on. And usually, it's somebody like the Strawbs—college kids in England are famous for always having three records in their collection by, like, Pink

Floyd, that kinda shit, Steve Hillage. But here was this *rock'n'roll* band, *rockin'*, knockin' 'em out."

The Scotsman replaced Scott after the former shrieker froze to death in his car after imbibing too much alcohol in 1980.

Brian says the big difference between his singing and Bon's is that "Bon was a bit more bluesy. When I joined, the boys didn't want an exact clone of Bon, otherwise it'd be just somebody *parodying* Bon. I could never get that great *swing* Bon had."

Which brings us back to the *beat*, like everything about this band.

"Rhythm first, yeah, we always start with the rhythm," Angus says.

When I ask him if AC/DC set out to make people *dance*, not just bang their heads, he's a little evasive at first: "If you're playing in bars, you play music that makes 'em *rock*, y'know. If, at the time, they wanna dance to rock, so be it. But do you mean, did we play dance music *à la* disco-type thing? No, there was none of that."

But then Angus delves further into the issue: "Well, Bon was a *drummer* first, and Brian likes to bang a bongo or two every now and again. They got a beat, you know . . . if you listen to 'Back In Black,' it's a *rap*. When we did 'Back In Black,' I think there was a guy from the band Chic who said, 'Hey, we're not far away from where AC/DC is at.' And I think that's the blues connection."

And while a bunch of AC/DC songs feature obsessively repetitive drum-beats that suggest disco ("It's a Long Way to the Top," "Jailbreak," "Highway to Hell," "You Shook Me All Night Long"), AC/DC's most disco groove by far shows up, appropriately, in a six-and-a-half-minute bass jam called "Soul Stripper," on their '74 *Jailbreak* EP. But since it came out in 1975, when disco barely existed yet, you can't call it a disco "move," like "Miss You" by the Stones; it's more like AC/DC reached disco by *accident,* by parallel evolution from a shared soul ancestor.

Angus and Brian don't know (or seem to care) much about current Aussie jailbait-grunge heartthrobs Silverchair. (And I forgot to ask them about that new movie called *Angus*. Sorry.) But they know their own roots: "At my house," Brian says, "you'll hear the Paul Butterfield Blues Band, and you'll hear John Mayall when Clapton was on it. 'Crossroads,' Satchmo, or Cab Calloway, Etta James . . ."

"Etta," he reflects. "What a voice, I love that woman's voice, I'd *kill* for that voice."

I've always felt that pre-Brian AC/DC songs like "The Jack" and "Big

AC/DC: BIG IN PRISONS.

Balls" dealt in a punning bawdiness that linked boogie blues to the Cockney glitterboot-stomping and soccergang-shouting of Slade, but Angus denies it: "They were going more for the commercial element, and we always tried to stay away from the pop side of it."

Slade was music hall, he says, but AC/DC was "probably more the *bordello* music." (Having "the jack" was down-under wharf slang for either the crabs, sez Brian, or the clap, sez Angus. But the song is all *poker* metaphors!) On the other hand, Angus acknowledges that the good-natured humor pervasive in Australian rock "*could* probably come from the Cockney element (he sure says 'element' a lot, doesn't he?), 'cause the language, they say, is very similar to the English East End Cockney."

And they *did* start out as a British penal colony. This penal/penile pedigree might explain one of the more disreputable sectors of AC/DC'S audience. "I remember a prison warden saying to me," Angus chuckles, "you've gotta be about the biggest act out there in these prisons. He says, 'Are you *aware* of that fact?'" (Angus is cracking up and slapping his knee at this point.) "I said, 'No, but it's good to know if ever I'm in the tank, I'm amongst friends!'"

Humble Pie's "30 Days In The Hole" in 1972 sounded like AC/DC before AC/DC did, so was *that* outfit an influence? "I was a big fan of Steve Marriott," Angus admits. "Steve Marriott actually performed on one of my brother's records, a song called 'Good Times.' To this day I think Steve Marriott was a great, great vocalist."

"I'll tell you a funny story," Angus volunteers. "They had a revival of the Humble Pie, and we had *Back In Black* out, and we were playing in Philadelphia, and the lineup was, I think, a band from the south called Nantucket, and the Humble Pie, and ourselves. Steve Marriott apparently came up to the guy in Nantucket and said, 'I love you guys. I love that opening track you did, that song "A Long Way To The Top If You Wanna Rock 'n' Roll," a *great* track. But I *hate* those AC/DC guys!' He says, 'I didn't have the heart to tell him you guys wrote it!'"

"Long Way To The Top," incidentally, was AC/DC's first American album-rock-radio hit, says Angus, "big in certain parts of the country around the West Coast–San Francisco, San Jose. And I think deep down in Florida. There was *pockets*." They were already stars in Australia by that time, he relates, with "a couple of Top 10 things. The biggest record we had there was our second album, the album called *T.N.T.*, and then they released that as a combination throughout the world as *High Voltage*."

Which is *my* favorite AC/DC LP, with the funniest back cover in rock history, featuring letters to the band members where, for example, one lovestruck underaged groupie says her dad wants to erase Bon's tattoos by removing his arms. The letters were fake, Angus reveals, for reasons of decency. "Bon got all sorts of crazy offers, you know. There were many things that would come in, and when they were putting it together they sort of looked at them and said, 'Oh, we can't print that . . .'"

"Toilet humor—Bon was a lover of that," Angus laughs. "That's what he called himself, a 'toilet poet.'" But, contrary to popular belief, Angus insists that "She's Got Balls" on *High Voltage* was *not* an ode to a hermaphrodite.

"Bon had seen his wife in Adelaide, and he said, 'Well I've got this little verse here,' and he had the line 'She's got balls.' And he said he wrote it at the time about his wife. She was actually a very pretty, good-looking woman, and still is to this day. But, uh, he wrote it about her . . ."

"When we first came here to tour in 1977," continues Angus, "the record company says, 'You've come at sort of a rough time; this country's very into *dance* music.' They just said it's not an *American* album." Atlantic Records initially rejected the first couple LPS for U.S. release, and by the time I was first introduced to the band upon hearing "Touch Too Much" off 1979's *Highway To Hell* on the rate-a-record portion of *American Bandstand*, I assumed AC/DC were punk rockers. Their association with ex-Easybeats Vanda and Young, who by 1979 were New Wave semistars called Flash and the Pan (whose best song "Lady Killer" on their dance-oriented debut disc halfway resembled AC/DC) only confused matters more.

"AC/DC first went to England and the height of the big punk thing was on, and they got sorta lumped in with it all for the slashing guitars," says Brian. "But y'see the boys didn't argue about it and that's why I like them. We've been through all the phases where critics, journalists like yourself, have said, 'Don'cha think you should change, don'cha think you should start wearing leather now because it's heavy metal time, or satin because it's glam-rock time?'"

"I don't think we're a *heavy metal* band. I think AC/DC's one of the only bands left that are playing *rock'n'roll* music. I love rock'n'roll and I'll never follow fads again—I never try to—and become a total twit."

Angus doesn't identify much with metal either, even though thrash bands often cite AC/DC as an inspiration: "Well, Metallica, they were on tour with us through Europe, and uh, I don't hear it, you know . . . I can say maybe they might've taken the guitar riff element, but I think the one big element they missed was the rhythm. They got the energy, and I think a lot of ('90s metal bands) borrowed the *shorts*." He says Metallica-type music "always leaves me feeling a bit cold. It doesn't go over my head, it's just cold. It's a little bit music-by-numbers."

I agree, but in kind of an ironic way, because—let's face it—these guys have been making music-by-numbers *themselves* for a good decade-and-a-half now, and moving toward metal has a lot to do with it. (Or maybe they started going downhill when they started firing cannons on stage. "One of 'em has part of an old Civil War cannon, which a farmer gave us," Angus says. "So that was very kind of him.") Bon's screech felt less self-important and lighter on its feet than Brian's; I think the change in bassists from Mark Evans to Cliff Williams in 1977 might've also stunted the rhythm more than anybody has ever admitted. And starting with *Powerage* in 1978, the instruments seem to more and more be mixed in a way that drowns out AC/DC's singing, to trick people into thinking their music's rocking harder when really it's just blaring *louder*.

In general, the Bon LPS were more subtle, funnier, catchier, warmer, less cynically tossed off. Humorous vocal asides on those records (like the one in "Little Lover" about Bon's poster being on some teenage girl's wall next to Gary Glitter) actually remind me of Bob Dylan's early '60s jokes. 1983's *Flick Of The Switch*, connoisseurs' consensus choice as AC/DC's best '80s album, has consistent riff-energy and a high high-pitched-screech quotient, and it always rocks, especially when it goes real fast or its vocals approximate rap music.

But *Flick Of The Switch* never makes me care that it rocks; unlike *all* of AC/DC's '70s music. It's too mechanistically metallic and emotionally detached and lyrically perfunctory to touch my *heart*. Give or take a couple cuts ("You Shook Me All Night Long," "Who Made Who," "Let's Get It Up"), that's always been the case with the Brian-era stuff.

Angus doesn't necessarily agree with me, but he definitely understands my point: "When you're playing some of those old tracks, fans seem to see right away where you're coming from. Some shows, we've gone out there and they won't let you leave the building unless you play 'T.N.T.' You go into places like Philadelphia and all night they'll just shout. 'T.N.T.' Sometimes I would say, 'Well, how 'bout we just go out and play "T.N.T." and go home?'"

"You're probably right, there's probably more of the humor (on the '70s LPS), and a bit more of the warmth then. . . . There's a lot of tracks I like personally on those (later '80s) records that I think sometimes, well, maybe people didn't get it. I know on that album *Fly On The Wall*, I always loved that song called 'Fly On The Wall.'"

But it's *Back In Black*, significantly the *oldest* album with Brian (not to mention easily AC/DC's most popular album ever), that he keeps referring back easily to. "'Have A Drink On Me,'" Angus says, a song recorded too soon for some teetotallers after Bon Scott's drinking-related death, "was never meant as a bad taste. I think a lot of people missed the fact that the whole album is a *tribute*. Because the whole idea of it, you don't want to make an album and put 'In Memoriam' to somebody." So the album title, its dark cover, and the song "Hell's Bells," he says, were "the best way to show our respect."

"Bon's thing was more circumstance than anything else," Angus stresses. "Because we'd be on the road for nine months and he'd go, 'I don't need to drink,' and then six months later he wouldn't be working and people would see him in a pub somewhere and he would have a drink. If he was working, he was always sober. I think the only show he ever missed was purely by accident. He had a great excuse. Normally we played at one o'clock in the morning, but that day it was for schoolkids and it was one o'clock in the day. So me and Malcolm had a great time *singing*, y'know?"

"I don't drink," Angus says. "I've never really drunk. Bon told me, he says, 'Whatever I do, you don't do.' Now, Brian—*he* likes a drink. Malcolm stopped drinking. He thought he'd had enough." Plus, everybody in AC/DC is *married*—Angus for 15 years now to a Dutch woman.

These guys are as regular as you can imagine; in fact, I don't remember ever interviewing rock stars before who seemed so soft-spoken and down-to-earth and normal and not full of themselves. I'd wanted to talk to the band in a pub, gulping down Fosters ("Australian for beer")—a conference room seemed a wee bit antiseptic for AC/DC—but they didn't want to get swamped by fans. Brian excused himself whenever the room phone rang, and he talked real polite into it (in French sometimes!), almost like he was a secretary and his *job* was answering phones.

"We don't consider ourselves any different than we were five, ten, even twenty years ago," Brian says. He calls himself "a pretty happy-go-lucky carefree kinda lad. I really don't worry about too much, and if I do it'd be silly things, like if I upset somebody. If I've upset somebody, it sticks with me for hours that I've hurt somebody by saying something stupid."

When I ask Angus if he's proud about more teenage boys puking up alcohol to *Back In Black* and *Highway To Hell* than any other records in history, he says, "I grew up in the 'burbs, so these are the things that influence you." He recently saw his first Beavis and Butthead episode, prominently featuring the ubiquitous AC/DC T-shirt: "I think Bon would've laughed—*I* laughed."

But does he think AC/DC is hilarious? (Lots of people do, you know.) "I don't think we're out-and-out *Benny Hill*," Angus says, "but there is a lot of touches of humor and a lot of double-entendres, double-meanings. Some songs we try to break it up. When we get out there, we're certainly serious when we pick up the guitar and play it. And some songs we play very much with conviction, but sometimes we lighten it up too. We don't get out there to say this is a serious work of art, this is important. It's *not* important—it's entertaining you."

Brian says AC/DC's new *Ballbreaker* album is just "a humorous look at life and love, that's all that is." Fair enough. I mean, it's certainly not 1/100th as good an AC/DC album as Rancid's . . . *And Out Come the Wolves*, Gillette's *On the Attack*, Kix's *Show Business*, the Upper Crust's *Let Them Eat Rock*, or Paul Revere and the Raiders' *The Essential Ride '63–'67*. In fact, it's rather dull. But hey, I'm just a rock critic.

"I think the only song on this album that there isn't any humor in is 'Burnin' Alive,'" Brian says. "It's basically about Waco and all that, all the kids that died in that fire-bombing. Basically, it was just a dig at people in charge who shouldn't've been in charge of a fookin' box of matches. 'No firewater or Novocaine, no thunderstorm and no John Wayne'— there's no John Wayne to come in and save everyone, do you know what I mean? It's not political at all. It's not meant to be—it's just our own cry for people to *think* about things in the future."

"Our new album's also got 'Boogie Man,' which is sort of a slow thing, but that's sort of like Satchmo, that one," Brian says. Tim Burton's movie *The Nightmare Before Christmas* had a big fat character full of worms and maggots called the Boogie Man whose voice growled exactly as low as Brian's in the song, and though Brian saw the movie, he says he didn't imitate the character on purpose.

"Does it sound *spooky*, though?" he asks me. "'Cause the lads wanted a spooky kind of sound." He says the post-Slade "Hail Hail!" call-and-response gang chants in *Ballbreaker*'s "Hail Caesar"—which is inferior to the old Sir Lord Baltimore version and reminds me of the Rancid-like "Oi! Oi!" ones in "T.N.T." and the sinister "done dirt cheap" snarls in "Dirty Deeds Done Dirt Cheap"—are "just audience participation."

Ballbreaker was produced by Rick Rubin, which is supposed to be a big deal because Rick's always bragged about being a huge AC/DC fan, even to the point of stealing all their guitar riffs on certain records he oversaw in the late '80s.

Angus says of the Cult's Rubin-produced album *Electric*, "One guy played it in an interview and he said, 'What song is this?' And we said, 'That's one of *our* songs,' and it started out that way and he said, 'No, it's the Cult.' And we said 'What did they do, cover a version?' And he said, 'No, they call it something else.' I mean, that's very *bold*, you know?" He says the Beastie Boys' Rubin-masterminded pre-*Licensed To Ill* single "Rock Hard," which stole its backing track directly from "Back In Black," was even bolder: "And I never got a check!"

"They'll say, 'Listen to this, it sounds like *you!*'" Brian scoffs. "It's funny, they think you're gonna be upset or something. And I'll say, 'What do you expect me to do, sue 'em?'"

Anyway, there are rumors flying around among "industry insiders" that AC/DC didn't get along all that well with Rubin; record-label people I don't feel like naming tell me the band was somewhat irked by his supposedly unorthodox hands-off techniques. Unlike some other producers, apparently, he doesn't exactly spend 24-hour days in the studio, preferring to periodically check the work his artists do on their own. Somebody at AC/DC's label even told me he might have too many chickens in the pot, and was too busy producing the new Chili Peppers album at the time.

Yeah, well, who cares? I don't remember loving any Rubin records since 1987, so I was hardly expecting great things. Angus seems unusually reticent when I ask him about working with the guy ("It was different. I mean, I think he's supposedly . . . different"), but Brian feels Rick "did a grand job. It's like the driest thing I've ever heard, just wonderful, *wonderful*. It's just like right in your face, there's no polish, there's no bells, no shiny bits, or tweaks. It's just dry as a bone. It's like what you'd hear if you were standing in front of us."

On the other hand, AC/DC did wind up granting co-production credit to their recording engineer after the fact. "Mike Frazier was a big part of that whole operation," Brian says. "The lads just took to 'im, and he worked so hard . . . and Rick was in full agreement. He said, 'Yeah, this guy's done more than just *engineering*.'"

So believe what you want. Personally, I'm more interested in what kind of oil the woman in *Ballbreaker's* "Cover You In Oil" is supposed to be covered in—peanut oil, olive oil, WD-40, what? "*Paint* oil," Angus says. "Yeah, it's a canvas. I'm like one-eared Vinny! That's what they'd call Vincent Van Gogh in this town wouldn't they? One-eared Vinny!"

Brian begs to differ: "We were gonna say it's about the Exxon Valdez, like 'Sink The Pink,' we said was about a game of snooker. It's fun, just pure *fun*, and it's not supposed to be any more than that. It's not *bad* or *nasty*."

He seems somewhat defensive.

"Tabitha What's-Her-Name from MTV yesterday was talking . . . and I can tell she's a bit of a *feminist* now," the singer complains. "She said, 'Listen to these titles!' She says, 'But I heard the album, and it didn't *offend* me,' but she says it's still sexist. 'Then why didn't it *bother* you?,' I said. She said, 'I don't know.' I said, 'Because it's *fun*, and when you say *sexist* it naturally means that it's a *guy*.' Why can't a woman be sexist?"

"They're silly people—Tipper Gore, especially. She's just a twit, a total twit. It's something to point their finger at," Brian rambles on, forgetting what I'd asked him about. "I mean, it's just like saying Anti-Christ/Devil-Child was the initials of AC/DC and we said, 'Who thought of *that*?' That was *amazing*, we couldn't have thought of that ourselves. *Sick fuck*. Of course, what they did was invented a name that was never there."

Just wait until B'nai B'rith hear your new song "The Furor," Brian!

"That's the perfect double-entendre," he says. "And as soon as anybody says, like, 'You're talking about *Hitler*?' we'll say, 'Absolutely *not*!' you know. It's about the furor *within* you, that fyoo-*roar*, not fyoo-*rerr*. Of *course* it sounds like *fuhrer*. Those little things . . . like in 'Whiskey On The Rocks,' one of the lines is 'He licks her from the top,' and it's an *elixir*."

"It's a *pun*," Angus reiterates. "But we're no Nazis, certainly, God forbid. I think when people first hear it, they're going to *shit*."

That's AC/DC for you: a band proud of making people both shit *and* throw up . . .

Raygun, 1995

WHITE WIZZARD ESCAPE EACH OTHER

In the hilariously low-budget video for the best heavy-metal single of the year, L.A. band White Wizzard escape a curiously non-homely witch brewing up frog eggs alongside her bearded inbred hunchback monk sidekick (who's apparently obsessed with fluffy drapery), then go racing down a Western desert highway in their "High Speed GTO," which is the name of the song. "So glad I got away! No way I'm gonna stay!" celebrates their babyfaced singer; like a few other tracks on their *High Speed GTO* EP (at least the ones that aren't about marching skeletons and giant prehistoric sharks), it's a super-catchy breaking-free-from-treacherous-girlfriend sing-along and car-club number, themes that haven't exactly been metal staples in the quarter century since the prime of Van Halen.

Yeah, that's how Southern Californian they are. But on paper, at least, White Wizzard are potential lead players in a cross-national mini-movement said to draw inspiration from the New Wave of *British* Heavy Metal, an almost mythic early-'80s pre-thrash moment of jean jackets, fast tempos, and poverty-driven production techniques, wherein both eventual stars (Def Leppard, Motörhead) and future footnotes (Tygers of Pan Tang) theoretically took DIY cues from punk and returned metal to lager-pint basics, until Slayer and their ilk decided being "extreme" mattered more than having hooks—which is to say they're a welcome throwback to a time when metal lyrics were audible, and hence fun to make fun of.

On Earache Records' instructive recent New Wave of New Wave of British Heavy Metal compilation *Heavy Metal Killers*, White Wizzard are also one of the few non-European bands—though it's true that the sampler's most notable song not about hot rods, the mind-bogglingly redundant s&m anthem "Chained Up In Chains," comes from kids named Cauldron out of Anvil's sweet home Toronto. And if turn-of-the-'10s NWONWOBHM does have a U.S. headquarters, it's clearly Cali, especially now that ex-Brooklynites Early Man are based there. L.A. has also got Trigger Renegade, whose *Destroy Your Mind* ranked with 2007's ravingest rock albums; Jet Fuel and Night After Night made some killer tracks, too, before imploding.

Confusingly, so did White Wizzard: the lineup making its New York debut at Club Europa's Brooklyn Thunder Fest this weekend (alongside one-time sports-uniform-clad Newcastle numbskulls Raven and old Manowar dictator Ross the Boss) shares only bassist Jon Leon with the lineup that recorded *High Speed GTO*—which is to say babyfaced escapee James-Paul Luna did indeed escape; the singer and two other ex–White Wizzards are now in a rival Pasadena outfit known as Holy Grail, who seem more given to poetry about Valhalla. In fact, as they practice more, both by-products of this band fission seem to be upping the theatrical bombast a bit—not the most promising sign. But White Wizzard's new roster, rounded out now with provincial heshers from Florida and Michigan, is still coming up with cheerful new road-trip tunes like "40 Deuces" ("Shifting gears to ride the sky/My metal heart will never die"). A recent interview also has them welcoming tranny fans and admitting that, in metal these days, "There's always some church-burning Norwegian warlock in the forest who's badder than you." Who needs that ugly crap, when you've got music's most blown-out GTO since Ronny & the Daytonas?

Village Voice, 26 August 2009

4

Hip-hop is clearly the most important popular music of the past three decades. Well, I don't know if I really believe that, to be honest, but it's a universally accepted truism by now, and given the music's pervasiveness—like you know, culturally or whatever—it might *as well* be true. I'm not willing to argue that any other genre has been *more* important (or even better, which is not necessarily the same thing), though there are certainly a few other genres that I listen to more.

Anyway, my main credential for writing about hip-hop is basically that I've been listening to it since it's existed on record. I haven't been *liking* it for quite that long, but it's been close. In 1979 the Sugarhill Gang's "Rapper's Delight" struck me as one of the dumbest bubblegum disco novelty hits I'd ever heard, and I didn't even understand that rap was an actual whole new *genre* until I started reading about it in the *Village Voice* a year later. But by 1981 I was already stocking up on Kurtis Blow and Funky Four Plus One and Frankie Smith and South Bronx and Brother D With Collective Effort 12-inches like they were going out of style—which, in a way, they were.

Which means, ha ha, my old school is older than your old school. And it's quite possible you're still digging through crates for records that I bought and loved when they were new. In fact, by the time your old school happened, it's possible I'd already had my name on a sticker on the cover of a Schoolly D album (1989's *Am I Black Enough For You?*) because I'd named his previous album (*Smoke Some Kill*) my favorite of 1988, and apparently that was the best selling point Jive Records could come up with—hey, I bet my famous endorsement sold *scads* of copies on Philly's cruel-assed West Side.

By the late '80s, which many hip-hop fans now consider the music's legendary golden era, I was already *giving up* on rap music, since I thought it was becoming too mired in empty virtuosity (Eric B. and Rakim) and conceptual navel-gazing (De La Soul) and pompous politics (Boogie Down Productions) and gratuitous violence that couldn't match Schoolly D's sense of humor (N.W.A.). In 1990 in *Rolling Stone*, I dismissed A Tribe Called Quest's *People's Instinctive Travels And The Paths Of Rhythm* as "Nutritiously Eclectic Adult-Contemporary Comedy Rap" for "Afrocentric upwardly mobiles" who didn't want to dance anymore.

If you asked me why I'd take old old old school hip-hop over later stuff, I gave reasons like these: (1) obsessive repetition, deeper and deeper into a hole—same thing that makes droning rock songs great for 10 minutes sometimes; (2) the way the voices worked off *each other*, which no later hip-hop matched—same thing that made doo-wop so transcendent in the '50s; (3) how you could just *hear* the genre being invented—the rules weren't there yet, so the rappers could do *anything*. So when lyrics got violent or political, it was believable—it emerged naturally out of the "lime to a lemon and lemon to a lime" party, so a record like "Western Gangster Town" by Trickeration didn't feel all weighted down by what it thought it "should" be doing; (4) the voices *themselves* were more exuberant than in almost any later hip-hop; (5) especially in something like Spoonie Gee's early singles, the groove was just plain *harder* than what came later; (6) fuck it, the words were usually *more* interesting; (7) complexity as an end in itself is just stupid.

I was right, of course—my favorite rap records ever are *still* mostly ones that came out before Run-D.M.C.'s first album. But I was also wrong, very wrong, since hip-hop obviously never stopped restlessly mutating, subdividing, and recombining, going pop and underground and local and national and global and rural and suburban and serious and silly and funky and beautiful and repulsive and impossibly crude and impossibly self-righteous. It evolved into a ponderous and tedious bullshit rich man's music of McMansion-like two-hour-long coffee-table double CDs, then back into a music of regional novelties from poor unknown kids who just wanted to see friends dancing on YouTube in their previously uncharted neighborhoods across the map, and the latter wasn't even necessarily guaranteed to be better than the former. And an awful lot of it—most of it, truth be told, just like any other musical genre—also totally sucked bigtime.

It also swallowed R&B whole, more or less—eating it from the inside out, like some evil species of parasite. Which is to say that, as R&B artists and fans inevitably started giving more direct emphasis to "great beats" in the wake of late-period hip-hop, they tended to de-emphasize great *hooks*. Or at least the kind that hook *me*. Yet when I say I "can't get past the sound of most contemporary R&B", I don't think what bugs me most is up-to-date studio production touches so much as the increasingly bluesless vocal sound. At some historical moment I can't precisely pinpoint, vocalists inexplicably started steering toward two polar performing-arts-school extremes—melismatic post-Whitney bombast or icy post-Janet restraint—and circumventing the less haughty and antiseptic church-schooled middle ground that had served soul/R&B/disco singers perfectly well for decades. In his prophetic 1988 book *The Death of Rhythm & Blues*, Nelson George wrote that "in [Whitney Houston's] commercial triumph is a hollowness of spirit that mocks her own gospel roots"; he went on to cite crossover-preoccupied creative, marketing, and radio networks becoming geographically isolated from the black audience. From that point, for me, the singing turned even more joyless, largely curtailing expression of emotion—especially as lyrics grew more and more mercenary, sexually gross, and just plain juvenile as time went on. Or not juvenile enough, sometimes: I miss unabashedly effervescent bubblegum R&B almost as much as the kind that once regularly dealt with adult lives, without fossilizing them into a clinical D'Angelo/Badu/Maxwell art project.

Koffee Brown and Kandi made mature, open-hearted, crafty albums early in the '00s; at decade's end I still loved "There Goes My Baby," former Gap Bander Charlie Wilson's hit about picking up ladies at a mall food court, and I was obsessed again with raw-grit throwback micro-label chitlin circuit music sparsely distributed to grown folks through the South. And there was always R. Kelly, who at his occasional best at least got soul's mannerisms right, though the crassness of his booty talk ultimately proved more influential on contemporary R&B than the depth of his sound. Hip-hopwise, I've certainly appreciated multiple releases by Field Mob, Trick Daddy, Trina, Ying Yang Twins, Bubba Sparxxx, and Somali-Canadian outlier K'Naan, not to mention Jay-Z, Lil Wayne, Missy Elliott, OutKast, Kanye West, and Sri Lankan Tamil-Brit outlier M.I.A. Giants of industry, those last six artists. Often deservedly. So yeah, like I said at the start— "important," at bare minimum. But the bottom line still is, when you're talking R&B and hip-hop after the mid-'90s or so, I was mostly an innocent bystander, taking notes and sometimes holding my ears cussing like any other crotchety old cracker when the crunk rolled by. Right—for white geezers, being epochs behind the black-pop mainstream is forever a cliché, and probably a moral failing. But that doesn't always make it stupid.

MANTRONIX: STRANGE LOOPS

I don't buy this propaganda 'bout hip-hop opening the gates on some kinda new all-else-overthrowing jazzlike "age"—too much of the stuff's too conventionally half-assed, and too much of it's too stuck on the same old rock'n'roll delusion-of-*Übermensch* bull. I mean, what are those honkie daunters in Public Enemy if not just more middle-class college grads acting tuff by yelling a lot: The black Big Black, they sound like to me, and the stance is too limited to last. But Mantronix is one of the many exceptions, and what makes this dynamic duo special is that they never sound like they're trying to be substantial (though they *are*); they don't even pretend to be "street." They're 100 percent filler-for-its-own sake, with redundancy just one overlying factor of an omnipresent experimental nonchalance they raise paradoxically to an untold urgency-level. And on *In Full Effect*, the third installment in rap's best three-LP career so far, the most obviously space-padding throwaways just happen to be some of the best parts.

To wit: "Love Letter," a funny-intentionally-or-not schlock-piano mush-missive to a main flame name of Tracy, with some semisarcastic surreal-pretention-on-purpose ("Knowledge is my teacher and it can only be learned from existence not resistance") in a perspective that reminds me of "Seen And Not Seen," on T-Heads' *Remain In Light*. And "Get Stupid Part III," sequel to "Listen To The Bass Of Get Stupid Fresh Part II," in turn sequel to "Get Stupid 'Fresh' Part I," all-in-all a potentially (but not yet) monotonous eternal-fluctuation on a preinstigated theme, this time with an annoying gameshow host whitey whining about Tammy Bakker, plus a sampled nonsense hook that goes "te-tum-TE-TUM-te-tum-tum." And "Megamix" (one of only two songs here that lack subtitles!), just all yesterday's leftovers (movie music, Thin Lizzy) Osterized together and played backwards too fast and turned into "noise" (or so Mantronix calls it).

If not for their sheer lack of "art"-deception, I'd sooner liken these cats to old-time synth/mouth pairs like Suicide and Silver Apples than to any rap-team I can name. Mantronik-with-a-"k" gets more reason-for-being out of his electronic machines than most anybody else gets out of guitars these days, usually underpinning his kerplunk-you-upside-the-chin teleprompter sounds with three-or-so strategically positioned recurring variables, like for instance horns, "metal"-suggesting guitar, '70s Earth, Wind, and Fire licks; and some dodo growling "Man-TRAWWN-ick." Then he blinds us with science, structuring all these easier-to-graph-than-describe details (e.g.: "Shaft"-ish bassline in "Gangster Boogie" goes due south three klicks, NNE two, SSE two, ENE one, ESE two, then due east), all these physiological nonbrain stimuli, into some post-Kraftwerk/Clinton equational equivalent of the "strange loops" Douglas Hofstadter formulated in his Pulitzer-winning *Gödel, Escher, Bach*: "moving upwards (or downwards) through the levels of some hierarchical system, we unexpectedly find ourself right back where we started."

In Full Effect's most self-referential lyric goes "understanding my language is not really hard," which is true, 'cause these syncopations are content-free, unless occasional screaming girls who smell like sex count. M.C. Tee's quite the inarticulator, and his muffly ways used to bug me, back before I noticed how he hitches his verbal cadence to all these slight changes, and how it's such an ear-thrill when he switches into a capella or impromptu or Dylanizing. I should caution you that Mantronix sound better close up than far back, and that for me at least, electronic machines somehow tend not to sustain interest over the trail of time. Still, given the choice between playing this record or paying my overdue taxes, I'm almost positive I'd always pick the former.

Village Voice, 17 May 1988

SPOONIE GEE: UNREFORMED

Women! Spoonie Gee sure can't live with 'em, sure can't live without 'em. This rapid-fire rap vet doesn't want a woman with good taste; he wants a woman who tastes good. He commands, "You got somethin' I want, so baby let me eat that"; he names his reggae triumph "Yum Yum." What Spoonie likes in a woman is submission, mainly: "She get up in the morning/She fix my food/She walk around the house in the naughty mood." On *The Godfather Of Rap*, Spoon's amoral but osmium-solid debut LP, he sings two songs about his heroes. One's a "Hit Man," the other's Mighty

SPOONIE GEE: *THE GODFATHER OF RAP* (TUFF CITY, 1988)

Mike Tyson. Spoon's a fan of men who hurt people, especially if they can make women submissive at the same time: "She seen Mike fight, got excited, then fell on me."

In "Take It Off," *The Godfather*'s scariest track, Spoon cruises down the road in his spit-shine spankin'-new machine, he spies a fine young lady, and she climbs aboard. Exactly the same thing happens in both "Love Rap" and "Spoonin' Rap," Spoonie's unrelenting pair of 1980 singles. Except in "Spoonin' Rap" he almost runs her over, and in "Take It Off" he doesn't give her time to make up her mind: "Opened up the door, and let her in, and automatically my mind just turned to sin/I told her TAKE IT OFF!" And producer Aaron Fuchs gives the holler reverb.

Spoonie Gee's time is precious. He worries about marriage an awful lot (sometimes it's "out," sometimes he wants every woman he meets to be his wife) and about what a bother a kid would be (in "Love Rap": "The first thing she said is let's have a child/I said no, no baby I only got time/To make a lotta money and say my rhyme"). His voice can lay back and woo and coo, but he's like corduroy: you rub him the wrong way, you're in for a surprise. In "The Godfather," just as in "Spoonin' Rap," he keeps rapping faster and louder as the groove progresses, and his voice echoes more and more, as if he were leading you by the wrist through this darkened tunnel, and it gets claustrophobic in there. By the end, he's rabid, spitting out words, turning r's into growls, flailing, slamming those punching-bag mouth beats against the gymnasium wall. Real mean.

He's a survivor of hip-hop's Sugarhill/Enjoy beginnings, when street meant *street*, and even more than other honchos from back then, he's not into frills—doesn't show off his elongated terminology, doesn't bellow, doesn't twist cadences into pretzels. He flattens vowels all the time, jumps ahead of the rhythm (and himself) when he's mad, mostly just chronicles violence as a matter of fact. He's got no doubt that people out there wanna mess him up. In "Love Rap," he harks back to the O'Jays and Undisputed Truth, tells about smiling faces who only want what you've got, then expounds on the dangers of women. In "Spoonin' Rap," the lesson concerns the dangers of purse snatching, and he warns about prison as if he'd been there.

But the outside, where women are always trying to "boss" Spoonie, to "use" him, is almost as bad. He asks his concubine in "The Godfather": "Are you ready? For what? For *beatin'* me now." In both "Hit Man" and "Mighty Mike Tyson," his funk periodically bunches up into big, ossified blood clots; the same thing happens in "Monster Jam," his 1981 collaboration with Sequence, where our hit man, ahem, "took on" all three Sugarhill women at once.

The Godfather's backup concentrates on horn bleats and bass lines, scads of 'em, borrowed by Marley Marl and Ted Riley from old James Brown records, plus beatbox breaks that squeak and quack and kickdrums that sound like sheet metal banged with hammers, or machine guns. The syncopation's wound up tight as a spliff, and Spoonie likes it loud: "The beat's so bad that at nine o'clock in the morning if you play it they'll call the cops." Here's the rare rap album in which the master of ceremonies throws his weight in every direction, but it's never like fishing. The lover's rock in "Yum Yum" curdles as thick as the funk everywhere else, rich boiling buttermilk to the drippy skim ska of the Fat Boys and D.M.C. and Bambaataa. And the way Spoonie's Jah accent rides the riddim's ripples is dread enough to convince: "You tell ever-body thatchoo hate mah guts/But if you hate mah guts why did you keess me last night?"

Unlike the L.L. Cool J type, Spoon romance is mush free (especially in "Spoonie Gee," where proud laziness collides with the Ohio Players' "Funky Worm," and in both "My Girl" and the definitive hard-rap/soft-croon-transpositioning "I'm All Shook Up," which get their respective choruses and exclamations from the Tempts and Elvis). It's more Teddy Pendergrass than Freddie Jackson or Barry White: sleek, snazzy, seductive, but never sleazy or sissified. He's a baby maker, woman taker, smooth talker, midnight stalker. His rap is strong and his love is long, and he's known coast to coast as the 60-minute man. As he says: before you know it, you'll be in the nude. Whether you like it or not.

Boston Phoenix, 27 May 1988

JUST-ICE: RAP WITH TEETH

If hip-hop is the "revolutionary" force everybody hereabouts pretends it is, it *will* instigate violence, which will theoretically be necessary throw-down-the-money-changers violence, right? Neocons and show promoters have every reason to be scared, so why deny it? The Original Gangster of Hip-Hop Just-Ice toasts on "Self-Destruction," and it's one of the few parts of the stop-the-violence PSA as enjoyable as the worst parts of "We Are the World." I'm confused. On Just-Ice's albums, there's weaponfire, street executions, "homicide and never doin' no time." He *likes* violence.

He despises "sorry-assed wenches," but his bitch-hate's a bore. Brags about making 'em "bloody," revives Melanie's penis-as-key metaphor. Sometimes he bleeps out some of his dirty words, and though I can't figure out how he decides which ones to bleep, usually the bleeps are more startling, more musical, than the cussing would've been. He bleeps most on *Back To The Old School*, his '86 debut, the title of which introduced his other big theme: Nostalgia. "Hip-hop history can never go old," how bogus—*all* history is old, that's why it's history! He was rockin' in the park when yo' ass was a baby, and his dad can beat up your dad.

The subject matter can get real tedious. And KRS-One, the producer, is a bad influence: Too often Just-Ice forsakes rhythm for that sarcastic Vegas singsong that made Boogie Down Productions' *By All Means Necessary* the most school-marmish piece of rap-lethargia ever, and on *The Desolate One*, Just-Ice's third and solidest slab, the only truly awful cut's all KRS-style Wittgenstein-wannabe semantic-dissection. This self-important shit's gonna make hip-hop as boring as rock before we know it, and could be we're already there.

That said, Just-Ice runs a distant second to Schoolly D in the don't-care department, which is to say that instead of following the prog-punk cue and eradicating rap's play-element and thereby maximizing firm-growth, he's still got some all-knowingly comic bad attitude linked to nothing but the hard thing he folds behind his Talon zipper. He's always cracking his knuckles, his mind outracing his gold-plated motormouth. In *Desolate*'s "Welfare Recipients" (also the B-side of his new 12-inch "Somoshitbyjustice"), he accuses handout-takers of being "too lazy to work," says they deserve whatever hell they get. So maybe he's been reading Pete Hamill or somebody.

Nonetheless, the big Just-Ice innovation is the anthem-rap, perfected on last year's *Kool And Deadly*. He keeps shouting louder, cruder, nastier, farther; he loses control, and KRS has to remind him the track's over. It's supposed to sound impromptu, and sometimes, like when those flying monkeys are wire-brushing cookpots behind him in "On The Strength," or when these *Mission Impossible* vamps are rolling hedgehoglike into balls of confusion in *Desolate*'s title cut, it works. Rakim's annoying "complexity" fixation might make him the real Metallica of rap, but only Just-Ice can touch the Romilar wattage and dramatic depth-charge of "One" or "Fade To Black," and he knows it. His "Mosh It Up" may not concern thrash-dancing, but *Desolate*'s got a millenarian mountain climb called ". . . And Justice for All." The ellipses are drumrolls.

As Just-Ice builds to his majestic pinnacles, his breath coughs up brim-stone so you can't tell whether he's got too much stamina or not enough, his frog-of-Nyabinghi biddleybums get too mangy and mystical to decode, his guttural gruffness attains an impermeability of brown-sound sufferation out of *Dreadlocks Dread* by Big Youth (of similarly rancid tooth). The new LP's side two, where our warrior finally remembers the rapstafarian beat he's mislaid since his ex-conspirator Mantronix's technocratic calculus on *Old School*, could've emerged direct from Joe Gibbs's dub-studio. "It's Time Release"'s dookie-rope bassline clangs into these enormous triple-backwards somersaults, then "Hijack"'s shamanistic convulsions make a blaxploitation bumrush back 6,000 years to the Mesopotamian core. Just-Ice appropriately bids bye-bye biting a thrice-thick "Another One Bites The Dust" sandwich, but to prep us he admits that rap can't cut it anymore—now we gotta "let the bullets do the talkin'," splatter blood and massacre with guns. What a joker.

Village Voice, 16 May 1989

PAZZ & JOP BALLOT EXCERPT 1989: N.W.A.

I've got friends who call Niggaz With Attitudes "scary," and I'm even more perplexed by the gullible bigots who distinguish *Straight Outta Compton* from some avant-boho shock-tactic by saying, hey, these guys are from the *slums* and they can't help it, like it's part of their *nature* or something. So what I wanna know is this: If they're so darn unselfconscious and just chronicling *real life* and all, how come they never rap about doing their laundry? (They must have pretty smelly clothes!) And if they were *really* crazy motherfuckers from around the way, wouldn't they think themselves *sane*?

PAZZ & JOP BALLOT EXCERPT 1992:
ARRESTED DEVELOPMENT

Between their horseshoes and hairdos and old men in rocking chairs, Arrested Development come off sillier than Right Said Fred without even trying. They could be some mad scientist's parody of a foolproof Pazz & Jop winner—Like, what do you get when you cross Tracy Chapman with De La Soul? Chrysalis could've just mailed out *press photos* and they'd still have a guaranteed top five slot. They're the ultimate Sunday School band. All their hits sound like Bible parables. If I'd been raised Protestant instead of Catholic, I might even take them seriously.

SIR MIX-A-LOT: *CHIEF BOOT KNOCKA*

Sir Mix-A-Lot blew it! On his new album, he says he's trying to make Tipper Gore and Rush Limbaugh restless, but he leaves out Reverend Calvin Butts, the Harlem Baptist minister who ran over rap CDs with a steamroller last year (and who has fought cigarette ads in the black community—

Butts vs. butts, get it?). Sir Mix should never turn down opportunities to talk about Butts! As cancans about coveting thy neighbor's ass and 'ocks go, his 1991 chart-topper "Baby Got Back" was cheekier than "Big Ole Butt," "Big Bottom," "Fat Bottomed Girls," maybe even "Tush." He came through the back door, he seat on 'em, he rectum. What a ham! Mix told a buttiful tail, and gave it ample underside that raised quite a rumpus. Talk about mudflaps, it's got 'em.

My brother-in-law Marvin describes Mix-A-Lot as a cross between Bushwick Bill and Santa Claus. He keeps alive the ancient rap tradition of "Get funky, make money"—Mix-A-Lot says the only color he cares about is green. I wish *Chief Boot Knocka* had a song as great as "Baby Got Back" or 1989's even greater "My Hooptie" (about a car falling apart), but I kind of like the tax-audit song, the paternity-suit one with cute baby voices, the Godzilla-music one, and the Indian-outlaw title track. He gets melodies from Kraftwerky electro-drumming, and he comically sets quadruple-rhymed anaconda-length words to nasal nursery-rhyme rhythms. He talks Dizzuble Dizzutch and makes like a locker room full of mooning butts. I'm thinking of joining Sir Mix-A-Lot's fanny club so I can get a posterior of him to gluteus to my rear wall. His movie should be called *Truth or Derriere*. (Okay, I'll stop being analytical.) The end.

Spin, August 1994

FROM TACO BELL TO PACHELBEL: COOLIO

Still can't decide if I'm a "playa" or a "playa hata" (don't know how to "turn up my Alpine" either), and lately I suspect Coolio's in the same boat. Ever since he first hit with "Fantastic Voyage" three summers ago, he's been schizophrenically unable to make up his mind about whether he's a good guy or bad guy, but he sounds so *happy* about it. He wants to live where his kids can play without fearing a drive-by, but he says his big tent of an audience wouldn't understand why he packs a .45 'cause they don't gang-bang. On the other hand, if I had seven kids, I might be ready to blow somebody's brains out too.

The former cocaine addict and Taco Bell counterman's most vivid lyrics are detailed journalistic snapshots of neighborhood life—playing hide-and-seek and watching *New Zoo Revue* in small-town Pennsylvania before moving west, or a little girl taking training wheels off her bike. He's an expert at the nostalgic streetlights-at-dusk Fresh Prince "Summertime" mood that's one of rap's most underrated and optimistic commodities. And he's one of the first hip-hoppers who's figured out how to be an *adult*—neck and neck with Bob Carlisle and Art Alexakis for pop's Pop of the Year, he even interpolated the theme from *Eddie's Father* once. His sex songs are full of self-effacing foibles and homely women, and in videos he rides tricycles and washing machines, and his hair is a hydra. He's not afraid to look silly.

Gangsta's Paradise, constructed around the biggest single of 1995, was more verbally acute, but *My Soul* is Coolio's most *propulsive* album. More bounce to the ounce, more motion for your ocean, more krush for your groove—talk-box robofunk, old school shout-and-response, up-jump-the-boogie bump bass lines including a flamethrower from J. Geils. Coolio's songs are often thinly disguised cover versions; he even named his first CD *It Takes A Thief*. But his taste in samples isn't half as schlockful as, say, Puff Daddy's—this time out, his "soul" is the radio-friendly Zapp/S.O.S. Band/ Ray Parker Jr./Tom Tom Club/Fat Boys postdisco of the early '80s. He crosses over just like they did.

Pop stations add his singles before urban stations do, and I don't think he minds much; in the '90s, a claim like "That's how we do it in the western hemisphere" feels like arms opened to *everybody*. On his new CD he rewrites ex-Eagle Glenn Frey's "Smuggler's Blues" as "Nature Of The Business," and that track and "Knight Fall" and "The Devil Is Dope" (its double-definition sympathy-for-the-devil chorus howled around corners by the Dramatics) are blues in the '80s beer-commercial/*Miami Vice* sense, the slick sound of organized crime plotting in high-rises and rolling dice and stabbing when backs are turned.

Coolio's into preaching the Bible, too, pulling folks up by their boot-straps. Tries to keep faith in his people, but sometimes they act evil. It's a family affair—"little Timmy got his diploma and little Jimmy got life." That's from his current crossover "C U When U Get There"—"If you *ever* get there." A recurring theme: In "Fantastic Voyage," "you better be ready when the five roll by" wasn't about missing your car pool; it was more like swing low sweet '65 Chevy to Utopia, where "it really don't matter if you're white or black," where nobody cryin' and nobody dyin' but take your gat with the extra clip just in case.

No doubt a few fans resent MC Medusa talking down to them with all his subtle little moral lessons. He's filling Stevie Wonder's shoes, risking goody-goody pretensions (if not exactly being a good sport when Weird Al makes fun of them) in the name of wisdom and fortitude. In "C U When U Get There," he strives his whole life for the mountain peak, and then gospel choirs chime in, all very "I Want To Know What Love Is." Starting with "Gangsta's Paradise," his music has had one foot in the shadow of death, in the Gothic moans of high mass. "C U" gets its gorgeous opening (and later metronomic string parts maybe) from Pachelbel's Canon. Gangsta rap is rifling classical shelves for darkness and beauty these days—on Puff Daddy's death-obsessed glockbuster *No Way Out*, the funereal violins and operatics in the background are just about *all* I like.

But where Puffball decenters his album with phlegm-congested voices refusing to enunciate, Coolio's delivery is all warmth and ebullience, casual confidence and plain talk. Old enough at 34 to miss the days when rap wasn't so mean-spirited, he never feels the need to rhyme "young black and famous with money hangin' out my anus," and he's not some prog-chops creep hung up on showing off meaningless "mad skills and innovative flow." One trouble in gangsta's paradise is that most g's try too hard to impress you with hardness to bother putting their songs over. Which isn't to say I'm not totally stoked about this big rap war coming down between the South Coast and North Coast, where Geto Boys and 2 Live Crew settle their beefs against Snow and the Insane Clown Posse.

Village Voice, 14 October 1997

PAZZ & JOP BALLOT EXCERPT 1997:
ERYKAH BADU AND B-ROCK & THE BIZZ

I hoped Erykah Badu might be hiding some Teena-Marie-type unhinged-ness amid her status-symbol-jazz-poetry pretension, but no such luck; she's just more schoolmarm R&B for public radio snobs, like Dionne Farris and Des'ree before her. In *Spin*'s year-end issue, she asks us to explain what all the fuss with "MyBabyDaddy" was about; well, maybe if she'd take that ridiculous bath towel off her ears and stop being so obsessed with proving what a classy dame she is, she'd note that "MyBabyDaddy" starts out addressing more or less the same predicament as her own only remotely un-humorless track "Tyrone"—Erykah scolds her man for never dropping by without Jim, James, Paul, or Tyrone, and the poor guy (B-Rock? The

Bizz? I have no idea) playing T-Bone in "MyBabyDaddy" frets that his gal is always phoning "Elaine, or either Shawna, or Donna." Then, obviously, said bass-booty hit turns into a paternity suit against a delinquent dad, and T-Bone swears the kid is not his son, and Billie Jean's new boyfriend is at the door so she ain't fittin' to be gittin' no Pampers even though her Dixie drawl is more believable than any other human microphone-use in 1997. I wonder if T-Bone's mama ever warned him not to go around breaking young girls' hearts, and to be careful what you do because a lie becomes the truth.

TIMBALAND, MAGOO, AND MASE, AS THE WORLD TURNS

Welcome To Our World by the newly chart-busting Virginia duo Timbaland and Magoo is one of the weirdest and most deadpan-conversational hip-hop albums ever made. A lot of it reads like some Zen-sage *Seinfeld* junkie haiku-ing off the top of his head: "This is my dialogue on this album." "Last verse/As you can see I did not curse." "Don't slam my car door/It costs too much to get that shit fixed/I need all my money to pay my bills with."

Not since Schoolly D has a rapper rolled around so effectively in his own day-to-day mundanity. There are details about Timbaland's life here that you'd never doubt are just as he relates them; you know that he really does like Popsicles and pork 'n' beans. His Lou Reed I-pulled-out-a-chair-and-sat-on-it songwriting-school inclinations reach their surreal peak over the knickknack-paddywack beat of the strangely superstitious "15 After Da' Hour," about how everything always goes bad at quarter-after-something-o'clock, winding up at 7:15 with Tim's trusted sidekick Magoo passing out drunk in front of the VCR dreaming he's a monk. The album's three supposed "remix" tracks sound more like entirely different *songs*, with different words, rhythm, everything, recognizable only because Timba says stuff like "This is the remix of 'Up Jumps Da' Boogie'" in the middle. Maybe he just ran out of titles.

Timbaland's music sounds as rustic as his name but space-age at the same time, and with an angular tequila-sunrise-desperado meet-me-at-high-noon-after-my-cartoons air to it skirting spaghetti-Western moods like reggae and "Planet Rock" used to; chantlike voices chatter alongside

rubbery roller-disco riffs updated into a still-stuttering but less refriger-
ated distant cousin of drum'n'bass. "Clock Strikes" takes its melody from
"Mack The Knife," "Ms. Parker" parrots Mantronix's '80s tapdance-rap,
and "Up Jumps Da' Boogie"'s blipping hook owes more to Heatwave's 1977
bubbledisco hit "Boogie Nights" than the movie did. But somehow it all
swings like a whomping down-South house party.

Timbaland's diction is laid-back Virginia-style, low-rumbling but light
on its feet like Barry White or Isaac Hayes, though his personality hints
more at an improbable cross between Sir Mix-a-Lot and P.M. Dawn's
Prince Be. In "Luv 2 Luv U (Remix)," he bypasses his unremixed version's
post–Donna Summer pillow-talk proclivities and becomes "the big black
Kahuna," howling wolfman whoo-hoos and alluding to the old jump-blues
classic "Is You Is Or Is You Ain't My Baby" as Magoo quotes "Surfin' Bird,"
shouts out to Ringo, and—in what must be the last lyrical reference to said
public servant—mispronounces the name "Sonny Bono."

"I have a partner, as well as my friend," Timbaland rambles about his
little buddy in the album's intro track, then corrects himself: "Well, I have
two partners, as well as my friends." Numero Dos is Missy "Misdemeanor"
Elliott, whose universally acclaimed but undeniably uneven debut disc
(three great songs and a surplus of so-what R&B filler) Timbaland oversaw
last summer. In larger portions Missy's voice starts to sound klutzy, but
she sure can sock it 2 you sexwise, begging you to touch her hot spot so
she'll scream nonstop like a bedroom wrecker who makes you beat your
pecker. Magoo is notably less commanding, high and nasal and congested,
but even looking up girls' skirts he sounds so girly himself that sometimes
you *confu*se him with Missy. In fact, for the longest time I assumed (or
maybe just twistedly hoped) it was *her* supa-dupa-big-boned self bragging
about how "I can make a dyke go straight/If you think I'm cute then you
up too late."

In their publicity bio, Magoo calls Timba a quiet guy, "more into God
than I am"; on record, Tim seems like a Fort Bragg supply-room NCO
with Magoo his bumbling Spec. 4 understudy. They're a big contrast to the
other rap rookie whose debut CD has been explicitly representing a personal "World" all winter—like *Welcome To Our World*, Ma$e's *Harlem World*
has a couple cuts-with-R&B-guests stuck on in a blatant bid for urban-
contemporary radio play, and, like Timba, Ma$e doesn't mind poking fun
at himself. But where Tim comes off almost middle-aged, Ma$e seems boy-
ish. And where *Welcome*'s sample credits are limited to the *Knight Rider*

TIMBALAND AND MAGOO: *WELCOME TO OUR WORLD*
(BLACKGROUND/ATLANTIC, 1997)

theme and Missy beeping about Jeep keys, Ma$e would be nowhere with-
out the voluminous hook-thievery of Puff Daddy, who produced half the
album. Regardless, when Ma$e calls Puffy "Mr. Producer," it still sounds
like "Mr. Magoo, sir"!

Best known as the "young Harlem nigga with the golden sound" who
opened up Notorious B.I.G.'s epochal "Mo Money Mo Problems," Ma$e was
actually born in Jacksonville, according to his record-label press sheet. He
moved to Harlem at 5, but Mama shipped him south again at 13, as soon as
"he began showing the slightest sign of getting caught up in the world of
Harlem street economics." Now he pretends he's a "classic criminal/keep a
gun by my genitals," and you no more believe him promising "nigga smack
me I'm gonna smack him back" than you believed Elton John welcoming his bitch back or Prodigy smacking their bitch up—Ma$e looks and
sounds about as threatening as L.L. or Vanilla Ice. Despite complaining
about not understanding the language of "people with short money" who
"talk funny," he's low-self-esteemishly mumbly and mellow-toasted (in an
early-EPMD pajama-slacker way) his own self. When background babes
dote on him, he echoes Biggie's head-nodding cuddly/awkward aw-shucks
chuckles and *ungh-huh* grunts, but unlike Biggie he's not remotely scary;

he compares himself to Tickle Me Elmo over Teena Marie "Square Biz" samples, for crissakes. So his moments of sad-sack vulnerability feel way more trustworthy.

He asks fans to ponder which of their friends would die for them, then asks fans where they'd go and what they'd do and who they'd screw if they only had 24 hours left. The latter ominous riddle inspires a flock of varying voices to philosophize and fantasize about altruism, evening up scores, boinking bank tellers, spending final minutes with kids, and "out with a bang, you'll remember my name." My favorite is the guy who says, "Fuck it, I'd probably eat some fried chicken and drink some Nantucket," then insists on playing Lotto even though he won't be around to collect any winnings.

Puff Daddy, as even his ugliest and slugliest Biggie productions demonstrated, is of course a master of juxtaposition (Matthew Wilder with Grandmaster Flash?!), addicted to puffed-up grooves as catchy as ad jingles, nostalgic for the same Reagan-era club of culture as *Romy and Michele's High School Reunion*—"Puff drive Mercedes/take hits from the '80s/do a sound so crazy" goes Ma$e's big hit, "Feel So Good," with a chorus from Miami Sound Machine over the same Kool and the Gang horns that DJ Kool stole in "Let Me Clear My Throat." And *Harlem World* might be Puffy's definitive album just because it's his most upbeat, bumping and hustling across the dance floor as it wonders, "Why you standing on the wall with your hand on your balls" (plus more stuff about "Benjamins," natch).

Paranoid about "hatas" denying he's "real," Ma$e lets his "pants sag down to the floor/really doesn't matter as long as I score," his Puff-rap recalling poof-metal poodles Cinderella asking "Who's to care if I grow my hair to the sky?" in "Gypsy Road" a decade ago. Mainly, *Harlem World* is a concept album about a handsome young man's sex life or lack thereof: in "I Need To Be," Ma$e's homies pressure him to undress his date, but every time he makes a move to love her, 1-2-3 red light she stops him (apparently because he's scared of cunnilingus). Women cheat on him, or cheat on boyfriends with him, and he worries their beaus will beat him up—most hilariously in "Jealous Guy," a yearning six-minute Chi-Lites/Stylistics falsetto-zodiac-sign-harmony parody as over-the-top as Oran "Juice" Jones or Cheech and Chong's "Basketball Jones." In "Lookin' At Me," our young stud even wears a tank top to the Greekfest with his family and picks up one Sandy-sans-panties and demands "gotta be a quickie/please no hickeys/'cause wifey's with me." But Sandy confides to an older co-worker who secretly tapes the conversation, and she devilishly keeps a blue dress with Ma$e's semen stain on it as a souvenir. Or maybe I'm mixing him up with somebody else.

L.A. Weekly, 20 March 1998

PAZZ & JOP BALLOT EXCERPT 2001: JAY-Z

As for Jay-Z, I don't *want* to like him, but for some reason I do anyway. Bragging about expensive furniture or desserts or socks (or whatever all his lingo means) that I can neither afford nor want to, he doesn't make his jerkdom sound especially enticing, and I'm stumped by all the people who hear something extraordinary in his voice and his lyrics, both of which strike me as merely functional in and of themselves. Maybe I'm just dense. The Nas vs. Jigga rivalry means nothing to me, either; centuries-old cultural trash-talk tradition or no, it's really starting to annoy me how rappers keep mistaking music for sports. But no matter how much he tries to convince us otherwise, Jay-Z obviously has a sense of humor. And damn is he ever *efficient*—that's the main thing. I docked *The Blueprint* a notch because (as with the vast majority of rap albums, still, which I realize might be my own limitation as a listener but what the fuck) it starts to feel oppressive when I try to play it all the way through in one sitting. But from one-on-one with Eminem to "Double Dutch Bus" rewrite to Ricky Nelson-via-Lou Bega promiscuity to no joy in the heart of the city to shout-outs to cousins who changed his diapers to that ridiculously obsessive Doors sample, it's just one perfectly crafted novelty after another, bam bam bam bam bam. It feels like a greatest-hits album already, and it's only been in the stores a few months. The last rapper who had this much straight-down-the-middle pop-chart savvy was L.L., but *Mama Said Knock You Out* wasn't anywhere near this consistent. Maybe *Sports* by Huey Lewis was, though.

BONE CRUSHER FEATURING COTTON MOUTH, "THE FAT MAN STOMP"

In 1949, 200-pound New Orleans pianist Fats Domino released "The Fat Man," which some people call the first rock'n'roll record ever; it featured his mouth making guitar wah-wah noises. Fifty-four years later, a song with a similar title by 380-pound Atlanta rapper Bone Crusher contains vocal wah-wah sounds as well. And in the great whomping overweight onomatopoeic tradition that the Fat Boys, Heavy D, and Chubb Rock inherited from Fats, these wah-wahs audibly wobble, all over the floor. Or at least back and forth: "You go left to right, left to right, left to right." Easiest dance steps ever! Bone even says it's OK to step on shoes, like a crazy fool. And "stomp" rhymes with "cronk."

TURK, *RAW & UNCUT*

Hot Boy Tab Virgil's Crescent City roots run even deeper, seeing how he's from the Magnolia Projects. Which is to say the opening cut's horns strut with some barbecue. After that, backing tracks go Jamaican dancehall, Asian flute, soap-opera piano, over-the-top gabba techno, and acoustic guitar blues. Which is to say par-for-the-course crunk. "Penitentiary Chances," a ridiculously cute and deliriously happy singsonged and nursery-chimed rhyme about living dangerously, could perk up any windup music box. Turk's obligatory sub-Snoop mack-and-pimp posturing couldn't, maybe, but when he turns paranoid about plea-copping snitches or turns hustling for 8,670 hours into a math quiz or turns blue about everything he's tired of or turns bluer about going cold turkey, you might not mind. Plus, the duet where Bubba Sparxxx ponders how penises affect female facial expressions has Turk calling himself "a dog like Blue's Clues," but so's his mom! "You my girl, you my dog, you my best friend," he tells her in "I Love U For Dat," about how overprotective she was. On his last CD, he thanked Mama in a heartbreaker called "Growing Up." But this one seems even sadder.

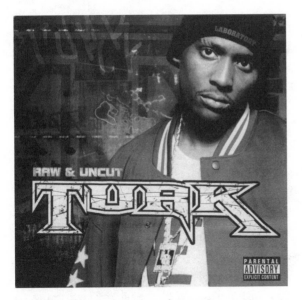

TURK: *RAW & UNCUT* (KOCH, 2003)

(VARIOUS), *CRUNK AND DISORDERLY*

Most important news is that tracks 11 through 14, linked by poverty as well as good cheer, are the best Christmas music in years. Bone Crusher cooks up a jolly old wallop featuring collard greens and cornmeal, the irrepressible Ying Yang Twins request weed and a 12-pack, David Banner ill-advisedly approves of unemployed folks robbing so they can eat, and the latter two, especially, make an eggnog party out of 19th-century midnight-mass cathedral-belfry tidings of comfort and joy like no goth music you've heard: Sinterklaas, go straight to the ghetto. In fact, the disc's truest common denominator is neither gang chants nor thuggery so much as minimalist Teutonic electro also getting weirdly ominous, obsessive, spare, and sci-fi in the Lil Jon, Three 6 Mafia, and Youngbloodz tracks. As bonuses, Trina's unabashed sex-drawl strikes a blow for Southern girls sippin' Malibu punch, Big Boi has trouble keeping up, and Pit Bull puts 24s on his truck. Hence, my fearless crunk prediction for 2004: 25-inch rims!

Village Voice, 23 December 2003

PAZZ & JOP BALLOT EXCERPT 2003

Much of my hip-hop knowledge is owed to my 12-year-old son Sherman, who knew who Joe Budden and Chingy and David Banner were before I did, who knows more Ludacris lyrics about midgets hanging from necklaces than he probably should, who doesn't think of Sean Paul and Wayne Wonder and Panjabi MC as anything more exotic than just more rappers, and who, unlike me, has yet to hear a 50 Cent song he doesn't like. And he's heard a lot more of them than I have. Me, I love "In Da Club" ("Happy Birthday To You" being the most popular song in the English language, and therefore making the most popular birthday song since and then flipping over the birthday cake in order to get-rough-not-make-love-with-you being a miracle move, plus it's got a detective-flick beat and your grandma will dance to it). But beyond that, I really don't get 50 at all: I mean, OPEN YOUR FUCKING MOUTH WHEN YOU RAP, OKAY DOOFUS??? Jeez!! But when I tell that to Sherman, he just stares and says, "But Dad! He raps like that because he got *shot in the face*!!" Which is very very important. As are his eight *other* bullet holes. Because to 12-year-old suburban white kids all over the country (who won't care so much about Eminem anymore, mark my words), 50 showed up as a true-life, built-in *Superhero*. Completely invincible. Bulletproof. And more than any sextuple-platinum-selling artist in popular music history, of course, he was *sold* that way. Which is pretty sick, obviously. But I'd be lying if I said I didn't somehow understand that appeal. Thing is, Ta-Nehisi Coates and Neil Drumming tell me that, where 12-year-old white boys might make 50 Cent a superhero, 12-year-old black boys want to *be* 50 Cent. Which sucks.

I have no patience for and feel quite sorry for idiot rock critics who think "pop hits and hip-hop are suddenly very good!"; idiot rock critics who think "our generation's newfound ability to inexpensively download individual songs online" opens up a world of discovery that hadn't pretty much always been available on the radio and TV and jukeboxes and mixtapes and dance clubs and used record stores in the first place; idiot rock critics who think albums are any less album-like now than they've always been; idiot rock critics who rejoice that "there are still acts out there who make quality albums built to last and not just a couple transitory hit singles"; idiot rock critics who think it was okay for Liz Phair to discuss her sex life when she was in her 20s but now it's somewhat unseemly since she's over 30 and all; idiot rock critics who think 40-year-old white guys who like hip-hop are unseemly; idiot rock critics who think grownups who like Justin Timberlake are perverse; idiot rock critics who like Justin Timberlake now but used to call me perverse for liking "Ice Ice Baby" and Will to Power and Amy Grant; idiots obscurantist enough to "still not get" the Strokes or White Stripes but who hype scores of more generic garage bands; idiots lazy enough to believe the Strokes and White Stripes are the best garage bands out there; idiots who think the Strokes and White Stripes are garage bands in the first place; idiots in the Strokes; idiots in the White Stripes; and um, lots of other people. (Many of which idiot categories sometimes include me.)

I think "screwed music" could turn out to be the new Black Sabbath and dub and blues and lots of other things, unless it doesn't. I think it's intriguing that so many of the best metal albums this year were the ones with no metal on them, by which I mean no guitars. I hope somebody starts screwing and chopping stoner-metal records soon. I often amuse myself by imagining somebody screwing down the speeded-up merengue version of Lil Jon's "Get Low," since that would make the song sound exactly like normal. I think David Banner's Tourette Syndrome problem and insistence on identifying with thugs who lack his college education may well make him an asshole. I think he knows he's one, and he thinks it's funny. I think he's right, sometimes, and even when he's not his music can still choke me up. I think he's complicated all the time, and unlike OutKast he doesn't feel the need to advertise this. I think I'm gonna stop right here.

5

This is one of the longest sections in this book, and it's one that material-ized largely by happenstance. Until I'd sifted through my file drawers and whittled down the list of articles I wanted to include, I never really real-ized how often I've written about artists—rock bands, rappers, singers—crossing the racial line. (I actually left out my 1987 *Creem* Beastie Boys cover feature, since it's already my most republished piece ever.) This has never *consciously* been an overriding theme of my writing, and it's not one that readers tend to comment on, either. But race-mixing's been an in-trinsic part of rock'n'roll from the beginning (by which I guess I mean the 1910s or 1920s.) And as I spell out in the Kid Rock/Eminem piece "Motor Suburb Madhouse," it's been especially inescapable in Detroit music for the past half century.

In the landmark 1974 case *Milliken v. Bradley*, seven years after devastat-ing, decimating riots had once and for all assured a mass departure of the city's white population to the suburbs, the U.S. Supreme Court legitimized white flight by striking down busing integration of school children within the Detroit metropolitan area. But coming of age in southeastern Michi-gan as the '70s turned '80s, you could sign on as a member of the Midnight Funk Association (on WGPR, where the Electrifying Mojo played songs by Devo and Billy Squier between Funkadelic and the Time) or Detroit Rock-ers Engaged in the Abolition of Disco (on WRIF, which only a couple years earlier had played songs by War and KC and the Sunshine Band between Alice Cooper and Ted Nugent); Steve Dahl, the disc jockey who in 1979 organized an explosive Disco Demolition Night at a Tigers–White Sox game in Chicago, had spent his first couple on-air years at Detroit's album-oriented-rock WABX. So maybe the mechanics of racial crossover became my accidental obsession merely by osmosis.

For the most part, I think the pieces here speak for themselves. But I should mention that, especially in some older pieces, you'll find an arguably patronizing presumptuousness that I'm no longer particularly proud of. And sometimes it's not even especially coherent: no matter how much the urbane smooth-jazz gentility of their brand of quiet storm may have irritated me at the time I wrote my 1983 Pazz & Jop comments, Al Jarreau and James Ingram were never "as white as I am," and I was an ass-hat to suggest otherwise; in general, R&B pop-crossovers of the electro-freakazoid early '80s—which I dismiss as "beige" "diet funk" in my comments from two years later—hold up better three decades down the line than I ever would have predicted. Fluid from all sides of the divide, flirting with but not yet giving into hip-hop's hegemony (that'd happen starting with New Jack Swing, in the *late* '80s), the period now ranks among my favorite pop eras ever.

But the two pieces in this section that really beg a mea culpa, or at least an explanation, come later. My reviews of Boogie Down Productions' 1989 *Ghetto Music: The Blueprint Of Hip Hop* and Living Colour's 1991 *Biscuits* EP take on a snide, almost neo-conservative bent where I appear to be fighting a one-man campaign against affirmative action in and out of music. In the BDP piece, I could almost be a Republican senator 20 years on, grilling Supreme Court candidate Sonia Sotomayor about screwing over white New Haven firefighters. No wonder Robert Christgau, in a Consumer Guide review of the same album, wrote that "KRS-One isn't just serious, he aspires to sainthood, and tough noogs if you think that makes him 'boring' or 'pretentious' or any of that racist, anti-intellectual cant." I still say Christgau's wrong—if I can dismiss self-styled canonization candidates Sting or Bono or Eddie Vedder as arrogant blowhards, as I do every chance I get, there's no reason I shouldn't be able to call a rapper who fits the bill the same. And I still don't like KRS's music or conspiracy theorizing much. But that doesn't mean I don't cringe myself when I read my rant about him. As for the Living Colour review, there's certainly some truth to it— blackness was undeniably a selling point for that band (and for the Bad Brains, who I'd profiled for *Spin* a few years before). But it seems somewhat disingenuous to dwell on the issue, since whiteness had already been helping rock bands get onto rock stations for decades. And though nothing in my review makes this clear, blackness was hardly Living Colour's *only* selling point. Prog pretensions, lousy singer, or no, they really sounded like no one else.

Interestingly, as a founder of the Black Rock Coalition in the mid-'80s,

Living Colour guitarist Vernon Reid himself was explicit in his opposition to black pop's industry-enforced crossover dreams—even though he wound up having his own greatest success in front of white rock audiences. In the critic Steve Perry's essay "The Politics of Crossover," included in the 1989 Simon Frith–edited anthology *Facing The Music*, Perry (not the Journey guy, or even Cherry Poppin' Daddies guy) notes the Reid contradiction; he also discusses the role that the late '60s black separatist movement played in subsequent suspicions about white pop influences impinging on R&B purity. Pedro Bell's crazed P-Funk album-cover cartoons lampooning funkateers selling out to disco were one highly visible side effect; as I was a fairly devout Funkadelic fan at the time, they probably affected my own thinking, too. (Nelson George has traced the crossover debate back much further still, to W. E. B. Du Bois's and Booker T. Washington's opposing declarations for assimilation and black self-sufficiency at the dawn of the twentieth century.)

But as for my broadsides against Living Colour and KRS-One, I'm not sure whether it was mere class resentment that got my dander up, or what. Like most Americans, I'm not even sure what "class" I'm *from*—I was born in Detroit proper seven years before the riots of 1967 made white flight inevitable; started kindergarten in archetypally white working-class Levittown, Pennsylvania; spent grade-school time in the suburbs of Cincinnati and a suburban Detroit orphanage. I went to schools named Immaculate Heart of Mary and St. Isaac Jogues and Our Lady of Refuge with other children of hardworking Irish/German/Polish/Italian-American Roman Catholic strivers. Eventually my family settled in an archetypally nouveau-affluent Detroit suburb, where my high school class had only two black students—twin sisters—out of well over 400. Yet while I didn't come from Keego Harbor, the part of West Bloomfield Township regularly disparaged as "white trash" at the time, and while my family somehow managed to add a built-in swimming pool to our backyard, neighbor kids frequently called me and my four siblings "poor" because we wore cheap black-rubber buckled boots all winter and drank milk stirred from powder and ate store-brand rice puffs and wheat puffs that came in plastic bags rather than boxes and my dad wanted to seed rather than sod our lawn.

Before my dad committed suicide, he'd just worked his last day at the personnel department of R.L. Polk & Co., a marketing firm serving the automotive industry; my natural mother was an RN, my stepmother an LPN. After my dad died, my stepmom drew insurance payments and social security checks, and I caddied and dishwashed and busboyed at Jewish country clubs and restaurants (Tam O'Shanter which confusingly had an Irish name, Fiddler on the Rye which went bankrupt owing me a few hundred dollars), and I wouldn't have gone to college right out of high school if I hadn't won an Army ROTC scholarship that paid my tuition and books for four years, on the condition that I pay the Army back with four years in uniform after I had my diploma. I spent my first year of higher education at the Jesuit-run University of Detroit, crossing the line from the white suburbs to the black city. So feel free to do the math yourself, and figure out where all of that puts me in the wide spectrum of the American middle class.

One thing that seems clear to me is that not all that much I've outlined here relates *directly* to race. Though it probably does have a lot to do with feeling conflicted about all sorts of things—something else Kid Rock, Eminem, and I have in common.

EMMETT MILLER: *THE MINSTREL MAN FROM GEORGIA*

I'm not going to pretend it excuses the kinky hair, the tilted derby, the exaggerated clown lips and the brown greasepaint he wears on his face on his album cover, but Emmett Miller was the missing link between Mark Twain and the Beastie Boys. He recorded his music in 1928 and 1929, about 50 years after *The Adventures Of Tom Sawyer*, 60 years before *Licensed To Ill*. Lots of tracks aren't so much songs as comedy dialogues, and the jokes come at you too fast to catch them all. His wife dies, so his friend asks about life insurance: "Did she leave you much?" "About twice a week!"

He plays black people as disreputable characters, ripping off innocents with sidewalk dice scams—"Dese here is African *diamonds*!" Or he portrays dusky sammies slap-happy with their mammies, husky sambos slop-hoppy with their mambos ("St. Louis Blues" slips into a Latin rhythm), sweatin' and smilin' fo de bossman in de Good Ole Sunny South. It's all lies, nostalgia for lost antebellum days when darkies knew their place, and I guess it's all "offensive." But I wouldn't say it offends me, exactly.

Emmett stretches vowels into one another, pronouncing "Alabama" "Ay-la-bay-ay-ay-ay-ma," finding 15 syllables in the phrase "I ain't got nobody." I've never before heard a singer this high *and* long *and* nasal; Jimmie Rodgers and Hank Williams ripped off Emmett's vocal mannerisms *outright*, but they sound strained in comparison to him. As does Harmonica Frank (famous hobo in *Mystery Train* by Greil Marcus). As does David Lee Roth, who remade two of these songs ("I Ain't Got Nobody," "Big Bad Bill Is Sweet William Now") then donned blackface on the cover of *Eat 'Em And Smile*.

Like proudly silly old-timey banjobillies Dock Boggs and Charlie Poole, like the 1926–1938 novelties compiled on Columbia/Legacy's indispensable 1993 *White Country Blues: A Lighter Shade Of Blue*, Emmett Miller was a bridge between Al Jolson and Bob Wills, too. I wish a couple of *Minstrel Man's* duller slow songs were replaced by the "early rap" called "The Gypsy" mentioned in the CD notes. But usually Emmett's Georgia Crackers (starring Tommy and Jimmy Dorsey!) get fast and busy; they *rock*—

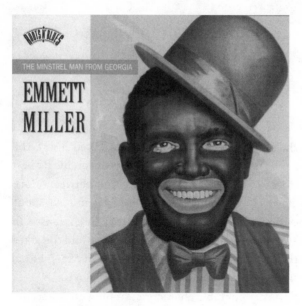

EMMETT MILLER: *THE MINSTREL MAN FROM GEORGIA*

(COLUMBIA/LEGACY, 1996)

tapdance-shuffling jug-and-kazoo hokum, cackling horns, hopped-up post-ragtime bang-on-all-the-pots-and-pans-in-your-kitchen dance-jazz.

Emmett reminds me of shy-but-clever kids in school who would master foreign dialects as a defense, to make popular kids laugh. Minstrelsy's dipshit devil-may-care delusions provide him with a context where he can hang loose and put on a *show*.

Eye Weekly, 4 April 1996

MISSISSIPPI SHEIKS VS. UTAH SAINTS

The Mississippi Sheiks and Utah Saints both have names that sound like sports teams—in fact, my colleague Frank Kogan says Utah Saints probably got their moniker when they heard the New Orleans Jazz (basketball) moved to Salt Lake City, but they thought it was the New Orleans Saints (football) instead. (Can't blame 'em—What jazz ever came from Utah, not counting the Osmonds I mean?) The Sheiks and Saints both excel at the sport where you take a genre (Delta blues in Mississippi's case, "techno" in

Utah's) and "sell it out" by making it catchy, thus improving it. But if they held a World Series, who would win?

The Sheiks certainly have the *seniority* advantage, or they did back when they existed in the '30s. Formed when lazy farmboy Lonnie Chatmon "got tired of smellin' mule farts" (honest—it's in the liner notes!), they started out as a square-dance fiddle-and-violin combo, then mined their hillbilly influence into major crossover success. They were an all-black group who played for largely white crowds, because that's where the money was, supposedly, but also because that's where their talent was—On *Stop And Listen*, the cuts that jump out at me are foxtrots and joke routines and Jimmie Rodgers yodellers, "Sales Tax" and "That's It" and "I've Got Blood In My Eyes For You." The Sheiks retain the famous fatalism of blues, but get rid of all the stuff that makes people act real serious and holy when they're hearing it. And while they might sound even more ebullient if they used kazoos and washboards like the Memphis Jug Band had a few years before, the Sheiks are yet more evidence that, in terms of energy, humor, hooks, rhythm, strangeness, and vocal personality, the music Robert Johnson started recording in 1936 was actually a *retreat* from a certain minstrelite kind of dance-novelty traveling-show songsterism that peaked around 1930.

Much in the same way that the pee-pee which people call "techno" nowadays is a retreat from Eurodisco, come to think of it: As usual, whenever a genre starts being billed as "intense" or "dangerous," you can bet it's shot its wad. Utah Saints are the only decent techno-rave act I've heard, mainly because these Limeys are really a *disco* act—when they start looping toward Philip Glass hypnosis, they're doing the same thing Montreal electro-whiz Gino Soccio did on his 1979 *Outline* album. Their hits "Something Good" and "What Can You Do For Me" propel indecipherably anonymous vocal snips atop a yummy geometric calculator-blip/popcorn-pop bottom, whilst male cheerleaders goofily chant "U-U-U-Utah Saints!" *Utah Saints* trances into the fusion-noodle ozone more than their earlier *Something Good* EP, but still gives Mississippi Sheiks a run for the pennant. There's even a guitarful MC5-via-EMF/KLF alphabet-rocker called "I Want You." The Sheiks win, though: not only because they have better songs, but because they're a better dance band.

Where's The Snake, June 1993

PAZZ & JOP BALLOT EXCERPT 1984

It's 1984, Michael Jackson's hot shit, and I can still put a Prince or Grand-master Flash (or Vickie Sue Robinson or whoever) record on my turntable, and somebody I otherwise like will ask me, "Hey Chuck, you know a lot about music. Didn't you know disco went out of style five years ago?" I don't know if New York's any different; I suppose it is. (For the most part, Detroit is, too—after all, Detroit has the Electrifying Mojo, and people who care listen to him.) But most of young white middle America *doesn't* care, of course, and its members still think disco sucks; they still identify anything remotely Negro as disco; and "Billie Jean" everyday on MTV isn't going to change a damn thing about it. Come to think of it, most black people I know still prefer James Ingram and Al Jarreau, who are as white as I am, to George Clinton or Afrika Bambaataa or Robert Johnson; it's a different symptom of the same problem, and it's got more to do with how people use music than anything else—they just don't want to hear anything that will disturb their precious body rhythms, or make them question their day-to-day way of doing things.

"REAL PUNK-DISCO FUSION": Soft Cell, Michael Jackson, Yello, Culture Club, Malcolm McLaren, King Sunny Adé, David Bowie, Rick James, New Order, Eurythmics, Junior Walker, Prince, R.E.M., Was (Not Was), B-52s, Philip Glass, Prince Charles and the City Beat Band, Yazoo, Herbie Hancock, and the Bad Brains, all of whom placed in *NME*'s Top 50 this year. "Dance-oriented rock": Slim Harpo.

PAZZ & JOP BALLOT EXCERPT 1985

It's about time that a lot of the characteristics that once seemed so horrible about AOR (Steve Perry's voice, Rush's philosophy, AC/DC's simplicity, 38 Special's pop sense, ZZ Top's boogie beat) finally got accepted on their own terms. These "clichés" help constitute a tradition just as much as Motown-to-Chic basslines or Byrds-to-R.E.M. modalities do, and the tradition still thrives: I think the reason I prefer John Mellencamp to all the other Americana-mongers has as much to do with his roots in '70s grunge-metal as it does with his roots in Southern Indiana.

So, back in the States after three years of Radio Luxembourg and American Forces Radio pop eclecticism, I find myself bypassing local CHR and Urbane Contemporary and Countrypolitan, and instead happily sharing my commuting time with a Louisville Apartheid- (or Anthem-) Oriented Rock station that has sold me on Robert Plant's astonishingly eccentric LP, confirmed my hunch that Springsteen's "Trapped" could have been my number-three single of the year, reminded me that Bad Company and Mountain could sure as hell kick some ass, and taught me that I kinda like the way Geddy Lee sings, if only because I figure it must take balls to annoy me as well as he does. This ain't rock'n'roll heaven, but it sure beats Tears For Fears and Simple Minds.

And—this is blasphemous, and scary, and may sound hypocritical coming from a white Negro who in 1981 got booted off the University of Missouri rock station for spinning "Flash On The Wheels Of Steel" and "When You Were Mine"—I have no doubt that, if this station suckered into the powers-that-wish-they-were and played "Oh Sheila" or "Roxanne, Roxanne" or "Pop Life" or "Part-Time Lover," I'd jump frequencies in a Taana Gardner heartbeat. Which is why they don't play those songs, and I suppose is also the reason they're scared to program George Clinton and Run-D.M.C. And which makes it pretty damn hard to be self-righteous.

For me, 1985's major triumphs in black music came from surprisingly traditional stuff—not bland mid-tempo diet-funk like RJ Smith's fave "Hangin' On A String," but grits and gravy: gospel, zydeco, Mardi Gras second-line, Malaco R&B, and Stax-influenced Southern soul, not a little of it originating from the Cooke-Womack family. But turn on a black station, not only in Detroit and (I bet) New York but also down here in central Kentucky, and you won't hear any of this stuff, and not too damn many Fishbone or Trouble Funk records, either. More than AOR's continued racism, CHR's continued Anglophilia, or C&W's continued (though somewhat abated, thanx to Reba and George and John and the Judds) suburbanization, the upwardly mobile sound of black radio is the biggest ongoing nuisance on the American airwaves; put simply, it implies a socioeconomic progress that doesn't exist in real life. Those shocked by my allegiance to a station that plays mostly Rush and Bryan Adams should explain how Ready For The World are somehow more worthwhile.

Come to think of it, black radio and Top 40/CHR/Hot Hits/etc. sound so alike these days they might as well be the same format. Coming off a period of intense segregation, and following the rock-crit lead, the Top 40 could now be thought of in the same way that Christgau described 1982's P&J outcome—as what white supremacists would probably see as a "huge liberal miscegenation plot." Now, I ain't no white supremacist; I love great, uncompromised black rock'n'roll, and I always have. But it's my love of that music that makes me despise what might best be termed the "beige" sound: lame post-*Thriller*, post–Boy George pop that tries so fucking hard to accommodate interracial crossover that it ends up sounding as cautious as the worst white-bread Newton-John pap or Kansas pomp. Only, this beige comes in all colors, and what makes it scary is its very legitimization by the rock critic intelligentsia. Black critics encourage the greyboys to make "soul" music more soulless than they'd ever accept by black artists, white critics encourage the bloods to make "rock" music more soft-centered than they'd ever accept by white artists, and eventually the garf all sounds the same.

This year we heard shitloads of the stuff—by Tina, Aretha, Stevie, Prince, Morris, Rick, Mick, Sting, Paul Young, Sade, Madonna, Eurythmics, Scritti Politti, New Order, the "new, improved" (har har) Talking Heads, and USA for Africa, and that only takes into account the "good" ones. What I hate is the dogged, unnatural insistence not to offend; the self-conscious determination to get a little bit, but not too much, of that beat in there; the contrived pretense that all we are is ebony and ivory, living in perfect, pretty, placid harmony.

BOOGIE DOWN PRODUCTIONS: *GHETTO MUSIC: THE BLUEPRINT OF HIP HOP*

On the cover of Boogie Down Productions' third slab of stolid slogan-rap, lead-blowhard KRS-One crouches on some backsteps, calmly discoursing art or education or finance (but not women—no sexism here, bub) at length like he thinks he's Socrates in Plato's *Republic*. His sole pupil, standing above and pointing a finger and grasping a nightstick that might as well have "might is right" written on it, is a cop (gotta call policemen that 'cause they might be *women*, my four-year-old sez). No surprise that rappers would proffer the same persecution complex such skinheads as Black

Flag and the 4 Skins used to ("Police Story," "All Cops Are Bastards"), and I suppose, sure, it's "justified." If I was Eddie Money, I'd've left the force, too! Not hard to figure what KRS is getting at; he leaves no room for guesswork, and his inner-sleeve note ("only ghetto consciousness will understand it") all but admits he's preaching to the converted.

Go 'head, call me David Duke, but by now I'm convinced kids flunk college entrance exams just so they'll have some "cultural bias" to complain about. Ya gotta be the victim, it's like a rite of passage. BDP's "Why Is That?" claims all these famous Israelites and Egyptians in the Bible were black (tell that to Shadrach, Meshach, and Abednego), which may or may not be true, but I really don't care 'cause THEY DIED THOUSANDS OF YEARS AGO. (Now they're the color of *dirt*!) "Jack Of Spades" aims to be some soldier of love, he's "cleaning up the ghetto of all its debris" (maybe he drives a garbage truck), he's "a hero 'cause he started from zero." But my heroes, they're heroes 'cause of where they *end up*, not where they start (and they *still* don't appear on no stamps!). "It's all a means to an end now," Axl Rose sang last winter; KRS goes "all the ends are justified by the means." Calls himself "the teacher." So if kids hate school as much as he says they oughta (in "You Must Learn"), why does he figure they'll listen?

Rap's initial social-consciousness moves (Brother D's "How We Gonna Make The Black Nation Rise," South Bronx's "The Big Throwdown," Grandmaster Flash's "The Message," all '81–'82) were interesting *as* moves, not unlike the four protest songs on White Lion's new *Big Game*; Public Enemy's fun, all the way down to the slapstick of their recent breakup, comes from the noise and contradiction and self-promotion. (Same goes for *Do The Right Thing*, which is cool for the same shit-and-heart-stirring reasons Guns N' Roses' "One In A Million" is cool, and if you think I'm crazy compare their xenophobia.) Role-modeling's got nothing to do with it. Schoolly D and Def Leppard ("Gods Of War") and Neneh Cherry and now the Beastie Boys (!) can get away with politics 'cause the politics are a small part of a bigger picture where politics make no sense whatsoever. The clashing colors make you stand up and take notice. In Spoonie Gee's "Street Girl" and Dimples D's "Sucker DJ's (I Will Survive)," the crime and violence come out of nowhere, out of happiness like in real life. They jump ya from behind.

But BDP's "reality" falls flat 'cause it's the whole damn package, and all work and no play makes KRS-One a dull, er, man. No offense to the late Scott La-Rock, but KRS needs a DJ who ain't dead yet. A gospel choirgirl and swingband horns replace last year's Deep Purple riffage, and that's as exciting as *Ghetto Music* gets. In "Breath Control," KRS makes a mistake then corrects himself, a trick he might've learnt from "Milkcow Blues Boogie" or "Bob Dylan's 115th Dream" or "Wrong 'Em Boyo." Once again, his sing-songily erudite cadence never diverts from iambic pentameter, and next to the thick groove-contortions in the Beasties' *Paul's Boutique*, next to Latifah or Asher D or most anything on *Reggae Dance Hall Classics*, his ragamuffin needs some stuffin'.

"Now in '89 the purpose of a rhyme is to strengthen and uplift the mind," the hype-spots plastered all over the *Village Voice* (and, I'm told, NYC phone-poles) proclaim, but rap's been strengthening and uplifting *my* mind, making me think, telling me brand new things, ever since I brought Steve Berkowski that "Rapper's Delight" 12-inch for his birthday back in Missouri ten years ago. Accustomed to buying "smart" records like, you know, the Fabulous Poodles and Joe Jackson, I was real embarrassed at the cash register. This was candy-crap, right? KRS-One, he don't want hip-hop to be candy-crap; 's gotta have 100 percent of yer U.S. RDA of B1 and B12 and Niacin and Folic Acid, otherwise it's no good. So he drops all these catchwords: "intellectual," "noncommercial," "radical sounds," "no glitter, no makeup," "purity," no "artificial additives." I mean, gag me with a cokespoon full of Sweet'n Low. "We're not here for glamour or fashion," KRS asserts, but he wears all black, like Sisters of Mercy. Like Poison's Bret Michaels admitted back before wussing out into Axl's "natural look," no image is an image too.

Village Voice, 6/27/89: "More politically conscious than the downtown fashion pack, this new breed celebrates its diversity, turning stereotypes into statements of self-affirmation. . . . Murray is wearing 'drummer' pants, about $65, a cowrie shell belt, about $40, Kente cloth suspenders, about $45, Malcolm X 'by any means necessary' T-shirt, about $24, and Senegalese beaded bracelets [five of 'em!], $5 to $30." To fight the power, you gotta be willing to pay the price.

B.A.M., 8 September 1989

YOTHU YINDI: *TRIBAL VOICE*

Man, it's about *time* the Aborigine Rock Coalition got its outback in gear. Bottom line is, the Australasiatic Man invented rock'n'roll, right? Or maybe I'm just thinking of Rolf Harris with "Tie Me Kangaroo Down, Sport" (1963)—well, at least he was from Perth, closer to wombat-hunting country than Sydney (AC/DC, Divinyls, INXS, Midnight Oil, Rick Springfield) or Melbourne (Men at Work, Olivia Newton-John, Kylie Minogue, the Little River Band). East coast Austies stole the soul, and to quote Peter Garrett in "Beds Are Burning," let's give it back!

The band Yothu Yindi comes from a remote coastal community of Arnhem Land and sounds not at all like the Strangeloves (who claimed to learn the Burundi beat of "I Want Candy" from aborigines). In fact, Yothu Yindi are closer to Midnight Oil—similar AOR-anthem bent, and Mandawuy Yunupingu stops and starts through his nose like a less pompous Garrett. "Treaty," their funky down-under hit, sarcastically protests imperialist land-plunder, just like all Midnight Oil's best songs. Only, Yothu Yindi are a *glam* band—their members wear wilder makeup than Poison ever did! (A tribal thing, perhaps.) The didgeridoo player takes gargling solos that scare my kids, and the clapsticks guy approximates Isaac Hayes protodisco rhythms. Emotive guitar noise on top: not bad, really.

Problem's the words—too serious. Personally, I'm rooting for Yindi to sell out like their Native American predecessor Redbone did with "Come And Get Your Love" in 1974. What a song.

Spin, May 1992

LIVING COLOUR: *BISCUITS EP*

We all know the real reason rock critics wet their pants over Living Colour, so I won't dwell on the issue, except to say that if I were in Mordred or Riot (or, uh, Rush), who do more or less the same pompous sound bite–sludge schtick and suck almost as bad at it, I'd be strongly considering blackface. What I will say is that Corey Glover is fast making a name for himself as one of the worst singers in pop history—the guy hasn't got a fraction of the natural soul of a Lou Gramm (much less an Axl Rose), so he goes all out trying to bust his bluesful gut, like David Coverdale maybe except with *way* more prog-schlock grandeur-delusion. Hence, he winds up combining what are probably the two most witlessly dead-assed vocal strains since Elvis died.

Vernon Reid's got his "intriguing" (in a "jazz" way) moments (strange noises here and there), and if I'm charitable I might say the same about the TV samples. But since this band has yet to write even one "important cause" lyric that engages anything beyond the obvious ("I don't care about your dreams of peace/I don't care about your please lawd please/I don't care about your Africa," etc.), and since the samples and riffs serve no expressive non-showoff purpose, and since tunes and dance grooves must not be nutritious enough, why split hairs?

On their new EP, L.C. minstrelize reggae and reduce extinct James Brown and Al Green standards into heavy-handed guilt-rock turds. Leaving it on the shelf will not make you a racist, I promise.

Spin, **September 1991**

3RD BASS: CACTUS LOVE

My first inclination was to think that 3rd Bass were to rap as Living Coloür are to metal—a horse of a different color, but so what? Problem is, Living Colour are straighter-shooting than these Caucasians, not angular enough; 3rd Bass are more like King's X, the prog-rock power trio with the black singer who flickered on and off *Dial-MTV* last fall.

Race ain't hardly their only conceit: not only are they self-conscious about content and form, they're *self-righteous* about 'em both too. (Living Colour are self-righteous only about content.) They bill themselves, most visibly in a January *Village Voice* cover story that fell on its face comparing them to Eric Clapton, as the authentic white face of black expression.

But at a time when so many rappers, political ones especially, grow up middle-class suburban, the idea that there is one "true" Afro-American experience is absurd. And *The Cactus Album*, Top 20 in the black charts, ranks with the Beastie Boys' *Paul's Boutique* as one of the artiest hip-hop LPs ever made.

As it ought to. M.C. Serch is an opera-trained Orthodox Jewish stockbroker's son who hung out with black kids in the projects since first grade and attended Manhattan's High School of Music and Art. Prime Minister Pete Nice is a onetime Naval Academy candidate who studied B-ball and B boys while earning his English BA magna cum laude at Columbia.

But they're "street," see, and they spend a good deal of their time telling us so. In their debut LP's first and funkiest song, they dis the Beasties as dust-imbibing pretty-boy "Village People clones" who exploit black beats. Which might be true, but when it comes to versatility, voice, or vocabulary, those brats show up these as amateurs. Nice puffs a stogie so we'll know he's one Mack motherfucker, and when he and his partner aren't inventing their own sub-*Heathers* slang ("cactus"=penis, "oval office"=vagina), they're basking in the lingo of the ghetto. Still, their Public Enemy imitation pales next to New Kids on the Block's.

The Cactus Album fuses two artsy hip-hop sub-styles. Like De La Soul's *3 Feet High and Rising*, it's a quasi-comedic collage, alternating raps with gangster-flick dialogue, backstage discussions, Yiddish one-liners, *Little Rascals* themes, and Abbott-and-Costello routines; the rhymes themselves aim for an arrogant introversion midway between Rakim and Big Daddy Kane, to most coldblooded effect in last summer's "Steppin' to the A.M." single. When their Blood Sweat & Tears trumpet loop spins into some dangerously obsessive groovology, when they imitate Tom Waits imitating Satchmo, maybe even when they expound on the work ethic over a sea of seamless salsa timbales, 3rd Bass show enough chutzpah to convice you they may be onto something.

But like Big Daddy Kane, M.C. Serch chills so frozen he can't help but fade away behind his bass samples, and like Rakim, Prime Minister Nice is so in love with his thesaurus that you strain to catch it all. Not much fun when you're dancing. The combination is deadly, and not in the way these crossers-of-railroad-tracks think it is. When I start hearing about "authenticity" and "complexity," I worry for rap's future. Then again, I was never much of a Clapton fan, either.

Boston Phoenix, 9 February 1990

Teena Marie is sitting next to me on a couch in her bright purple tour bus. She beckons me closer. She finishes her curried chicken, sips her honeyed tea, then removes her jacket, leans toward me, and looks straight into my eyes. She tells me people just don't realize how shy she is.

She suggests I hang out a while and puts on a short film called *Temptation* by some New York guy named Daryl McKane (about a disc jockey who dresses like George Clinton, then goes home to his suspiciously normal wife). We're alone, and Teena's behind me, singing a seductive song from the soundtrack.

I won't make too much of it, because she's probably just being a good hostess—which surprises me, because when I was introduced to her backstage at Baltimore's AFRAM Expo '94 at Camden Yards earlier that day, she shook my hand like it was a chore, and seemed sullen, pissed, and bored. Teena's cute two-and-a-half-year-old daughter, Alia Rose Noelle, was yelling out the window of a mobile home, and Teena was talking to her stage people about fixing the sound. Hands in her pockets, the four-foot-11-inch singer looked muscular and tough—her 37-year-old, nonwaifish body didn't seem tiny at all.

She wore sunglasses, boots, and a jacket and pants with colorful pictures of herself all over them: images of Teena as a blonde, as a redhead, one on the back with Rick James (whom she last spoke to years ago before he entered prison/rehab). "People say I'm a chameleon," she says in the bus. "Sometimes I walk down the street and nobody recognizes me." Her right pants cheek has MAYBE THAT WILL EXPRESS JUST WHAT I'VE BEEN GOING THROUGH written on it.

I can't imagine wearing an outfit with pictures of me all over it, but I don't get the idea that Teena's especially full of herself, except in the sense that she always sings like she's proud of her voice—volcanically loud and uncontrolled and doing backflips over five octaves and holding vowel notes really long and scatting to imitate guitar parts. She brags about being "the first woman rapper ever" and "one of the only white people who have been completely accepted by the black audience as one of their own." But when I compliment her on her musical accomplishments, she just thanks me or denies that it's any big deal at all.

THE SECRETLY SHY TEENA MARIE. (PHOTO: RANDEE ST. NICHOLAS)

"Touché olé/My opening line might be a bit passé," she fibs in the open-ing of her only big pop hit, 1985's "Lovergirl." And in the notes to her 1984 album, *Starchild*, she concedes, "no one's new or innovative except the Cre-ator." And maybe she believes it. On 1986's *Emerald City*, Teena topped off salsa rhythms with metal guitars in ways nobody'd pulled off before—both Lenny Kravitz (Teena says) and I think it's her best album. It was also her poorest seller. "To tell you the truth," she says, "I didn't know what I was doing." She doesn't do *Emerald City* songs live.

Teena's favorite Teena albums are her new *Passion Play* (she calls it ro-mantic; I call it pornographic), 1990's *Ivory*, and 1980's *Irons In The Fire*. They are her purest R&B records—make-out music for her faithful urban audience. "My voice is made for R&B," she says with a smile. "It's my first love."

She now shrugs off her mid-'80s foray into bebop slang, runny-nosed toddler voices, poems about girls named Pity who wish they were green, and escapist journeys to Oz, Shangri-La, and Xanadu, saying, "I was a young kid then." But on her newest album, I miss the self-mocking, English-major/hippie-rocker/*Star Trek* side of Teena Marie.

Passion Play doesn't even have a poem on its album cover! "I felt like the Shakespeare quote ['Here she comes and her passion ends the play'] covered it this time," she explains—and besides, she's just finishing writ-ing a book that will be titled *The Truth*. It's full of poems, prose, raps, and a play about her black godmother from Detroit and a tramp who's sort of like Puck in *A Midsummer Night's Dream*. "I don't look at myself as being eccentric," she swears, her nose ring wiggling. "Sometimes reporters make me look crazy, and then at the end they say I'm a genius, and I know that's the kind of article you're writing, right?" (I say of course not. She asks me if I like Joni Mitchell.)

Part of the insanity people detect in Teena, I tell her, might come from the unguarded way she exposes every emotion in her convoluted bohemian-beachtown-to-Detroit-and-Motown Records life to the whole planet. But she denies it: "I don't tell everything about my life in my songs," she says. "You'd be surprised. I'm saving some things for my daughter."

"After having my baby," Teena continues, "I felt complete in ways I didn't before." She's starting fresh: The new album was released on her own Sarai Records label instead of Epic (Teena says it was a cordial split). Her little girl travels with her on the road, along with the two daughters of a girlfriend Teena lives with, and they're all in bed by 10. Teena would like to portray Janis Joplin someday, onstage or in a movie, but says that unlike Janis, she won't die unhappy for having never found a man who'll return her love. "I don't need a man in my life. I do need my daughter."

No artificial stimulants for her either. "I don't need any cocaine to keep me up; I'm already up." On a now forgotten episode of *The Beverly Hillbillies*, when Teena was an eight-year-old aspiring TV star, she swallowed a Granny-concocted elixir to calm her down. It didn't work—on TV or in real life. And I'm glad. I don't want Teena Marie to ever calm down.

Vibe, 1994

SHAKE YOUR LOVE: GILLETTE

Call-and-response practice: "Do you like 'em short?" "YEAH!" "Do you like 'em tall?" "YEAH!" "Do you like 'em bad?" "YEAH!" "We like 'em all!!" This 20-year-old (now 22) semi-Latina (Puerto Rican half, Mexican quarter, French quarter) chick from Chicago going by her *familia* name Gillette put out this oppressive CD last year called *Gillette On The Attack*, and she was a cheerleader boxing your lights out, especially if your dick was too short or you didn't last long in bed or you had Coke-bottle glasses (but a great personality) or your lies ruined her reputation. ("If sex is always so unsatisfying for you, then maybe you better change your technique," my fellow Gillette fan Frank Kogan wanted to say back to her. "Or don't you think that *you* have any responsibility for the interaction? Moron.") She was a total superficial bitch, and she rocked my world.

I can be a superficial bitch too. I made a celebrity-crush list for my hot-for–Antonio Banderas amiga Gomezgrrrl, and she pointed out that I obviously go for light-skinned-but-dark-haired-Latina types (Gloria Estefan, Corina, Gloria Trevi) and tomboy-but-not-weightlifter white-trash types (Suzi Quatro, Joan Jett, Jo on *The Facts of Life*), and Gillette fits *both* categories—cool, huh? Fishnet stockings, high heels, Daisy Dukes (sorry, I misplaced my hip-hop spelling dictionary), silver hoop earrings,white tank top with bra strap protruding beneath, caterpillared eyebrows, fuck-me-red (my neighbor Diane calls it) nails and mouth, and this excellent beret on top. Man, if I knew her I'd, I'd . . . well, I'd probably just wind up being her close friend, seeing how I'm married and all.

Gillette On The Attack sounded like late-'80s Miami-jailbait bubble-rappers L'Trimm had graduated high school then crossbred the Beastie Boys' *Licensed To Ill* with Joan Jett's *Bad Reputation*. Gillette was some tacky-hairdoed runaway barking catcalls from the back of the bus, cracking gum and cracking up loudly at her own lame insults. Production team 20 Fingers (who've now grown to actually having 60 fingers, including 10 from onetime "next Prince" house-music hype Jamie Principle) have kick-ass trash-rock tastes. Between Gillette's albums and their 1995 sampler *20 Fingers* (packed with dance-floor novelties about pithecanthropus erectuses and erect penises), they swipe hooks outright from BTO, Toto, Steppenwolf, Van Halen. And though jungle and trip-hop may well be the brave new prog snooze, 20 Fingers' muscular stomping and gang shouting and brevity (nine or 10 songs per Gillette disc, all between 3:14 and 4:05, no time for Muzak bullshit) prove that disco's true old AOR allies were glam fags ballroom-blitzing in big glitzy boots.

Shake Your Money Maker skips the debut's Beastie-metal guitars, and Gillette's hilarious abrasiveness isn't constantly in your face, so it confused me at first. But it's just as frenzied and vernacularly versed and opposed to premature ejaculation as *Gillette on the Attack* was, and it's also sillier and friendlier and more disco—fast-forwarded dinky-synth motion, break-dance-era graffiti spray paint on its cover, and the lyrics make fun of a platform-shoed/Superfly-'froed/fake-gold-chained/black-eyed cad with a diamond in the back and a sun-roof top. Last album, when Gillette said "dog!" we said "baby!"; now when she says "booty!" we say "bounce!" And apparently becoming a mama last winter taught señorita how to do more than just yell—now she can also *squeak*!

GILLETTE: *SHAKE YOUR MONEY MAKER* (SOS, 1996)

Her oral-sex euphemism "Underwater Boogie" does the swim with Billy Squier strokes and gets the "rhythm of the head-ding!-dong!" like kiddies on *Sesame Street*—a cute match for the Cookie Monster growls in "Bounce" and "1-2-3-4-5-6-7-8" counting lesson in "Oops Too Late." "Weekend" counts down days, luring impatient party voices through Monday-with-Friday-on-their-mind blues, over the hump-day hump, and finally into that 5 p.m. Friday high dive with all the delirious off-the-deep-end abandon of trash-radio quitting-time anthems like Debbie Deb's "Lookout Weekend" or Loverboy's "Working for the Weekend." And the single, "Do Fries Go With That Shake" (title from McDonald's via George Clinton), would be a so-what ripoff of Salt-n-Pepa's clumsy man-ogling shtick if it wasn't catchier than any S-n-P hit since "Push It." Gillette shouts three shouts this time out about studmuffins shake-shake-shaking their booties, groovethings, tail feathers, money makers, whatever. And she's getting funky making money herself, as Funky Four Plus One used to say back in the day, back when hip-hop still hipped and hopped. So shake it up, baby. Twist and shout.

Village Voice, 30 July 1996

THE ICEMAN COMETH BACK: VANILLA ICE

Yo V.I.P., let's kick it: Vanilla Ice has this amazing bucktoothy rube smile he flashes when he's really proud of himself. He looks like his own mascot—a pumped-up plastic Aryan action figure, biceps covered with Celtic tattoos, blond goatee, Caesar cut where his slicked-down pompadour used to be.

Here cometh the Iceman last Tuesday: "This song is called 'Fuck Me' 'cause I know how I've been perceived." His black cheerleader buddy tries to get the crowd to yell "fuck you!" at the stage, just like Ice Cube's sidekick on the Family Values tour—Vanilla's ludicrous comeback is produced by Korn/Limp Bizkit guy Ross Robinson, see. Live, his band of head-banging white sleazeballs hide their occasionally glam-ish Burundibilly beats and cute Eurocheese keyboard zigzags under three guitars and Ice's frog-monster growling.

CBGB was a claustrophobically packed hotbox—tons of curiosity-seeking, bridge-and-tunnel car-crash gawkers in their twenties who'd heard Vanilla getting dissed by *Howard Stern* callers during their morning commutes, all fist-fucking the air to his industrialcore "Ice Ice Baby" update. Nobody cared enough to yell for an encore after that, but the band returned anyway with noisy numbers about stomping through bayous and "goin' crazy like Prozac." (Huh?) Upon which the faithful started shouting "Go Ninja, Go Ninja, Go!" but maybe Vanilla couldn't remember his old Teenage Mutant Turtle words (to your mother).

"Hootie-fucking-who?," Vanilla kept chanting—must not approve of black guys sounding white. He was funniest "taking us back to the old school," doing a Freddy Krueger human beatbox pantomime and bump-and-grinding about climbing his coconut tree 'cause Ice cream is good for our health. (*Hard To Swallow*, his new album's called, yup yup.) Preppie fans reminisced about being 14 in Miami, believing Vanilla the true face of hip-hop, then growing up to track down his motocross-and-jetski-equipment store, To the Extreme, but never a copy of 1994's holy grail *Mind Blowin'* CD. Everybody was waiting for "stop, collaborate and listen/Ice is back and he's a born-again Christian," but instead he asked how many of us had ADD. We raised our hands and decided to go home.

Village Voice, 3 November 1998

MOTOR SUBURB MADHOUSE: KID ROCK AND EMINEM

On the cover of *The Source* and on a two-page spread inside *Rolling Stone* last month, 26-year-old Marshall Mathers a/k/a Eminem and 29-year-old Bob Ritchie a/k/a Kid Rock were respectively photographed, both wielding chainsaws extending from their groins, out past the cornfields where the woods get heavy, possibly somewhere in the Upper Peninsula. Chopping down trees must be what New York glossy-magazine editors figure Michigan white boys—at least Michigan white boys with albums at the top of the charts—do in their spare time. Even in the sweet summertime.

"I put Detroit City back on the map!" Kid Rock raps in his current single. "Got the rock from Dee-troit, soul from Motown!" His first definitive song-as-statement, released in 1990, was heartland chauvinism worthy of Jack and Diane themselves: a middle-American midnight cowboy treks to Manhattan, where the cabbie drives like a moe-ron, and there's "a fucking transvestite, walking in the daylight," who'd "get dissed in Detroit, but I'll leave him alone, 'cause New York's not my home." Kid's got more local color in his lyrics than any Michigan musician ever: Livernois, St. Clair Shores, Taylor, the Great Lakes, being born and raised in the Outerlands, drinking 30-packs of Stroh's (spelled backwards is "shorts"!), rolling deep in his Lincoln, self-made like Henry Ford. He's got a tattoo of one of those olde English D's from Detroit Tigers hats (also used on the cover of D'Angelo's current longplayer, *Doodoo*). His new album, *The History Of Rock*, starts with a song title clearly inspired by Grand Funk Railroad's "American Band" and ends with songs unapologetically ripping Bob Seger's "Get Out Of Denver" and Ted Nugent's "Stranglehold"—three landmarks of Michigan hard rock. Last year he visited the Bowery Ballroom and delivered maybe the most exciting rock concert since Guns N' Roses in Detroit in early '87, and here's the medley he centered it around: "Sister Anne" (MC5)/"American Band"/"Ramblin' Gamblin' Man" (Seger)/"Stranglehold"/"My Name Is" (Eminem).

On his own new album, Eminem—who changed schools constantly as a kid, but seems to have been reared mostly on his mom's welfare earnings in 13-miles-north-of-Detroit Warren—disses fellow honky-rapping Michiganders the Insane Clown Posse for "claiming Detroit when y'all live 20 miles away" and because they "ain't seen a mile-road south of Ten"; a

KID ROCK WANG-DANGS MORE SWEET POONTANG THAN K.D. LANG.
(PHOTO: JOSEPH CULTICE)

couple weeks ago, he allegedly pointed a pistol at one particular ICP idiot outside an electronics store in Royal Oak, Detroit's most bohemian suburb. His only other ode to his hometown on *The Marshall Mathers LP* is "Amityville," a generically comic-bookish apparent tribute to the eccentric terror-rap of Esham, whose 20-some ignored-outside-Detroit albums apparently kick-started all the murder capital's current white punks gone dope—most of whom may well hang themselves, if they get enough rope.

Esham is black, as were the Detroit kids who invented techno in the mid-'80s and their "acid rap" and "ghetto-tech" descendants today. The metropolis has a unique history of musical miscegenation, of the ghetto taking cues from commuters and vice versa: Motown slicking up soul; Seger and Nuge and the MC5 (and Iggy and Mitch Ryder and so on) rooting their hard rock in hard R&B; George Clinton making funk psychedelic; the Electrifying Mojo spinning Kraftwerk and Billy Squier alongside Prince and Kurtis Blow on urban-contemporary WGPR in 1981; Madonna Ciccone usurping drag-queen disco for 10-year-old shopping-mall girls; Derrick May and Juan Atkins taking notes from Mojo's Kraftwerk records. It all sounds especially good in big cars.

But Detroit, the land of Devil's Night arson festivals and bombed-out crackhouse ghosttown blocks and cops pulling you over then robbing you at gunpoint, not to mention the largest predominantly black city in the

United States, has never produced a nationally successful hip-hop star darker-complexioned than Kid Rock or Eminem. Weird. The last U.S. census ranked the city second only to Gary, Indiana, as the nation's most segregated; drive across the demarcation line that is Eight Mile Road, and before you know it you're surrounded by the two-car garages and built-in pools of 86 percent Caucasian Oakland County and 95 percent Caucasian Macomb County—white-flight demographics spurred as much by the auto industry itself as by riots downtown 33 years ago.

Which is not to suggest that there aren't profound demographic differences *within* the burbs' bourgeois utopia—surrounding Detroit, for instance, you've got your Jewish-American-princess suburbs, your assembly-liner-feeling-like-a-number suburbs, your redneck-with-hunting-rifle suburbs, and lots between (and none of those populations is pure itself, either). Still, though Kid Rock proudly bills himself as white trash, he probably doesn't need to go see *The Virgin Suicides*—set in old-money Grosse Pointe—to learn how the other half lives. He grew up on a six-acre plot with a 145-tree apple orchard in 40-miles-north-of-Detroit Romeo, tolerating his parents' barn-dancing to Seger's *Live Bullet*; his first hip-hop gig was popping and locking for a breakdance crew sponsored by the local Burger King. In his embarrassingly openhearted, Bill Withers–looping, allegedly autobiographical racemixer "Black Chick, White Guy," revolving around a ninth-grade abortion that "really fucked his head up," the title's white guy comes "from a family of middle class." Kid's stuff about how he grew up herdin' cattle and has more rhymes than everyone in Seattle seems inspired by Weird Al's "Smells Like Nirvana," but his great secret subject is Pleasant Valley Sunday in Status-Symbol Land: layin' sod, chillin' in the old man's boat, workin' at the car wash (yeah), gettin' set to go cut the lawn. If you're really straight out the trailer, you don't *need* a lawn mower!

Kid talks more about sex with black women than Eminem does (in fact, he seems to enjoy sex more in general), but they've got plenty of obsessions in common: their middle fingers, their mushrooms, their misogyny, their my-name-is songs, their misplaced (and much mentioned) hostility against homosexuals. The Nugent rip on Kid's *History* is a gonzodelic father-and-son-debate fuzzbuild epic called "My Oedipus Complex"; on *Marshall Mathers*, Eminem raps oedipally about—grab your barf bag—raping his own mama (who, in real life, sued him last year). Mostly what the pair share, though, is vulnerability: a vulnerability that manages to keep their middle fingers interesting. They both give every indication, even, that they're loving fathers in real life. Watching his youngest son helps Kid Rock (whose seven-year-old Junior comes up constantly in interviews) pass the time; Eminem (whose four-year-old Hailie does) imagines being 40, cooling with a 40, babysitting two grandkids while his daughter's out getting smashed. "Kim," the intensely-wailed-and-teary-eyed new marital-squabble duet where he kills his old lady (who in real life he's since married, then just last month reportedly pulled a gun on) 'cause he caught her messin' 'round with another man, actually starts with Eminem convincingly goo-goo-ing and powdering and diapering their little girl.

Not vulnerable enough for you? Depressed that such a sick mother-fucker could have the summer's most popular record? Worried what that says about the youth of America? OK, here's my Minnesota friend Molly, on hearing "Kim" for the first time: "I can't figure out why I feel sorry for [Eminem] when he breaks down and confesses to his wife, while he's slitting her throat, that he loves her instead of 'hating [her] so fucking much.' Plus, I can't remember the last time I took an album so personally. I feel violated listening to it, or like I've accidentally seen some domestic dispute that I can't get out of my mind. . . . I want to like it because I think 'art' should make you feel, it should make you think, and it's been so long since a record freaked me out. But, at the same time, I wonder if he's just full of shit." Which he is, of course. But that's half the fun.

Kid Rock recently helped legendary country outlaw David Allan Coe compose a similarly themed wife-murder spectacle called "Wreckless" for an upcoming collaborative EP; for Coe, who was splattering spouse-blood then his own all over walls on the "Sui-side" (as opposed to the "Happy Side") of his *Human Emotions* album 22 years ago, and who claimed to have served time on death row in Ohio, this is not exactly something new, but whatever. The Kid/Coe EP has plenty of bottleneck and slide and crap about titty-bars, plus a slowed-down-and-censored version of Kid's gorgeous power ballad hit "Only God Knows Why" (which version Kid recently re-covered himself on *Saturday Night Live*). Coe is slated to appear, along with Iggy and a TLC or two and maybe Axl Rose interpreting Lynyrd Skynyrd, on an album due this fall by Kid Rock's vastly underrated Twisted Brown Trucker Band. Mostly though, DAC exemplifies yet another tendency Kid and Eminem share: they really like helping out their friends. Though their friends are rarely as newsworthy as David Allan Coe.

Double Wide, the just-out roots-rock Hootie-hop debut album from Kid's DJ and best friend, Uncle Kracker, peaks with a charbroiled-on-the-crossroads ZZ Top rip about whiskey, a fingersnappy Myrtle Beach tuck-you-in doo-wop, and a beige hopper about how "if Heaven ain't a lot like

Dee-troit"—if it ain't got no Eight Mile—it might as well be Hell or Salt Lake City. Kid also cameos on the album by Blowfish-brand jamless jam-band Robert Bradley's Blackwater Surprise; mush-mouthed deep-soulster Bradley moans sweetly about how he was born on a farm in Alabama, but now he's motoring down the road take-one-guess-where.

And then there's 3'9"-with-a-10-foot-dick Joe C, of course, whose debut album has been postponed, which might be just as well seeing how his purpose in life, obviously, is to serve as a sidesplitting free-lunch sideshow break in Kid Rock's circus. Last year he squeaked about having the highest voice like Aaron Neville and being down with the devil; on *History of Rock*, he insists he's vertically challenged but ain't no goddamn midget. On *Saturday Night Live*, hugging Florence Henderson and mugging for the camera in Mickey Mouse ears and dolled up in a wedding dress as Jerry Lee Lewis's underaged cousin, he stole the show from Kid Rock and Jackie Chan both.

By contrast, Eminem's own height-identified protégé, Royce Da 5–9, has an amusing name but not much vocal presence. In fact, pretty near the only rapper whose dexterity and energy have kept up with Em so far is Kid Rock himself—in "Fuck Off," which notably got lost in the shuffle on Kid's octopussal-platinum *Devil Without A Cause* but which jumps right out of Eminem's useful-if-illegal duet-and-remix-and-compilation-cut-compiling bootleg CD *Fucking Yzarc*. "This planet belongs to me and this hippie with long hair," Eminem raps in it. The Snoop/Dre G-funk-era interlude on Eminem's new album is summery and smooth, but too often, whenever anyone else joins in, we get snooze city: mere underground method acting by dimwits trying too hard to sound hard.

The Dre connection—bolstered by Eminem's yzarc willingness to both use Mr. Nigga With Attitude as his conscience and put him in his place—seems the main reason that rap's answer to Jeff Gillooly (Kim being Tonya Harding, natch) is given props by R&B stations that would never touch Kid Rock or the Beastie Boys: before you reach the whistling G-thang conclusion of Em's ridiculously catchy current smash "The Real Slim Shady," though, you've got to work your way through stanzas dinky enough to be nursery rhymes and taunts about how "you act like you never seen a white person before." Molly (remember her?) says he sounds like Porky Pig. In the tradition of onetime funk-crossover stars Kraftwerk and Devo, his nasal whine is the ultimate parody of an Anglo-Saxon nerd: he makes no attempt to sound black. Yet at the same time, he's the rare rapper who gets on rock stations without any attempt to sound rock, unless you count the

"Back In Black" riffs in certain bootleg "My Name Is" remixes. "How can I be white?" he asked last year. "I don't even exist."

Like Teena Marie, perhaps the last Anglo-Saxon to so fully achieve approval across the great divide, Eminem complexly switches voices within songs for different characters (five or six in "The Real Slim Shady" alone) and different emotions. He can be as verbally complicated as anybody else in rap, without limiting himself to anti-mainstream hip-hop's gratuitous aren't-you-impressed-by-my-thesaurus spelling bee. But most of the remarkable displays of technique ("skillz," "flow," who cares) on his breakthrough album last year weren't compelling enough to return to much, maybe because his word-slinging sensibilities totally dominated over the music. For all its competently eclectic production, *The Slim Shady* LP was hardly conducive to background play—it had to be paid attention to, like a singer-songwriter record, almost. But *The Marshall Mathers LP* is another story: the ever-increasing variety in Eminem's voice (drawled Southern-bounce cadences, impatiently curt throaty staccatos, flat Beck-like deadpans, crying and screaming) somehow feels completely conversational; and the musical backdrop (calypso/Caribbean, Gothic etherea, jiggy disco evolving into P.M. Dawn) is frequently, of all things, beautiful. Heart-stopping use of musique concrète sound effects adds to the suspense and tension and weirdness: Smith-Coronas typing fan letters, machetes impaling tracheas, music boxes jingling for baby, cars splashing in the lake, hostages shrieking in the trunk, insane clowns slobberingly sucking each other off. And it's worth noting that, as on the debut, some of the best parts ("Stan," "The Way I Am") are not produced by Dr. Dre. One conceivable influence for all the funeral bells and blues-guitar-dirged waltz passages is the British Gregorian-rap group Faithless, whose trip-hop diva Dido croons behind Eminem in "Stan," an impossibly eerie stained-glass rainstorm.

"The Real Slim Shady" blatantly announces itself as a sequel, and it's got loads of unexpected bits, even beyond how Eminem rhymes "mammal" with "Discovery Channel" mere months after the Bloodhound Gang (and enunciates the word "clitoris" mere months after Danish hard rockers D.A.D.'s undiscovered cunnilingo classic "Kiss Between The Legs"). At least one line can be heard as explicitly pro-gay: "Who says a man and a man can't elope?" (rhymes with cantaloupe, and antelope). But mainly, the thesis here is that a million other Slim Shadys are out there, walking and talking and cussing as scary as our hero—strange, because give or take maybe MC Paul Barman, no rappers have exactly plundered the dude's dialect so far. Plus, if "every single person is a Slim Shady lurkin'," then Eminem by definition is not the real Slim Shady—Michael Jackson or Iggy Pop or Attila the Hun is. Or Adam and Eve.

None of which matters, though, because Eminem recites it all like it's just nonsense words to jump rope to. When it comes to exploring ways to deflate his own pretension, he's up there with Richard Meltzer, almost: "Women wear your panty hose, sing the chorus and it goes . . ." Check out the hook while the DJ revolves it. He can singsong demands to "take drugs, rape sluts, make fun of gay clubs" like they're Dr Seuss; he can turn the seven words George Carlin couldn't say on television into skooby-doo-wop scatting. Or last year, in the most *Sesame Street* smile around: "Hi kids!:-) Do you like violence?:-)." Identifies himself as the bad guy who persecutes people who die in plane crashes, but what he persecutes more is his own persona.

"THIS IS FOR CHILDREN WHO BREAK RULES," Eminem says, "and every single teenager who hates school." For somebody who hates school, though, he really does love playing with language (a pastime which school as often as not discourages, admittedly). He gets off on vowel sounds: "Don't blame me if little Eric jumps off the terrace, you shoulda been watching him, apparently you're not parents." By the time he's 30, he predicts, he'll be in a nursing home pinching nurses and jerking off with Jergen's 'cause the Viagra's not workin'. He can't rap anymore, he confesses once; he just murdered the alphabet. Seems to be keeping the *Physician's Desk Reference* alive, though.

When we last met him he was getting revenge on bullies, needing Tylenol PM to sleep, slicing up Dad in a dream, complaining about stabbing victims bleeding all over his rug, making the world fellate him without a condom on, winning a million bucks then robbing armored trucks, blaming himself for somebody's psilocybin OD ("We need an ambulance!/ There's a girl upstairs talking to plants!"), and giving another girl herpes (which later in the album he can't decide whether he has) in exchange for syphilis. But these were all really Slim Shady, of course, who is of course a cartoon, so the born-brain-damaged/one-sandwich-short-of a-picnic-basket slapstick mostly came off cute—not terribly more authentic in its nastiness than, say, Alice Cooper in "No More Mr. Nice Guy" or Wile E. Coyote shopping for bombs at Acme. Puts on a bulletproof vest, ties himself to the bed, shoots himself in the head. The first time I heard "My Name Is" on the radio reminded me of the first time I heard "Loser" by Beck, in that it felt like a wacky novelty song—a good one, but hardly something presaging a career anybody would remotely take seriously.

Eminem has since, though, proved responsible for the funniest not-a-motherfucking-role-model-(or am I?) disclaimers in pop history—stuff about how children shouldn't partake in the album with laces in their shoes, and Slim Shady is not responsible for their actions. "I try to be positive and keep it cool/Shoot up the playground and tell the kids to stay in school." Slim Shady gives Em the luxury of narrative distance: he's constantly also portraying Greek choruses of peanut-gallery inhabitants criticizing Shady ("Stop the tape! The kid needs to be locked up!"), and nobody confuses those voices with Eminem, oddly enough. He laughs at his own audaciousness—all over his new album, he sets up an endlessly neurotic supply of trapdoors within trapdoors, turning-back-on-self techniques frequently more audacious than whatever audaciousness they're escaping him from. Tells us he's really just Marshall Mathers, a regular guy. Dippiest moment is when he suggests (in apparent seriousness) that it's more dangerous to let 12-year-old girls wear makeup than to let them listen to him. But that doesn't stop a couple brats in another song from breaking through his window and stealing his machine guns and trench coats.

Where *The Slim Shady LP* mainly comprised variations on "Glory Glory Hallelujah, Teacher Hit Me With A Ruler," Eminem's new set ranks with rock's most outlandish travails-of-stardom dissertations ever, setting themes that Kurt Cobain never quite pulled off to atmospherics that Tricky never quite pulled off: or you could say it's all variations on "Positively Fourth Street," except when it's variations on "Hey Joe" or "It's Only Rock And Roll." Suicide right on the stage: Would you think the boy's head full of ideas was driving him insane? Eminem's always fantasizing about killing himself—"and I'll try it again/That's why I write songs where I die at the end." And on the new album, the catalyst is mainly his fans. But as with Kid Rock on *Devil Without A Cause*, there's a self-awareness and emotional complexity to *The Marshall Mathers LP* that Eminem previously seemed incapable of. He's "sick and tired of being admired," and he's got no patience for either the cocky Caucasians at rock'n'roll stations or the underground rappers labeling him a sellout 'cause he can't rap about being broke no more. He's fed up with your shit and does not give a fuck what you think, and if you're stupid enough to believe he'd really kill somebody, he says, well, maybe he'll just kill you. He dismisses his own audience as "fucking retards" who, upon purchasing his record, have hereby kissed his

EMINEM LOVES IT WHEN YOU CALL HIM BIG POPPA.
(PHOTO: ANTHONY MANDLER)

ass. His best new song, "Stan," consists of three obsessive letters from a stalking nutcase who thinks Slim Shady is a real person and one uncharacteristically thoughtful Eminem missive back to him advising him to seek counseling. But (à la "In The Air Tonight" by Phil Collins, one of the letters points out) it's too late; the dork's already downed his fifth of vodka and driven into the lake with his girlfriend riding shotgun.

Not to say it's out of his system yet (his rap remake of Bob Seger's beautiful-loser-on-tour tour de force "Turn The Page" is due next year), but Kid Rock actually immortalized in verse the travails of stardom *before* he was a star, in "Only God Knows Why": "Guess that's the price you pay for being some big shot like I am." Easily one of this year's most irresistible radio singles, said backporch ballad comes closer to realizing what made the Allmans' "Ramblin' Man" or Skynyrd's "Am I Losin'" great than Wilco or the Jayhawks, say, ever could. Rhythmatized by the danciest hard-rock drummer (her name is Stefanie Eulinberg, by the way) since Steven Adler on *Appetite For Destruction*, Kid's eight-piece Twisted Brown Trucker Band regularly finds the funk at the heart of Southern rock that has eluded generations of jam bands. His "Welcome To The Jungle"/"Hotel California"/"Hollywood Nights"-style move-to-L.A. fantasy "Cowboy" rocks like Beck would if Beck could rock; his boast about "living on Match-box 20 money" seems even goofier in the wake of Santana hiring smoothie Rob Thomas; his a cappella Fleetwood Mac basslines in "Wasting Time" (*Devil*'s best dance song, now penciled in as its platform-shoed fifth single) are even funnier than the Backstreet Boys' a cappella basslines in "Larger Than Life"; his "Dust In The Wind" reference beats Enrique Iglesias's. And his alcohol fixation—bottles of Beck's, gallons of cognac, 18 Heinekens, Boone's Farm, shots of Jack, and his man Jim Beam, all to wash down the one-hitter puffs and New Orleans jumbo shrimp he loves so much—would stop anybody's 12-step program from keeping them clean.

Gold links and minks and shrimps on the bayou, these are the things he ain't gonna buy you: he's bad, he's nationwide—life's a bitch, but he deals with it. He's slept in dumpsters, got high with kings. He's an easy rider dreaming of Winona and he rides all night 'cause he sleeps all day 'cause he wang-dangs more sweet poontang than k.d. lang (got a whirl-pool, don't even ask, lickin' pussy underwater blowin' bubbles up your ass) 'cause yodelin' in your valley is a delicious break from potatoes. Causes chaos, rocks like Amadeus, finds West Coast kootchie for his Dee-troit playas, who might also be his heroes at the methadone clinic. He'll serve no rhyme before its time, and he's got more time than Morris Day, and he's so greasy you can call him mud, and he can feel a little Hank run-ning through his blood. Ayn Rand couldn't stand him, so she banned him, but he doesn't steal from the rich and give to the poor; he steals from his bitches and gives it to his whores. He's a Capricorn, and Detroit City's where he was born—at night, but not last night, baby. Maybe he's also a sexist pig. But you better not need to be born in Detroit City yourself to detect a ferocious wit—not to mention an enviable IQ—here.

Even his kiss-my-grits "aggression" feels good-natured. Being punk is not his talent: warmth is, and humor, and craft. It took a lot of work to get all the jokes and choruses and piano breaks on *Devil Without A Cause* into the right places, and even more to make them sound so tossed off. Kid's louder Rage Against the Machine-type harangues (despite commendably frequent "Immigrant Song"-like twisted propulsion)—the ones where he shows you some metal—actually tend to be his *least* interesting stuff. For months, in fact, they led me to underrate *Devil* as a whole.

It was in 1996 on *Early Mornin' Stoned Pimp* (which provided *Devil* with two songs and *History Of Rock* with three) that Kid Rock truly forged both his redneck image (on the CD cover: long unwashed hair, tattoo, wifebeater tank top) and his groove: descending symphonic blaxploitation wah-wah slinkin' round the block (three years after his White Room Studios stablemates Big Chief—the Michigan band most responsible for *Motorbooty* magazine—made a fake blaxploitation concept soundtrack), hardboiled barbecue-rib-joint boogie drama, soul-sister backup winding upward, high squealing drop-the-bomb-on-the-white-boy-too nuclear synth sirens, Rufus/Frampton vocoders, "Freddie's Dead" falsettos, shotgun blasts, spy-movie organ. The vocals, chanted as much as rapped, were schooled largely in Too $hort's bootiliciously beeyatch-baiting Oakland pimpitude, but also in badass shit older than old-school: the JBs, Blowfly, Rudy Ray Moore, John Lee Hooker, Swamp Dogg, Parliament's live album, the dozens. So despite his welcome anti-nostalgic claim that "everything that gets old gets overrated/old to me just means outdated," Rock really does have a sense of history—on *Devil*, remember, he based "Bawitdaba"'s MTV-smashing chorus on an old Sugarhill Records mantra, and he threw up his Zodiac sign in "Ain't Nothin' But A Party" like one of the Furious Five (Cowboy, maybe?) at a roller rink.

The History Of Rock, despite being not nearly as funny or fruggable, despite mostly haphazardly handpicking rerecorded renditions of old songs, and despite leaving such fuzzily boinging Beastie-beatboxed scratch-rap goodies as "Live" and "Classic Rock" in the vault, is still a keeper. Previously unheard tracks—for instance, the soaring road anthem "Dark & Grey" (complete with expert Appalachian banjo break)—head in a dirgeful sort of biker-metal direction. "Abortion" (neither manifestly pro- nor anti-) is snarled with the same tough horror-movie Zappa tongue that Monster Magnet used in "See You In Hell," which similarly ascribed a personality to the unborn. In "American Bad Ass," Kid even catalogs his record collection: everything from the Clash to Johnny Cash to Grandmaster Flash. Not to mention, ick, Korn and Limp Bizkit. But "boy bands are trash," he tells us (and on *Saturday Night Live* he dissed Britney Spears for lip-syncing the week before); Eminem's current single, too, words-up Fred Durst and disses your typical teenybop targets. Em's Will Smith and LFO parodies are admittedly entertaining in their grossout way, but both Detroit boys are suckers for clichéd "keep it real" baloney. "Vanilla Ice was fake," Eminem told the *L.A. Times* this year. "3rd Bass was real." Even though "Ice Ice Baby" (and "I Want It That Way" and "Oops! . . . I Did It Again") have more life in them than 3rd Bass or Fred Durst (or Royce Da 5–9 or Robert Bradley) ever will.

Kid also furthers his 1993 *Polyfuse Method* hair-loss obsession in "American Bad Ass" by bragging about not needing Rogaine. Then he boasts about going platinum seven times, though he was more likable when he was bragging about how he was *going* to go platinum—back in *Devil*'s title track, after a truckload of albums that didn't sell diddly outside Detroit. He made like Babe Ruth calling the shot, and wound up not eating crow: no more floozies, just high-class 'hos! But in the rock world, success can be failure, and failure can be accomplishment. This is something he and Eminem instinctively understand. Kid says he doesn't like small cars or real big women, but somehow he always finds himself in 'em; Eminem says he hasn't had a woman in years, his palms are too hairy to hide. These guys brag about being fuck-ups in ways black rappers never would (though, then again, black rappers would never disrespect their own moms the way Eminem does, either). "Fuck high school," Kid proclaims. "Pissed on my diploma." "I never went to college/Ain't got no skills/I got hair on my shoulders and a bottle of pills." "I ain't no rough guy/Ain't no tough guy/ Don't get out much/And don't dress up fly." This beat is for Sonny Bono: in "Black Chic, White Guy," he even concedes that people listening might be laughing at him.

Part of his shtick, of course, is to exaggerate his dumbness, to pretend "my only words of wisdom are Suck My Dick." "You can look for answers, but that ain't fun": it's not a problem you can stop, as Axl would say, it's rock'n'roll. It's not something to *fix*. "Crucified by the critics every day," Kid kvetches, "cause I really don't have that much to say." Yet it's obviously not farfetched to argue that his and Eminem's embrace of "white trash" (starting with the pejorative itself) has much to say about class—not for nothing did Kid cover Creedence Clearwater Revival's anti-entitlement anthem "Fortunate Son" at Woodstock last summer, almost a year before Sleater-Kinney's rendition of the same classic led to claims in the *Times* of their reinventing punk rock. If Kid and Eminem are reinventing anything, it's probably just the idea that, as much as (say) Wu-Tang Clan fans, white kids who hate school need something empowering to call their own, and to blast out car windows while driving through menacing neighborhoods like their parents blasted snakeskin cowboy Ted Nugent and sick mother-fucker Alice Cooper back in *Dazed and Confused* daze. Which is important, y'know? Ain't it funny how the night moves, when you just don't seem to have as much to lose?

Village Voice, 11 July 2000

THE DADDY SHADY SHOW: EMINEM'S FAMILY VALUES

So when you're born a pauper to a pawn on a Christmas Day, and then suddenly your daddy's not a pawn and you're not a pauper anymore, do you get more presents on your birthday, or less, or what? Hard to say, but Hailie Jade Mathers, who turns seven December 25, already has a whole Toys"R"Us worth of stuff, not to mention an indoor pool to swim in (at least that's what her great-grandma, Betty Kresin of St. Joseph, Missouri, who hereby wishes Hailie happy birthday and Hailie's dad Merry Christmas, says), so she'll probably do OK. Word is that her daddy maybe spoils her a little, and why not? "If Hailie wanted a hamburger at one o'clock in the morning, he'd go get it," Great-Grandma Kresin says. "If Hailie wanted to go to a movie, Marshall (her dad, born in St. Joseph himself) goes with her; he doesn't have a nanny do it. They just have to sneak in through the service door." He even has her name and picture tattooed near his right shoulder.

"He lets her play with the neighbors, and has cookouts," Kresin continues. "He loves children. I think if he had his way, he'd have a lot of children. He always wanted to have a family." As a matter of fact, she says, Hailie's dad has also been taking care of *another* little girl lately. "Marshall adopted one of Kim's sister's kids," Kresin explains.

Kimberley Anne Scott is Hailie's mom; her relationship with Marshall has been a little rocky, seeing as how he pulled an unloaded gun on her once when he caught her playing tonsil hockey with some doofus ex–nightclub bouncer. Plus he has this habit of enlisting Hailie to help him record hilarious and obnoxious and highly moving songs where he murders Kim and stuff, but the couple seem to be back together now. "I think it's for Hailie," says Kresin, who won't absolutely confirm that the pair have reunited. Kim's sister's daughter is two years older than Hailie, Kresin explains. So is the adoption legally binding? "She's got his last name," Kresin answers. "What would *you* call it?"

Marshall and Kim and Hailie and Hailie's cousin—plus Marshall's aunt Betty and uncle Jack, who help out with child care—are all said to live together in a great big house in Clinton Township, Michigan, a lovely suburb situated around three branches of the Clinton River. Kid Rock and Uncle Kracker live in town, too, as do about 95,600 other people, according to the 2000 Census. (92.8 percent of them are white; 4.7 percent are black.) Marshall, who is just 30 years old (and contrary to his previous predictions isn't yet in the nursing home pinchin' nurses' asses while jackin' off with Jergens), reportedly paid more than a million and a half for the mansion.

It's part of a gated yuppie community called Manchester Estates; the subdivision is located near Cass Avenue (named for onetime slave-owning Michigan governor Lewis Cass), more or less in between 18 and 19 Mile roads—that is, about 10 miles north of where Marshall grew up. The title song from his new movie goes like this: "I'm free as a bird/And I turn and cross over the median curb/Hit the burbs and all you see is a blur."

He moved from his last house because the city of Sterling Heights wouldn't let him build a 12-foot fence to keep kids from littering his lawn with M&M wrappers. But Manchester Estates is working out better. Marshall's neighbors like him a lot. "I personally have dealt with Marshall. I know Marshall. We live right next door, so we see him all the time," says Cathy Roberts. "He is a wonderful performer, he is a wonderful father, he is an awesome neighbor—you can imagine—and he is a great person."

"He's normal, down-to-earth, and puts his pants on the same way everyone else does," Roberts continues. "A very, very good father."

"Couldn't ask for a better neighbor, that's all," agrees Mary Russo, who has grandkids. "He's been really good around here. Sorry, I know you guys don't want to hear that."

"He's introduced himself to my husband and we see him around the neighborhood trick-or-treating. He always waves when he goes by. They're real friendly," says yet another neighbor. "He plays with his little girl. He never lets her out by herself. He scooters around the block with her on her bike. Now he's teaching her to ride her bike without training wheels."

At Halloween, according to the *Detroit News*, Marshall's lawn was decorated with haystacks, yellow chrysanthemums, and three smiling scarecrows. Neighborhood kids come over and shoot hoops with him.

But at the center of his universe, there's his little girl, who likes watching *The Powerpuff Girls* with her dad and jumping on the trampoline. She started making friends in town not too long ago, thus reportedly squelching any plans the family might have had to move to California. Pretty much every afternoon when Marshall's not on tour, he heads over to the school where Hailie attends first grade and brings her back home. (Word is that Marshall's leasing a Benz, but foreign cars in Metro Detroit are ill-advised, of course. Around town, he opts for Fords.) Though Hailie's dad could no doubt afford to send her to Cranbrook, he makes fun of the famous Bloomfield Hills private school toward the end of his movie; no hypocrite, he sends her to a public elementary—albeit one located at the end of a quiet, secure, secluded little street, where paparazzi or stalkers or anyone else out of the ordinary would stick out.

Though no one will divulge whether he cooks up brownies for the school's bake sale, sources say that Marshall's been known to show up for PTO meetings. The school's website, in fact, boasts that 99 percent of parents attended fall conferences. "Parent involvement is directly associated with student success," the Web page says; parents are asked to read with their children for 15 minutes every evening, and to "also please work on math facts." ("Everywhere I go, a hat, a sweater hood, or mask," Marshall rapped this year. "What about math, how come I wasn't ever good at that?" But sometimes parents learn from their kids.)

"The Elementary Schools Student-Parent Handbook" for Chippewa Valley Schools prohibits weapons and unauthorized medication and "boomboxes," as well as tank tops, halters, and "pants not worn at the waistline." "Verbal threats or assault may result in suspension and expulsion," the handbook informs. "Any behavior or language, which in the judgment of the staff or administration, is considered to be obscene, disrespectful, profane and/or violates community held standards of good taste will be subject to disciplinary action."

"With the right of expression comes the responsibility to use it appropriately," the student-parent handbook concludes. Which might sound familiar to Hailie's dad, given the words concluding this *Hartford Courant* review by Eric Danton: "He raps on *The Eminem Show* about freedom of speech as an inalienable right, but Eminem seems unwilling or unable to accept the accompanying responsibility."

Eminem, of course, is Marshall's alter ego. And sometimes Eminem goes by the name Slim Shady. And sometimes he plays a movie character who shares a name with the protagonist of John Updike novels about suburban midlife crises. In *8 Mile*, when Rabbit's buddies are doing their ceremonial Devil's Night–style arson on the eyesore shell of an abandoned Motor City crack house, he salvages a torn, burnt snapshot of a happy (black) nuclear family, gets all choked up, and says, "When I was little, I used to want to live in a house like this."

When Marshall Bruce Mathers III was tiny, his maternal grandma Betty remembers, "The little boy would give me letters, and say, 'Could you give them to my daddy?'" He never met his dad, who left when he was six months old. And he hates him for it, says so in his songs, and imagines kids who listen to him feeling the same way: "He's a problem child, and what bothers him all comes out/When he talks about his fuckin' dad walkin' out/'Cuz he just hates him so bad that it blocks him out/If he ever saw him again he'd probably knock him out."

Marshall didn't call his grandma on Thanksgiving, she says, but that's OK; she heard he was in the studio till 4 a.m. Besides, she's got 12 other grandchildren, and she didn't hear from all of them, either. "He's an excellent grandson. I'm very proud of him," she says. "You get him offstage, and he's so polite—he says, 'Yes, Grandma, no, Grandma.' And he never talks bad around his little child. He's still kind of shy." Betty's doctor recently asked her for an Eminem T-shirt.

She's met other fans, too. "I had a person who was abused growing up tell me not too long ago, '"Cleanin' Out My Closet," he wrote that for me,'" Kresin says. "He's not just making up words. I can relate to the songs, too. When my grandmother [who raised her] wasn't switching me till I was black and blue, she used to put me in a spooky closet full of mothballs, and lock me in it." She says she's been looking for a ghostwriter to help her finish a book about all this.

Deborah Mathers-Briggs—Betty's daughter and Marshall's estranged mom—was due to be born on what would eventually be Hailie's birthday, Kresin says. Instead, she wound up being born on January 6, just like Kresin's grandmother. "Debbie was born on her birthday, and I feel she was under a curse. My grandmother is shoveling coal now; God doesn't want her, and Satan won't have her."

In 1972, Debbie gave birth to Marshall. And Kresin wound up raising Marshall—who was born the same year as her son, his uncle Ronnie, who first introduced him to rap music—when Debbie couldn't, or wouldn't. "I had a baby and a grandson at the same time," she recalls. "It was like having twins." Sometimes when they were acting up in the backseat of the car, she'd scold them; Marshall would "start chanting, 'If we don't stop, we're gonna have to walk! If we don't stop, we're gonna have to walk!'" When Debbie would take him up to Michigan and leave Ronnie in Missouri, Kresin says, both boys would feel empty and beg to see each other at Christmastime.

Kresin says she thinks Debbie took her "hurt and bitterness" out on Marshall. "When you have verbal and mental instead of abuse that's physical, you can't really see it," she says of the boy's upbringing. "If it's snowing in New York, and your mom tells you again and again that it's 80 degrees out, you'll believe it." In the early '90s, Ronnie committed suicide, and Kresin says Debbie blamed it on Marshall.

"She put my poor little grandson on such a guilt trip," Kresin remembers. "She told him that Ronnie was trying to call and call when Marshall was out rapping. Which isn't true, because I was with Ronnie the entire time! She said, 'I have some bad news for you—Ronnie's dead, and he wouldn't be dead if it weren't for you,'" Kresin says. Marshall wound up taking an overdose of Tylenol on the day of the funeral and couldn't go. (Debbie—who Kresin says is "in hiding, up north"—could not be reached, and Eminem himself was unavailable for comment.)

Deborah Mathers-Briggs, for her part, has insisted she never abused drugs, that she actually spoiled Marshall and never raised her voice to him when he was growing up, and that she sacrificed to support him and his 16-year-old brother Nathan (who still lives with her). She told the BBC that her relationship with Marshall started imploding when she also took in his girlfriend Kim, who was 12 at the time; she said Marshall, who is two years older than Kim, didn't move out until he was 25. A couple years ago, she even sued him for defamation and put out a CD single called "Set the Record Straight." The case was settled before trial by Marshall paying $25,000.

"He was an excellent son," counters Kresin. "He never said anything bad about Debbie, and it's coming out now. It's his way of healing." (Possible examples: lyrics about how he doubted his mom's breast-feeding abilities due to her lack of tits, how his mom took his bike away 'cause he stuck his guinea pig in the microwave, how his mom always taught him the important lesson of "goddammit, you little motherfucker, if you ain't got nothin' nice to say then don't say nothin'," how all bitches is 'hos even his stinkin'-ass mom, and how he never meant to hit her over the head with that shovel.) "I love that boy," Kresin says. "I'll defend him till the day I die."

And if his relationship with Kim is any indication, he seems to be reliving part of his grandma's life. Starting at age 15, Kresin was married to, but repeatedly split up then reunited with, the same man. "He was the boss of me, and he was cruel to me," she says, "And I'd never heard the word divorce." Kim and Marshall were married in St. Joseph in June 1999; Eminem filed divorce paperwork in August 2000; they made up in December 2000; Kim filed for divorce in March 2001; and now they're apparently back together. Last time around, they wound up agreeing on joint legal custody of Hailie after a months-long battle, and a Macomb County court recommended Eminem pay $2,740 a week in child support, $156 a week in health insurance, and 90 percent of health care costs.

"TOO MANY FATHERS are absent from the lives of their children," Al and Tipper Gore write in their feel-good tome *Joined at the Heart: The Transformation of the American Family*, published last month. "We believe that most single mothers do an excellent job of raising their kids, but it must be acknowledged that families are almost always better off with two loving parents present in the home, sharing both the work and the joy." In early editions of *Baby and Child Care*, they say, Dr. Benjamin Spock warned against "trying to force the participation of fathers who get gooseflesh at the very idea of helping to take care of baby." But these are different times, and what constitutes a family is changing. The Gores' book is organized around a bunch of examples—their sole in-depth discussion of fatherhood, in fact, immediately follows their story about the Logan family, a white gay couple named Josh and John raising two adopted sons of color.

Forty pages later, Tipper talks about getting upset at the dirty words on an album her daughter brought home, then co-founding the Parents' Music Resource Center, leading an effort to put warning labels on objectionable albums, and writing a book called *Raising PG Kids in an X-Rated Society*. Which might partially explain why Eminem has a song where he tells Tipper "fuck you."

But in "My Dad's Gone Crazy"—a track prominently featuring Hailie's looped vocal—Eminem concedes, "I don't blame you, I wouldn't let Hailie listen to me neither." And by now, there should be no doubt that he's obsessed with the exact same transformation-of-American-family issues that Al and Tipper are obsessed with. For one thing, he's probably written as much about being a father as any popular songwriter of the past half century.

Who else is there? John Lennon and Stevie Wonder and Bobby Goldsboro and Harry Chapin and that creepy "Butterfly Kisses" guy had a song or two each, maybe. John Prine, Art Alexakis of Everclear? Not out of the question. But Eminem came out of hip-hop, where the prevailing attitude about fatherhood was stated by the great Spoonie Gee, over 20 years ago. "When I got into my house and drove the female wild/The first thing she said is let's have a child," Spoonie postulated in 1980's "Love Rap." "If I had a baby I might go broke/And believe me to a nigga that ain't no joke."

Give or take isolated instances of parental pride from, say, Will Smith (who don't have to cuss to sell records but Hailie's dad does) or Coolio or Out-Kast (but not Big Daddy Kane), that's where rap music remains.

And in 2002, for some reason, pop-icon pops have been especially visible. Ozzy became the latest in a long line of TV fathers-know-worst, right up there with Dan Conner and Homer Simpson and Tony Soprano. Michael Jackson, whose greatest hit ever had him insisting "the kid is not my son," made a spectacle of himself on a Berlin balcony. Liv Tyler's old man played Santa on *Lizzie McGuire*. And a *People* magazine cover even proclaimed, "Jon Bon Jovi: Secrets of a Rock Star Dad."

Hearing about all those other papas, though, sometimes gets Betty Kresin's goat, especially when congresspeople pick on Marshall. "I just think, well, they don't know my grandson. Have you ever seen my grandson take Hailie to the fourth or fifth floor of a hotel room—like, well, I won't mention any names—and dangle her out the window?" she protests. "Did you ever see him bite the head off a bat or a dove?"

In a way, though, the real precedent for Eminem's handy tips on modern parenting might not be a fellow dad at all, but rather his fellow Michigander Diana Ross—the one who wailed in the Supremes' "Love Child" about how she "started my life in an old, cold tenement slum/My father left, he never even married mom. . . . We'll only end up hatin' the child we may be creatin'"; the one who, in "I'm Livin' In Shame," hid her life from her embarrassing mother, "who had a grandson two years old I didn't even show her." Is Detroit the real deal, or what? Though Eminem's mom probably won't pass away making homemade jam.

"Ninety-nine percent of my life I was lied to," he complained in an early lyric. "I just found out my mom does more dope than I do." His songs went on to tell us how he felt like someone else since hanging his original self from the top bunk when he was 12, how his brother and sister never called him until they saw him on TV but now everybody's so proud he's finally allowed to set foot in his girlfriend's house, how he yelled "you fuckin' homo" at his dad's funeral, and how he won't let his daughter attend his *mom's* funeral.

A couple of which stories, one can possibly conclude, might even be true! But mostly, ha ha ha, he's just playin', ladies (and America). You know he loves you. "If my music is literal, and I'm a criminal, how the fuck can I raise a little girl?" he asks. Which isn't to suggest he doesn't have issues. Has anybody mentioned how *oedipal* his first movie is—how he and Kim

Basinger are always falling all over each other, even in bed? Weird. Still. "How the fuck you supposed to grow up when you weren't raised?"

And by that, he doesn't just mean himself—he means his audience, all those little hellions feeling rebellious, embarrassed their parents still listen to Elvis. He never knew he'd get this big, never knew he'd affect these kids, never knew they'd slit their wrists. He's a role model: "Don't you wanna grow up to be just like me/Smack women, eat 'shrooms, and OD?" White America, he could be one of your kids—little Eric looks just like him, and Erica loves his shit. "How many retards will listen to me, and run into the school shooting when they're pissed at the teacher?" He's the one they can look up to better, so tonight he'll write his biggest fan a "fuck you" letter.

He only cusses to upset your mom, he says, so kids hide his tape like bad report cards. Then they get drafted: "All this terror, America demands action/Next thing you know, you've got Uncle Sam's ass askin'/To join our army, or what you do for their navy/You're just a baby, getting recruited at 18." But since he makes "fight music for high school kids," at least the grunts will be well-trained. He'll take seven censored kids from censored Columbine, stand 'em all in line, add an AK-47, a revolver, a nine, and that's a whole school of bullies shot up all at one time. "I was put on earth to annoy the world/And destroy your little four-year-old boy or girl."

Or maybe not. Last year, though nobody much noticed, he decided to donate part of his pay-per-view special's ticket proceeds to Boys and Girls Republic, a suburban Detroit school whose mission is "to help at-risk youth, one at a time, become contributing members of society." The Republic, though, refused Eminem's gesture, opting to avoid endorsement by a performer whose lyrics seem to run counter to the school's sense of nurturing.

Drawing on statistics from the Census Bureau, Center for Disease Control, Department of Justice, and more, an (admittedly probably not entirely unbiased) organization called the Father's Rights and Equality Exchange computed a few years back that kids from fatherless homes are five times more likely to commit suicide, nine times more likely to drop out of high school, 10 times more likely to abuse chemical substances, 14 times more likely to commit rape ("this applies to boys, of course"), 20 times more likely to end up in prison, and 32 times more likely to run away from home. But by all sane measures, current workfare and child-care laws are stacked starkly against single mothers; think of *Bowling for Columbine*'s Flint, Michigan, mom, working two minimum-wage jobs while her six-year-old son finds his uncle's gun and accidentally shoots a classmate. And as Queens College political scientist Andrew Hacker pointed out earlier this month in his *New York Review* essay on the Gores' new book, single-mother families "now account for more than a fifth—21.9 percent—of all households with children, over double the proportion of a generation ago." Even more surprising, Hacker notes, is the increasing number of families in which no *mother* is present. Single-father households "now make up 5.7 percent of all those with children, almost five times the ratio for 1970," Hacker writes. "Fathers now make up 20.1 percent of all single parents." While he's yet to quote any such statistics verbatim, it's impossible to listen to much of Eminem's music and not conclude that he's thought a lot about what they add up to. "It's a sick world we live in these days," he says. Think of little Eric, who's gonna jump off the terrace because the people who should've been watching him apparently aren't parents. Or Em's number one fan, Stan: "I never knew my father neither/He used to always cheat on my mom and beat her/I can relate to what you're saying in your songs/So when I have a shitty day I drift away and put 'em on." Next thing you know he's on the freeway with his pregnant girlfriend in the trunk, and he just drank a fifth of vodka. So Slim Shady suggests counseling, but doesn't get the letter to him fast enough to change Stan's life, which Slim has somehow decided is his responsibility.

Frankly, Eminem seems convinced that the state of a *lot* of America's youth is his responsibility right now. Or his fault. Or something. No wonder his grandma thinks Marshall wants a whole brood of kids. If he's not Michael Jackson (and they sure do seem to share certain neuroses: about how sex is kinda icky, for instance), maybe he's Bing Crosby in *The Bells of St. Mary's*. Except where Bing said if you hate to go to school you may grow up to be a mule, Eminem says he can rap so fuck school, he's too cool. But that's just a minor detail.

And it's not hard to understand why he's so determined to properly raise the one kid who really is his responsibility. "How do I rate myself as a father?" he pondered on WKQI-FM's *Mojo in the Morning* show in Detroit earlier this year. "My Aunt Betty's screaming 10, 10; I don't know, I do the best I can. On a scale of 1 to 10, like a 20." And OK, maybe that doesn't take into account the time he told both Kim and Hailie that he was taking Hailie to Chuck E. Cheese's, then instead took her to the studio to record "'97 Bonnie and Clyde," the goofier of his two Kim-murdering classics. (But hey, have *you* ever hauled rugrats to Chuck E. Cheese's? Flying pizza slices everywhere! It's hell on earth.)

And anyway, that was ages ago; times have changed. "I look at Hailie and I couldn't picture leaving her side/Even if I hated Kim, I grit my teeth and I try to make it work with her at least for Hailie's sake/I maybe made some mistakes, but I'm only human/But I'm man enough to face them today." He loves his daughter more than life itself, he says in the sappy ballad with her name in its title; she's maybe the only lady he adores. But his insecurities could eat him alive. "I'm a responsible father, so not a lot of good I'd be to my daughter, laying in the bottom of the mud/Must be in my blood 'cause I don't know how I do it/All I know is I don't want to follow in the footsteps of my dad, 'cause I hate him so bad/The worst fear that I had was growin' up to be like his fuckin' ass." There's a hellhound on his trail. "I sold my soul to the devil, I'll never get it back," he says in "Say Goodbye Hollywood." "It's fucking crazy, 'cause all I wanted was to give Hailie the life I never had."

And here he is in *8 Mile*'s title track, talking about his little sister from the movie, played by Chloe Greenfield ("Yo, she's the cutest girl in the world, besides Hailie," he told Mojo), who, while working on the film, he invited home for a play date with Hailie so she could know him better: "Ain't no tellin' what really goes on in her little head/Wish I could be the daddy that neither one of us had." He's *always* wishing life could be more normal. In "The Way I Am," he hopes "you freaks" would at least have the decency to leave him alone when he's out feedin' his daughter.

EVER WONDER WHY people are so determined to reach for white picket fences, supposed normalcy, a nuclear family? Well, try growing up without one. My own parents both died when I was a kid (mom: ovarian cancer; dad: suicide), and my stepdad walked out on Christmas Day when I was in high school. Before that, I'd spent over a year at the St. Vincent and Sarah Fisher Home for Children, just up the Farmington Hills road a piece from the Boys and Girls Republic. Got married at 21, had three kids by the time I was Eminem's age, got divorced (very amicably, fortunately) a few years later. Sherman, who's 11, likes Eminem the most. He was psyching himself up for an early-Sunday-morning peewee hockey practice in Bucks County last month, listening to "Lose Yourself" from *8 Mile* ("Lonely roads, God only knows/He's grown farther from home/He's no father/He goes home and barely knows his own daughter"), and said, "Eminem makes being a dad sound *hard!*" So I answered, "Yeah, Sherman, and Eminem only has one kid!" But Sherman was right. And so is Eminem. And Sherman also has a point when he can't figure out why some people get so upset about so many things Eminem says (even on the clean versions that Sherman's allowed to listen to, not that I'm naive enough to think kids can't hear whatever kids want these days), after everybody already heard him tell Stan outright that he's saying that shit just clownin', dawg.

"My little girl knows me even if nobody else does. She knows that, at the end of the day, Daddy is not what he says in his songs," Eminem told *Megastar* last year. "There may be part of me that's like that, or that gets angry and wants to say those things, or maybe wants to actually do those things. But when I'm with my little girl, I'm not like that at all. I'm Daddy to her."

So hopefully the guy who jokes about grown-ups sucking his wee-wee back in preschool wasn't *too* fucked up by his childhood. Thing is, I have a feeling he's not clownin' at all when he criticizes parents who let their 12-year-old daughters wear makeup. For Hailie, that's five years away. He says hip-hop was never a problem in Harlem, only Boston, after it bothered fathers of daughters starting to blossom; what happens when *Hailie* starts to blossom? What happens when she starts to *date*? In two years she'll be in third grade, when a song by her dad says Slim Shady used to sniff glue through a tube and play Rubik's Cube. And in three years she'll be in fourth grade, and by then kids have the Discovery Channel so of course they're gonna know what intercourse is. And in 2012 he'll "be 40 with a 40 on the porch tellin' stories/with a bottle of Jack, two grandkids on my lap/Babysitting for Hailie, while Hailie's out gettin' smashed." At 17, if you haven't already done the math. Happy birthday, Hailie. And papa, don't preach.

Village Voice, 25 December 2002

Additional reporting by Daniel King

SPAGHETTI EASTERN: THE LORDZ OF BROOKLYN

Mr. Kaves, along with his brother ADM the last remaining founder of the Lordz, is not 100 percent Italian. But their cigars and fedoras and mustaches sure made the quintet then known as the Lordz of Brooklyn look like wiseguys on the cover of 1995's *All In The Family*. At first, this was a rap group who rocked; now, they're a rock band who rap. In that debut album's

LORDZ OF BROOKLYN, CONNECTED LIKE SINATRA—IF NOT TECHNICALLY ITALIAN.

statement of purpose, "Saturday Night Fever," they bragged about being "connected like Sinatra" and likened themselves to "Lucky Luciano with a tommy gun," rhyming "Tony Manero" with "Verrazano" as brassknuckle Guess Who riffs punched holes through glass. Picking up where House of Pain's shamrock shenanigans and Cypress Hill's Latin lingo left off, and dunking the blunted greaser-rap in spaghetti sauce and cheap beer, *Family* was one of the best hip-hop albums of the '90s, even if nobody noticed. Yet despite all the ethnic hints otherwise, the siblings' true birth names are Mike and Adam McLeer.

"They're mutts," says Kaves, just like his two big floppy dogs Midnight and Sonny, who were lounging all over his modest Bay Ridge family room on a recent Saturday afternoon. The brothers' dad, a carpet-layer fond of playing the ponies, came from Russian/Irish/English/Scottish stock. But after he left when the boys were eight and nine, they were raised by strong Italian women. Their grandmother, a beautiful photo of whom adorns the cover of the renamed Lordz' surprisingly entertaining new record *The Brooklyn Way*, danced in Bay Ridge wearing black as one of the Quatrone Sisters back in the '40s. Their mom, 18 when Kaves was born, was known around the neighborhood as "Little 92nd Street" and supported the boys on public assistance and waitress tips. "She was like a hippie chick," Kaves says. "Kids would stare at her ass and I'd have to fight them." When Son of Sam was loose, he waited in his bed with a baseball bat, since his mom matched the victims' description.

Baseball figures prominently with this band: "Grab the Louisville out the Coupe De Ville," lead rapper Kaves threatened in *Family*'s "The Bad Racket." Back when his crew was called the Verrazano Boys, he tells me, preppies and gym rats might've found themselves on the action end of the wood; now that *Brooklyn Way* is out on Warner's sub-subsidiary Perfect Game, he says it's like being called back up from the minors. The Lordz have released sporadic tracks while watching label deals collapse over the past decade, but *Brooklyn* feels like their first shot at the gold in forever: contributions from Rancid's Tim Armstrong and Avril/Bowling for Soup teen-punk producer Russ-T Cobb; crunchy hard-pop chords that onetime club DJ and longtime Lordz studio specialist ADM seems to have swiped from Rick Springfield and Bob Seger; canny covers of two classic New York shout anthems . . . add it up, and you've got one of 2006's more effortlessly playable pop-rock albums. And if it's not quite as loaded with mama-mia pizzeria specifics as *Family*, it still packs plenty of blue-collar pride and local color.

A half-block from Kaves's house, Fort Hamilton Parkway runs beneath the Verrazano-Narrows Bridge overpass; in *Saturday Night Fever*, this is where John Travolta's buddies hassled a gay couple. The end of the R line. Even with roaches crawling all over the little apartment where Kaves grew up, Mom always told him to appreciate their million-dollar view of the bridge. "The real mom-and-pop Brooklyn still exists in this neck of the woods," he says. But these blocks are changing—newer immigrants are likely to be Indian and Arab, and there aren't always 40 or 50 kids running around outside like in the old days. So Kaves sometimes feels like a ghost. His CD covers are photo albums full of faded old uncles in Army uniforms and tattered holy cards and rosaries and First Communion snapshots. The new Lordz CD, which comes with a photo album DVD, winds down with an update of Jim Carroll's good-die-young roll call "People Who Died," in which a friend gets whacked by a wiseguy in a Cadillac instead of offed by bikers. Then the closer, "Mama's Boy," remembers Kaves's and Adam's mom, who died along with their baby sister in 1994.

That was the year before *All in the Family* came out. Kaves had just re-turned from the road when he got a phone call telling him they'd been killed by a speeding hit-and-run driver in a white truck. The NYPD inves-tigated, Kaves held press conferences, and the incident made the papers, but the case was never solved. Rudy Giuliani even wound up renaming the intersection of 92nd Street and Fort Hamilton Parkway "Donna and Michele Blanchard Plaza"; a copy of the sign is on Kaves's living-room wall, across from graffiti pieces he's made. "Everything you work for in your life, everything you are, changes at that moment," he says, his voice cracking.

We're sitting at his dining room table. Kaves, born in 1969, is sipping water since panic attacks convinced him to dry out nine years ago; now he calls stogies "my only vice." He's wearing a black-and-white football jersey along with his tan fedora ("Run-D.M.C. called them Godfather hats," he says). He's grilled up some broccoli rabe sausages, and his wife has laid out a generous spread of snacks. Her name, just like his mom's, is Donna; a graphic designer who also runs the band's website, she grew up in a strict middle-class Sicilian family, which is finally starting to accept him. The couple has two boys, ages seven and three, who Kaves showers in affection (little Quinn does an excellent penguin walk); ADM, who comes over later, is a year younger than Kaves and has four kids of his own. By afternoon's end, the backyard deck is full. Beyond the deck, there's a small shack that once housed a diaper business, and now is where the Lordz do their recording, surrounded by Kiss memorabilia, Run-D.M.C. dolls, graffiti-painted ghetto blasters, a giant Krylon spray can, and a *Lords of Flatbush* poster— Kaves's dad insists his old Flatbush gang, Pigtown, inspired Sly Stallone's and Henry Winkler's movie gang.

The Kiss obsession goes back to childhood, when the McLeer brothers dressed up as that band whenever they could. In their new remake of Ace Frehley's glam-disco bleacher-beat smash "New York Groove," Kaves demands that Kiss be put in the Rock and Roll Hall of Fame. He hopes it'll get played at Mets games. But if Kiss were superheroes, it was graffiti that made *him* feel like a superhero. In Bay Ridge in the late '70s, the rocker kids started tagging first, and before long Kaves was making a name for himself by climbing down his fire escape to bomb the BMT line. "As long as we weren't out robbing cars it was OK with our mom," he says; car theft, climbing the Verrazano while stoned, and drag racing his '67 Nova—just like his dad had raced the '55 Chevy that Kaves was conceived in—didn't come till later. A graf arrest eventually led Kaves and ADM to concentrate more on breakdancing—they made it into the Roxy and a Chaka Khan video—and, ultimately, rapping.

Race wasn't an issue, at least till they returned to Bay Ridge, where older teenagers told them not to tag since they weren't in Harlem, and where they watched black kids get chased back to Fort Hamilton Army Base. The late '80s were a time of white violence on young blacks in Howard Beach and Bensonhurst, and nearby Bay Ridge "is looked at as a racist neighborhood," Kaves acknowledges.

So imagine this scene: In 1988, Kaves is helping book a club at 95th and Fourth called Ernie Barry's, and he recommends this new group he'd heard called Public Enemy. He liked them because "Rebel Without A Pause" felt like Led Zeppelin—he wanted hip-hop that was "drink fight and fuck" music, and "this was a rumble." So he gets Professor Griff's number, makes arrangements, and drives a van to Long Island to pick them up, wearing his three-finger ring and Verrazano Boys leather jacket. After a long wait for a drug-delayed Flavor Flav, he brings them back to a club full of impatient rowdies, all white. But the show went on, SIW goons and all.

It was the Public Enemy camp who urged Kaves and Adam to come up with a concept and gave them an opportunity to record demos. Sampling Italian NYC tough guys Dion and the Belmonts, they initially presented themselves as graf-obsessed transit bandits before deciding to play up the Italian stuff and rap about bada-bing bada-boom. When *Family* finally came out, one prescient track was "American Made," an almost countrified choogle about real men drinking Bud and driving domestic and getting drafted and never crossing picket lines; three years later, Kid Rock, who hadn't previously been known for patriotic hick-hopping in a Run-D.M.C. Godfather hat, took a curiously similar sound and shtick to the multiplatinum bank. But the Lordz of Brooklyn, signed to the short-lived Venture imprint of Rick Rubin's American Recordings, saw their debut fall through the cracks. Since then, say the notes to 2003's self-released odds-and-sods disc *Graffiti Roc*, "The rollercoaster ride through the music industry has been a dizzy one full of empty promises." And now they're just the Lordz.

The shortened name, Kaves says, was Perfect Game label coach Howie Abrams's idea; it puts their hard-luck past and unrealized early hype behind them and brands the group as more rock than rap—a rock band with a rhythm section from upstate and a hefty Bay Ridge guitarist known as Tommy Salami and two McLeers on the microphone, a rock band that brings its own PA to the Warped Tour. Basically, Kaves says, "It gives our music a fighting chance." Back in the Brooklyn groove, they might still be contenders.

Village Voice, 23 August 2006

6

Growing up in the suburban Midwest and mostly Michigan, I didn't hear much country music—at least not consciously. Maybe the occasional big-deal crossover, like "King Of The Road" or "Rhinestone Cowboy" or "Convoy," but that's about it. Not sure whether any kids in my high school listened to the genre; maybe certain pickup-trucking shitkickers taking all industrial arts classes did, but I kind of doubt it. What exposure I did have to country wasn't much fun: for four years or so in the mid-'70s—pretty much the duration of my high school career—my stepmother was married to a downriver yokel named Dave Moore who'd occasionally badly drawl "Lovesick Blues" and "Crawdad Song." Sold waste-management pumps for a living, filled our own garage up with presumably outdated auto-repair equipment, and liked working on cars broken down on the driveway. Wanted my brothers and me to do the same, so I have him to thank for teaching me a few indispensable sparkplug-gapping and oilpan-draining and manifold-swapping skills I've never used since. I didn't like the guy, and when he eventually walked out in the middle of a holiday dinner, no love was lost.

I didn't miss the country songs he liked, either, and by the time I started listening to music more intently, if Detroit had a country radio station, I never noticed. The rock stations did work in Charlie Daniels's "The Devil Went Down To Georgia" and "The Legend Of Wooley Swamp" fairly often around 1980, but those probably don't count. My second year in college, though, I transferred to the University of Missouri and met kids who were fans of CDB and Willie and Waylon, which at the time they referred to as "progressive country." My smartass response: "What does that mean, 'Old McDonald Had A Farm?'" But within a couple of years, country was part of the growing patchwork quilt of my own listening, as well—Merle Haggard's *Big City*, Rosanne Cash's *Seven Year Ache*, Joe Ely's *Musta Notta Gotta*

Lotta, and Elvis Costello's all-C&W-covers *Almost Blue* all made a year-end Top 10 list I compiled for my college paper in 1981.

Once I joined the Army, I schooled myself on select strains of mostly very *old* country, sending away for Dock Boggs and Smokey Wood and Milton Brown and Moon Mullican reissues through mail-order services like Roundup and Down Home. Albums by the great '80s neo-traditionalist John Anderson somehow proved widely available at the PX, and I wound up writing about him twice in four years for the *Village Voice*, exactly as many times as I wrote about the Fall. But as for contemporary post-*Urban Cowboy* (and especially '90s and beyond) stuff, I had little use for it at the time: in fact, I recently dug up some mix cassettes I made for myself in the late '80s and early '90s, and one surprise was how *little* country—at least current country—was on them.

Or maybe a more accurate way to map it out is that I paid cursory attention to some country (mostly neo-trad and cowpunk stuff) through most of the '80s, but then *stopped* paying attention for several years, and didn't start obsessing about it above most other genres until I was living in New York, of all places. In 15-albums-per-year discographies in the back of my 1997 book, *The Accidental Evolution of Rock'n'Roll*, only a few country albums make my '80s and '90s lists—Best-Of LPs by John Anderson, Charlie Daniels, John Conlee, Bellamy Brothers, K.T. Oslin, and Garth Brooks (only one of those primarily a '90s act); that's it. When I did review country records, I was just dabbling. My instincts were also, for the most part, your usual pseudo-traditionalist hypocrisy, suspicious of country watering down its down-home purity with pop impulses; this, incidentally, still tends to be the country party line toed by most rock critics.

In the '90s, though, something started to change. I had started watching videos on CMT now and then; there's a piece on that in this section. By mid-decade, country hacks as seemingly inconsequential as Alabama ("Cheap Seats") and Sawyer Brown ("Some Girls Do") and Rick Trevino ("Bobbie Ann Mason") were making better John Cougar singles than John Cougar himself. But the real sea change presumably had something to do with Garth and Shania Twain breaking country sales records by shamelessly incorporating album-oriented stadium rock, teen pop, and hair metal (Shania's husband and producer was Def Leppard *Hysteria* architect Mutt Lange) into their sound; before long, alumni of discarded glammetal bands were shifting their operations to Tennessee. So-called "altcountry" partisans who secretly preferred coffeehouse folk to arena rock (and doubtlessly would've freaked out when Dylan went electric had they been old enough to pay attention) were having none of this; to their ears, blankly recited songwriter demos were keeping alive the authentic tradition of Merle and Loretta, even if Merle and Loretta had never sounded so parched and hookless on their sickliest days. Whatever. By the time the '00s rolled around, country—Nashville country, the kind on the radio—was suddenly my music. As a white mid-American male who turned 40 in 2000, maybe this wasn't so weird—especially when so much country, by now, sounded like the Eagles/Bob Seger/Tom Petty/Cinderella records I'd been gobbling up all along.

It's not for nothing that Kid Rock, probably the '00s superstar whose background has the most in common with my own, wound up having so much success on the country chart; his huge 2008 "All Summer Long" even talked about vacationing in Northern Michigan in the days before the Internet. And it's also not for nothing that the most dead-on portrayal of the disintegrating auto industry—John Rich's John-Anderson-cowritten 2009 hit "Shuttin' Detroit Down"—was a country song. It's not like country lyrics hadn't traveled up to the Great Lakes before—Bobby Bare's "Detroit City" in 1963 and Lefty Frizzell's "Saginaw, Michigan" in 1964 are acknowledged classics. And as my onetime Farmington, Michigan, junior high school classmate RJ Smith put it, in a piece on Stooges alumnus Ron Asheton's final days in what turned out to be the final issue of *Blender* magazine, "Michigan hippies had hillbilly ancestry: Their parents had come from the Deep South in World War II to work in defense plants. They brought a *don't tread on me* rebel vibe." So maybe it was inevitable that, by the late '00s, Ted Nugent would be tea-partying with Toby Keith, and Bob Seger would be landing singles on *Billboard*'s country chart. No wonder I fell in line.

Also didn't hurt that commercial country albums, which as recently as the early '90s rarely shook out as more than a single or two plus filler, kept getting better. Year in and year out through the '00s, the top spot on my Top 10 lists went to Nashville country-rock albums: Montgomery Gentry's *Carrying On* (2001), Brooks & Dunn's *Red Dirt Road* (2003), Big & Rich's *Horse Of A Different Color* (2004), Montgomery Gentry's *Some People Change* (2006), Little Big Town's *A Place To Land* (2007), Jamey Johnson's *That Lonesome Song* (2008). My favorite band (any genre) of the '00s was Montgomery Gentry; my favorite singer of the '00s was Toby Keith—both of whom, in a nightmare conservative decade getting its wars on, flaunted a politics of resentment and lost white male entitlement that felt questionable at best, reprehensible at worst. Which, rightly or wrongly, is part of what made their music more powerful than anybody else's.

"The progression from Grand Funk to BTO to ZZ Top pretty much exemplifies rock's turn toward nihilistic violence," *Circus* magazine editor Frank Rose had written in "Kitsch Me Deadly," a long and somewhat paranoid essay about commercial hard rock in the *Village Voice* in February 1976, mere months before punk exploded. "With BTO and the recession came the realization—among blue-collar rock fans especially—that fun was temporary at best, something which might be enjoyed before adulthood set in; and just as BTO was incapable of seeing music as an escape, their fans seemed incapable of seeing adolescence as one. Cornered animals turn nasty— and so, ZZ Top." Counting the big-city-baiting libertarian backwoods barricade of Hank Williams Jr.'s "A Country Boy Can Survive"—an astoundingly prescient #2-country-charting single from 1981—as a gateway drug, you could say Toby Keith and Montgomery Gentry were how those blue-collar '70s teens *did* wind up carrying their nihilism into adulthood three decades later.

As for rock critics, I'm hardly the only one to come around to commercial country—at least in the form of vengeful gals next door the Dixie Chicks and Miranda Lambert and Taylor Swift, mountain-goateed renegade Jamey Johnson, and nice-guy Obama fan Brad Paisley—in recent years. But most critics still have little use for the genre. One specious platitude you'll hear is that, horror of horrors, country is suddenly being listened to by soccer moms in minivans—even though the U.S. population has been drifting toward suburbia at least since the end of World War II, and country has been incorporating suburban-style pop just as long, well before the countrypolitans and urban cowboys who '70s outlaws and '80s neo-trads reacted against. (How long has it been since, say, farming was the dominant subject of country songs? Was it ever? If anything, Hank Williams Jr.'s dad and Jimmie Rodgers sang more about *moving on to new places*.) "Country music" has been a commercial marketing concept pretty much since the beginning—at least back to early '20s Opry cowboy Vernon Dalhart, the slumming classical singer whose 78 of "Wreck Of The Old 97" is said to have sold 6 million copies.

Another common complaint is that Music City is immune to innovation. And sure, if your definition of "new" is something as prescribed as, oh, "edgy production values," contemporary country might seem more resistant to change than, say, current R&B or hip-hop. And country does of course frequently define itself, aesthetically, by its commitment to tradition—just like certain respected strands of R&B do. But that doesn't mean Nashville's output sounds the same as it did 20 years ago—more distorted metal-leaning guitars and more confessional teenpop-leaning melodies see to that. But that's just the surface anyway. And obviously "new" doesn't always mean "good."

So anyway, this chapter. Some of it—John Cougar Mellencamp working fiddles and dulcimers into his Indiana scarecrow rock, Mexican banda groups topping their tubas and accordions with matching rhinestone cowboy hats—is country only by proxy. Some of it—Mindy McCready singing of thunder in her mind and life catching fire like a box of matches several years before a laundry list of widely reported overdoses, suicide attempts, arrests, and violent relationships pinpointed what she may have meant— seems spookily clairvoyant. Some of it—Big & Rich opening country up to a hip-hopping big pink-and-black tent four years before John Rich, having reined in the duo's sound, turned to dealing jingles plugging "real man with an American plan" John McCain—seems depressingly off the mark. Then there's single white female Chely Wright, who in 2010 came out of the closet and put out the greatest lesbian breakup album in Nashville history. But overall, in the long run, it's hard to imagine that country's productive 'oos won't wind up a strange historical blip—a genre so stubbornly resistant to everyone else's theories of evolution can't stay relevant long, can it? Like white small-tent-in-a-small-town evangelical RepubliCorp males and their middle-class-mauling Mama Grizzly co-conspirators, country represents (or feigns to speak for) an increasingly marginal cultural segment that realizes it's on its last legs but needs somebody else to blame. Know-nothing Flat Earth Society quasi-populism doesn't sound like a viable long-term plan, and country probably lacks the stomach for it anyway. Boxed into a corner of its own making, the genre seems destined to get bulldozed by shifting ideals and demographics, later if not sooner. And maybe that's a good thing. But if it happens, nobody with ears can pretend it didn't put up one badassed last stand.

YIPPIE TIE ONE ON: RURAL ROOTS AND MUDDY BOOTS

Everybody always thinks the good old days were so dadburn "uncomplicated" and "innocent"—what a crock! Richard Nevins's silly liner notes to Yazoo Records' definitive new two-volume roundup-ballad collection, *When I Was A Cowboy: Early Songs Of The American West—Classic Recordings From the 1920's & 30's*, pretend that wrangler life was about polite gents saving the day with heroic deeds, then shrugging it off with "Twarn't nothin', ma'am." The set's songs, on the other hand, tend more often to praise whiskeyed losers cheating at poker and shedding blood.

Nevins compares cowpokes to knights at the round table, no doubt ruffians in their own right. But I still doubt he listened to the lyrics—not unless he believes that, say Snoop Doggy Dogg's words also "depict, simply and convincingly, the freedom, self-sufficiency and courageousness he is famed for, and they embody, too, a rare quality of genuine warmth and innocence that is irresistible."

"Bandit Cole Younger," by Edward L. Crain, has a confessional this- I'll-never-deny tone to it about a highwayman robbing a bank in "Minny-so-te-oh" with knives, revolvers, and the James Brothers. Then Jesse shoots a teller, and the gang wind up wasting all their lives away behind bars; incidentally, according to *The Encyclopedia of American Crime*, Jesse wasn't the Robin Hood he's mythologized as but rather a ruthless murderer who never gave a cent to the poor and slaughtered anyone in his path. But I'm happy to report that that doesn't stop Harry McClintock, in "Jesse James," from calling the guy who killed Jesse a "dirty little coward."

These songs are like reading somebody's diary, or their end-of-day e-mail to a confidant: Today I got invited to a ball, listened to a "colored man" strum his guitar, went outside to cool off, and got caught in the crossfire of a shootout. Yesterday I fell in love with a neighbor girl, but so did my best buddy, so we pulled our knives and I stabbed him. "The Last Longhorn," by Carl Sprague, is about nostalgia in the 1890s for the 1870s, back before the nesters invaded with their dogs and barbed wire. Happens every time: Nesters move in, then there goes the prairie.

At the same time (and here's why they're not "uncomplicated"), these songs feature plenty of Zen-like trancing out at the simplicity of nature, the pureness of air, the balminess of the breeze, the 10-feet-highness of the grass, and the freedom of the zephyr—and if a zephyr ain't free, what is, right? "Cowboy's Dream" by McGinty's Oklahoma Cowboy Band is a cosmic instrumental swirling into oodles of high-lonesome noodling-poodle odelay yodels.

The notes to *When I Was A Cowboy* don't say how to distinguish Rural South cuts from Western ones; more chronological or biographical info would've been helpful. Has some great names though: Buell Kazee, Rowdy Wright, Jack Webb (as stiff as the *Dragnet* guy), Patt Patterson and His Champion Rep Riders. The most famous songs are "Home On The Range" and "Get Along Little Dogies," both on the far-preferable Volume Two. "Seldom is heard a discouraging word, and the skies are not cloudy all day"—ambiguous enough for you? Like, does that mean the skies are only cloudy *part* of the day, or *never* cloudy? Or maybe *neither*, since America *has* no places "where the deer and the antelope play," since antelopes are only native to Africa (unless they mean pronghorns). Likewise, unlike "Marie Provost" by Nick Lowe, "Get Along Little Dogies" is not about a long little dachshund, but rather about a herd of cows who, the singer hopes, experience more misfortune than he does. But then he says he wants to marry a widow with six kids—hey, a ranch house full of stepkids sure sounds like misfortune to *me!*

The compilation's women singers—Billie Maxwell, Lois Dexter—sound like widows with six kids themselves, *old* ones. Lots of this is aged music sung in an aged *voice*, not an uncommon trait in so-called old-timey '20s/'30s recordings. Which might mean our present-day concepts of "old-people voices" are all screwed up. I'd guess that most of these singers were probably in *their* 20s and 30s at the time—i.e., not old at all—but if they sound "old" to us anyway, maybe what we're hearing is simply how rural (as opposed to urban Crosby/Astaire/Garland-type) people *talked* back then, regardless of their age. My wife says that theory's absurd, and what I'm really hearing are just raggedy folk-music-style voices made even raggedier by primitive recording technology. Maybe we should take a poll.

With the more ethereally lo-fi-muffled and quiet numbers, especially singsongy ones that drone on forever without changing pitch, I tend to lose patience before I can figure their plots out. I can only put up so long with quivery women whimpering about shady valleys. "Long Side Of The

Santa Fe Trail," by Jules Allen, has something to do with towheaded gals with water kegs tied to their tails, riding as if carrying mail. Good song, but it begs for a *band* treatment, or at least background singing—it's way too parched, like watching a documentary. Personally, I'd rather barn-dance: to the Crockett Family going 'round the outside and do-si-do-ing their partners in "Buffalo Gals" 50 years before Malcolm McLaren; to Lonesome Luke and His Farm Hands razorbacking through "Wild Hog In The Woods"; to Jules Allen's "The Gal I Left Behind Me" bridging the gap between Virginia reels and Western swing.

"Sam Bass," by Harry McClintock, sounds almost Irish, like something the Pogues might cover. Appears to chronicle an alcoholic bank robber getting robbed and shot as the culprit hides in the bushes, thus creating a bustle in the hedgerow, you might think, except now I'm told bustles in hedgerows are actually *menstrual*. But don't be alarmed, now—it's just a spring clean for the May Queen. And speaking of queens, in "My Love Is A Cowboy," Powder River Jack sings as a woman, even claiming, "He tipped me a wink as he did gaily go/For he wished me to look at his bucking bronco"—isn't it weird how, in folk singing, this sort of move was never thought of as cross-dressing? Likewise, when in "Tom Sherman's Ballroom" Dick Devall croons, "I'm a gay cowboy, I know I've done wrong," he too sings as someone in love with a man.

ON *BALLADS AND BREAKDOWNS*, the banjo-and-fiddle-syncopated, Virginia-oriented second volume of Rounder Records' new field-recording collection *Southern Journey: The Alan Lomax Collection*, recorded by musicologist Lomax on a Dixie research trip between August and October 1959, a woman of unstated sexual proclivities named Ruby Vass drawls both a ditty about how single girls are always happier than married girls and a ditty where she strolls along with another lady then stabs her to death and throws the corpse in the Ohio River because they can't get married. The CD also has a remake of the Carolina Tarheels' great '20s shoemaker-trampled-by-wheels-of-industry protest "Peg an' Awl," a play-by-play depiction of a "Fox Chase" complete with noisily barked hound and hunter effects, and an acoustic power-trio (banjo/guitar/fiddle) rendition of "John Henry" featuring a 76-year-old banjoist but not featuring any words about anybody dying with a hammer in his hand. Not to mention a lovely lullaby where a woman promises that after nap time her baby will be able to eat cake and ride "a whole heap of little horses," suggesting perhaps that the infant resembles a whole heap of little jockeys.

The songs on the Lomax collection are occasionally a cappella, and almost always sung by elderly amateurs with long memories—not even the folk revival, set into high gear a year earlier when the Kingston Trio broke the bank with "Tom Dooley," qualified these often century-old-or-older songs as popular music in 1959. But homicide buffs still won't hear much history-book detachment on *Southern Journey*'s fifth volume, invitingly called *Bad Man Ballads*. *When I Was A Cowboy* oldies like "Cole Younger" and "Jesse James" make later appearances here; the fugitive yarn "Lazarus" is performed in three distinct versions, including one by a gospel quartet. In "Early in the Mornin'," a gang of penitentiary inmates in Mississippi even seem to be using their balls and chains as percussion.

"Hangman Tree" is related in obvious ways to Led Zeppelin's "Gallows Pole" (though probably not to Soundgarden's "Pretty Noose"); "The Lawson Murder" spells out the precise order all members of a North Carolina family were offed by the man of the house one Christmas morning. Andrew Kye's liner notes theorize that these songs' lyrics often treated cold-blooded destroyers-of-passersby as heroes symbolic of the "libertarian, anarchic spirit of the frontier"; his quote from Alan Lomax could easily be a description of gangsta rap or *Grosse Pointe Blank* fans seeking vicarious thrills: "Those of us who do not indulge in violence certainly enjoy hearing about such behavior and its consequences."

The most rocking track on *Bad Man Ballads* is Hobart Smith's depiction in "Railroad Bill" of a guy who rolls $10 bills into cigars and murders his mom and dad. Its sound, so energetic and sprightly it's almost comical, is in the tradition of J.D. Farley singing on Yazoo's cowboy collection about how Billy takes J.D.'s saddle, Johnny takes J.D.'s spurs, somebody else takes J.D.'s pistol, they all help dig J.D.'s grave, and he uses his knapsack as a pillow. Listening to a couple of concurrently recorded retrospectives two years ago (*White Country Blues: A Lighter Shade Of Blue* on Columbia/Legacy, *Mister Charlie's Blues* on Yazoo), I learned that scores of white banjo-novelty hayseeds buoyantly imitated Jimmie Rodgers's fusion of blues with Appalachian yodels (and maybe a bit of vaudeville shtick) in 1929 the way white hayseeds would later mimic the Rolling Stones in 1966 or Nirvana in 1995; the result was far less leaden than "authentic" blues of the day.

On Columbia/Legacy's recent Gene Autry reissue *Blues Singer 1929–1931: "Booger Rooger Saturday Nite!,"* Gene takes 10 writing credits and Jimmie Rodgers is granted six. Gene himself started recording only a couple of days before Black Friday kicked off the Great Depression, but the rhythmic

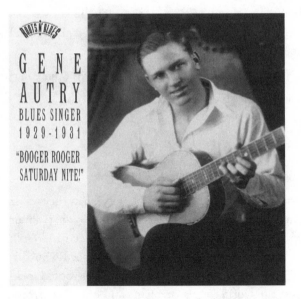

GENE AUTRY: *BLUES SINGER 1929–1931: "BOOGER ROOGER SATURDAY NITE!"* (COLUMBIA/LEGACY, 1996)

frolic he gets out of his guitar proves he's not considering swan-diving out of any 15th-story windows just yet. In one song, he gets a job sweeping hotel floors, he talks to a skirt, and she doesn't see his dustpan but he tells her all the dirt. In "Do Right Daddy Blues," he turns bawdy, drooling, "If you feela mah leg you gotta ride me high"; eventually its lines about not having to work because of names inked onto shirttails were stolen by rockabilly progenitor Harmonica Frank in 1951's "Rockin' Chair Daddy."

Like everybody else in the late '20s, Gene does "Frankie and Johnny," the "Hey Joe" or "Macarena" of its era; his version is remarkably jubilant, considering the words are about a woman yanking a .44 out of her kimono and shooting her sweetheart through a saloon's hardwood door for screwing around with Nellie Bly. "Stay Away From My Chicken House" has Gene making cow, horse, pig, and hen noises, and threatening to slice up trespassers with a razorblade. Yet by 1932 he was selling out to goody-goody non-blues whitebread that made him the biggest country crooner on Earth, and by 1935 he was single-handedly helping Hollywood convince suckers that cowboys really were "twarnt nothin', ma'am" kinds of guys.

In 1948, Gene Autry sold 9 million copies of "Rudolph the Red-Nosed Reindeer," but on *Blues Singer*, three of his first six songs have "jail" in the title. Like his cow-punching contemporaries, he sings like he knows he's heading there but plans to live it up on the way: rambling, gambling, and fighting the law till the law wins.

L.A. Weekly, 6 June 1997

JOHN COUGAR MELLENCAMP: LIFE GOES ON

Driving Indiana-31 from South Bend down toward Louisville in the winter of '85–'86 with hits from John Mellencamp's *Scarecrow* on the radio is about the closest I've ever come to a spiritual experience listening to rock'n'roll: this was the lonely, indignant, overboiling sound of a hayseed who'd finally found his voice. The world's hottest old-fashioned blues-rooted rockers barrelhoused behind the world's most arrogant and effortless front-journeyman, the latter bemoaning blood and ghosts and rattlin' old bones he knew were there because he'd seen 'em with his own two eyes, because they'd betrayed people he loved. I'm convinced that nobody currently making music, platinum or otherwise, has done more than Mellencamp to earn the audience's respect—nobody's grown so drastically with every record. We're talking about someone who had to work his way back from selling his identity and damn near his manhood to David Bowie's manager Tony DeFries, someone who was positive that nothin' matters and what if it did until he learned that you've gotta stand for something or you're gonna fall for anything, someone who in an age of fraudulent everyman-rock had the humility and nerve to bypass Bruce-style lookit-me-my-art-will-live-forever poetic/operatic mythologizing for the real deal. Nobody else demands so much out of himself.

So it's hard to get too ticked off by the relative wet-noodle status of *Lonesome Jubilee*, the first of the songster's six post-DeFries LPs that hasn't made complete mincemeat of its predecessor. It's good-humored, unvarnished, bound to be the least tight-ass music all over FM this fall. And with its fluid Carter-Family-meets-Booker-T ('mid the green onions of Virginia?) sound and an astounding evolving-feminist undertow (*three* numbers championing divorced women) thoroughly supplanting the macho hey-hit-the-highway of old, it's sure no rerun. The dulcimers and dobros may induce some pundit to peg the disc as John's folk-move, a more rhythmic and less pessimistic *Nebraska*, but what it's mostly about is

JOHN MELLENCAMP,
AFTER THE THRILL OF
LIVING HAS GONE.
(PHOTO: KURT MARCUS)

dealing with maturity, so really it's his *Night Moves*—in fact, "Hot Dogs
And Hamburgers" opens with a riff sped-up from that (last decent) Seger
collection's great title track (both songs reminisce about girls in the back
seat), and the line "Seventeen has turned thirty-five" in "Cherry Bomb"
is apparently an adaptation of "Sweet sixteen's turned thirty-one," from
"Rock And Roll Never Forgets." In the album's best lyrics, Mellencamp discusses what he hinted at in "Jack And Diane" and "Pink Houses": hopes
denied, expectations thwarted, impending mundanity, "days burnt up like
paper in fire."

He's always been accused by certain counterculture totalitarians of having mixed-up politics, but then so do I, and while *Jubilee* has some trite
and redundant (if well-intentioned) Age-of-Reagan parts, something like
the verses of "Hard Times For An Honest Man" (a guy takes his frustra-
tions out on his family, a wife loves a husband who "lies like a dog") strikes
me as a pretty empathetic observation of the human behavior all this financial inequity births. The songwriting's starting to display disturbing
inclinations toward creative-writing crap, but unlike all the other rootsol-
ogy out there it's never sappy, and of course it doesn't hurt that these ret-
ros can actually hold down a beat. Kenny Aronoff's the biz's last dangerous

hard-rock skinsman, slam-bam solid all over the kit (with each drum re-corded through its own mike), clean, muscular, no let-up, not just taking a pulse. It's too bad *Lonesome Jubilee*'s Cajun/Appalachian/mbaqanga bias never really lets him kick it in, but not even the intentionally lightweight (Prince-inspired?) beach-pop side-closers qualify as true wimp-out. Just wish the singer didn't believe he needs some soul-sister wailing behind him to symbolize an "authenticity" he's already got.

Mellencamp's not stagnating. But anxious to break free of his small-town pigeonhole, he's aiming higher, struggling for universality and thereby leaving his pals back in Seymour to fend for themselves. So he's missing targets—"Down And Out In Paradise" is bombastic populism-by-rote, "We Are The People," a laughably vague electro-acoustic quasi-anthem with a chorus as blowhard as Kansas or U2. Too much of this is "significance"-for-the-sake-of, like the man's still fighting authority but he's forgotten that rebelling without a cause can be the most fun anarchy of all. Maybe the John Cougar who broke the bank with *American Fool* in 1982 was a Dionysian cartoon, drooling over chili dogs outside the Tastee Freez and sex in the shade, but this new guy's starting to sound like his Apollonian obverse. And that's worse—chip knocked off his shoulder, bad attitude down the drain, he's growing up and beginning to take himself seriously but he's not allowing himself time to go wild or get horny just for the heck of it, which with JCM of all people is a total drag. Nothing on *Jubilee* is anywhere near as jubilant as, say, "Rumbleseat"; worse, nothing tells us anything new about Mellencamp the human being, except he's get-ting old. The little bastard needs to get a grip: you can only mature so much and still call yourself a rock'n'roller, or after awhile you just start fading away. Go ask Bob Seger.

Village Voice, 15 September 1987

K.T. OSLIN: *GREATEST HITS:* *SONGS FROM AN AGING SEX BOMB*

K.T. Oslin sings like Janis Joplin and Dusty Springfield (my wife says Phoebe Snow), but who she mostly reminds me of is two people who've never made a record—Tanya, an old army buddy of my wife's and mine who was a lieutenant in Germany when I was, and Nancy, my stepsister.

Both divorced young (one with three kids already), both waited until they were grown up to get college degrees, both have to watch their weight, but not too much. One got married in her teens; the other was the only girl in a family of boys. Both are baby boomers, and I miss seeing them around.

Like Reba McEntire, K.T. Oslin is more suburban than rural—in the *Boston Phoenix* once, James Hunter imagined her "behind the steering wheel of a station wagon in Atlanta, though not necessarily enroute to Kroger's." But K.T. is more ribald than Reba, prouder of the bras and bridges and dinners and candles-at-both-ends she used to burn. She's the musical equivalent of Tim Allen's wife on *Home Improvement*. Her most Tanya-and-Nancy-like songs are "Younger Men" (which predated Dolly Parton's bun-ogling theme in "Romeo" by six years) and "'80s Ladies" (where a "borderline fool" who crosses the border every chance she gets winds up with a daughter who looks just like Mom used to, just like Nancy's kid Jennifer). "'80s Ladies" is on *Songs From An Aging Sex Bomb* (great title!); "Younger Men" (a 1987 single) isn't. Too bad, because it could've replaced "I'll Come Back," the only merely ordinary or gooey Nashville-type throwaway here.

Outside of maybe the Bellamy Brothers' 1982 *Greatest Hits*, I think this is my favorite "country" album of the last 15 years. It's loaded with risky sounds: groove-stretching Europop synth sheens, Crystals da-doo-ron-rons in a verse about how fooling around was fun before it got dangerous, Lou Reed dooh-d'doohs in a verse about making out under a porch light-bulb, jump-rope rhymes about what '50s girls want to be when they grow up, basslines from "Spiders And Snakes" and the Police and Hall and Oates's "Maneater" (a good joke, since said hook shows up in one of three songs that talk about *dieting*, a world record!).

K.T. probably watches too much *Oprah* and reads too much *Cosmopolitan*, and I wish she'd always growl as tough as she does in "Do Ya." But she can get hoarse and high and saucy (in "Younger Men" she did *all three*—OK, I'll stop complaining), and I love her songs about picking up a boy in her new car and procrastinating 'til next week about giving up bad habits. Nobody roars the word "Mama" (as in "stone rock'n'rollers in the '60s, Mama") like K.T. does, and all the marriages she sings about might be big mistakes. I have a feeling Tanya and Nancy could relate.

Eye Weekly, **23 September 1993**

THE TEMPTATIONS OF MINDY MCCREADY

Here's Mindy McCready fretting about her fan mail: "The self-esteem level of the little girls is so low. They're terribly insecure about what they look like and how they feel about themselves. I'm sure it's because of the images they see constantly in the media that they have to compare themselves with." But now, here's how the country cutie goes about reviving Ophelia on her new CD sleeve: spread eagles, kissyfaces, lip-parted gazes of come-hither ecstasy. Like nobody in Nashville this side of Shania Twain, Mindy is clearly using her body to sell music. *If I Don't Stay The Night* is billed as "country music's first enhanced CD with multimedia material and AOL software," and there's even a promo version where the cover unfolds like a kid's 3-D pop-up book centerpieced by an enticing paper doll of Mindy and her suntanned cleavage playing lifeguard on the dock of the bay. Does she look like a motherfucking role model? Did she shave her pubes for this?

The paradox is that *If I Don't Stay The Night* is mainly a concept album about *not* having sex. McCready claims "What If I Do" "is worded just as if I were talking to one of my brothers. When they bring home a girl, I say, 'Do you like my brother?' And if she says yes, I say, 'Then don't have sex with him.'" In "What If I Do," Mindy's on a movie date with some horny hunk, walking the vocal plank between sincerity and theatricality, vamping sarcastically on the asides—emphatic "No!"s and racy "Yes!—it's a test!!"s.

She sings about temptation a *lot*; her first hit, the title track from her platinum 1996 debut *Ten Thousand Angels*, even quoted the Lord's Prayer about leading her not into it. Born into a Pentecostal Florida family 22 years ago, she graduated high school at 16 and has since had her navel pierced and tonsils removed; as Rob Sheffield has pointed out, Mindy's "young enough to have been named after Pam Dawber." Her fiancé is Dean Cain of *Lois and Clark* fame—or, as her grandma told my doctor neighbor Diane who was doing a hospital rotation in Georgia last year, "She's gonna marry Superman!" But as a child, Mindy quarterbacked in Little League. Her gender-flipped "Guys Do It All The Time" was a No. 1 single, and now she says stuff like, "I am so much like a man in some ways, but in others, so much like a woman." For her new media image I'd suggest a "soft butch" look (as the *Philadelphia Gay News* calls it).

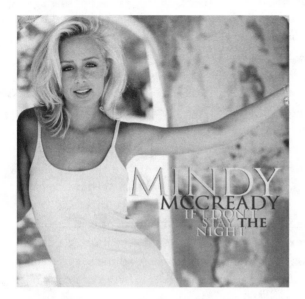

MINDY MCCREADY: *IF I DON'T STAY THE NIGHT* (BNA, 1997)

The suburban-woman-warbled songs that've dominated my country listening these past few years—Faith Hill's "Wild One," Deana Carter's "Strawberry Wine," Trisha Yearwood's "Walkaway Joe," Helen Darling's "Jenny Come Back"—almost all revolve around the temptations of impatient teenage girls. But give or take "Walkaway Joe" (gas station robbery!), none of these songs' subjects quite spins out of control. McCready goes further, somehow—her best music does more than just skim the shiny surface of an internal moral tug-of-war. In "Oh Romeo," she plays a "romantic depressive" contemplating suicide. In "Cross Against The Moon," "a restless girl in a pink bedroom" festooned with Marilyn Monroe posters packs up her Bible for Hollywood, where "nothing's black or white/nothing's wrong or right." She's stuck on a scary tightrope between relativist humanism and fundamentalist Christianity, brimstone burning in her ears.

So she sings like she's tossing hair all over the place: driven, ravished, marinated in the vinegar of Stevie Nicks. Covering "Long, Long Time," one of the saddest songs on earth, all the extra syllables and serifs and cracks in her voice convince me *she's* about to crack; more than Linda Ronstadt, who too obviously emphasized the melody's indelible prettiness, McCready sounds unprissy, full-bodied. She rides a wider range. And producer David Malloy immerses her in an icy and desolate sound that's been missing from country music since isolated early '80s cheated-on songs like "Ashes To Ashes" by blind tomboy Terri Gibbs and "She Can't Say That Anymore" by moonlighting mortician John Conlee—cuts which seemed to pick up their Gothic sense of sparseness and echo, suspense and void and unanswered questions, from European disco. Spooky harmony backdrops and hints of Spanish guitar and dusky wind effects help McCready inhabit mentally unbalanced terrain that '90s C&W (including No Depression nostalgia) is almost always scared of.

Here she is caught in a minor-key spaghetti-western-skirting mood on *If I Don't Stay The Night's* title cut: "Can't you hear the storm outside/Well it's nothing like the thunder in my mind." And you *can* hear it. Emotionally, what this CD most reminds me of is dance-pop records from a decade ago by girlies like Pajama Party and Stacey Q where all the songs seemed accidentally to wind up worried about falling over the edge of 17 into heroin abuse or bi-curious personal ads. Maybe it's inevitable when you try too hard to be an angel. "Life is like a box of matches/sometimes the whole thing catches."

Village Voice, 17 March 1998

CMT

Women with short new wave haircuts and skinny guys with mustaches are far more common on Country Music Television than on MTV or VH-1. I usually prefer the women. My favorite haircuts are the ones on Lorrie Morgan, who barely smiles at all in her torchy "Something In Red" video, and Tinnita, who has no last name like one of those Madonna imitators from a couple years back and dresses and moves around like one too, especially in the video where she plays a waitress in a greasy-spoon joint. What these people have to do with country music is anyone's guess (Lorrie's music is all keyboards and strings, and I've yet to find a copy of Tinnita's record or see her listed on *Billboard*'s country chart), and that's what I like about them.

Every hour or so, CMT runs an ad with hip young adults explaining why they watch country videos. None are hillbillies, and maybe three of every four are female, a good gender for saying how cute Clint Black and Dwight

Yoakam are. They mostly appear to be urban apartment-dwellers in their mid-'20s, with college educations and money to spend on new clothes. One talks about passing through an "alternative stage, punk rock stage"; another about being the eccentric kid who liked country at her high school. A 30-ish black woman smiles, "*Me*? Watch CMT? All the time!" A freckled lady with a slight drawl (and short hair) explains "I like country music videos 'cause they make sense."

Travis Tritt whines about Billy Ray Cyrus acting like a big star before he really was one in his wild "Achy Breaky Heart" clip (where a big crowd of women watches him shake that healthy butt), but Travis isn't really the Vietnam vet he plays in his "Anymore" video, is he? I don't care how "honest" videos are. The most honest CMT videos are by interchangeable hat (or hat-like) acts named Ricky or Rodney or Vince; they all use drab earthtone colors and too many simple-man-standing-still performance shots. And they all seem perfunctory, just fulfilling an obligation y'all old boys gotta put up with from now on.

Frankly, my favorite C&W videos usually *don't* make sense. Since nobody's quite figured out yet how to sell hick music to the sophisticated city-slicker demographic Nashville so desperately wants, C&W videos are a hypeform still in the market-research stage. My wife wonders how come city slickers in suits always wind up being *bad* guys on CMT, taking over downhome establishments. But she says it's good that CMT body shapes often tend to be less than perfect. And some vids even have black people in them!

Tapeworm, 1992

BANDA, SÍ, POR QUÉ NO?

• In Banda Kampesino's "Pancho El Borracho" video, a man with hairy legs and a beer gut puts on lipstick, pointy boots, a red beret and a revealing polka-dot halter top.

Twelve musicians are all smiling and laughing beneath their facial hair, and all wearing matching blue cowboy outfits and hats, which they swat at the cross-dressing guy. He acts like he's their groupie, which seems to amuse more than annoy them. He walks by a dead dog, then reaches down and fondles it—what a pervert! He keeps sneaking Spanish words I can't decipher into the song, in a stereotypically swishy lisp. A rooster cock-a-doodle-doos, and the musicians all dance real fast. Two extremely agile gents, both holding trumpets, hook each other's legs at the knees, then spin around in circles.

• Banda Pachuco's "Te Quiero A Ti" is more serious. Everybody's in a gym, apparently in Brooklyn. A Muhammad Ali poster is plastered on the outside wall, and inside there's plenty of male bonding. In comes an actress who's supposed to look overweight, though really she just seems to be wearing too many layers of clothes.

Sweaty jerks make fun of her, bullfight brass sounds, she works out on the Exercycle. After she's taken 30 days to thin her thighs, two young bucks suddenly start winking at her, vying to be her boyfriend. They break into a locker-room brawl, so a sleazy promoter decides to stage a boxing match. The skinnier buck wins—a knockout! But the girl's a knockout herself now too, and the buck who lost the fight winds up winning her over.

• Banda Arkangel R-15 actually play an accordion in "La Que Me Hace Llorar," a rarity in banda-land. A busty red-haired Latina emerges from a pickup truck with a handsomely svelte singer, and appears exasperated by his female fans. She writes a letter dumping him, which he crumples upon receiving. The music is ignorable romantic mush—more tejano than banda, seems to me. The singer plays dominoes in a saloon, hears a tune on the jukebox reminding him of old black-and-white-filmed days when he and his sweetie were wining and dining: please mister please, don't play Arkangel R-15, it was our song, it was her song, but it's over. He chugs tequila, his bandmates all shaking their heads at him. But she comes back.

DEFINING OR ANALYZING THIS STUFF MIGHT limit it, so I won't, except to say that banda basically happens when you get a dozen Mexican (or Mexican-American) guys, preferably a few of them pushing middle age at least, to wear glitzed-out color-coordinated ranch-hand costumes and play double-time polkas where they can swing saxophones around. This might be the most open-ended dance music of the mid-'90s, and it's done on the cheap: my cassette copy of Banda Vallarta Show's *La Fiesta*, purchased at a flea market in Northeast Philadelphia, has Xerox-blurred lettering and artwork, plus song titles on the wrong sides, so I assume it's a bootleg. Likewise, Banda Movil's "Cuando Los Hombres Lloran" video clip looks like a fuzzily produced local-UHF-outlet commercial, maybe even a home movie. After lo-fi park and barbecue scenes, it mysteriously sentences us to prison: some inmate banging bars with a tin cup.

"Bandas wreck every song there is!" my *roc en español* buddy Yvonne scoffs when I confess to her I'm hooked. Electro Banda redo "I Will Always Love You." Banda Pistoleros do "El Pistolero," a schizophrenic Western-movie/square-dance hodgepodge reminiscent of Carlos Malcolm & His Afro-Jamaican Rhythm's 1965 "Bonanza Ska" (recently reissued on Rhino Records); in fact, banda's tempo has the same relationship to conjunto and norteño that ska has to reggae and rocksteady, except that where the Jamaican genres slowed down over time, the Mex-border ones sped up. When Banda Zeta do "Presumidas S.A." on the Telemundo or Univision network, they even crisscross feet ska-style while dancing—a big switch from the stark horror-noise and Gothic death-metal depictions of hell opening up their video.

On *Ghostbusters*, the best banda album I've ever heard, Banda Bahia bop out five ridiculously diverse cover versions: "Ghostbusters" by Ray Parker Jr. (so loony out of context, especially with "Who you gonna call?" quizzes in Spanish, that I can't help but eat up its cheese); "Mambo No. 8" by '50s Cuban crossover king Perez Prado (blasting periodic missed horn notes like a drunken funk combo); "My Way" by Frank Sinatra (crooned, not Sid Vicioused); "El Matador" by '90s Argentine rockers Los Fabulosos Cadillacs (funeral-wake horns, tropical timbales, reggae-toasted shakedowns); Pat Boone's borderline-racist 1962 novelty hit "Speedy Gonzales" (with doo-wop cartoon mouse squeaking and a rockabilly guitar break halfway through, landing it somewhere between Mexican preschool-TV clown Cepillin's rendition on his 1980 *Rock Infantil* album and alleged Walt Disney peyote pal Cri-Cri's '30s cartoon cowboy-mouse jig "Raton Vaquero"). On an earlier CD, Banda Bahia even included a medley of melodies by easy-listening legend Ray Conniff (of *Dr. Zhivago* theme fame) where they spelled his name wrong ("Popurri A Ray Connif").

Outside of remakes, my favorite *Ghostbusters* tracks are tongue-twistedly recited speed raps: "El Sinverguenza" and "Charanga Changuirongo." "Charanga Casteña" by Banda Vallarta Show (where the singer quacks like a duck, then stumbles over his shoelaces a few times) sounds somewhat similar, so a new subgenre may well be in the making here. But "El Chango y El Toro" by Banda MR-7 raps charangalike too, with totally over-the-top auctioneer dexterity and stamina; onstage under a disco mirror ball in the video, their choreography involves lots of nimble one-step-up-two-steps-back moves.

Banda MR-7 wear matching black costumes; Banda Zeta's and Banda Vallarta Show's are both blue—I wonder if they take a vote, or what. Banda

Machos wear brown-and-white fringed cowboy suits with "male" circle-with-arrow-emerging-from-it symbols on the sleeves, but in one video they have on long black coats instead—home and away uniforms, I guess. On their current *Mi Chica Ideal . . . Arrre Machos!!!*, voices float the Machos' team slogan—"harrrrrrrrre machos!!"—high above the rodeo-roundup trotting, and "Jinetéando" communicates a manly Moorish mournfulness. Eleven Machos men have mustaches and only one doesn't, whereas in Vallarta Show, seven guys have them and five don't—this seems significant, somehow. The "La Secretaria" video has all 12 Machos trying to peek under the skirt of a flirtful female secretary who disturbingly appears to enjoy being sexually harassed by her Judge Ito look-alike office manager. He has a mustache as well.

THIS IS FAMILY ENTERTAINMENT, unjaded and thus unconfined, with a feel closer to a neighborhood talent show than a rock concert—puppets, juggling exhibitions, cockfights for the kiddies if need be. Banda Vallarta Show want to *be* a show, and they announce themselves as such at the beginning of their *La Fiesta* tape. Then they end numbers with circus music, decorating the midsections with dancehall toasts, primitively plucked twixt slack-key and slide-guitar parts, vibey little keyboard *ploinks*, animalistic caballero "ye ye ye" yodels and high-lonesome "little-old-lady-who" yodels too. Drums rumble around, the oompah-pah beer-barrel beat turns into waltzes, and even their slower sappiness has an equestrian gallop to it. Sometimes I wonder how they get so much mariachi beauty out of only four horns. Their singer can't touch Frankie Valli's girly-man falsetto, but they instigate nostalgia for 1976-nostalgia-for-1963 in 1996 anyway by jubilantly translating the Four Seasons' virginity-loss anthem, "December 1963 (Oh What A Night)." Which appropriately enough, has almost exactly the same rhythm as "La Bamba."

L.A. Weekly, 8 November 1996

BIG & RICH BOOGALOO DOWN BROADWAY

Horse Of A Different Color by Big & Rich, probably the most unabashedly and forward-thinkingly dance-oriented Top 10 country album since western swing, opens with a preacher's exhortation: "I present to you country music without prejudice!" Then straight man John Rich and fall guy Big Kenny start in on proving it. A hard swing materializes from Southern metal-funk power-chords interspersed with mountain fiddles and banjos under shouted street-gang hey-hey-heys, a chorus referencing "Raw Hide" through Fred Durst, hamster squeaks quoting the Wiseguys' techno hit "Start The Commotion," nonsensical Charley Pride and Johnny Cash shout-outs, and blatant lies such as "Why they trying to complicate this simple music that we make?" in one of the most complexly constructed country tracks ever. All of which leads you into a bilingual old-school rap from Cowboy Troy, a very tall black man with an economics degree: "Back home we love to dance/We could be two-steppin' or ravin' to trance/And when the party is crunk the girls back it up/We've got the systems in the cars and the 20s on the trucks." Big & Rich claim their fans listen to Ludacris and OutKast as well as Kenny Chesney, and "Nashville's going to catch up with that."

Maybe it already has. A couple months ago, I caught an Allentown country station playing the looooong (15 minutes flat) version of "Rapper's Delight"; next day, the DJ was quite funkily scratching "Sweet Home Alabama" riffs into Charlie Daniels's "Legend Of Wooley Swamp." Around the same time, Big & Rich were debuting with this year's weirdest and loveliest country single, "Wild West Show," which mixes a placid keyboard intro, spacious spaghetti-western guitars, and Andes flute solos into a tepee-and-peace-pipe lyric that repeatedly chants "hey yaaaa!" à la fellow Native American stereotypist Andre 3000.

You can bet Kid Rock envies *Horse*'s punchline quotient too. There's this totally self-effacing gimme-three-steps two-step where the singer keeps getting his ass kicked by bar bullies and hog-tied by the police, who cut doughnuts in his yard when he's blasting Zeppelin. A woozy goof about falling in love with newscasters turns into a bizarre speed-hoedown comparable only to Swedish club-novelty act Rednex's 1995 electro-square-dance "Cotton Eye Joe." Then the duo's bawdily bumper-stickered follow-up single, "Save A Horse (Ride A Cowboy)," has them bling-blinging and tossing Benjis out windows and "what-what"-ing Lil Jon–style, until they mosey into a lazily mint-juleped riverboat shuffle with a distorted guitar solo played as jazz. Magic tricks, hog calls, Prozac pranks, and Spanish diversions oddly reminiscent of Mex-hop jokers Molotov stretch out several songs past 4:50 (unheard of in country), but in a disco-remix way, not an arena-pomp way: in service of crack buddy-movie harmonies and a dance rhythm that doesn't feel remotely retro.

None of it's mean-spirited, either. These guys love *The Wizard of Oz* like Nellie McKay; they wear dresses in their CD booklet; they tell websites they met through a dating service; they proclaim "I've got a whole buttload of friends" and "riding up and down Broadway on my old stud Leroy" and "Who gives a hoot if you're red, yellow, purple, or pink" and "I am what I am and I can't do nothing about that." If Montgomery Gentry's Gitmoized new longplayer is about building a hard-rock fortress, Big & Rich are about building bridges between red and blue states and pissing on the culture wars' wagon wheels and boarding the O'Jays' love train. (Yep, that's another title; starts with choo-choo disco toot-toots, plus Republicans and Democrats bickering.)

Spawn of an old Virginia cowhand and a church pianist, Big Kenny raves in interviews about how Jesus unconditionally loved hookers, drunkards, robbers, and tax collectors; before a schlock stint in Lonestar, John Rich grew up in Amarillo with a guitar-playing minister dad ("somewhere between a Baptist and a Pentecostal," he told angrycountry.com). The three least irreverent songs on *Horse of a Different Color* all peddle religion. Despite empathetic acknowledgement of sex and suicide and fluid gospel backup from sweet Martina McBride and tough Gretchen Wilson (whose wonderful debut is half John Rich compositions), "Saved" and "Holy Water" and "Live This Life" aren't as over-the-top as the rest of the album. But they still make it bigger and richer, still help it point a way out for country. And if enough fence-riders hear it, maybe even for *the* country.

Village Voice, 2 June 2004

PAZZ & JOP BALLOT EXCERPT 2004:
MONTGOMERY GENTRY AND CHELY WRIGHT

Montgomery Gentry did in fact give me an idea about who they are, or who they play on TV, at least. And their horseshit, as hateful as it is, is completely compelling. In fact, when Chely Wright (whose "Back Of The Bottom Drawer" was a better 2004 country single than any by Todd Snider) put out her asinine "Bumper Of My SUV" song in December, I realized its video would be pretty cool if it had her driving through New York with a dead deer strapped to her hood, and then she got out and chased drug dealers with a baseball bat, and she closed with a crucifix of light emerging on the back of her coat. Bizarrely (or maybe not), the old video that MG's "You Do Your Thing" most brings to mind is Laibach's immortal quasi-fascist (though allegedly anti-fascist) "Life Is Life"—especially when Eddie Montgomery is standing there singing, with the stars and stripes and Constitution and purple mountain's majesty behind him, just like the alps and elks behind Laibach's brown shirts. The thing gives me chills, and if any music will remind me 20 years from now how fucked up life got in 2004, the MG video will. It totally gets the sickness dead on, from its baloney about liberal hypocrites dining on venison in those fancy restaurants while they look down their snooty urban noses at two redneck buddies and kids returning from the hunting trip on down.

The lyrics, most of them anyway, are more libertarian than fascist—the chorus is "you do your thing I do mine." But the video argues otherwise, just like Chely's flaunting of her gas guzzler, and her deceitful equating of Iraq with our "safety" and "freedom," not to mention her deceitful equating of people pissed off enough about her U.S. Marines bumper sticker to flip her the bird with elitist rich people who send their kids to private school, make me wonder how many questions she's been asking about the war she says her brother's in. But no matter how offensive MG's vid is, I have to admit I get off on it. There is something about the visuals' power, and how the music kicks so hard, that makes its danger irresistible. I can't take my eyes off the thing. Maybe that makes me a masochist, but it's hardly the first time that awesomely hard-rocking music has flirted with evil. I can acknowledge a masterful and absolutely audacious piece of propaganda when I see it.

MONTGOMERY GENTRY FEEL THE POWER. (PHOTO: MARINA CHAVEZ)

PLEASE STOP BELITTLING TOBY KEITH

If recent research into *Voice* readers' country-music listening patterns (conducted by demographic analyst Alan Jackson) is any indication, I'm guessing you pretty much just think of Toby Keith as "that doofus who did that song after 9/11 about how putting boots in asses is the American way." Maybe you've also heard that he tours battle zones and doesn't play well with the Dixie Chicks. Beyond that, admit it: You're kinda clueless, right?

Well, at least he *has* a public image beyond Nashville, which is more than Bucky Covington or Jason Aldean can say. And Toby's image is clearly his own fault: when he made the Statue of Liberty shake her fist in 2002's outrageously rousing "Courtesy Of The Red, White And Blue" (*awesome* karaoke song, btw), Toby defined himself despite himself, and the self-proclaimed conservative Democrat has been trying to live it down ever since. Except when he hasn't: he's currently making a movie somehow based on "Beer For My Horses," the even more despicable ode to lynching (of "gangsters") that he sang with Willie Nelson around the same time. Add his camel-jockey cartoon, "The Taliban Song" ("Ahab The Arab" updated for the age when "Turkmenistan" is a very rhythmic word), his obligatory "American Soldier" (about how freedom isn't free), and his soggy dishrag "Ain't No Right Way" (implicitly anti-choice and explicitly pro-prayer in public schools), and it looks like we've got ourselves some Neanderthal species of nationalist numbskull.

But here's the thing: that handful of songs (a couple of which appeared on a surprisingly funky 2003 album entitled *Shock'n Y'All*, har har) is pretty much where Toby's editorializing ends, at least on record. His output is no more limited by his war-machine anthem than Merle Haggard's was by the comparably opportunistic "Okie From Muskogee" and "The Fightin' Side Of Me" when Nixon was president. And not many country artists since Merle have managed a creative streak like Toby's these past few years—in fact, to my ears, his '00s output (six albums plus change, including half of 2006's *Broken Bridges* soundtrack and a few spare tracks collected on his new 35 *Biggest Hits*) just might stand up to anybody else's this decade, in *any* musical genre.

Go ahead and attribute my fandom partly to biographical coincidence: Toby was born in July 1961, a half-year after me; we both have three kids; we're both straight white guys who've done time in inland suburbia. Then again, I've never personally worked an oil field or a semi-pro football field, my grandma didn't run a supper club, I'm not six-foot-four and 240 pounds, I don't own a bar and grill in Oklahoma, and I don't do Ford commercials. But we both apparently cut our teeth on the same Bob Seger and John Cougar LPs, so I'm a sucker for the chili-dog-outside-the-Tastee-Freez heartland-rock riffs he stuck in four songs on last year's *Big Dog Daddy*, the first album he produced himself. And where I come from, "water-tower poet class of '73" is a right pithy depiction of hip-hop's fourth element, and calling your most ZZ-worthy boogie "Zig Zag Stop" is a darn clever pun.

It also helps that the big lug isn't afraid to make fun of himself—for being a bumbling husband, say, or for being a boyfriend who likes his girlfriend but loves his local bar, or for his aging-athlete body not working as well as it used to. His class resentment (in "Get Drunk And Be Somebody" and "High Maintenance Woman," say) is totally good-natured as well. But where Toby most manifestly trounces the competition is with his singing (and, frequently, talking), which only gets smarter and warmer and more conversational—richer in both his high and low registers—as his career goes on. The song that first made me take notice, 1999's "How Do You Like

TOBY KEITH (ASS-BOUND BOOTS NOT SHOWN).
(PHOTO: RUSS HARRINGTON)

Me Now," had him bellowing like Billy Ray Cyrus in Meat Loaf mode, but since then he's figured out how to communicate a masculine vulnerability with an easy-as-Sunday-morning soul phrasing equal to Ronnie Milsap or T. Graham Brown, if not quite Charlie Rich (listen to "That's Not How It Is" or "Your Smile"); his latest move is a Barry White cover with power forward turned jazz bassist Wayman Tisdale. On his best album, 2006's *White Tra$h With Money*, Toby jumped ship from DreamWorks to his own Show Dog Nashville imprint, where green-eyed country-soul convert Lari White surrounded him with Tex-Mex accordions, Western swing saxes, *Dusty in Memphis* orchestrations, and Dixieland kazoos, coaxing laid-back nuances and big blue notes out of him that made perfect sense alongside the same year's Collector's Choice reissue of Dean Martin's 1955 *Swingin' Down Yonder*.

So Toby's a bit of a late bloomer: he had six regular-issue albums and a handful of country Top 10s under his belt before his ass-boot woke up the world beyond CMT. The chronological *35 Biggest Hits*, for its part, starts off as cautiously but competently as any good Alan Jackson retrospective—the hit about the 18-year-old getting her first upstairs apartment downtown kills me, seeing how I just helped my daughter move to Brooklyn, and "Who's That Man" and "A Woman's Touch" employ open space in a ghostly way. And though I hope Mercury canned whoever thought a Sting duet was a marketable concept, even that song makes for a decent divorced-dad depiction. But Toby qua Toby doesn't really bust out until "Dream Walkin'"/"Getcha Some"/"How Do You Like Me Now," beginning 14 tracks in; after that, there's no looking back. If you're new to the guy, start with disc two, then check out a few '00s albums before you shift back to disc one.

Getting loud—even a bit blowhard—was the first step. But for years now, Toby's sincere ballad side has been catching up with his funny rocking side. Even in a genre where vocal aptitude is a prerequisite for career longevity, masterful voices and discernible personalities (especially personalities with hot beefcake sex and a sense of humor and a chip on their shoulder attached) don't always coincide: Shooter Jennings might match Toby in a war of wits, but he can barely sing a lick, while Toby out-sings squeaky-clean goody-goodies from Travis to Jackson to Strait. And on top of that, though he's been known to borrow winners from wooden-voiced wordsmiths like Paul Thorn or Fred Eaglesmith on occasion, Toby's also the rare Nashville star who seems to do most of his own writing.

And again, dude can write. I admire his move-over-small-dog-a-big-dog-daddy's-movin'-in shtick, and how he does way more songs celebrating one-night stands than somebody married 24 years should be able to get away with—and how they don't come with angst or a moral attached. He's the kind of burly old teddy bear who'll stash his sleeping bag (and dog bowl?) behind your couch and finally remember your early-November birthday in December, when he shows up with a ribbon tied around your present—"Brand New Bow" beat "Dick In A Box" by eight 2006 months. And if he's playing wingman for a night, he'll take one for the team, even if it means sleeping with the fat girl.

OK, that one, "Runnin' Block" (great football metaphor, huh?), is indefensible—or it would be, anyway, if its chorus melody wasn't so amazing. Like "The Taliban Song," it's one of the "bus songs" that Toby sometimes tacks on at the end of albums—a disingenuous escape hatch he uses when he feels like pulling your chain. Not surprisingly, they're usually among his livelier tracks. So when do we get a whole disc of those? Soon, I hope, unless the R&B album comes first.

Village Voice, 14 May 2008

BRAD PAISLEY IS READY TO MAKE NICE

"I am very disappointed in Brad Paisley," some yokel named Jack wrote in the comments section of Country Music Television's blog in September, a couple of months after the star performed at the White House with Alison Krauss as part of an educational workshop on country music. "He's never been true country anyway. He probably became liberal from being married to a Hollywood actress. You can tell he's whooped and she runs the show."

But being whooped isn't all that bad. The truest true-country honky-tonker on Paisley's current *American Saturday Night*, the best album he's ever made, is a witty sing-along called "The Pants," about how you might wear 'em, bucko, but whoop-dee-doo, it's who wears the skirt that counts.

The skirt-wearer in his own house is Kimberly Williams, who *Huffington Post* lists as having donated $2,300 to Barack Obama's campaign last year, and whom Paisley first fell for after seeing *Father of the Bride*. "Welcome To The Future (Reprise)," off *Saturday Night*, relates the details. The celebrities wed in 2003—the same year Paisley hit it big with a song chiding celebrities. Six years later, on "She's Her Own Woman," he confesses he still doesn't know where she keeps the tarragon, or even what tarragon is. (Psst, dude: Check the spice rack! If you really wanna impress her, the August issue of *Cooking Light* says tarragon can be useful with seafood; if none's on hand, substitute parsley. You catch lotsa fish, right? Go for it.)

The Williams-Paisleys now have two boys, Huck and Jasper. *Saturday Night*'s "Anything Like Me" predicts that, before long, they'll be breaking windows and skipping class just like Paisley used to. Boys will be boys, after all. (Except for those metrosexual sissies who lotion their hands nowadays, as Brad pointed out on "I'm Still A Guy" a couple years back, 'cause how the heck do they grip their tackle box? Not that he has to worry: "I don't highlight my hair/I've still got a pair." And where his better half sees a priceless French painting, he sees a drunk naked girl. Who is probably always changing her mind, and taking way too long to get dressed, and scratching up the car.) Paisley has also talked about being proud that Obama is his sons' first new president, and how moved he was last November 4. Which makes him the new Dixie Chicks in certain country fans' eyes . . . but, hey, there's always liberal rock critics!

Besides, country radio hasn't backlashed yet, as evidenced by his latest Top 10 hit, "Welcome To The Future," the most optimistic musical statement about the state of America you'll hear in this recessed year: Now we can play video games on our phones and make deals with the Japanese who Gramps fought back in World War II, and, wow, look how far black people have come! The touching if confusing racial-progress verse *sort of* implies Obama, except the "man with a dream" Paisley refers to was somebody different (and not "Martin Luther," whom the lyrics actually name.) Weird. Still, stellar song, even its "futuristic" '70s synth-pomp coda—gutsy how it runs against the Nashville grain by explicitly arguing that a changing world is a good thing.

"Welcome To The Future" is clearly *Saturday Night's* centerpiece—you can tell, since there's that reprise later, plus a hidden instrumental version. Video's a real throat-lumper, too: kids from all around the world planning a bright tomorrow (plus a Japanese country band twanging in front of a Confederate flag, in a song that mentions cross-burning, WTF?). It's a genuine melting pot, just like the record's SNL audition of a title track, which celebrates a nation fond of Brazilian boots, French kisses, Spanish moss, Greek fraternities, Canadian bacon, Mexican beer, and pizza. Even actual immigrants, if you count Great-Great-Great-Grandpa!

What's impressive is that as Paisley reaches toward Big Statements— not to mention conceptually arranged albums increasingly exceeding an hour in length (very rare in Music City, as is his lack of a best-of disc)—the music also somehow seems to be loosening up. Only a half-decade ago, he was easy to dismiss as just another neo-trad blando in a white hat, with as little charisma as any and a less expressive singing voice than most; he got lucky with a non-mediocre number now and then, but they all do—an album every other summer since '99, one heartfelt Jesus song per, reams of shrug-worthy high-lonesome slow-song snooze, cornpone "Kung Pao" picking-and-grinning guest-star interludes starting with 2003's *Mud On The Tires*. Then he hit with two singles about drinking that were tough to ignore: the dark death-folk Krauss duet "Whiskey Lullaby" and the significantly lighter booze-narrated waltz "Alcohol," the latter novel enough to place in 2005's Pazz & Jop poll. His surprisingly playable 16-track *5th Gear*—complete with its own crit-approved novelty hit in the outdoor-sex itch-scratcher "Ticks," some sub–Weird Al Web-geek-baiting called "Online," more obligatory boring ballads, and nifty studio sound effects galore—followed in 2007.

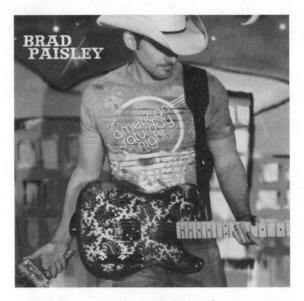

BRAD PAISLEY: *AMERICAN SATURDAY NIGHT* (ARISTA NASHVILLE, 2009)

If nothing else, you had to give it up for the fella's guitar playing. When it comes to vintage equipment, Paisley's as much a tech wonk as his "Online" protagonist. And by *5th Gear*, his understated virtuoso fills and washes—hoedown, swamp, surf, spaghetti western, blues, Merseybeat, festering Muzak voluptuousness—had become downright encyclopedic. Since he avoids the semi-metal stomping that more and more stands as Nashville's norm, it's easy to miss how rock he is. But 2008's mostly instrumental wankfest *Play* had its Billy Gibbons and Eddie Van Halen moments, and his catchiest recent hits aren't far from Tom Petty. Good ol' boys like Montgomery Gentry and Toby Keith push way more buttons for me: their politics are more threatening, their sessionmen more propulsive, their vocals more involved. By comparison, Paisley's a big ol' wuss. But "big ol' wuss," from a high-IQ rundown of his life history with *water*, of all things, is also one of *Saturday Night*'s most grin-inducing hooks. Wusses deserve respect, too, especially funny ones with chops. I wish the Williams-Paisleys all the best.

Village Voice, 13 October 2009

7

POP MUZIK

Once upon a time, rock critics didn't care about pop music. Okay, that's a lie; it depends on what kind of rock critic you're talking about—and even more so, what kind of pop music. Or "Pop Muzik," maybe: the weird chart-topping New Wave disco single by one-letter-named one-hit-wonder M (real name: Robin Scott) finished second on another chart in 1979—namely, the first-ever year-end singles competition of the *Village Voice*'s annual Pazz & Jop poll. (If Ian Dury's "Hit Me With Your Rhythm Stick" and "Reasons To Be Cheerful, Pt. 3" hadn't combined their votes by appearing on the same 45, "Pop Muzik" would've won.) Before 1979, critics only voted for albums. And after 1979, plenty of singles that you'd have to consider more pop than rock fared well: "Bette Davis Eyes," "Funkytown," "Billie Jean," "Karma Chameleon," "Electric Avenue," "Girls Just Want To Have Fun," and so on. None of which were especially surprising.

But there were other, more crass music-biz creations that rock critics seemed oblivious to—AOR mall ballads, teen trifles, Nashville crossovers, adult-contemporary croons, smooth jazz swoons, soft-rock schmaltzolas. In early 1982, Ken Tucker wrote a highly influential (for me anyway) lead *Voice* review called "A Readable Guide To Unlistenable Crap," rounding up and trying to make some silly sense out of recent airwave items by Little River Band, Quarterflash, Sneaker, Paul Davis, Loverboy ("these Canadians know how to kick and kiss ass with equal skill," ha ha), and the like, which for some reason nobody had thought to do before. When John Waite's post-Babys proto-power-ballad "Missing You" tied for 25th place in Pazz & Jop in 1984, it came as something of a shock. ("The most unequivocal such commodity to chart," Robert Christgau called it in his essay, "though the loathsome 'Like A Virgin' came damn close.") And when Greil Marcus periodically proclaimed his love for a Foreigner or 38 Special or Bryan Adams or Stacey Q song, I noticed even if nobody else did. By the late '80s, as I was burning myself out on the angry and abrasive indie rock that had become my bread and butter, I somehow brainstormed that there was shameless stuff all over the radio that might be more fun to write about. So I decided to start.

In retrospect, reviewing teen princess Debbie Gibson's 1987 debut album in the *Village Voice* doesn't seem strange at all; in fact, given that it stayed on the charts for 89 weeks and sold three million copies in the United States alone, it would almost seem neglectful *not* to pay attention to it. Debbie's "Only In My Dreams" and "Shake Your Love" both made my Top-10 singles list at the end of the year; so did two singles by Nerf-metal puffballs Poison and one by Latin freestyle girl-twirl trio Exposé. I doubt any of those records got many other votes. Yet somehow, I wasn't alone.

Here's Christgau again, in his essay that ran with the 1987 Pazz & Jop poll:

> 'Radio is a good, weird machine,' Greil Marcus insisted last year, and this year the theme was reflected in the singles lists of many critics who've never met—for instance, Frank Kogan, Rob Tannenbaum, Chuck Eddy, and Ted Cox. All were Amerindie partisans five years ago, and to an extent they still are, with Cox and Tannenbaum in the Lobos-to-Hüskers tributary and Eddy and Kogan down with noise bands like White Zombie and Pussy Galore. But for singles they listen to the radio and get off on getting manipulated. Cox and Tannenbaum go for pop-to-schlock, Fleetwood Mac or Eddie Money, while Eddy and Kogan list a lot of street-rap. But all fell for diva/girl dance records that five years ago they almost certainly would have dismissed as, dare I say it, disco: Whitney Houston, Deborah Allen, Company B, Exposé.

There are definite misconceptions in that passage—believe me, Bob, I was "manipulated" at least as much by White Zombie as Exposé. But though none of the schlock-pop and diva-dance votes he's referring to were reflected in the poll's overall results, maybe something was afoot anyway. Flash forward a few years, and New Kids On The Block never score even a single single on the Pazz & Jop tally; in 1990, "Ice Ice Baby" gets shut out, too. But a decade after Debbie Gibson, a tide has turned: Hanson's boy-band debut "Mmmbop" actually places first in 1997; the Spice Girls' "Wannabee" finishes 15th. And in subsequent years, singles by such Radio Disney regulars as Britney Spears, Christina Aguilera, the Backstreet Boys, 'NSync, Kelly Clarkson, Avril Lavigne, and Taylor Swift follow suit. Eventually, Britney, Taylor, and Justin Timberlake even score on Pazz & Jop's *album* lists. Ashlee Simpson, despite making two of the best albums of the '00s, didn't fare quite so well. Regardless, by the time the 2010s rolled around, critics were almost considered perverse if they *didn't* pay attention to such stuff; even indie haven pitchforkmedia.com wound up running a definitive "Decade In Pop" survey, by Tom Ewing.

This reversal makes certain onlookers uneasy, and some resort to confusing convolutions to explain it away. Frequently those explanations seem to revolve around an illusory movement known as "poptimism"—a supposed reaction to the allegedly entrenched but also largely hypothetical "rockism" that, for decades, kept critics unfairly favoring seemingly organic ingredients over artificial additives. Both terms are fairly meaningless oversimplifications, and you'll be hard pressed to find a widely published critic who defines his or her tastes by either. The term "poptimism," in fact, was apparently coined by unreconstructed art apologist Simon Reynolds in an attempted backlash against a comparatively open-eared attitude that his misrepresentations generally indicate he never much comprehended in the first place. Still, both titles have at least served the purpose of inspiring some rather entertaining straw man–baiting essays in recent years, from the *New York Times* on down.

"Punks came around and spat at their Woodstock-worshiping elders; they evolved into indie rockers, a new establishment. Hip-hop produced a separate critical stream complete with its own brand of purists. This 1980s generation has lately been taken down by younger poptimists, who argue that lovers of underground rock are elitists for not embracing the more multicultural mainstream," the frequently far more perceptive Ann Powers wrote in the *Los Angeles Times* in 2008. "Prefer Ray LaMontagne to Toby Keith? You're an NPR-listening square! Irritated by T-Pain? You're a Luddite! Sick of Fergie? You're sexist!"

Revealingly, Ann does not name names. Who are these upstarts, anyway? Do they really call underground rock fans "elitists"? Where, exactly, have they done this? Are there really critics out there who dogmatically privilege only music that they consider inauthentic and that features guitars the act didn't play or lyrics the act didn't write, and who look down on all music by important artists considered part of the historical canon? Or might such critics more likely be figments of somebody's imagination? And beyond all that, what exactly are today's alleged poptimist youngsters doing that, oh I dunno, Chuck Eddy and Frank Kogan and Rob Tannenbaum and Ted Cox and Ken Tucker and Tom Smucker and James Hunter and Carol Cooper and Michael Freedberg and Deborah Frost and John Leland

and Barry Walters and Lester Bangs and Richard Meltzer and Greil Marcus and Dave Marsh and Robert Christgau, say, hadn't done long before Ann's mythic "1980s generation" came along? "Look, there is no poptimism," an exasperated Kogan wrote on his livejournal blog in 2009. "Unless by poptimism you mean every interesting rock critic ever."

But enough ranting. This is a chapter about pop music. For instance, there's a piece about "Italodisco," published about 15 years before certain super-hip non-Italian indie-techno DJs started hosting "Italodisco nights." (I swear I'm not making that up.) But there are also some articles about stuff that rock critics have always been pretty fond of. Not just the Spice Girls, but the Pet Shop Boys, for instance—who sadly stopped making records that I cared about not long after I interviewed them in 1991. And Michael Jackson, who, much more sadly, died on 25 June 2009. Until that afternoon came along, he had never quite seemed mortal. "I can guarantee you one thing, we will never agree on anything as we agreed on Elvis," Lester Bangs had written in a 1977 obituary, only a couple years before Jackson definitively proved him wrong, emerging full-blown into adulthood as the world's most popular musician by presaging generations of young adults who would postpone their own decline by refusing to grow up. But if the King of Pop can't last forever, what does that say about the rest of us—and pop itself?

CUTTING IT AS A BAY CITY ROLLER IN 1989

We watched "Adventures In Babysitting" that afternoon (our cable had just been connected and they were giving us HBO and Cinemax free for the weekend—word is if you disconnect the wires when they get around to zapping the subtraction-factor, you'll get 'em free forever), but my sister doesn't know any crack dealers southeast of Eight Mile and Woodward, so Martina and I weren't worried about leaving Linus with her. Anyhow, tonight was important: The Bay City Rollers had just been awarded the key to Bay City (the map-spot where their pin landed long ago), and after practicing around Michigan for four weeks they were kicking off their comeback tour in our very own suburb, across the street from the Livonia Mall, two miles from our apartment. In a bar. We were trying to figure out why.

The doorman said Barry Kramer published the first *Creem*s out of his basement twenty years ago, and he may or may not have been lying, and we were gonna give his seedy meat-market Jamie's all this national publicity, but he charged us twenty-eight bucks anyway. What an asshole. After some deliberation, we went in. The crowd was mostly women who, like us, would've been 15 years old 13 years ago. Some brought old *Tiger Beats* and copies of the *Dedication* LP for Eric to autograph. Halfway through the show, several of 'em yelled "happy birthday." Eric said he doesn't have birthdays anymore. He's 33.

Eric, of course, is Eric Faulkner, the string-strumming singer, the squinty-eyed one who always seemed exuberant but lacks a shirt on the *Greatest Hits* cover. He's the only "original" Roller left, but saying this ain't the "real" Rollers is like saying Van Hagar's not the "real" Van Halen. (Which they're not, but you get my meaning.) Eric told me he keeps in touch with either Woody or Les or Derek, I can't remember which, who's in South Africa now and who says just 'cause he Rolled once doesn't mean he's gotta Roll now, an attitude both Eric and I find absurd.

Now there are six Bay City Rollers, five of whom (the shrimpily Benataresque backup nubile whose name is "Cat" or "Kaz" or something told me) were "about nine or ten" during Rollermania. Which, since this is the Rollers, was old enough. Cat/Kaz says she's "been with Eric for six years, so

YESTERDAY'S HEROES, THE BAY CITY ROLLERS.

sometimes I lose sight of the aura surrounding all this." Eric was the only person on stage wearing much plaid (the others had token sashes, stockings, etc.). I asked why, and he said they weren't sure whether or not they should be downplaying their plaidness. I told him of course not.

I liked the show a lot. The band did the boring small hits ("It's A Game," "You Made Me Believe In Magic"), the catchy medium ones ("Money Honey," "I Only Wanna Be With You," "Keep On Dancing," their brougified version of which I've always preferred to the Gentrys'), the fantastic big ones ("Rock and Roll Love Letter," the Vanda/Young-penned "Yesterday's Hero," which clumped my esophagus good even though Eric can't remember the second verse), the immortal giant one (to which I clapped my hands above my head while Eric spelled the title), and some newer stuff that alternated 'tween solo Scotch balladeering and subway-shout stomps with highly literary headlines such as "Party Hearty" and "She's Hot." The drummer's a wildman, and the gum-bubbles are even more riff-oriented than before, extremely Poison-like though Eric claims he's never heard those guys 'cause every time he turns on MTV he just sees the same songs over and over again—real strange because since I got my cable connected the songs I keep seeing over and over again are mostly by Poison. The encore was "Rebel Rebel," which Keith Partridge's little brother covered on an album in '77 or thereabouts, but Eric says that's news to him.

Eric and Cat/Kaz scoffed when I mentioned ABBA and Shaun Cassidy; I'm not sure why, maybe 'cause that music's for little kids. Eric revealed his plans for stardom in the college/indie-circuit, where they'll score real big 'cause there's no competition. He agreed with me that you can't be a teen-idol at 33, but that the Rollers are in this horrific Catch 22 'cause the words "Bay City Rollers" are inseparable from teen-idoldom but if they changed their name (as they have on occasion over the last decade, in other configurations) it'd be like starting from scratch, which'd take all the fun out of it. He says they're shopping a demo around to labels "but this industry's like the Jewish Mafia, so you know how that goes." He apologized that he hoped we weren't Jewish and thereby offended by his Public-Enemy-style slur, but we weren't.

The Rollers are big in Japan still, and the tartan-clad vocal-lad talked about recently playing Dingwalls in London, where I coincidentally saw Nick Lowe play each of the two times I was there. So I asked Eric what he thought of "Rollers Show," and he answered, "I don't really understand why he did that—probably just to make some money," a motive which never helped inspire *anything* Eric's ever accomplished, I'm sure. (He's in it for the Art, you know.) Otherwise, I forgot to ask him what his ideal dream date would be like, but maybe I will next time.

Swellsville, 1989

PEOPLE PLEASERS: THE VILLAGE PEOPLE

To comprehend the mid-'70s, that exuberant epoch of Chevy vans and chartreuse micro-buses, ballroom blitzes, afternoon delights, and kung-fu fighting, you have to realize that the more tasteless, gimmicky, and exploitive a record was, the better chance it had of climbing the Top 40. Corporations raced to see which performers' doltishness could be unhealthiest of all: in a way, it was a fulfillment of the mass-pop mandate. Cheese reigned, extremism and excess ruled; in the dire '80s, we should be so lucky. And in retrospect, the Village People seem the perfect capper for such a silly period. Cavorting on backs of bulldozers, Monkees-style auditions behind them, facial and torso fur to spare, this salacious sextet attained some pin-nacle of flashy stupidity.

When Eurofunk magnate Jacques Morali unveiled the Villagers' beef-cake drag in late '77, disco was just reaching its Travolta-chaperoned sales peak, a Georgia native prone to sighting flying saucers and killer rabbits manned the White House, and aides still meant nurses' helpers. Each of the singers had a fantasy uniform: Victor Willis dressed up as a cop, Alex Briley as a GI Joe, Glenn Hughes as a bike stud, Randy Jones as a cow-poke, David Hodo as a hardhat, Felipe Rose as a Cherokee chief. And for a few months, the nation embraced all of 'em. They probably couldn't have gotten away with it at any other time in American history; for sure they couldn't get away with it today.

The music, anthologized on the recent *Greatest Hits* (Rhino), wasn't much—assembly-line dance schmaltz, lotsa corny violins and marching-band brass, real clodlike next to the Phil Spector/James Brown fusion of so much prime disco. But faceless the Village People weren't. Up front Victor Willis's lumberjack Philly soul gruffness led his cross-racial crew through these fist-thumping pool-hall choruses, and the message was all bawdy innuendo. At the YMCA, "You can hang out with all the boys," "You can get yourself free/You can have a good meal/You can do whatever you feel"; in the Navy you can learn to "skindive." Macho men jog at dawn and work out at the spa, and if you're one you can "have your own lifestyle and ideals."

Pretty sheltered in high school back then, I didn't decode the alternate-preference subtext (and I'm not sure I would've appreciated it if I had), but I used to guffaw out loud (and still do) when Willis told me to dig Mr. Ego's chains, and when some potential ship recruit complained that he got seasick even watching water on television. As a stringer for a sub-urban paper a couple years later, I covered a Catholic elementary school recital where the students did that dance where you spell out "YMCA" with your arms, so the ribaldry must not've clicked with their nuns, either. And in his '81 Reagan jab "B Movie," Gil Scott-Heron, with characteristic hu-morlessness, chastised "Macho Man" for being "very military." Obviously, this was pretty sneaky stuff.

Greatest Hits has the three great hits ("Macho," "YMCA," and "Navy"—in longer versions on the CD), plus bunches of small ones. Several of these stump for substitute utopias (Key West, San Francisco, Greenwich Village) where there's plenty of "unity," "happiness," "liberation," "togetherness," and hippie food like that. Then in "Sodom and Gomorrah," the salty six buy into the mindset that says cities full of wicked lust oughta be incinerated, which is confusing.

The Village People tossed in everything, they let it all hang out. But Willis's voice wore out fast, and so did the jokes, and attempts to outlast disco backfired. *Greatest Hits* does ignore the sicko "New Romantic" '80s-comeback-try *Renaissance*; unfortunately it also omits their earlier heavy-metal maneuver "Sleazy," which had some perverse peacock-rock class. As it is, the comp's last three cuts, from career-waning live and soundtrack LPs, are lousy by even the most trash-tolerant yardstick. My only real complaint, though, is that these guys didn't survive long enough to strut their smut on MTV.

Boston Phoenix, 3 February 1989

ARRIVEDÉRCI, BAY-BEE: NOCERA AND FUN FUN

Frankly, if I tried hard enough, I could probably convice myself that *any* tripe was terrific. Three years on the continent, I tolerated the Eurobeat in every *Gasthaus* and record shop I killed time in (even remember Aryan kids breakdancing on Frankfurt sidewalks to it), so I'm well aware it's a zero-level reduction, the ultimate bastardization of rock'n'roll, a millimeter removed from Muzak. I associate yonder technopulse with stuff that's always repulsed me for no other reason than my own repression, so you can chalk this one up as willful fascination with an acknowledged annoyance.

Anyhow, Italy's some kinda Eurodisco hotbed, apparently; probably has something to do with the Vatican. And though what little Italodisco I've force-fed myself lacks the "percussive inventiveness" (e.g., congas) of your standard nuevo-huevo, pervasive goofiness more than makes up for rhythmic defects. In '85, Sire Records shipped me a compilation called *Fuzzdance*, as interplanetarily offbeat as classic doo-wop. (Note: The most classic doo-woppers were wops!) Also, I'm not sure what country Vivien Vee's from, but her recent "Heartbeat" is such an absurdly confectionary hyperelectronic arithmetic lesson that I wanna plug it nonetheless, seeing how it's produced by Dario Raimondi and Alvara Ugolini, who also master-minded Fun Fun's *Double Fun*.

Fun Fun are two scrubbed-skinned blond Italoflirts whose LP cover is a sickening sort of Doublemint-flashback, and who sound so sexless, so shallow, they make Jem and the Holograms seem like Last Exit. Anonymous cloud-nine harmonies ride rice-paper-thin synths over eternally jiggly choral hooks, not superfast, with add-on Ventures riffs and ballpark Farfisa (or Vox). Mostly it's like strobe-light soundtracks in lousy TV movies—nothing jarring or unpleasant; in fact, no "personality." The vocals are cheerier than the words, which suggests that the girls don't comprehend what they're singing.

The album, "Gimme Some Loving" and "I'm A Believer" covers on down, is negligible. I'm left wondering how actual human beings could stoop to such blankness. (Not to mention: Who *buys* this garbage, anyway?) But the lush and relentless 12-inch remix of *Double Fun*'s "Baila Bolero" is *about* blankness; it's *proud* of its anonymity. Voices are fleshed out, as is the bottom end, and the Abba-manqué melody (reinforced by a "Take A Chance On Me" lyrical allusion) orchestrates unto hypnosis with synbass triplets, claps, horn charts, castanets (that's the "bolero" part), and lute-or-whatever strums. "A never-ending desire/Will never know your name," laments the key line; the twins (?) are afraid of waking up to find out their "dream has gone," so instead they "dance the night away," and accelerate that last line like dancing is some inescapable toil or compulsion they'd rather not even be reminded of. The emotion sounds drugged, frozen, resigned to No Future.

Of course, No Future *is* the future (what else is new?). Like Fun Fun, Nocera overuses the noun *fantasy,* and more often than not her spiel on *Over the Rainbow* deals with not wanting to be alone (which—lemme guess—is the main reason people go to discos, right?). Trilling sing-songily through her adenoids, Nocera's awkward at points, emphasizing wrong syllables, enunciating mispronunciations, splitting herself in two. She sounds "artificial," but in a *real genuine way*; to Mantronik (who produces her sometimes, which I suppose makes her only semi-Italo despite her birth-pedigree, but what the hey), her squeal is just one more machine to terrorize with. The kinetic energy doesn't ricochet with quite as much poly-architectural intricacy as on the Mantronix LPs, but Nocera's got more soul than M.C. Tee. Studio jockeys tense up the proceedings like they're hitching electrical wires to cigar boxes, and all these tricky little beat-gnomes shuffle out as the racket unravels.

"Summertime, Summertime" has a breezy tune simple enough for a toy xylophone, plus an unknowable water metaphor; "Let's Go" has soap-opera wave-crash effects making way for an impossibly high-pitched "bay-BEE" that sets off an Escheresque ascent/descent. Both are substantial club hits, and both cook. Save for her inevitably languid slow one, Nocera's filler is uniformly perky and playful: I especially like the (non-Garland) title cut's shoobedoo-down-down Neil Sedaka rip, and that thing getting sawed in half in "Play The Part." Seriously doubt anybody could "dance" to the midtempo stuff—outside of the singles, there ain't much funk. At home, though, it sounds super.

These records are vacuous, contrived, redundant. But to fling that adjectival triumvirate at *any* popmode these days is to tautologize. And unlike vacuously contrived redundancies from Springsteen to Savage Republic, true disco (as opposed to some tepid-by-both-catharsis-and-get-down-terms art-placebo) has no aesthetic delusions, so it's free to be free. If music's gonna matter anymore, it's gotta buck *all* tradition, including the worn-out tradition-of-bucking-tradition—protesting history at this point is no less a limitation than being in legion with it. We need pop for the present, not for posterity; we've fucked everything up, and it's too late to turn back. (Or, in other words, I've *sold out*, okay?)

Village Voice, 3 February 1988

DEBBIE GIBSON: ANGEL BABY

First off, if Madonna is the Shangri-Las (which she's not, but let's be hypothetical), Debbie Gibson's the Angels, or maybe Rosie and the Originals: She's less wise to the ways of the world, more gullible, more ladylike, cheerier, cleaner. *Untainted*. Plus, just 'cause she's a 17-year-old pipsqueak Lawn Guyland hoodsie (12 years younger than Madonna!) don't mean she's a Ciccone-clone. Saw her hosting the Nickelodeon Network's kidvid show, *Nick Rocks*, and she said her hero's Billy Joel. When she was eight she went to see him on his *52nd Street* tour, and her sister saw him walking in Manhattan once, but was too chicken to get an autograph. Deb offered to babysit Billy's kid. She said, "Concerts are for dancing" and hates when grown-ups tell her to sit down. She ate McDonald's fries, and reminded us that George Harrison used to be a Beatle.

On the back cover of Deb's *Out Of The Blue*, released when she was still sweet 16, she thanks (among others) Billy Joel, her grandma and grandpa, her attorney, "Steve E. Joel S. for giving me the hots," "MIDI-mouse for all those great sounds in binary," and (why not?) God. Old fogeys like you probably figure her and Tiffany (Tiffany *Darwish*, trivia buffs) are the same person, but you're wrong: Tiffany's younger, wears more denim, and covers Rubinoos numbers. Debbie Gibson's got more gusto and writes every word she sings.

Her snazziest words on *Out Of The Blue*, including those in her two top-five hits, "Only In My Dreams" and "Shake Your Love," concern being trapped in a suburb where you constantly fall heels over head and go weak in the knees for people who basically don't care (or maybe even know) you exist. Oodles of dreams that don't come true, looking-for-the-perfect-love-at-first-sight stuff. NO SLEAZE. Dunno what Debbie means by "I need your love like a flame needs a fire," but I'm glad she's cautioning her teeny troops that they better shop around: "Stop your crying over one special boy." She sings, um, like Madonna. Kind of restricted, but in a pleasant, unassuming, even meek way, with long vowels doing the mambo, and those sparkling churchbell-angelscat things like Madonna used in "Crazy for You." Debbie's at her bubbliest over a quasi-maraca nurserybeat that's frisky but not really sexual or anything; she doesn't seem to be enjoying herself much in the couple big melancholic Sade/Anita-style abused-by-love torch-travesty snoozaramas. And her sax player needs to track down a copy of Albert Ayler's *Witches And Devils*.

"Only In My Dreams" is spiritedly slinky, with bongobeats lifted from the Sugarhill Gang's version of "Apache," and its girl-group backdrop adds credence to a somewhat ambiguous situation wherein Gibson's whole mall-world falls apart as she bemoans the loss of a guy who apparently was never hers to begin with—a no-baloney teen-life predicament, as I recall, and you can't assume her dreamtext had anything to do with birds and bees, either. In the "Only In My Dreams" video, Debbie wears pajamas. In the "Shake Your Love" video, she wears a miniskirt (in only one shot, so watch fast!), smiles crooked, and does a funky hand-jive that looks like referee signals. "Shake Your Love," the song, has a prefornicating id-level triple-entendre title, an exuberant domino-effect rhythm, an underlying synth-buzz that suggests "Let The Music Play," a google-eyes syncopation-break that suggests Spike Jones in Miami, some inspired phrase-repetition, and one cute part where Debbie telephones her desired one, hangs up, and cries. Hate to admit it, but this may be as close to a transcendent single as anybody this side of Poison is capable of anymore. And I'd take it over "Allentown," even "Only The Good Die Young," any day.

Village Voice, 5 January 1988

IT WAS IN THE CARDS

Lucy once asked Schroeder in a *Peanuts* cartoon how he could consider Beethoven a superstar since there's never been a bubblegum card with his picture on it. Well, Pro Set Inc. of Dallas has a set of Super Stars Music Cards out now, and even though there's 260 of 'em, none feature Beethoven's picture (Ludwig or Camper Van!). Not only that, there's no Michael Jackson, Guns N' Roses, New Kids on the Block, John Mellencamp, or Shonen Knife. (That one's a *real* shame. It could've been the rock equivalent of the 1965 Giants rookie card of Masanori Murakami!)

Tiffany only gets one card, but Debbie Gibson gets five. It's not fair, but Tiffany's card (No. 96) is cooler than all of Deb's combined (her head's sideways, her hair's all over the place, and real greasy, too!). The other really cool card is Kix (No. 198), not just because they're the best rock band in the world, but because Pro Set used a photo negative. Everything's backwards: the drummer's Zildjian T-shirt, the singer's Kix medallion, the danger sign.

I don't get why they gave certain people more than one card. The only time it makes sense is with Kiss (No. 196 without makeup, No. 197 with). Madonna gets five cards; the prettiest is No. 69 (honest!), which I think is an old picture. Sexier than Madonna: Taylor Dayne (No. 40), Karyn White (No. 104), and Doro (No. 164).

Sonic Youth doesn't get a card, but on Voivod's card (No. 244), Blacky is wearing a Sonic Youth *Confusion Is Sex* T-shirt. That's on the front; on the flipside, Snake's wearing 3-D movie goggles! Other fun cardbacks: Basia (No. 33), which says that her last name is Trzetrzelewska and that she wrote "possibly the only pop song to celebrate Poland's great astronomer, Copernicus." (Amy Grant's got a song about Galileo, but no card.)

Another astronomical fact, on Adamski (No. 30), the only acid-house performer honored: "A space alien, Adamski landed on Earth when the moon was in Sagittarius." (Another evil pop hoax! Quick, call *Newsday*!)

Oh yeah, there's also 100 *Yo! MTV Raps* cards (a separate set), and they're almost as dull as that show is (hey, face it, as dull as rap itself is). Dr. Dre and Ed Lover get four cards, but not a single homegirl gets one. Where's L'Trimm and the Real Roxanne? Where's Salt-N-Pepa?

Um, back to superstars. There's a bunch of "legend" and "historical

DEBBIE GIBSON: PRO SET MUSIC CARD NO. 44, 1991

concert" cards too. The former are old people, the latter are psychedelic posters. Not that I care really, but if the Doobie Brothers and Eric Clapton are "legends" according to Pro Set, then Ted Nugent oughta be a legend, too.

Request, **August 1991**

PET SHOP BOYS' MAD BEHAVIOR

All my jeans were either too long or too short or too brown or in the wash or had New-Kids-style holes in the knees, but eventually I decided to wear the semi-flood-expecting off-white ones, and I even ironed them the night before. But I was still nervous. I was going to meet the Pet Shop Boys, and I wanted to make a reasonably good impression. I'm not used to being around people who actually enjoy shopping for clothes, and these guys enjoy it so much they do songs about it!

There it is in black and white and a couple other colors in *Pet Shop Boys, Annually* (Areagraph Ltd. U.K. 1988): Chris Lowe with his nine favorite pairs of sunglasses, four of 'em by Issey Miyake; Neil Tennant with eight favorite suits and coats, three of 'em by Jean Paul Gaultier. They were gonna laugh at me for sure, just like the time the Beastie Boys told me I was dressed like Keith Partridge. Then in the cab on the way to the EMI offices, I noticed I had on one navy blue sock and one black one. This was like high school all over again!

Fortunately, the EMI people put me behind a big desk so my socks wouldn't show and nobody'd think I was Sal Mineo in *Rebel Without a Cause*. Then in walked the Pet Shop Boys, and I'll be a junkie's uncle if they weren't dressed worse than me! Tennant's got on this old black T-shirt and some jeans, Lowe this tan Motorways T and a baseball cap from some sport shop or something, like they just got out of bed almost.

I thought about all those references to "authentic" Latin sound in the liner notes to their last LP, *Introspective*, and I thought about all those guitars on their new LP, *Behavior*. I thought about the U.S. tour they've got planned for early 1991, even though back in the old days Tennant always said that the only reason musicians tour is to prove that they're manly hunks. I thought again about those crummy clothes they were wearing, and the truth became clear in my mind: The Pet Shop Boys have sold out and become a macho heavy metal band!

Which of course is a lie, but face it, lies make the world go round. My friend Michael Freedberg had written me a letter just the week before in which he defined disco as "a music of intentional deception, of having fun telling lies." The Pet Shop Boys have so much fun telling lies that sometimes they even lie about being disco. What they really are is a scared-of-dogs singer-songwriter duo using disco-derived production techniques; as such, they are philosopher kings. When they pretend to be a pop band, they're almost as good as Def Leppard, but not quite. Like Merle Haggard, their love songs never match their sociological songs.

They're the apex of postliberal metapop Thatcherland tradition ("Pop Muzik," "Sweet Dreams Are Made Of This," "Wham Rap," Heaven 17, Scritti Politti, Westworld), which, if it's about anything, is about the joy of selling out, of selling and shopping and being sold and being bought: "I heard it in the House of Commons/Everything's for sale."

It's not so much that the Pet Shop Boys have no use for integrity as that they only have use for their own kind of integrity. One of the best tunes

THE PET SHOP BOYS LET THE DOGS OUT. (PHOTO: ERIC WATSON)

on *Behavior* (it's vicious like "Positively Fourth Street"), and likely the most cynical thing the Pet Shops have ever done, is "How Can You Expect To Be Taken Seriously," which can only be described as an anti-protest song (and how many of those have you heard since Live Aid?).

Tennant says it's meant to chronicle "the development from a pop star to a rock star, about how nowadays a lot of rock stars want people to think of them as authorities on all these causes." The song's villain takes drugs, preaches about the ozone layer, sups with royalty, then aims for the Rock and Roll Hall of Fame. I hear it as a knock at the Sinead/Suzanne/Tracy set (it seems to be addressed to a woman), but maybe you'll see it as as a knock at George Michael or Phil Collins or John Cougar Mellencamp or Sting. Tennant left it vague on purpose; he says it could even be about himself.

Which is stretching it, but he has a point. "It's just that I think ecology is too important to be left in the hands of pop musicians," he explains.

"No," I say, "you've got it backwards. You're falling into the protest trap yourself. You should say that pop music is too important to be left in the hands of ecologists!"

"Yeah, that too," he admits. Tennant's no dummy, and he has to be careful to keep his own pretensions in check. He worries that, if he claims "My October Symphony" is about Russia's failed October Revolution or "I'm Not Scared" is about the student uprising in Paris in 1968, onlookers might scoff at him like he scoffs at Sting. "I find it incredibly embarrassing to admit it, because I know that's not what people will hear in those songs, but those events are really what inspired me to write them," the onetime history major (Polytechnic of North London, 1975) says.

He also says he wrote "Rent" as a love story, but egghead rock critics like Simon Frith and Greil Marcus heard it as a definitive statement of dole/capitalist Thatcher-era blues, which Tennant intentionally addressed in "King's Cross" on the same album. "I try to keep my politics subtle," Tennant explains. "I've always thought that songs as obvious as [the English Beat's] 'Stand Down Margaret' were a little naff."

No matter how much they try to hide it, the Pet Shop Boys do indeed concern themselves with their credibility. When I chide them about the guitars on *Behavior*, they even get defensive about it. "That's wah-wah," Tennant insists. "That's a disco sound!" (More like proto-disco, actually; the riffs in "My October Symphony" and "To Face The Truth" are straight out of Marvin Gaye's "What's Going On," Hot Chocolate's "Brother Louie," and Isaac Hayes's "Never Gonna Give You Up.") "And we decided to put that guitar in 'How Can You Expect To Be Taken Seriously' because it's about a rock star, and besides they're mostly just electronic simulations of guitars, anyway."

These guys really take pride in their phoniness!

"When we were recording with Bobby O, we wanted to make an authentic Bobby O record. On *Introspective*, we wanted to make authentic Latin hip-hop," Tennant says. "We didn't mean we were authentic Latins!"

In case you're not up on Miami disco history, that means they wanted to be the Flirts or Company B, not Tito Puente. But, hey Neil, I know Company B, and you are no Company B. For one thing, they look better in underwear (check the cover of *Gotta Dance*). For another thing, you don't sing as well. You replace passion with passivity. When you cover Elvis Presley's "Always On My Mind" and Sterling Void's "It's Alright," you sound like you're making fun of the words (a cheap camp move), and in the middle of incredible tracks like "Left To My Own Devices" and "What Have I Done to Deserve This?" your vocal cords suddenly go limp, and you pull the rug from under our feet. I think you wanna give us just enough pleasure to get by. You're worried that if everybody gets too excited about the Pet Shop Boys, you'll wind up just another flash in the pan without the steady income longevity guarantees. What do you have to say for yourself?

Tennant basically acts like he doesn't know what the hell I'm talking about, which might be true. I'm starting to like the Pet Shop Boys so much that I almost don't know what the hell I'm talking about myself (which is nothing new, of course). Be that as it may, Tennant says the Pet Shop cover versions were "totally sincere. I thought I put a lot of feeling into them, actually." Though he admits he doesn't and wishes he did have the vocal range of a classic disco diva, he finds my criticism of Anglo-synth dweebs who hold back mouth-wise and thus bleed the guts from disco completely off the mark. "It's what those singers can't do that makes them great!" Tennant theorizes, using New Order's "soulful" Bernard Sumner (who teamed up with Tennant and ex-Smiths guitarist Johny Marr recently for a one-off single under the name Electronic) as a case-in-point.

"Yeah!" Lowe pipes up. "Bernard really goes for it."

Remember Lowe? He's a Pet Shop Boy, too. During our interview, give or take two or three sentences, Tennant and I talk while Lowe just sits there. Since he tends to just stand there in almost all the Pet Shop videos, and since I was told that when the Pet Shoppers tour, he'll probably just stand there on stage, I am kinda curious what exactly it is he does. A spokeswoman for EMI says that, for all she knows, he is there "for moral support, like a teddy bear or something."

Tennant first says Lowe doesn't do anything, then later asks me if I believe him, to which I answer that I want to believe him except I once read that, back when the twosome united, Lowe was the disco fanatic and Tennant a mere verbose Bowie/Costello fan, which indicates that Lowe is probably instrumental in providing the Pet Shop Boys with their instrumentation. And it so happens that I guessed correctly.

The lyrics are world historical 'cause Tennant studied history, and the music is built from the bottom up 'cause Lowe studied architecture at Liverpool University and even designed a staircase once. If it wasn't for Lowe, the Pet Shop Boys might have turned out to be garden-variety gazebo folk pervs like the Smiths (except Tennant's a lot smarter than Morrissey, so I doubt it). In *Pet Shop Boys, Annually*, Tennant's "favourite 10 records of the last year or so" include oldies by Joni Mitchell and Stevie Wonder and Dusty Springfield, not to mention Sting's "Fragile" and the *My Fair Lady* soundtrack, but Lowe's faves are all timely disco-pop and house music. So credit Tennant with *Actually*'s haunting Pet Shop world-weariness, and Lowe with *Introspective*'s hefty Pet Shop syncopation (lotsa strings and pianos).

My wife, Martina, says *Behavior* is the Pet Shop Boys' best ever, and I think I understand why: humane hummability, warm recitation, deep emotions, everything Lester Bangs liked about Bowie's *Young Americans*. Produced by Harold Faltermeyer, who played keyboards on Giorgio Moroder's *Midnight Express* and *American Gigolo* soundtracks then scored big with his own "Axel F" in 1985, this is (according to Tennant) the Boys' tribute to the Munich electro-buzz of the mid-'70s: Moroder, Kraftwerk, Silver

Convention. As such, it has the thinnest, most brittle, most wallpaperlike Pet Shop sound ever (it makes *Introspective* seem like "One Nation Under a Groove"), and though all of it is pleasant enough, only the cruel rock-disco of "How Can You Expect To Be Taken Seriously," the baroque militia-disco of "My October Symphony," and the outrageously reflexive critic-baiting of "Being Boring" have personality or bombast enough to jump you from the background.

"The whole idea of being boring has always followed us around," says Tennant, the only guy I can think of who's ever yawned on one of his own album covers. "We can't help how we act in our videos. It's just the way we are." Most Pet Shop LPs have maybe a 50/50 great vs. OK ratio; *Behavior* runs more like 30/70. Give or take 1986's ill-executed remix compilation, *Disco*, I think it's their worst album. But I still give it even odds of making my 1990 Top 10.

Then again, I'm a rock critic, and like Blue Öyster Cult or the Patti Smith Group or Yo La Tengo, the Pet Shop Boys are a critics' band in more ways than one. "Rock critics think about our songs more than we do," Tennant observes, but what he's not telling you is that he used to be one himself. "But I wasn't a *rock* critic," he points out, "I was a *pop* writer." He wrote for *Smash Hits*, see. I tell Tennant that, if he was just a "pop writer," I'm a rock critic trying desperately to be a pop writer, only *Smash Hits* won't take me.

The pop vs. rock conundrum might not mean much here in the States (where would you put Poison or Public Enemy?), but in Blighty, it still means a lot, and the Pet Shoppers are obsessed with it. "In the music business, people hate pop music," Tennant claims. Like any sane person, he has more respect for Frank Sinatra, "who at least doesn't spend hours a day in the gym, and he doesn't go to bed early," than for Mick Jagger. But then he and Lowe start groaning about how, when a Deee-Lite single and Steve Miller's jeans-commercial-revived "The Joker" both sold the same number of copies in the U.K. recently, the powers that be gave Miller the No. 1 chart spot.

"They'd rather have an old rock record top the charts than a fashion-able new pop one!" Tennant gasps. When I argue that "The Joker" is a bet-ter record—catchier, goofier, less cumbersome—they stare at me like I'm crazy. When I blurt out that Guns N' Roses are a better dance band than the Pet Shop Boys, Tennant attributes it to "cultural differences." (I blame it on the beat.) "People in England wouldn't dance to that kind of music," he says.

But will people in America dance to the Pet Shop Boys? Well, obviously, they *have*. Though *Musician* magazine curiously listed the boys as one of the "Top 25 One-Hit Wonders of the 1980s" for "West End Girls" ("Does anybody ever read *Musician*?" Tennant asks me, and I have no idea), the duo actually has placed no less than six hits in the U.S. Top 20, five of which made the Top 10. And Tennant thinks his Yank fans are pretty diverse. "We did three record signings in 1985, and the audiences were completely mixed—teenage girls, rock fans, club people, suburban mothers with their kids—and it was the moms who bought our records," he says, laughing. "I think we share a large part of our audience with the Cure. They're like the weirdest, then New Order and Depeche Mode, and we're considered the most commercial of those groups." And the least iconlike, I'm guessing.

Record buyers, like *Musician* editors, may not even realize all those Pet Shop hits came from the same band. "West End Girls," inspired by Grandmaster Flash's "The Message" according to Tennant, is a Nerf-rap equal of "All The Young Dudes." "It was a song about escaping, just like every other rock song in the world," Tennant snickers. "What Have I Done To Deserve This?" has Bee Gees hooks and Dusty Springfield in the flesh; "It's A Sin" is a monkishly ornate fallen-Catholic epic, complete with sound effects from Brompton Oratory candleholder cleaners and Westminster Abbey pastors. "I've been lapsed since I was 16, but I don't think Catholics ever really lapse," Tennant says. "If they were dying, and somebody asked if they wanted to see a priest, they'd say yes."

And this is the group who brought back Liza Minnelli. "When Bowie came out in '72, everybody I knew in Newcastle had *Ziggy Stardust*, Roxy Music's *For Your Pleasure*, and the *Cabaret* soundtrack," Tennant recalls. "We considered her a glam-rock star." (Which helps explain why Zal Cleminson, who played guitar in early Tennant faves the Sensational Alex Harvey Band, used to paint his face like Joel Grey.) But Tennant/Lowe turned Liza into a disco star, providing her with *Results*, the hippest music any over-40 Westerner has made in the last few years and a hit to boot.

Not surprisingly, Tennant has no idea how record sales will translate to concert-ticket sales: "That's one of the reasons we wanna tour, to find out who'll come." Without Depeche Mode's New-Kids-for-kinky-kids pinup appeal ("We never looked good enough to be pop idols"), the Boys could conceivably play to some empty seats. Until last year's 14-date jaunt through Hong Kong, Japan, and Britain, the result of a Far East promoter's offer they just couldn't refuse, they've been as resistant to live shows as Steely Dan ever was. "We've always noted that the effect of touring is that it makes you into a fist-clench rock band," Tennant explains, using the Eurythmics (certainly *my* idea of a fist-clench rock band!) as an example. "So we didn't have a fantastic urge to tour and couldn't have afforded it even if we wanted to. Getting 12-inches played in clubs was always our idea of touring."

"Rock shows are really boring," Tennant figures, "unless you have a charismatic frontman," and the Pet Shop Boys may be the only band on earth who could upgrade their frontman's charisma by replacing him with Michael Dukakis. So though the concert will "still be a little bit like a rock show, with some live performance element, all the songs will be visualized with costumes, choreography, and films all interacting." Overseas, the duo had help from jazz saxophonist Courtney Pine and arty movie dude Derek Jarman, among other folks. "We're both interested in theater, without being like Genesis," the crooner continues. "And no one will have gone as far in that direction as us."

I tell Tennant he should not only lip-sync, but lip-sync and make an issue of it, like it's the only honest way to use a microphone these days. But he says he's gonna wimp out and sing for real.

Request, **February 1991**

GIMME BACK MY BULLETS: WILL TO POWER SHOOT FOR DISCO VALHALLA

Once upon a time, back in the days of the Angry Samoans castigating stupid assholes for being social types and the Fall's Mark E. Smith bragging that his friends didn't add up to one hand and admitting how hard it is to share space with other people, I could listen to records by well-read white iconoclasts and figure out that they lived on the same planet I do. But now well-read white iconoclasts all become computer hackers or something, and all the music I like comes from party boys with tattoos and party girls with aerobics classes. I take what I can get, but something's *missing*.

Something was missing with punk rock too, of course: there wasn't much active pleasure in it, so, perfect as it may've been for the first morning of the year, it usually wasn't enough to get you through the subsequent 364. Not so with Will to Power's *Journey Home*: this is well-read-white-iconoclast music that acknowledges that America's a fucked-up place for loners, but makes an aerobics party out of it. It covers every inherently contradictory base I care about, so, needless to say, I'm addicted. Things happen on this record that you wouldn't expect to happen anywhere, and even if you did, you'd expect them anywhere else but here.

Will to Power are a neo-disco team from Miami, but they don't play "Miami sound" or "Latin freestyle," which is to say they're usually too mellow to bang timbale-and-conga percussion as crazily as most Miami girl groups do—in fact, their sound ranks with the schlockiest disco ever, which by definition means it ranks with the schlockiest music. Their self-titled 1988 debut album had not only a No.1 pop single, but also two No. 1 dance singles. "Baby I Love Your Way/Freebird" (a/k/a "Free Baby"), an outrageous keyb-and-string-driven thing of beauty that sparkled like the fireflies in the Peter Frampton original and unfolded toward you like song sheets scattering in a warm wind, improved Frampton like Dinosaur Jr.'s punk "Show Me The Way" couldn't and improved Lynyrd Skynyrd like Kill-dozer's punk "Sweet Home Alabama" couldn't.

But *Will To Power* was a far stranger animal than anyone who uncondi-tionally dismissed "Free Baby" would suppose. For one thing, there was this self-analysis statement wherein songwriter/producer/mastermind Bob Rosenberg gurgled, "People try to say I'm antisocial/I don't know if it's true"—weird, because disco is probably the most social Western music of the last quarter century. Then there was the wild cutmix instrumen-tal called "Zarathustra," with a title that harked back through Deodato's theme from *2001: A Space Odyssey* to Richard Strauss and Nietzsche, the latter of whom provided Will to Power's name and was even quoted on the inner sleeve.

The sound on *Journey Home* is fuller, more organic. Maria Mendez, who sang lead on *Will To Power*, is gone, replaced by Elin Michaels, who doesn't wear as much makeup. Seven vocalists, all but one of them women, back up Michaels. Inside the CD cover, Rosenberg quotes not just Nietzsche, but also Goethe, Walt Whitman, Thomas Jefferson, and Thoreau, whom he calls his "friends," and most of whom say it's smart to live dangerously. And he thanks not only the Solid Gold and Pure Platinum Dancers, but also Mahler, Wagner, Odin, Thor, Earth First!, and the NRA.

TWO PEOPLE I'VE PERSUADED TO LISTEN to this record have said they don't hear anything, that it's just Muzak. Which in a way it is, or at least the first five songs are, but they're squeaky-clean *pop* Muzak—in the tradition of "Classical Gas," the Carpenters, Hugo Montenegro doing "Good Vibrations," Hank Marvin's guitaring in the Shadows. Yet I also hear a lot of Phil Spector in the bombast, and Fleetwood Mac's *Rumours* in the stacked harmonies; what with his weird production tricks and laid-back layered voices and obsession with the details of young suburban romance, Rosenberg's a pop eccentric squarely in the Spector/Lindsey Buckingham mold. To call this music bland is to ignore the down-the-drain vocal fade-aways, the extended sax sustains, the whispered Greek-chorus asides, the rhythm scrapes that suggest worn-down brake pads. Or how the multiplexed Elton-to-ELP piano recital in "Clock On The Wall" gives way to a ticking time bomb, or how "Fly Bird" echoes "Free Baby"'s gorgeous sway with a lushness that feels like a rice-paper origami forest frosted with Lee Hazlewood's morning dew.

There are no cue cards telling you "Look for Richness Here." But the music *is* rich, and so are the words, subtle new twists on Tin Pan Alley's mid-'20s man-woman theme. Stuff like the clock haunting you while you sit home alone watching rented videos Saturday night not of your own volition. Or a gal catching her guy with his best buddy's flame and telling him in this real sarcastic tone to pack his bags and try not to get hit by the door when he leaves.

Basically, that's the first half of the album; after that it messes with your head. "Koyaanisqatsi," with Rosenberg reciting in a serious *Dragnet*-introduction bark over repetitive David Byrne *Catherine Wheel* talking-drum beats, might be based on the Philip Glass soundtrack and then again might not. Citing some of the quotes on the CD sleeve plus some new ones by Oscar Wilde and Solzhenitsyn, referencing Hopi Indian lore, Rosenberg delivers an oration about freedom and rebellion in art and life. "The only thing worse than a knee-jerk liberal is a kneecapped conservative," he hypothesizes, and a soul singer in the background keeps asking, "Where do you draw the line?"

Wild-eyed, Rosenberg starts spilling clichés and slogans and brilliant ideas and crackpot theories and leaps of faith all over the parlor room rug: "Imitation is suicide," "To be great is to be misunderstood," "Down with New Age, up with reality," "When we want something from the rich, we will take it by force, the honorable way." Eventually the track turns into a pro-NRA editorial, making Rosenberg the first pop performer to take 1990's trendy Bill-of-Rights-boosting to its logical libertarian conclusion. Then he spouts out a radical survivalist platform that calls for violent defense of the wilderness, a far cry from the dainty ecology pussyfooting even speed-metal bands dabble in these days.

Next, as if no segue could be more logical, WTP veer straight into their cover of Heatwave's bubblebump classic "Boogie Nights," then into their robot-breathy redo of 10cc's cynical "I'm Not In Love." Over "Boogie Nights," an exponentially more-close-packed version than the original, Rosenberg explains that he doesn't like to let his anger linger, 'cause "it's bad for my aim, and my trigger finger." He also says he hasn't got many friends, and he's got "brains; but no personality," whatever that means. It's funny, but I don't think he's being "ironic."

SO WHAT THE HECK is going on here? "Anti-Social," the hermit life, Nietzsche, guns galore, not to mention the way Rosenberg scowls like a straw boss on the record cover—this is pure rub-your-schnozz-in-snot nihilism. Punks like Dinosaur Jr. and Killdozer might go pro-NRA as some kind of campy lumberjack joke, and with Ted Nugent or Hank Williams Jr. or Ice Cube, firearms are just one more element in their chosen genres' respective he-man shticks, but Will to Power are as far from Monday-night-football machismo as music can be. (That they got famous covering a song by Skynyrd—rednecks whose "Saturday Night Special" just happens to be the most effective *pro*-gun-control protest song in pop history—only confuses matters more.) In 1990, life-denying Scientological superstition was passed off by disco and rock nincompoops alike as "positivity," and Living Colour said Elvis is dead, but Will to Power know *God* is dead. I imagine Rosenberg sees himself as a Superman rising above the herd, which indeed he is.

I even imagine him consciously bypassing more traditionally Nietzschean Stooges-rock in favor of schmaltz disco because, like Nietzsche, he knows that Dionysus isn't enough. Here's his spiel toward the end of "Koyaanisqatsi": "Build your cities on the slopes of Vesuvius. This may very well end my career in music, which is not a career in any case but a passion, fueled in equal parts by anger and love, for how can you feel one without the other?" He's saying the contradictions in Will to Power's music are part of his game plan—as in all great disco, he wants his music to encompass the whole wide world; as with Guns N' Roses, the Velvets, Sonic Youth, the Stones, he wants to use hate to counterbalance (and validate) his lovely-dovey stuff, and vice versa. The way Will to Power completely confound aesthetics and stomp on hippie bullshit reminds me of Led Zeppelin, another posse despised by critics when they came out. And this group uses Muzak like Zep used the blues.

I wonder if Rosenberg thinks about this sort of thing; I also wonder if he's thought of any ways to invest his live audience (assuming he has one) with a will to power of their own. (Maybe he could hand out violins at the door, and tell the crowd they can do whatever they want with 'em as long as they don't hurt anybody.) And I worry about bringing it up because it makes me feel I'm hunting witches and because it wouldn't necessarily make his music worse if he was one, but Rosenberg's chosen philosophers and Norse gods and lobbying groups do betray a certain proto-fascist bent, and though his liner-note admission that "absolute power corrupts absolutely" is a buffer, I can't pretend I'm fully comfortable with all the guy's ruminations. I'm glad Rosenberg has left pieces out of the puzzle, or I might start thinking he's just another pretentious creep.

"Koyaanisqatsi," which like "Anti-Social" before it is significantly the only song on the album where Rosenberg takes the lead vocal, *is* pretentious, in a way. But this is a gushing-deluge-of-pent-up-over-the-years-ulcerous-frustration kind of pretension, and when the dam breaks the waterfall comes at you too fast to bog down, and when it's over it's over, completely erased by the joyous silliness of "Boogie Nights." So I still don't know whether to consider WTP an art band. Inside the sleeve of the new CD, they thank some "famous artist" I've never heard of, but if this is art music, it's a kind we've never experienced before. Which might even make it (gulp) Art Itself.

L.A. Weekly, 17 January 1991

MICHAEL JACKSON LOVES THE SOUND
OF BREAKING GLASS

Hey, so how come nobody's compared the fucker to *There's A Riot Goin' On*?

Well, maybe *Riot* without the cocaine. Or okay, okay, *Fresh* then, with all the reversion to mere professionalism that implies. But I swear there are parallels: Sly warned us of "a mickey in the tastin' of disaster"; Michael's drawing back from a woman with "a mojo in her pocket." And then there's the unintelligibility, the Delta dirge tempos, the creaky abrasions tearing the music apart, the shapeless melodies, the disorienting changes (well, they disorient *me*, anyway), the whole defeated fugitive-turning-hermit *mood* of the thing (or at least the second half of the thing). Michael's obsessing on his "darkest hour and deepest despair," "the agony inside the dying head," confession and pain and anguish. Not to mention world hunger, illiteracy, AIDS, homelessness, gang violence, drug addiction, police brutality, and "streetwalkers walkin' into darkness."

He keeps slipping into these monotonal little mumbles where you gotta rewind to catch whether he said what you think he said, for instance all this stuff in "Jam" about the baby boom and confusions contradicting themselves and being conditioned by the system and being recognized in the temple and (huh?) going fishing. At the end of "In The Closet" and the beginning of "Heal The World," you hear people in the background wailing like they're being flogged. I detect a wee bit of *hostility*.

So what else is new, right? This one is called *Dangerous*, as I suspect you've heard by now even if you have been shaving yaks in Siberia, and Michael Jackson's been doing fear and loathing like nobody's business ever since "The Love You Save," when he first threatened some playmate to "look both ways before you cross me, you're heading for the danger zone." Tire tracks all across her back, he could see she'd had her fun, and he felt compelled to warn her about the Lou Christies of the world who'd strike whenever lightning did, how they'd label her a flirt and someday she'd be all alone. He was *11 years old*. Jump ahead 10 years, he's checked into "Heartbreak Hotel," people act like they know him; "this is *scaring* me," he winces, turning back into a little kid. "Every smile's a trial thought in beguile to hurt me," he says. "Hope is dead."

Add the boys kicking him and beating him then telling him it's fair in "Beat It," the girl who's on his tail 'cause the rabbit done lived in "Billie Jean," the cops in his rearview mirror as he's heading toward the border like Thelma and Louise in "Speed Demon," the evil temptress locking him up and losing the key in "Dirty Diana," and the guy smashing through a window on a black Sunday and leaving bloodstains on the carpet in "Smooth Criminal," and you've got yourself a *concept*, no?

But who noticed? Just like who noticed when Sly left the party in "Thank You (Falettinme Be Mice Elf Agin)," even though the devil was grinning at his gun and bullets started chasing? In "Life," Sly *admitted* that he didn't trust anybody. On *Riot*, he just rubbed everybody's noses in the gloom that was already there; aesthetically, it was redundant (and at least he could've kept some wild energy in), but mental health-wise, maybe it was necessary. I'm convinced this is what's happening on parts of *Dangerous*, certainly in the crawl-on-your-belly-like-a-reptile throb and minor keys of the back-to-back "Who Is It" and "Give In To Me." And in how Michael's nervous little squeal keeps popping up from unseen cracks in the sidewalk to decry betrayal in the former, how the Special Guitar Performance by Michael's Friend Slash in the latter keeps shoveling graveyard soil onto the singer's howling stone-carved blues fury. And it's *definitely* what's happening when Michael demolishes those windshields in the unbelievable (and now deleted) last third of the "Black Or White" video—it's like the guy's known all along that all his songs are about violence and paranoia and stones in his passway and now he wants to SHOVE IT IN OUR FACE, because we were too stupid to understand the subtlety he's been shoving in our face for the last 21 years. And then, having changed from a Black Panther, he throws a garbage can through a window, like Spike Lee.

One thing *Dangerous* makes clear is that the King of Pop loves the sound of breaking glass. In the video, even before the singer exhibits his own appetite for destruction, Macaulay Culkin turns up his amps and feedback and blows out the windows of his parents' house after Dad tells him to turn it down. It's really cool. Halfway through the album, with surrogate voices, the same scene comes off kinda hokey; I root for Dad to come in with his belt. But earlier, the very first sound you hear when you switch on *Dangerous* is glass shattering. And in the provocatively titled "In The Closet," amid quality lust-mush and "Heartbreak Hotel" horror-violin wash, and a Madonna-sounding "Mystery Girl" telling Michael to rub her ache then oohing and ahhing and biting her pillow, the percussion appears to consist primarily of dinner plates being broken over heads and silverware drawers being slammed open and closed.

If there's nothing new happening on this record, as certain fools have claimed (as some of the same fools claimed when *Bad*, which they now like, came out), how do they explain all this *noise*? Right after the apparent Madonna duet (better than her Prince duet if it is one), the next song opens with musique concrète "Summer In The City"/"Expressway To Your Heart" traffic clatter. I'm reminded that Michael wasn't the first person ever to end side one of a great album with a funny fright-song called "Thriller" (Pere Ubu was, on *Dub Housing*), but exactly what "trend" is he trying to "keep up with" here?

Complaints about trendmongering would seem to spring from Michael's newfound association with New Jack Swing entrepreneur Teddy Riley, who is indeed quite the royal pain in the butt here, I admit. New Jack is both colder and more retro than Michael has ever had any reason to be; evolving as it has from late hip-hop and Princebeat, it tends to tighten postdisco rhythm where Michael has always loosened (and thereby stretched) the same. On *Dangerous*, Riley produces half the tracks—seven total, including the first six. The opening title is "Jam," as in "Teddy's Jam" by Guy, the best "song" Riley ever wrote, and that's a clue—used to working with interchangeable singers with the charisma of a church pew, Teddy naturally puts himself in the foreground, hiding Jackson behind oppressive big-beats, corralling him in, de-emphasizing the tunefulness that's always enabled Michael's rhythms to walk on the moon. He tries to help him out of a "jam," I guess, but he uses a little too much force. Apparently not comprehending how much Michael has in common with Johnny Rotten (they're both incomparably feral performers grossed out by their own animal desires, for one thing), Riley tries to *obligate* toughness. Sort of like if Steve Albini got a hold of Kix and tried to make 'em, you know, "rock harder."

For all that, even the Riley numbers have a lot to admire in them. The raps are fine—Teddy picks his rappers on the basis of their sound, a good rule, and Heavy D's wobbly patois in "Jam" is especially fun. And anybody who considers the raps mere street-credibility ploys should consider that Michael was mixing a full-fledged straight-outta–Roosevelt High rap part into the Huey Smith boogie and ravaged guitars of "Going Back To Indiana" when Bell Biv Devoe were still in diapers. Anyway, all of Riley's cuts build to exuberant meshes of synthetic beatplay and organic voiceplay, and in most of them Michael winds up scatting his plastic surgery off— "Remember The Time," Ted's most *orthodox* botchjob, climaxes with a deranged Billy Stewart–style machine-gun-tongue stream of consonant rolls. Michael's ecstatic gasps and whoops are still wonders of nature, and Riley makes more violent use of them than Quincy Jones ever did. "Can't Let Her Get Away," a nonstop, nonlinear barrage of bopgun pops and bumble-beed beats, vamps and squeaks and gurgles, Cupid's arrows flying through space, and what at one point could be a drippy faucet, has as much disco momentum as anything Jackson's waxed since *Off the Wall*.

The Michael-produced half of *Dangerous* can basically be broken down into two categories: Spiritual stuff and stuff that's not. Both categories are 100 percent downtempo, save for the song you're probably already sick of. I hear "Black Or White" as a cave-in to the Motown/rock fusion popularized by dimwit nostalgists Lenny Kravitz and Terence Trent D'Arby in recent years, but it's got a catchy teenpop hook, and if anybody oughta be allowed to sing bubblegum Motown, it's Michael Jackson. The insistent riff and jungle-lite undertow sound cute and rock out at the same time, and the lyric's got a secret history: Prince sang "Am I black or white, am I straight or gay" 10 years ago, and last year Madonna (inspired perhaps by Hot Chocolate's "Brother Louie") said "It makes no difference if you're black or white, if you're a boy or a girl." I expect Michael could identify, but I suspect the words' real blueprint is Slade's goofy 1984 Top 20 electro-grunge/Burundi/square-dance/parade-music comeback, "Run Runaway," where they praised a "chameleon" who was "all things to everyone"; the chorus went, "you like black and white."

Michael wants to be all things to everyone for sure—in his new video he tries to one-up Madonna, Axl, Hammer, Gene Kelly, the U.N., you name it. But "Black Or White" isn't about you or me or Clarence Thomas—it's about Karma Chameleon Michael, why *his* color doesn't matter, how hypocrites kick dirt in his eye. "Once you were made/You changed your shade/ Was your color wrong?" asks the new "Word To The Badd!!," by big brother Jermaine, whose main claim to fame is having recorded with Devo once. But really, Michael's facial makeover was just the ultimate taboo-trouncing glam-rock mindfuck. It's no mistake that glam Elephant Man David Bowie, from the "fights under neon and sleeps in a capsule" in "Jean Genie" to the oxygen tank and silicone hump and mannequin with kill appeal in "Diamond Dogs," foretold so many of Wacko Jacko's tabloid/MTV antics back in the '70s.

In a way, then, "Black Or White" is a pro-sellout sermon, Michael Jackson's "Positively 4th Street," or better yet, his "Public Image" ("was it just the color of my hair?")—he's done a lot of compromisin' on the road to his horizon, and don't it make his brown eyes blue. "Black Or White"'s also one of two ditties on *Dangerous* where he discusses how Important Issues affect you if you're rich, famous, and wanna be left alone. (The other's "Why You Wanna Trip On Me," basically Zapp's 1982 electrofunk hit "Dance Floor" with dumber lyrics.) Maybe Michael's never read past the *USA Today* headlines, but at least he's honest about why all these current events concern him. And if Living Colour and Fugazi, neither of whom know the first thing about music-as-pleasure, can get away with piles of protests about not a damned thing we didn't already know, why shouldn't the most popular entertainer in the world be allowed the same courtesy? If either of *those* losers made a CD with church music, breaking glass, kiddie dialogue, and axe distortion, it'd be "innovative."

Anyway, the church music on *Dangerous* gets pretty awesome. Eurocentric scum that I am, I prefer the towering Sistine Chapel classical spans to all the gospel-tent revivals, but if Michael doesn't put the latter to better use than Foreigner or Helen Reddy, he certainly makes them sound more magnificent than the Clash, Rolling Stones, Mott the Hoople, Melanie, or Parliament ever did. "Will You Be There," performed with quite a bevy of choirs behind him on MTV's 10th-anniversary special (grade schoolers, old ladies, Protestants, Turks, Michael's guardian angel, probably some others), is both a real tearjerker (at least if you're Michael) and a reminder of how the Gregorian sections on the Jacksons' forgotten 1980 *Triumph* album paved the way for what monk-rockers like Enigma are doing now. "Gone Too Soon"'s gooey-schmaltz-for-Ryan-White is gone too soon to complain about; "Keep The Faith"'s George Michael-doing–Norman Vincent Peale universalism and "Heal The World"'s incomprehensible "We Are The World" cloning are girly-man-with-holy-roller-help showcases, expendable if you want 'em to be. But Michael croons all three as prettily as any ballads since "I'll Be There," and if you can put up with somebody advising you to "stop existing, start living" (go ahead, try—it'll make you a better person), you just might be blessed with make-out music that leads you to wonder why you ever cared about "She's Out Of My Life."

So, needless to say, I can't figure out why everybody hates this record so much. That it's lagging behind sales expectations is no big surprise—young '80s fans have grown up, and "Black Or White" is no "Billie Jean," no "Bad" even. But *Bad* dived in with a bellyflop too, remember, and if the 25 million copies it went on to sell weren't quite 48, well, hey, I like watching the music industry sweat a little. *Dangerous* will sire plenty of hits, mark my words—only three or four cuts out of 12 strike me as anything like unmemorable, and if that seems an awful lot, let's hear you hum a few bars of "Just Good Friends" or "Baby Be Mine" (from his last couple LPs, honest!). I'll even go so far as to predict that "Give In To Me," which smolders its lonely sexism to a sleaze-density somewhere between Aerosmith's "Seasons Of Wither" and Free's "Wishing Well," might finally break Michael on AOR in a way that "Beat It" and "Dirty Diana" couldn't quite pull off—he's completely comfortable with the loud riffs now; it doesn't feel at all like a genre move.

I mean, Guy or Another Bad Creation or Al B. Sure! or Johnny Gill *might* make an album with this much depth or personality when hell freezes over. (Johnny Kemp and Keith Sweat won't.) So if *Dangerous* is Michael Jackson's least remarkable set of Sony microchips, and I'll concede that it is, that don't mean it's still not one of the most complex artifacts out there. I've got my own quibbles—first and foremost, that the writing leaves way too much to the imagination; frankly, I wish there were more songs that really talked about murdering people the way *Bad* and *Thriller* did instead of just implying it. I suppose there's a decline in energy—all those sad slow songs—but that's nothing new. *Every* '80s Michael Jackson album had less syncopative propulsion than the one preceding it, and in the case of *Bad* and *Thriller*, I'm no longer convinced said dropoff made the albums worse. Truth be told, "I Want You Back" rocks harder than "Shake Your Body (Down To The Ground)," which rocks harder than "Don't Stop 'Til You Get Enough"—how 'bout that, the man's been getting older all along! But watch that footwork: Nobody else around has aged with more grace. And also with *less*, which is why we need him.

Village Voice, 17 December 1991

IF IT AIN'T BAROQUE, DON'T FIX IT: MICHAEL JACKSON AND FAITHLESS

When I first learned that Michael Jackson was putting out an album called *Blood On The Dance Floor*, I immediately thought of one of the punkest songs I've ever heard, "Somebody's Gonna Get Their Head Kicked In Tonite" by '70s British R&B thugs the Count Bishops: "There's gonna be a pool of *blood* on the old dance floor." It's a really sick image. I also thought of *Carrie*, and Michael's old "Smooth Criminal": "He came into her apartment/He left bloodstains on the carpet." I wondered if "Blood On The Dance Floor" could've been the song that New Jersey girl requested a couple of months ago when she wandered back into her prom after murdering her newborn baby in the ladies' room.

Several *Blood On The* . . . tracks are obsessed with bodies being *penetrated*, by knives, hypodermic needles, penises. After a few minutes of solar-system explosions and click-clacking funk, a cut called "Morphine" breaks for an intermission of ballet Muzak and bird chatter and Michael crooning, prettily but ominously, "Relax, this won't hurt you, before I put it in, close your eyes and count to 10." Next song hints that marriage only confirmed MJ's disgust with sex: "Push it in and stick it out/That ain't what it's all about."

His voice is just so fucking *hard*, all insane, vicious, fist-clenched brimstone and bite. He's been backgrounding his R&B with baroqueness ever since the Jacksons' *Triumph* in 1980, but *Blood* is his most Gothic death-rock album ever. Six of its 13 songs have a monastery eeriness, a dark Europomp sense of space. One three-title sequence goes "Ghosts," then "Is It Scary," then "Scream Louder." "Is It Scary" is toweringly symphonic, full of cellar doors going bump in the night. If you were Michael, you'd have bad dreams, too.

"If you want to see eccentric novelty, I'll be grotesque before your eyes," he promises. By now, he might even be too avant-garde for the mainstream. Unpromoted by his record label as retail-chain managers whined about the "unappetizing album title," the title-track single didn't even go Top 40, and the CD took barely over a month to plummet out of *Billboard*'s Top 100. It's subtitled *History In The Mix* because it half consists of retooled tracks from Wacko Jacko's last album, whose financial floptitude could be blamed on the redundancy factor if almost all its remixes weren't such overwhelming *improvements*. The artwork formerly known as "Scream" adds a "Thank You (Falettinme Be Mice Elf Agin)" bass line, keeps sister Janet's sweet middle-boy-in-Hanson (or Michael-at-10) imitation, but chucks her stupid poetry-recital part. Halfway through, it breaks into chopped-up jazz.

One song later, Michael's talking about selling his soul to the devil for the sake of lust. Boston critic Michael Freedberg says Jackson is living Robert Johnson's life in plain view of billions; the ghosts he's chasing, obviously, are his own. "What do you want from me?" he asks some jezebel homewrecker trying to shake his family tree in "2 Bad." "Tired of you hauntin' me." The entire album is about being chased, followed. "Susie got your number/And Susie ain't your friend/Look who took you under/With seven inches in." She comes back later, in "Superfly Sister": "Susie like to agitate/Get the boys and make 'em wait/Mother's preaching Abraham/Brothers they don't give a damn." Loud guitars barge in, and cute bumper-car honkbeeps, and nonword vocal grunts moonwalking into rhythm. The man sings like nobody can touch him; it's his defense mechanism. Especially in Michael Jackson's world, just because you're paranoid doesn't mean people aren't out to get you.

BACK ON *HISTORY*, MICHAEL DID YET another Susie lyric, a gruesome old-country funeral waltz called "Little Susie," about a little girl falling downstairs and cracking her skull open. There was the sound of a music box being wound up and a section where the melody alluded to *Fiddler on the Roof*. Now there's this new song, "Angeline," a sort of ice ballet evolving into "Little Susie"–style music-box/death-klezmer fusion, but you won't find it on Michael's new CD; it's on *Reverence*, by the British quartet Faith-

MICHAEL JACKSON: *BLOOD ON THE DANCE FLOOR: HISTORY IN THE MIX* (EPIC, 1997)

less, the only dance album this year *more* Gothic than Michael's. The "Angeline" vocal is quaint Harlem-speakeasy-movie fake blues; the words have a man at home with crying kids and dying houseplants, while his wife's out dancing on tavern tables, soaking herself in cheap perfume, being undressed by kings and seeing some things a woman ain't supposed to see. He's begging her, please come home.

Produced by house duo Rollo and Sister Bliss (responsible for past club hits by Kristine W), the music on *Reverence* is all knocks, whooshes, Arabic scales, drawn-out droning, heroin-blues guitar lines, Bach-like fugue sections, dub-echo potholes and trap doors expanding into garish cathedrals of incrementally changing Philip Glass–trance opera-aria disco. All of which adds up, I guess, to "trip-hop," but even if like me you gag at the word "pre-millennium," don't worry. Proud to be programmed ("I make no apology for linking my thinking with computer technology"), Maxi Jazz raps with Tricky's kicky Afro-Anglican accent but not Tricky's icky numb-mumble mannerisms. When he hitches his edgy monotone up an octave, he inches toward Coolio in "Gangsta's Paradise." And he's backed by almost the only trip-hop ever to be as fast and bubbly as it is dark.

The gorgeous Latin high Mass "Salva Mea" opens with a waif whispering nobody-loves-me Portishead psychoanalysis claptrap, but before long her lethargy speeds up with drastic fantastic abruptness into long organ lines, then racing synthesizer loops, spareness that sounds spooky and alive at the same time. The music takes four or five orchestrally complex minutes just for its solipsistic rapping ("Reality is dreaming/just below my skin, I'm screaming") to start; now and then after that, its bottom falls out. Cosmic as hell, yet there's something remarkably earthy about this band: "Hole in my tooth, uncouth," Maxi brags. There's a song about a (literally) dirty old man; one about a 14-year-old bully getting his ass whupped over his base-ball cap on the way home; a defiantly anti-PC one about being too obsessed with someone to give a shit about the ozone layer or apartheid.

"Don't Leave" is a divorce song, produced to sound like a scratchy old vinyl folk-rock 45. A woman comes in humming gospel soul, then a man starts missing her, humble and browbeaten as Hootie and the Blowfish be-fore they started getting in fights in front of convenience stores. Bummed that she's "packing [her] bags like people in the movies do," he remembers her favorite Joni hit, admits he ain't an easy man to love. "He" being singer and songwriter Jamie Catto, who, the liner notes hilariously brag, "has been arrested in nearly every European city for possession of cannabis, which shows his love of travel."

Maxi Jazz, on the other hand, is a Buddhist former Jah Wobble crony who insists, "I only smoke weed when I need to eat." He's verbose with bullshit, erotically fixated, agonizing over premature ejaculation, yearning to "dream about making mad love on the heath, tearing off tights with my teeth." But it's half past 3, and an alarm clock is his rhythm track, and church bells are clanging, and he can't get no sleep. It's a haunted sound, as tormented as Michael Jackson. Maxi's mind plays tricks on him like a Geto Boy: "Creaky noises make my skin creep."

In "If Lovin' You Is Wrong," perched on a minimal hammer-and-chisel beat, circled by pornographic mmmmms and ohhhhs and singing bed-springs, his girlfriend's fingers on his keyboard, Maxi walks a fine line be-tween horniness and self-mocking silliness: "I finished my beer, so come here/and get nice while I lick your ear/Put your legs over there and kinda swing on the chair/I swear you look wicked with your panties in your hair." Just like Springsteen getting "sick of sitting round here trying to write this book" in "Dancing In The Dark," hanging alone around Maxi's pad only made him "tired of magazine articles we be forced to write." Me too! I should go get laid.

L.A. Weekly, 18 July 1997

THEY KNOW WHAT THEY REALLY REALLY WANT AND
THEY KNOW HOW TO GET IT: SPICE GIRLS AND GINA G

Not that I'm averse to getting more notches on my belt, but I don't particularly wannabe any of the Spice Girls' lovers, not yet anyway. Which I
guess means I'm also not required to (orgywise or otherwise) "get with"
their friends; two of the first four songs on *Spice* are basically "We Are
Family" rewrites (and two of the first four are also basically "What's Love
Got To Do With It" rewrites), how sisterly of them. See, my problem is two
of these sisters outright *bug* me: babydollish, blond-pig-tailed "Em in the
place who likes it in your face" and cold, unsmiling George-Michael-video-
Eurobitch-sophisticate. "Easy V [who] doesn't come for free she's a real lie-
dee" (rapped in Cockney à la Eliza Doolittle—so does that mean the others
are all fake lie-dees because they're not prostitutes?).

Then there's the redheaded one—my jury's still undecided on her. On
Saturday Night Live, clad in what looked like a white bed sheet with slogans
and her name (Geri) smudged all over it, she sang way off-key but at least
her mike was turned on. And so was she: she kept mugging for the camera, making hypothetically alluring kissy faces and sticking her *Kiss Alive*
tongue out. Like the blond one, she seems slightly chunky and unwaiflike,
almost like an actual adult female, so I feel a little guilty that she jarred
me by coming off so repulsive; the music world hasn't witnessed sluttiness
this slimy since who, Samantha Fox? I assume she was *joking*—she didn't
remind me of *Baywatch* so much as the sort of call girl–booby bimbo you'd
wince at on some bad BBC comedy.

The two Spices I like for sure are both buff and named Melanie; they
also have the best voices. The athletic one who wears sweat suits and does
backflips belted soulful and loud on SNL, but it's token dark-skinned Melanie, the right-on-rapping live wire who wears the coolest clothes (battle-
fatigue trousers and a bra on SNL) and shows the most cleavage, that everybody in my peer group, from my seven-year-old daughter on up, picks
as their favorite. Still, the whole point of assigning individual "personalities," obviously, just like with the Monkees or Village People, is to cover *all*
social-class fantasy-taste bases.

People don't even seem to agree on the undeniable: that the first and
biggest worldwide Spice hit, "Wannabe," just plain *rocks*, with humor, from

its chortling laugh at point one on. It's got a hard '60s garage-guitar riff, but unlike, say, "Devil's Haircut" by Beck, where the garage riff just stands alone in the corner with no comparable rhythm or voice pushing it forward, this riff actually helps communicate punk-rock emotion—"If you really bug me then I'll say good-bye." The smartest of the several slogans inside *Spice*'s sleeve proclaims, "Silence Is Golden but Shouting Is Fun," and between party chatter and unison yells and "you've got it, you've got it" chants, you can tell the girls believe it. The only other piece of 1997 music that you could compare to "Wannabe"'s pummeling oi-like "huh!huh!huh!huh!" hoodlum-gang grunts is, of all things, "Firestarter" by Prodigy.

The song is actually quite *complex*, mixing pretty singing and fast rhyming with an eccentric energy comparable to Neneh Cherry doing "Buffalo Stance"; something about black women with British accents (see also Cookie Crew, Wee Papa Girls) always makes rapping sting like a bee. Gets as cryptic as Beck, too: if the zigazig-hah part really does mean they want a cigar, this stogy song out-smokes Pink Floyd's. The "Pass the Dutchie"–stylee early-'80s-reggae-toast part—"slam your body down and wind eet all around"—really does slam, so maybe Spice Girls lie down by the Rivers of Babylon, too. Another CD cover slogan, "Can You Handle a Spice Girl?," is the 1997 equivalent of the New York Dolls' "Do you think that you could make it with Frankenstein?"; "If you want my future, forget my past," the Spices demand, because, as David Johansen could tell you, a Babylon girl ain't *got* no past.

Problem is, nobody will let the Spice Girls forget theirs. Their partially Spanish album closer, "If U Can't Dance," rightly places people with unlocked hips higher in the prospective-mate hierarchy than people with two left feet, but like most music preferred by suburban kids who know how to dance, the Spice Girls are continually dissed as "phony" or "manufactured" by stodgy Son Volt fans. So what if their first four singles all went to No. 1 in England, the argument goes, when they had to pass an audition (from a manager they later fired!) just to join together in the first place? But big whoop—in Japan, this year's hottest new cutie-pie-pop starlet, Date Kyoko, is a tube-topped 5-foot-4 17-year-old *created via computer animation*. The Spice Girls, by contrast, have real-life baggage to live down: praising Thatcher, posing nude, having libidos, maybe even dating Tricky. So inevitably, now there are websites where you can slap their faces.

Kinda unfair when nobody ever slaps En Vogue or TLC, neither of whose faces manage half the Spice Girls' bounce. "Do you think I'm really cool and sexy?" one Spice queries in "Last Time Lover," blatantly honoring TLC. But if anything, it's this album's slightly streetwise urban-constipatory bent that keeps it from quite becoming the mythical "mountain of spices in the arms of the desired" that multicolored dancegal trio Seduction poeticized about in 1989. In other words, it ain't quite disco enough: whichever Spice keeps borrowing the hushed-sickliness-as-sultriness fallacy from the neighing hoarsemouth chick with short red hair in TLC should go invest in a few Latin freestyle records instead.

Mostly though, funky bass lines from Kool and the Gang, Chic, Marvin Gaye (in their get-it-on ballads, of course), and the Gap Band keep the Spice Girls' lacy harmonies and old-school microphone-handoffs from dragging; "Mama" is a warmly sappy Supremes-inspired thank-you note, veering into a ridiculous gospel-choir climax worthy of the talent show in *Fame*; "Something Kinda Funny" gliiiiiides like "Let's Groove" by Earth, Wind & Fire (a major influence, too, by the way, on current dancegal trio Wild Orchid, whose most-EWF song invents "tambourine" as a new euphemism for "vagina"). And though the lyric sheet swears otherwise, I always hear "Who Do You Think You Are" as discussing how "the rush is on to get out of the bathroom" to attend a "traditional wedding"!

WHEN THEY TRY TO GET A BIT ARTY IN "Naked" by rapping in snoozy subdued sweet-taboo lounge-dub whispers over an apparent phone line, though, the Spicers actually forfeit some vitality, and there's a lesson in that. Same thing happens to Australian twirl-girl rookie Gina G in the "Motiv8 Vintage Honey Mix" of her hit "Ooh Aah . . . Just A Little Bit" at the end of her debut disc, *Fresh:* may well be trip-hoppier therefore trendier than the original mix, but it's not nearly as catchy.

Then again, hardly anything lately is — "Ooh Aah" in its pop-radio form is an expert confection of interlocking speed-stuttered repetitious-trance electro-breakdance beats, above which Gina G breathily metronomes too-childlike-to-be-suggestive "ooh ahh"s as if she were a Kit-Cat clock ticking and tocking its way to the bank, its Cheshire smile bursting with catnip. To boot, the rest of *Fresh* creates a veritable sunshiny environment of big, happy hooks and clear-enough-to-see-yourself production. Madonna hasn't made an album this fun, or this disco, since 1983.

Being from Melbourne, Gina G probably includes Olivia Newton-John and Kylie Minogue in her evolutionary lineage, and being a Eurovision Song Contest winner probably ABBA. On her CD cover, her full frontal nudity is coated in chocolate and topped by wiry orange hair somewhere

BABYLON SPICE GIRLS AIN'T GOT NO PAST—OR DO THEY?
(PHOTO: DEAN FREEMAN 8/00)

between Wilma Flintstone, Albert Einstein, and a Brillo pad. Inside, she's sprawled on her back in an off-white snow-leopard-print bikini plus red high heels and matching nail polish, and her skin is albino-pale. On the back she's more jaunty, with a blue Annie Hall-ish hat tilted to its side, a flowing scarf, spider eye shadow like Alice Cooper in 1971, and a pinstripe suit opened at the bosom, revealing plastic mannequin skin beneath.

She coos three heart-wrenching miss-you ballads, but they're not mere schlock; the melodies reveal hidden red-clay roots—"It Doesn't Mean Goodbye" is old-country country worthy of ABBA at their bluest, with raindrop doo-wop backup, tailing off into jazziness after five minutes of husbands packing bags and running for trains and playing with fire. More often, though, Gina's music is unashamed high-bpm Eurodisco, symphonically rising and raising hands to the sky, even more rooted in Giorgio Moroder than techno is, with plenty of PG-rated innuendo about getting fresh and feeling love deep down inside. The flamencofied guitars and castanets creating a storm-cloud-tinged Mediterranean-island-at-midnight undercurrent in "Ti Amo" don't recall the Laura Branigan tune of the same name so much as Madonna's "La Isla Bonita." And "Rhythm Of My Life" is simply over the top, jabbering giddy sugar-rush spunk that'd make Stacey Q proud; "bay-bee bay-bee bay-buh-buh-buh-bay-bee," into a brazen verse tackling cultural fragmentation at its very core: "Cut your hair, rip your jeans/I'm a victim of your fashion scene/My brother doesn't like you/My sister thinks you're cool." Sounds like a fan letter to the Spice Girls.

L.A. Weekly, 2 May 1997

PAZZ & JOP BALLOT EXCERPT 1998

1998 was, perhaps disturbingly, the year all my kids started thinking like music critics. It was the year my 13-year-old son Linus downloaded Harvey Danger songs from the Internet like people my age used to buy Grand Funk Railroad 45s, heard "Footloose" by Kenny Loggins on the radio and told me it's got the same guitar riff as "Rockafeller Skank," and decided that all the tracks besides "Lullaby" on Shawn Mullins's album prove "he's just some boring folksinger always talking about his culture." (In the land of eighth-grade Social Studies textbooks, the word "culture" is clearly a pejorative.)

It was also the year I verified Linus's theory that the best song you hear over the radio whenever you drive from Philly to New York will always be the one that comes on (and you immediately lose) just as you finally begin to enter the Holland Tunnel. Last time we drove in, the culprit was "Du Hast" by Rammstein, a band whose audience Linus smart-assedly defines as "Marilyn Manson fans and rock critics who used to live in Germany." When I offered my learned opinion that Krauts seem to come more naturally and convincingly to ominous machine-metal muzik than Brits or Americans do, he shot back with "And that's a *good* thing?"

Speaking of machines, my outgoing voicemail right now has nine-year-old Spice fan Coco and seven-year-old Beastie fan Sherman squeaking "Right about now, the funk soul brutha! Check it *out* now, the funk soul brutha brutha brutha brutha . . ." Coco and Sherman are also considering performing "Tubthumping" for their school talent show (leaving in the piss-all-night and cider-whiskey-lager-vodka references, and falling down and getting back up again on cue), but in music class their teacher just makes them harmonize on tediously unsubtle R&B mush where the singers treat every note like a solo—"All My Life" by K-Ci and Jojo, "My Heart

Will Go On" by Celine Dion, and R. Kelly's unfortunately eternal "I Believe I Can Fly," which Coco informs me has recently inspired the following morbidly political fourth-grade playground parody: "I believe I will die/I got shot by the FBI/All I wanted was a chicken wing/A bag of chips and some collard greens. . . ."

SINGLES AGAIN AND AGAIN

People listen to music one song at a time; always have, probably always will. But strangely, rock critics have almost never *reviewed* music one song at a time—at least not until recently, when iTunes and digital leaks have seemingly sent purchasing practices scurrying back to the pre-album era that rock criticism itself theoretically helped kill off. Meanwhile, corporate partnerships and disappearing ad dollars and diminishing budgets and faint-hearted publishers, coupled with meaninglessly release-date-geared biz/press symbiosis (which can be traced back to the early '90s, when *Entertainment Weekly* began publishing and SoundScan started highlighting first-week retail figures), have shrunk record-review word counts to haiku levels; print media continue to lose ground to websites that may well never turn a profit themselves. All of which is to say that, in a sense, rock criticism lived by the album. And now, as singles sales climb while album sales continue to collapse, professional rock criticism may well be dying with the album.

But just as in the high album era (say, *Sgt. Pepper's* to *Nevermind* or whatever) music fans never stopped listening to singles on the radio or movie soundtracks or K-Tel compilations or 45 spindles, there have always been anomalous columnists who paid as much attention to singles as to albums—Steven Harvey and others in *New York Rocker*, Ken Barnes in '80s *Creem*, Jim Green in *Trouser Press*, Michael Freedberg in the *Boston Phoenix*, John Leland then Charles Aaron in *Spin*. In 1989, Dave Marsh put out a book called *The Heart of Rock and Soul: The 1001 Greatest Singles Ever Made*, arguing that the single, as much as the album, is rock and pop music's natural unit of measurement. I've always liked that idea, and so over the years I've managed to con a number of editors into giving me a regular forum for singles reviews: "45s Magnum" in *Creem Metal* in the mid-'80s, "Juke Box Jury" then "Singles Going Steady" in *Creem* proper around the start of the '90s, columns called "Singles Again" in both the *Village Voice* in the early '00s and online magazine *Blurt* later in the decade, and a "Single of The Day" feature for rollingstone.com in 2008.

I also twice, out of the goodness of my heart and obsessive-compulsiveness of my soul, signed on as part of an international stable of unpaid amateur-to-careerist critics offering up freewheeling, numerically scored reviews of (mostly chart-hit) singles. And though neither added a red cent to my income, critiquing songs for Phil Dellio's Toronto-based print fanzine *Radio On* in the early to mid-'90s and William Bloody Swygart's Leeds-based website *Singles Jukebox* as the '00s made way for the '10s were as much fun as I've had writing about music anywhere. Though the former came out only once or twice a year, and the latter was updated three times a day, both ranked current singles by averaging scores (0 to 10) from about a dozen smart, idiosyncratic writers at a time. And though both seemed to be primarily read by the people writing for them, and neither was immune to in-jokes or infights, both did what the much bigger publications I wrote for almost never seemed capable of—they turned music criticism into a conversation that, at its best, could seem like a microcosm of the real social world.

Several of the reviews in this chapter are taken from one outlet or the other; they end with the scores I gave the songs at the time. And like the long *Voice* essay I also include about what I then wrong-headedly considered the rock-bottom state of pop radio in 1986, many of them tend to illustrate the folly of reviewing records in real time, when ten or 20 years down the line might be more reliable. The situation I've been in at a given moment—married or single, tied to home fires or damned to go out every night, 19 or 29 or 39 or 49, stuck in a subway city where I don't hear the car radio or a normal place where I do—has probably been just as relevant in determining how I judged the quality of pop radio and pop hits as how they actually, you know, sounded.

And shifting technology played a role, too. I'm the kind of guy who didn't even own his first cell phone until 2009, see, and as the '00s dragged on, my listening had actually managed to turn *less* singles-oriented than most of my younger, less digitally ambivalent peers. I mostly, at the time, listened to music on a five-disc CD player on random shuffle, almost never attending to albums from beginning to end. So theoretically, the idea of "tracks" (the term that seemed to be displacing "singles" in the rock-crit lexicon) should have made perfect sense to me. But my CD changer was at the other end of my living room from my couch and didn't light up very well. And I'm nearsighted. So by the time I could get over to it to figure out what numbered track was playing, so I could mark it on a CD-cover-affixed post-it note, the player had invariably switched to the next cut. It also bugged me that, while great singles should connect you with other people, as far as I could tell great iTunes tracks mostly connected you with *yourself*. And with the Internet, you can't really stumble onto songs by accident like you used to back in radio days.

So I got pretty cranky about it for a while there. After more than a decade in New York, and a year and a half of queasily watching music-industry sausage get made at *Billboard*, particularly at a depressing time of alternate revenue streams failing to counter plummeting sales, I'd pretty much given up on ever caring about hit singles again. But in 2009, I moved to Austin, where I again had a car radio, and I started contributing to *Singles Jukebox*, which gave me another fun reason to keep up. And before I knew it I was on my way to a favorite-100-singles-of-the-year list. Then a year later, I was playing CDs in the car. I foresee this cycle recurring, in some form or other, 'til the day I die.

The silly hippie Shangri-La symbolized by the Summer Of Love supposedly collapsed at Altamont or the funerals of a handful of acid-rock icons,
but if you grew up in the '70s, you know better. The fact is that free love
and bellbottoms were so pervasive by 1971 or so, they were absorbed by
even the squarest segments of popular culture. Vanity Fare, five trusting
souls from England, sang about "Hitchin' A Ride," not worrying for a second that the driver might be packing heat beneath his eight-track deck,
and a man called Lobo dreamed of conquering the wild frontier with you
and a dog named Boo.

This was AM-radio *pop*—as distinguished from FM-radio rock, which was
fabricating medieval poetry or looking to Charlie Poole or Robert Johnson.
Suddenly rock seemed obsessed with its authenticity. Commercialism was
a mortal sin; rock was something serious, to be "appreciated," not used up
and then disposed of. The Top 40 succumbed to teenybop wimps, studio
musicians disguised as groups, and TV stars disguised as singers, but if you
scoffed at them, it's time you reconsidered. Rhino's *Have A Nice Day,* with
10 volumes done and five more in the works, is your chance.

Compiled, no doubt, by some very sick minds, *Have A Nice Day* captures
the exploitative ephemerality of classic K-Tel Hell in all its raging glory.
To my ears, at least one in every five cuts holds up as well as anything on
Layla or *Who's Next* or even *Moondance,* partly because the decent tracks
on those albums have been drummed into my consciousness so often for
so long that they're not special anymore, but also because quite a few hits
on this compilation had more electricity in the first place.

It's hard to envision very many of the acts on this anthology making
a career of the music business; ubiquitous idols are bypassed in favor of
what mainly amounts to one-hit wonders. The newest tracks on volumes
one to 10 date from mid-1973, a full two years before the dawn of disco.
There's too much Jesus rock ("Spirit In The Sky," "Put Your Hand In The
Hand," "Superstar," et al.), and guitar grunge is generally ignored, though
Mountain's "Mississippi Queen" dumps a two-ton truckload.

Since early '70s R&B, from the Spinners to *Superfly*, was such a righteous riot that it couldn't help overshadowing everything else in sight, the overwhelming Caucasian slant of the selections is perhaps excusable; as is, Dobie Gray's "Drift Away" seems somehow out of place, too *legitimately* good, not cheesy enough. Otherwise, only the countripolitan sequence on volume four—"Rose Garden," "For The Good Times," "Help Me Make It Through The Night," "Mr. Bojangles"—threatens to dissolve into mere integrity.

The smarm can get real embarrassing. But in miracles like the DeFranco Family's "Heartbeat—It's A Lovebeat" and Melanie's "Brand New Key" there's a Zeitgeist at work, and an aesthetic. The Zeitgeist says everything is beautiful; the aesthetic says everything's allowed. So the Partridge Family can back Monkees harmonies with Kurt Weill cabaret rhythms, and if the ragtime revival exemplified by the Pipkins' "Gimme Dat Ding" and Hurricane Smith's "Oh, Babe, What Would You Say?" is nothing but camp, so what? Bobby Bloom's "Montego Bay" wants to be a calypso; Mungo Jerry's "In The Summertime" aims for skiffle. The Sandpipers' beatific "Come Saturday Morning" is out-and-out middle-of-the-road swill, but its Oscar-nominated arrangement is to die for. Succulent strings, bawdy brass, foreign words, primal chants—Nixon-era pop proves how gimmicks can be good things.

Too often, the mood suggests all was for the best in this best of all possible worlds; thus the title *Have A Nice Day*. But in "Alone Again (Naturally)," Gilbert O'Sullivan promises to throw himself off a nearby tower when his bride stands him up on his wedding day. The Big Issues aren't ignored, either: We get imperialist carnage in Coven's "One Tin Soldier (The Legend Of Billy Jack)"; life on the run from the law in R. Dean Taylor's "Indiana Wants Me"; discrimination against "longhaired freaky people" in the Five Man Electrical Band's "Signs"; and rock journalism in Dr. Hook's "The Cover Of 'Rolling Stone'." And forget Lou Reed—it was the Buoys who overcame the modern world's *final* taboo, charting with "Timothy," a gruesome tale of cannibalism.

Face it: This crass trash was ahead of its time. In "Popcorn," Hot Butter let a new synthesizer come in and do the popcorn machine like Eurodisco producers would seven years later; likewise, in "Son Of My Father," one such producer, Giorgio Moroder, initiates hooks he would revive almost a decade later in Blondie's "Call Me." Jerry Reed's "When You're Hot, You're Hot," Commander Cody's "Hot Rod Lincoln," and the introduction to "Gimme Dat Ding" provide solid rap links back to the talking blues and Pigmeat Markham and forward to the hip-hop nation. And you'll be hard pressed to find a present-day fortysomething rock survivor who can match the midlife angst of Bobby Russell's "Saturday Morning Confusion," a suburban nightmare where pregnant dogs and grill-swiping neighbors torment a hungover dad who just wants to watch the game of the week. It was the first single I ever bought; for better or worse, the songs on *Have A Nice Day* are our roots. I can't hear "Don't Pull Your Love" without imagining Hamilton, Joe Frank, and Reynolds peering down at me from Mount Olympus—and I wouldn't have it any other way.

Rolling Stone, 8 March 1990

ZAGER AND EVANS: "IN THE YEAR 2525"

One time in a *Rolling Stone* review I said the first record I ever bought was "Saturday Morning Confusion" by Bobby Russell (the guy who wrote "Little Green Apples," "Honey," and "The Night The Lights Went Out In Georgia"). But while I definitely remember *liking* the song a lot when I was ten in 1971 (probably not so much because of its sarcastic-but-cheery suburban-family ethos as because of "let it be known that at five the TV is going to be tuned to the game of the week," my favorite TV program at the time), I now can't remember actually *owning* a copy. So maybe I *didn't* buy it— maybe I just asked for it on my Christmas list once. Regardless, to this day I enjoy how its strings and drum machines bounce, at least until the sappy "day is done" final verse. And I identify with the words more than ever now that I'm a suburban dad myself (even though I'd rather listen to Martina than Courtney Love yell at me any day): "I can hear my wife yelling take 'em all to the show/I'll take the whole neighborhood to the show/I'll just walk out in back where the money tree grows/Grab me a handful and off to the show we'll go." This March I appropriately put the song on a birthday tape I made for our divorced neighbor Diane, whose kids I had just taken to see *The Brady Bunch Movie* and *Man Of The House*.

Anyway, the first record I *positively* remember being obsessed enough about to *buy* was "In The Year 2525" by Zager and Evans, which was actually a hit two years before "Saturday Morning Confusion," when I was eight— though I think I must've been at least eleven when I bought it, since I vaguely remember I was living in our house in West Bloomfield, Michigan, at the time, and I didn't start living there until I got out of the Sarah Fisher orphanage in Farmington in early 1972. My mom died of ovarian cancer when I was nine, in 1970; my dad remarried, then hung himself in 1974 (and before he died, another of my favorite songs was "Suicide Is Painless" from *M*A*S*H*)—to put this in perspective, my son Linus is ten now, and he still usually seems like a *little kid*. So I guess my family life was a lot more confused than the family life in "Saturday Morning Confusion," though I don't exactly *remember* it as being fucked-up; for self-defense reasons probably, I must've blocked from my memory a lot of unpleasant details from when I was growing up. One thing I've been noticing in the last year or so is that I feel much more natural being a parent to Coco and Sherman—who are five and three years old—than I do being a parent to Linus, which is actually a huge *effort* for me, and part of the reason might have something to do with me never having quite been Linus's age in a normal sense. Anyway, the point of all this psychobabble is that I wish I could tell stories about my childhood and adolescence in my writing more than I do, but the stories are hiding someplace I can't get to. Mostly I just remember always waiting hours in the snow for my stepmother to say we could come inside to play, and even hoping it might rain. Of course, maybe it's just possible my childhood was really *boring* despite all the traumatic stuff, and nothing much ever happened to me.

Okay: Joel Whitburn's book *Top 40 Hits* says Zager and Evans were a singing duo from Nebraska; they originally put out "In The Year 2525 (Exordium & Terminus)" on a small label in 1968, but it didn't become a hit until June 1969. It went number-one for six weeks, and they never had another hit before or since. Technically, I bought their album instead of their single; in fact, I bought *two* of their albums, both as cutouts (in a K-Mart I think) for a couple dollars. I don't remember much about the records (which I haven't owned or even seen copies of for years) except that the one that didn't have "2525" on it had a greyish-white cover, which I'm pretty sure pictured Zager and Evans recuperating on crutches in an antiseptically sanitized mental institution.

One of the albums had a song called I believe "Reginald Ludwig," about a snobby rich person who I associated with our snobby next-door neighbors the Lords and whichever even snobbier neighbor put a hate letter in our mailbox once about my dad's "Roto-Tiller and all that dirt dirt dirt" in our unsodded front yard. And Dave Marsh's *New Book of Rock Lists* last year jogged my memory about another track called "Mr. Turnkey," apparently about a guy who rapes a woman who makes fun of him in jail, then bleeds to death after he nails his hand to the cell wall. I doubt I fully understood the plot at the time—at least I hope not.

"In The Year 2525" is a very dark record—psychedelic-rock-influenced sci-fi armageddon-cliché pop about the downfall of mankind and the end of the world. It was the most popular single in the country the week Neil Armstrong became the first human to walk on the moon—appropriately, since more than a few people at the time connected moonwalking with doomsday. A whole bunch of early '70s songs—"Ball Of Confusion," "Freddie's Dead," "Inner City Blues," Black Sabbath's "Into The Void," the MC5's "Gotta Keep Movin'"—equated rockets and moonshots with pollution and the abyss and kids escaping reality and growing up too soon. And my biological mom, who probably was already dying, was a devout Catholic who was convinced that Apollo 11 was opening Pandora's box by trying to take a short cut to heaven. She might've heard some priest do a homily that compared risking getting burned up by the sun with risking hellfire; all I know for sure is that I got nightmares myself after looking at the astronaut pictures in my Cub Scout manual.

Possibly Zager and Evans were just jumping on the same bandwagon that the Grass Roots ("I'd Wait A Million Years") and Troggs ("When Will The Rain Come") and Turtles ("Grim Reaper Of Love") and Sonny & Cher ("Love Don't Come") tried hopping at the time, the Gothic death-gloom bandwagon probably invented when the Yardbirds did "Heart Full Of Soul" and "Still I'm Sad" and "Shapes Of Things" in 1965 and 1966. But of course at the time I didn't know any such bandwagon existed (in fact I still didn't know it existed until *a couple months ago*!), so I found "In The Year 2525"'s corny synthesizer-and-acoustic-guitar-strum blastoff-melodrama haunting (and a quarter century later I still do). There was probably some forbidden risk involved in me liking something that scared me a little and would've scared my Mom more, and maybe her funeral made haunting sounds feel like real life to me—I don't know. The most relevant fact in my self-image at the time concerned my crumminess at sports. I'd always gone to Catholic school, and I liked gloomy Gregorian high-mass hymns better than happy hippie folk-mass ones, and I really dug paleontology, but I'd never cared much about science fiction (except maybe *Planet of the Apes*).

I expect I was smart enough to realize that Zager's and Evans's stuff about how people won't talk to each other or use their bodies thousands of years from now, and how God's gonna tear everything down and start over, was mainly just bullshit. But weirdly, their one prediction that definitely did jar me was the one about how "you'll get your sons and get your daughters too from the bottom of a long glass tube" in the year 6565—a couple millennia late, it turns out, though I don't know if Z&E had artificial insemination in mind. "Come And Get It" by Badfinger in 1970 was the first song that I remember consciously associating with sex, and a few years later in my basement by my pool table I thought the sexiest songs on my temporary stepsister Debbie Moore's copy of *Goodbye Yellow Brick Road* weren't the ones about lesbians or dirty little girls, but rather "Social Disease," "Saturday Night's Alright For Fighting," and "The Ballad Of Danny Bailey (1909–34)"—"And he found faith in danger/A lifestyle he lived by/A runnin' gun youngster/In a sad restless age." (I've always hated "Harmony" and the Marilyn Monroe song.) But I guess "2525" had been about sex too, in its own way. Maybe it just *comforted* me—maybe when you're eight or nine, a long glass test tube seems *less* scary.

Why Music Sucks, June 1995

RADIO '86: DEAD AIR

Rock'n'roll radio has never been as boring as it's been this year. Not in the middle '70s, not in the early '60s, not ever. By which I'm mainly talking Top 40, but with "classics"-damaged Apartheid-Oriented Rock and crossover-damaged Urbane Contemporary rapidly closing whatever minuscule gaps remain between formats, and with Top 40 adopting Adult Contemporary's no-fast-ones rule, distinctions are pretty useless anyway. (Even college stations have tightened their playlists.) For the first time in history, the formulas for pop success have been reduced to mere studio technique. Every hit is fatuous, syrupy, middlebrow swill; every hit (except for born-again oldies, which there are more of than ever) has the same automaton drumbeat. Almost every hit has a fussy little guitar part—this is "rock," remember? Nothing sounds nasty, nothing sounds innocent, nothing sounds spontaneous. There is no sense of humor, no sense of dread, no sex, no anger, no hard rock (in one of the most productive hard rock years ever), no funk, no soul.

Don't get me wrong. I'm not just bitching because there's lots of stuff I like that radio doesn't play. Of course I'm unconvinced, as always, that there's anything inherent in Green River's or Bogshed's or Peter Stampfel's noise that would prevent them from becoming stars if they had FM, MTV,

Warner Bros., and tons of money on their side; claims of "inaccessibility" are mostly reactionary bullshit. Besides, radio has ignored adventurous music ever since *Trout Mask Replica*, or Dock Boggs, and that negligence has never made the airwaves unlistenable before. I mean, I may love the Stooges to death, but I dig the patooties out of the Stylistics and Allman Brothers anyway. Damned if I can say the same about David & David or New Edition.

Let me put it another way. In 1984, a barely visible rock underground spewed out perfectly wonderful recordings by the Folk Devils, Scraping Foetus Off the Wheel, and Venom. But I didn't give a fuck, because like everybody else with ears (save for a few pud-brained collector scumbags) I was too busy listening to the radio. Which was amazing. After *Thriller* and following the over-hyped and under-existent British invasion of 1983, American white music and black music were finally communicating (with each other and to us) again—"When Doves Cry" was soul with distorted guitars, "Jump" heavy metal with disco percussion, "What's Love Got To Do With It" R&B with Anglo percussion, "Glamorous Life" saxy funk with Latin percussion, "Dancing In The Dark" and "Girls Just Wanna Have Fun" Caucasian pop with Arthur Baker remixes. The Top 40 was desegregating, opening to hard rock, emphasizing what was new, and sounding livelier and more progressive than it had in ages—since the glory days of 1965, maybe. Fantastic hits multiplied like unpaid bills: "Borderline," "Boys Of Summer," "Hold Me Now," "Swept Away," "Missing You," "Run To You," "Out Of Touch," "Jungle Love," "If I'd Been The One," "Foolish Heart," "Jam On It," "99 Luftballons," "Round And Round," "Authority Song"/"Pink Houses (Acoustic)"—death-metal fetish or no death-metal fetish, I still love these records. Even that faceless aggregation of trans-Atlantic AOR vets called Foreigner came up with the gospelly gem "I Want To Know What Love Is."

What sucks is that "I Want To Know What Love Is" has more personality, more tension, more feeling, *less facelessness* than just about any 1986 hit. In fact, so do "Hot Blooded," "Dirty White Boy," "Urgent," maybe even "Cold As Ice." Except for an indie-label rap-associated novelty-fluke Aerosmith cover by Run-D.M.C. (both the only hard rock, and until they followed it up with "You Be Illin'," the only funk item on this year's chart), I've drawn repeated enjoyment from a grand total of two Top 40 songs since January: the Pet Shop Boys' "West End Girls," which comments on the very vapidity it taps and thus asserts itself as an "All The Young Dudes" for the mall generation, and Electric Light Orchestra's "Calling America," about six fine English boys coping with modern-world telecommunications difficulties and sounding exactly like the Move should have but didn't. (AC/DC's genius epistemological query "Who Made Who," easily the greatest '86 major-label 45, never reached Top 40.) These singles, like the 1984 list above, sound like the work of human beings. Every other 1986 Top 40 hit sounds like it came out of a machine.

Perhaps you disagree. After all, there *are* other records that produce pleasure. But "pleasure" is more a science these days than an art; there's plenty of music you might like, but nothing you *need*. A purely competent, purely professional perfection intrudes on nearly every recent major-label release. You can't even call the sappy ballads on the radio "schlock" anymore—upscale and proud, they know better than to sound tacky. In an era when you can program a computer to develop hooks, mere inoffensive catchiness is hardly enough.

Think about it: functional, scrubbed-clean trifles like Stacey Q's "Two of Hearts," Nu Shooz's "I Can't Wait," and the Jets' "Crush On You" convey so little emotion they sound mercenary; you listen to them and feel coerced. Same with Madonna's "Live To Tell," 38 Special's "Somebody Like You," Van Halen's "Why Can't This Be Love," and Prince's "Kiss," once you peg them for the cynical lighter shades of "Crazy For You," "If I'd Been The One," "Jump," and *Dirty Mind* they are. "Word Up" passes for funk because Cameo's Larry Blackmon sings through his nose, "Sledgehammer" passes because Peter Gabriel sings about his dick, but neither has a beat mammoth enough to get me off my ass to jam. And Jimmy Jam, and Terry Lewis's gimmicky doodling passes for funk for God knows what reason—making the Human League blander than ever is a remarkable feat, I guess.

"Money$ Too Tight (To Mention)" and "For America" and "The Way It Is" (by Bruce Hornsby, dummy) and "Ain't Nothin' Goin' On But The Rent" and (if you insist) "Papa Don't Preach" may hint at concerned topicality, but every one of them clouds its dissent in ambiguity and its worldview in sanctimony. Their submission to syndrum technocracy signals unguarded restraint hidden within polite liberal dreams; their cowardice ensures they don't scare my ass like "Freddie's Dead" or "Living For The City"—they're all, like, snoozeville.

THIS YEAR'S ODDITIES stand out only if you're grading on a curve. The method a smarmy indie-label rap-associated novelty-fluke by the Timex Social Club uses to divert my attention shares more with "Escape (The Pina Colada Song)" than with "Little Egypt" or "Sugar, Sugar." And though Oran "Juice" Jones's and Falco's novelty-flukes' unfashionable sexism and stoopidity are somewhat refreshing, I don't think we're talking the best (or even weirdest) of anything—a period without salable subcultures (rockabilly, doo-wop, garage, bubblegum, disco, whatever) is bound to lack astonishing one-shots. Invented for teens, who demanded new styles, Top 40 radio now stands pat along with its original baby-boomer listenership. By feeding the Big Chill generation's illusion of eternal youth, radio is retarding creativity and aggravating audience passivity.

In the last few months, *Billboard*'s Hot 100 has included "Stand By Me" by Ben E. King, "Twist And Shout" by the Beatles, "Daydream Believer" by the Monkees, "25 Or 6 To 4" by Chicago, and "Don't Stand So Close To Me" by the Police, plus covers of "Earth Angel," "Jumpin' Jack Flash," "Venus," "California Dreamin'," "Stairway To Heaven," "Runaway," "Spirit In The Sky," "That's Life," and, um, "War." An Eddie Money song with Ronnie Spector burbling "be my little baby" reached the Top 10 and six Monkees records returned to the charts. We've meanwhile seen uniformly lame comebacks by James Brown, Little Richard, ELP, Alice Cooper, Boston, Bad Company, Isaac Hayes, Kansas, and the Temptations.

Yes, this unprecedented, good-old-days fixation ties into the traditional-value hegemony of the current presidency. But fuck that easy explanation. Even during Nixon's reign, hits kept the wireless hot. Now, by telling its youth market to beat it, the pop industry is murdering its future. Moguls deceive themselves if they believe they can get away forever by marketing PMRC-placating middle-of-the-road mush as everything from "outrageous" (Lionel Richie) to "alternative" (R.E.M.) to "unusual" (Cyndi Lauper) to "art" (Talking Heads) to "heavy metal" (Bon Jovi).

The profusion of mechanical rhythms, coupled with the large number of black acts on the charts, have induced more than one pundit to term the current situation a "disco revival" (or, rather, the return of the genre to the mainstream after years of cult status). But I'm not initiating "Disco Sucks II" here, folks; the analogy doesn't wash. First, even during disco's '78–'79 commercial apex, there were Top 40 hard rock successes by Skynyrd and Petty and Patti and the Knack and Fleetwood Mac—somehow, I can't imagine a "What's Your Name" or a "Tusk" breaking through present barriers. Second, despite stupid claims that it "all sounded the same," dance music was sonically and expressively far more eclectic then than now, when there's nothing nearly as brutal as "One Nation Under A Groove" or goofy as "Stayin' Alive" or obsessive as "Disco Inferno" or left-field as "Pop Muzik" or ironic as "Good Times" or inspirational as "Ain't No Stoppin' Us Now." And where 1978 had the Rolling Stones branching out by recording one (astonishing) disco track on *Some Girls*, it sure as shit didn't have Lou Reed and Bonnie Raitt and Neil Young and the Bangles and Fishbone and Tommy Keene and Joan Jett and Jason Ringenberg and Chrissie Hynde and John Fogerty and Iggy Stooge cashing in whatever slivers of integrity they had left to some digital production assembly-line in a last-ditch bandwagon bid for acceptance in condominiums.

But then, hardly anybody calls disco rock-radio's nadir. They point to the pre-punk '70s and the post-Elvis, pre-Beatles '60s. I was in high school for the former, and I recall a Top 40 that rocked tough: BTO, BÖC, Lizzy, Sweet, Stones, Aerosmith, Nazareth, even Elton catching fire now and again. Plus yearning soul by Spinners and Warwick, Three Degrees, Hues Corporation; plus eccentric, alleywise funk by Parliament, the Ohio Players, Hot Chocolate; plus glistening three-minute AM hookcraft like "Jet," "Love Is The Drug," "Tonight's The Night," "Fame," "Overnight Sensation"— can a person truly think an entity as superficial and redundant as Eurythmics, Corey Hart, or Whitney Houston stands up to *any* of this? And if '60 and '61 are considered unspeakably bleak despite the mind-blowing output of the Brill Building, Phil Spector, various instrumental combos, Sam Cooke, the street corners of Newark and the Bronx, and even once in a blue moon-June-spoon Philly's teen-idol machine itself, what can you call Top 40 1986 except dead on its feet?

CONTEMPORARY HITS RADIO made people lazy. Performers, producers, radio programmers, A&R departments, critics, everybody. (Especially drummers.) The idea looked smart at first: After *Thriller*, potential blockbusters were forced to visualize every album cut as a possible 45; consequently, we got five or six palatable hits off more LPs than ever before. But once CHR had established its multiplatinum, multisingle elite, every one of its chosen few started to coast. Lauper, Richie, Tina Turner, ZZ Top, Van Halen/D. Roth, Madonna, Huey Lewis, Prince, the Pretenders, and Billy Joel/Idol have all released inferior LPs in late '85–'86 compared to their '83–'84 titles; radio has reacted favorably to each of these new discs, except for maybe *Parade*, the only one flawed more by failed experimentation than stasis or backsliding. Meanwhile, with FM programming based on track record rather than sound, with the blockbuster mentality still holding, and with recycled gold and ten sides of live Springsteen filling the spaces, new artists aren't getting airplay. Michael Jackson's new album, needless to say, won't help—rookies that get lucky will continue to do so only because their sound conforms explicitly to the corporate blueprint.

The melting-pot programming of two years ago was lauded for helping listeners of divergent backgrounds realize what traits they all share. But instead of accomplishing this by demonstrating how base emotions are held in common despite very real cultural differences (what Top 40 had always done anyway), and instead of reaffirming black and white pop's mutual roots, it crossbred both camps into the most compromised stylistic mongrel, diminishing personal expression to sitcom level. The overblown gloss, stifled beats, neutralized vocal acuity, salt-and-pepper duets, and escapist yuppie positivism that have made 1986 the most frustrating year for black American music in at least three decades are a direct result of 1984's creative exchange.

This year's homogenization may have been CHR's intention all along: The format was, after all, in part the brainchild of superconsultant Lee Abrams, who had determined in late '83 that music aimed at only a select demographic—music he called "vertical"—was unsuitable for radio play. The more homogenized music is, the more "horizontal," obviously; what you've heard before won't make you change the dial, and what they don't play won't frighten you.

Though some '60s holdovers theorized that CHR hinted at a return to the days of real countercultural unity, the format's artistic failure only proved what the old hippies should have known already—fragmentation is forever, as is commerce. While it's tempting to pretend that today's pop speaks for a mass community of youth and underprivilege, it can't, because no such community exists. To refuse *carte blanche* to partake in the products dumped upon the multitudes is foolish, and more than likely a psychological disorder. But to advertise your desire for social solidarity by reverting to an aesthetic of prerock pop just because we've finally reached a time wherein rock'n'roll is no longer the predominant popular music is to pretend to be moved by that which cannot possibly move you, and thereby to ignore every promise that rock'n'roll has ever made.

Village Voice, 30 December 1986

MONTELL JORDAN: "THIS IS HOW WE DO IT"

For the longest time this struck me as 100% generic post-new-jack doo-doo, but now I'm starting to think it might be a document future histo-rians will consult when they want to find out what exactly "designated drivers" were for. I was shopping in a thrift store in Germantown and they had the Urban Contemporary (or whatever it's called nowadays) station on, and I thought to myself, "Good, they'll play some of those black songs from the *Radio On* list I haven't heard, and I'll fill in numbers on my ballot." And they *did*, probably—they played a whole *bunch* of songs while I was in there, and I wouldn't doubt if some of them were by Brandy or Smooth or Da Brat or whoever. But this is the only one that held my attention all the way through while I was shopping, and the only one I remembered having heard when I left the store. Which tells me, I *think*, that Montell isn't water-ing his music into submission like every other R&B act does in the post-G-Funk era by mumbling in quiet lazy voices or substituting formless ebbing-and-flowing for hooks. He mixes enough real words into his meaningless street slang that I can follow what he's talking about; there's something unfashionably *upfront* about it. He's not trying too hard to force a sexiness he hasn't got, and there's some evidence of energy and humor in the voices he's employing—the ironic Slick Rick Brit-proper accent on the rap part, for instance. Kiddie viewers of the Nickelodeon Network—which seems to embrace R&B (especially positive role models Boyz II Men, though I bet some unhealthy R. Kelly–type perverts too) these days—voted this song their "Song Of The Year," Linus told me, and at first the choice struck me as symptomatic of the retardation of Generation Z youth, but now I'm not so smug. The spirit of Montell's hit is closer to 1988 Bobby Brown/Johnny Kemp hackwork than to '90s doo-jack-swing hackwork (which is as joyless as crossover R&B ever gets.) Yet part of me is afraid I'm just lowering my standards—if "This Is How We Do It" was *early* '80s party hackwork, like Junior or T.S. Monk or Yarbrough & Peoples or D-Train or somebody, it'd funk sillier and more joyfully still, wouldn't it? Nothing in it compelled me to listen close *before* I got my *Radio On* ballot, and I don't retain much

DESIGNATED DRIVER MONTELL JORDAN.
(PHOTO: KWANKA ALSTON)

about how it sounds when it's not on, so I probably should be skeptical. Most of me just wants to wait and see what everybody else thinks. (7.5)

TLC: "WATERFALLS"

I guess "chasing waterfalls" is like Don Quixote (pronounced "Don Kee-shot" in Magazine 60's great '80's electric salsa single "Don Quichotte Costa Del Sol") chasing windmills, and when this trio of bankrupt arsonists tells me I'd be better off sticking to the rivers I'm used to, I'm reminded of what Dave "Sidecar" (because of the Eddie Money/Trisha Yearwood–like way his mouth was positioned on his face) Morris wrote in my senior yearbook in high school: "Try not to defeat life: Only live it." Well, I've been trying to defeat life all my life, and I'm not gonna stop now. Though I suppose I don't go chasing waterfalls much, either—I mean, I get nervous when Martina switches the *furniture* around, so I guess you could say I'm a creature of habit in some ways. Martina loves this song and wants me to buy her the album, but when Linus saw the video he asked whether the short-red-haired girl sang in her hoarse voice on purpose or as a joke, and when Left Eye started rapping, he cracked up laughing. He said her squeakiness reminded him of our neighbor Siggi. So I'm obviously not the only person who thinks their voices are ridiculous. I thought "Creep" was a slinky cheating song with a Southern grits-and-gravy soulfulness to it, but as usual, the same girl trying to be "sultry" wrecked it for me. In "Waterfalls," Miss Hoarsemouth's neighing almost sounds sickly enough to qualify for some Wax Trax industrial band, a shame seeing how (thanks to the under-utilized long-black-haired chick) the chorus harmonies are actually fairly waterfall-like, and the words aren't bad—at least they don't *mention* the condoms you see in the video. TLC have always seemed way too condom-obsessed to me, and there never has and never will be a good condom song by *anybody*, I promise. (6.5)

R. KELLY: "YOUR BODY'S CALLIN'"

Call me a prude (or just the dad of a nine-year-old), but I'm getting sick of all the gratuitous sex stuff in movies/ TV shows/songs aimed at teenagers. I think it's all a big lie—where are all these teenagers who are supposedly having sex all the time? I don't believe I've ever met them. If they *have* to put so much sex in there, they could at least make it fumbling and neu-rotic. Even if 75% of high schoolers really do lose their virginity before graduation (which I doubt), I don't buy how the music pretends they're completely *casual* about it all. People like R. Kelly, H-Town, SWV, and Jodeci have figured out a way to take all the excitement, fun, and *sexiness* out of sex. If fucking is as boring as these singers make it seem, it won't be long before adolescents start abstaining in droves. Maybe this music is a fundamentalist plot! (0.0)

BLACKSTREET: "NO DIGGITY"

To a certain extent this hits me as merely adequate '90s greaseball urban-crossover players-freaking-you-till-the-cows-come-home buffoon-ery, though the talkover part where they announce "Yo! We're Blackstreet!" always cracks me up . . . unless that's just some tagline they recorded espe-cially for Q-102 here, which is the only place I've ever heard the song. Ei-ther way, it might be neat if all groups starting doing that at beginnings of songs: "Yo! We're Metallica!" "Yo! We're Underworld!" "Yo! We're Crosby, Stills, Nash & Young!" (6.0)

TONI BRAXTON: "YOU MEAN THE WORLD TO ME"

She has an annoying short haircut that's supposed to come off "elegant" and "jazzy" like her low notes, but sometimes she gets a bit of that Karyn

White "Superwoman" breakfast-nook sound. If I was Eric Weisbard I might say that "to be Toni Braxton is to find yourself in things—culture, if a more delicate term is required—instead of origins." But I'm not. (4.0)

JOE: "DON'T WANNA BE A PLAYER"

Ever notice that how hip-hop critics (who tend to be even more addicted to empty jargon than rock critics by the way) use the word "skills" is a perfect parallel to how old prog-rock fans used to use the word "chops"? I also have no idea what "lyrical flow" or "flavor" means. I think such baloney started with Eric B. & Rakim, whose appearance as prog to me stems from the fact that what was supposed to be great about them always seemed to revolve around some sort of "virtuosity," with not a smidgen of fun or disco attached. Rakim was sort of the Emerson, Lake and Palmer of rap lyrics (and rhythm). (Though Jane Dark insists he was more like Jimi Hendrix, which still doesn't dispute my point.) If he didn't turn rap prog, he did at least reduce it to bebop-style art music, which is almost as bad. Not that there hadn't been precedents; the most obvious one being "Beat Bop" by Rammellzee and K-Rob, from 1983, which basically laid the groundwork for almost every rap record of the next ten years. But whereas "Beat Bop" went artsy and nonsensical and obtuse while retaining rap's original old-school bounce and spirit, it was Eric B. & Rakim who turned rap humorless. (Even if at the time I did get the idea they were funkier than hip-hop had been for a while—probably they had virtuoso basslines.) (—)

CHERRY POPPIN' DADDIES: "ZOOT SUIT RIOT"

I care less about the extent to which this number connects to a jumpin'-jive-or-what-have-you revival than I care about the ferocious hugeness of its (admittedly Gene Krupa–inspired I suppose) drum parts, and the fact that I thought the main characters in the song were "satyrs" instead of "sailors" (and they're on leave), and the fact that at first I thought the singer was saying "I'm coming home through your coal black hair," and the fact that coal black hair is inherently sexitudinal in a way that makes me want to swing you down and throw back a bottle of beer. None of which is to kneejerkedly knock the rag-mop revival per se—the kids into this sort of music really know how to *dance* (and dress), and the music frequently seems to be more aggressive than whatever forgotten '40s forebears it's nostalgic for (though admittedly Bette Midler and Joe Jackson and David Lee Roth and Manhattan Transfer and Jive Bunny and the Mastermixers and the Honeydrippers were nostalgic for it a whole lot earlier, and Dr. Buzzard's Original Savannah Band were nostalgic for it a whole lot better). (7.75)

PRODIGY: "BREATHE"

"Inhale inhale you're a victim exhale exhale exhale come play my game psychosomatic addict obscene . . ." A couple times when I was turning into a teenager I managed to work myself into psychosomatic dizzy spells then blackouts then actual fainting spells when a teacher was discussing the effects of drugs in school. My last drug-related passout happened maybe 12 years ago in New York, after smoking pot and drinking something or other with Doug Simmons and RJ Smith. I fainted in a bar, if I remember right, then came to (or "came through"?—"came to" has never sounded right to me) and felt fine. And now that I think of it, it's not inconceivable that RJ could've been present for one of my *early* passouts, too, since he's the subject of the weirdest coincidence of my life: He was my best friend who I used to trade baseball cards with when I was in fifth grade and he was in sixth in suburban Detroit at the beginning of the '70s. When we had to perform record pantomimes for a class assignment, instead of doing rock songs like everybody else, we both did *Sesame Street* songs—he did "Rubber Duckie"; I did "I Love Trash." I moved away from Farmington at the end of that year and didn't talk to RJ for over a decade, after which we both somehow wound up being the two main rock critics for the *Village Voice* at the end of the '80s. (7.5)

TOM PETTY: "MARY JANE'S LAST DANCE"

I like the Neil Young guitar swipes at the end of this, and the John Lennon ones. And Tom's Dylan-rap verses are okay too, especially the parts about Indiana girls (like Martina) growing up with Indiana boys (like Axl Rose) on Indiana nights (like Bobby Knight). (7.5)

SHERYL CROW: "A CHANGE WILL DO YOU GOOD"

I've enjoyed every single radio single off my fellow Mizzou alum's second album; one of these days I should listen to the whole thing, I suppose, but first I still need to get to Alanis Morissette. I remember all three hits as having a surprisingly expert sense of rhythm, and I remember this one as having a vocal that reminded me of white women like Merrilee Rush who got soulful in a vaguely rural but rather unabashed way toward the start of the '70s. The answering machine line about "if you wanna reach me, leave

IF YOU WANNA REACH SHERYL CROW, LEAVE HER ALONE. (PHOTO: NORMAN JEAN ROY)

me alone" always jumps out, and it's totally true; the people on my mind are always the ones who *owe* me phone calls. I'm paranoid like that. On my voicemail now, I've got Joe Walsh's "just leave a message, maybe I'll call"; before that, I had the *Cool Hand Luke* "what we have here is a failure to communicate: some men you just can't reach" sample from Guns N' Roses; and before that, an appropriate snippet of Sugarloaf's "Don't Call Us, We'll Call You." My stepmom left a voicemail message during Stanley Cup weekend asking if I was planning to go to the Spectrum to root for my "home team the Red Wings," apparently not realizing that [1] I've never cared a whit about hockey and [2] wearing a Red Wings jersey in Philly this spring would've only made sense if I wore a bulletproof vest under it. But the disconnection from reality thing is nothing new, really, and I remember her friends as always being disconnected, too: After my stepdad walked out on us, she used to be involved in this group called "Parents Without Partners" (which my ten-years-older-than-me stepsister Nancy used to call "Penises Without Pussies" or vice versa), and they threw drunken parties at our house on weekends every month or so, parties that contained lots of embarrassing middle-aged fat people who were no doubt instrumental in turning me into an anti-social social-gathering-and-large-crowd-hater for most of my life. After one particular party, some aging drunken lout was about to depart with his date, and she asked him to go upstairs to retrieve her coat from the bed, so instead he yelled in an inebriated slur up to us teenaged offspring hiding away upstairs to "toss down the fur coat up there made out of artificial rat shit!" If his date had worn her fake fur on the inside like Sheryl Crow recommends, instead of removing it upon entering the house, my brothers and I would've been deprived of a reliable source of guaranteed guffaws for several years thereafter. (7.5)

Radio On, 1994–1997

TEN CENTS A WATUSI

The tapes I make for other people usually consist of songs that I like which (according to my understanding of the other person's tastes) I think they'd also like and which (according to my understanding of their record collection) I don't think they already have. Tapes I make for non-critic-type people are more likely to include songs which *remind* me of the other person by reflecting their personality or life. I used to make tapes for myself too, but I stopped having time for that years ago. Now the "mix cassettes" in my collection are of one kind only—anal-compulsively pruned if sloppily recorded "accumulation tapes" of songs I like but don't otherwise own on vinyl or CD.

The songs can come from promo CDs I get in the mail or used flea-market/thrift-store records I buy but decide not to keep because I only love one or two tracks, or from tapes people make for me. If you make me a tape, I'll eventually wind up taping songs from discarded records over songs you taped that I either already own or I dislike (or if I only want a couple songs you taped, I'll tape *them* onto another tape.) I only keep songs—occasionally only *parts* of songs, like a drum intro—that I'd give a 7.5 or higher to in *Radio On*. Songs jumping from tape to tape lose fidelity over the years, and eventually mosaic themselves into something like the monstrosity below:

SIDE ONE

The Police, "Landlord" (recorded live 1979, released 1995): They for some reason saved all their punkiest songs (this, "Dead End Job," "Fall

Out") for non-LP singles. It's punk in velocity and emotion, but in the rhythm section especially, it's *virtuoso* punk, which naturally is more musical than most other punk, as is Sting's high-pitched speed-toasting. They were great through their third album, *Vagina Dentata* or whatever. My two favorite early-Police B-sides the Police didn't make: "Too Bad, Too Sad" by Nazareth (1973) and "Sabotage" by the Beastie Boys (1994).

Angel, "Any Way You Want It" (1976): More high-and-pretty-screeched angularly fast hard rock, only more *boogiefied* than the Police, from usually-proggy Kiss klones (like Starz, except not half as funny). Some Angel person (*not* Punky Meadows) says to throw your arms to the sky—You know, like "wave your hands in the air like you just don't care." Or maybe it's a stickup.

La Castañeda, "Torque Nahuaque" (1995): Only upbeat cut on these Mexican death-Goths' over-dirged second album. In fact it's almost *too* slam-dancey, but the stop-start drums and disco basslines and "Batman"-guitar spritzing make the ultra-serious deep-echoing vocal melodrama powerful anyway, then midway through it turns into a guttural Killing Joke jungle chant. On stage, my Hispanic friends tell me, they do Gwar-style "performance art."

Blues Traveler, "Run-Around" (1995): Trendy critics refuse to give them a fair shake, but '90s Deadhead hacks like these goons and the Spin Doctors have a hook-vigor to their hits that I rarely if ever heard from the Dead (much less from '90s pub-hack bands rock critics *like*, like Wilco and Son Volt). Anyway, I still haven't figured out if this is a song about a guy chasing a headgame-playing girl or just a song about a harmonica solo. High male voices now lead low ones on this tape, three to one.

Dire Straits, "Once Upon A Time In The West" (1979): Not as spaghetti as Babe Ruth's "For A Few Dollars More" or "Fistful Of Dollars" or Hugo Montenegro's "The Good, The Bad, And The Ugly"—Not a Morricone song at all, in fact. The rhythm has a laid-back funkiness to it, like Clapton on *461 Ocean Boulevard*, and the guitar has a tumbleweed flow, like ditto probably (I'm not gonna check). The words appear to be more "Sultans of Swing"/"Money For Nothing" rationalizations for being a stodgy codger.

Shelby Lynne, "Feelin' Kind Of Lonely Tonight" (1993): Jazziest timing and arrangement on C&W-rodeo radio in the last couple years; her voice dances a husky bop, and boy is she ever hot-looking—short red hair, plus she smokes cigars. A maybe-we-shouldn't-have-broken-up-after-all song with a sexy train video.

Bucketheads, "The Bomb! (These Sounds Fall Into My Mind)" (1995): Dub-screwed-up start, six words, jazz horns allegedly sampled from some old Chicago record, but it feels more like a chant than a collage. Does the hustle like disco in 1975.

Redd Foxx, "Just Plain Funky" (c. 1970?): Unlike all the "underground art comics" in *Tapeworm* #2, this has a punchline.

Gang of Four, "Armalite Rifle" (1978): Not as funky as Skynyrd's "Saturday Night Special," which has exactly the same message. Lyrics and vocals range from matter-of-fact to blankly stupid: "I disapprove of it/So does Dave." (Who's Dave?) But it's neat how the bassist tensely tightens the constipated rhythm.

Motörhead, "Don't Waste Your Time" (1995): I like them when they sound like a rock'n'roll band, like early Bob Seger and/or speeded-up Chuck Berry; I hate them when they sound like a heavy metal band, like speeded-up Iron Maiden. So their oldest stuff is their best, and their worst stuff is everything they've done since 1983. Boogie-woogie piano made this the only song on their most recent album that sounded *catchy*, not merely noisy.

Slaughter, "Searchin'"(1995): These ex-Nerf-metal stars are now defiant retro-AOR dudes, and their high point since "Up All Night" is Bad Company/Eddie Money beergut-shake with unexpectedly pretty (see also "Armalite Rifle") guitar parts and sympathetic grunting about a cheap-perfumed New York lady who's up all night searching with all her might for Mr. Right (aka Mr. Goodbar).

Mott The Hoople, "Saturday Gigs" (1976): Mincing music-hall glam turning gorgeously anthemic, like if Queen were smart. Dainty war-story nostalgia for the '69–'75 rock highway: upstaging the Stones, wearing platform boots, getting tired of dressing up.

Dancing Cigarettes, "Pop Doormat" (1982): Merry-go-round-herky-jerk New Wave, with David Byrne-ish robot singing improved by being more twee. One of the artier of lower Indiana's early '80s bands; I tend to prefer the punks (Jetsons, Panics, Gizmos).

Hey! Let's Go Latin, "Hey Leroy Your Mama's Calling You" (c. 1967): I don't actually know the band's name; I think that's their *album title*. Studio musicians, maybe, doing a sufficiently timbaled version of Jimmy Castor's 1967 Latin bugalú hit. Which I never heard until *after* I heard this cover version last summer.

Jerry Colonna, "On The Road To Mandalay" (1938): Rudyard Kipling words, apparently about bumping into Gunga Din while slogging boots through Burmese mud in World War I. Heavy Irish-tavern-brogued comical crooning (with rolled consonants and eternally-held notes) alternates with poetry recitation, march-cadence yelling, audible breath-catching, and (toward the end) a surprisingly bouncy Louis-Armstrong-mimic blackface break.

Bill "Bojangles" Robinson, "Doin' The New Lowdown" (1932): *Incredibly* bouncy—his voice pops and pepper-sprouts and jumps so high. We even hear him tapdancing the old worn-out-shoe soft-shoe, just like the Nitty Gritty Dirt Band promised he would.

SIDE TWO

Los Tres, "All Tomorrow's Parties" (1995): Chilean art-rockers whose Spanish-language music doesn't much excite me, but I never realized how eerie this number was until I heard them do it, maybe because Nico's icy affected warbling in the Velvets' version always bugged me. I like the instruments' mechanically-automatic-but-not-mechanically-cold Saudi-Arabian-bellydance tranciness, and I like the semi-accented cross-dressing-boy voice.

The Dorsey Brothers With Bing Crosby, "Let's Do It (Let's Fall In Love)" (1929): More fun than Billie Holiday's rendition, thanks more to the Dorseys' extended dance arrangement than to der Bingle (whose blues-smoked post-Jolson warmth I'd still take over Sinatra's smartass coolness any day). Words I never noticed before: "The Chinks do it and the Japs do it/Up in Lapland little Laps do it." Maybe they even do it sitting in *each other's* laps!

Ruth Etting, "Ten Cents A Dance" (1930): Her initially near-wallflowerly nasal whine gains womanly dimensions, toward Kate Smithness I guess, as the waltzy tempo picks up and she switches from her daytime teaching job into her moonlighting gig as a palace prostitute whose gown gets torn by sailors and bowlegged tailors and barbers and rats from the harbors.

Boswell Sisters, "Shuffle Off To Buffalo" (1933): Jazzy Nerf-scat girl-pop, at least as horny as "Buffalo Stance" by Neneh Cherry—It's about honeymooning at Niagara Falls! Slow parts turn the lights down low like Kurt Weill, but I like it best when old-timey banjos bring back the buffalo-shuffle stampede.

Mills Brothers, "Diga Diga Doo" (1932): Missing link between Al Jolson and Louis Prima, with murky falsetto minstrel gloom accelerating into a sweaty scat-jump with crazed old-school-rap-like jivetalk. A bassman acapellas booming basslines; saxes do a badass brothel blat. (On the other hand, judging from an old compilation I found, the Millses had gone totally limp by the '50s.)

Argent, "Liar" (1970): So horribly recorded you can hear the Goops bleeding through during the opening. Then a passive-aggressive man scolds his deceitful spouse, and venus-in-furs whipcrack effects make him creepier than Three Dog Night when they made it a hit. Argent (whose "Hold Your Head Up" Pearl Jam cover live) are the only rock band our kids' classical-music-loving piano teacher (also in love with one of our divorced-mom neighbors much to her chagrin) ever asked me to tape for him.

Ratt, "Lay It Down" (1985): Tuneful forward motion with post-Slade / Zep high-register shouting and danceable basslines, like Kix (if not the early Police). Second-best song (after "You're In Love") on Ratt's second album, with the kind of lyrics critics call "sexist" seeing as how they're about wanting to have sex.

Tesla, "Little Suzi" (1987): More sympathy-for-city-girl haircut-metal, like the earlier Slaughter track, but this girl's run away to Hollywood trying to be a movie star, and she shares her name with girls in Everly Brothers and Michael Jackson songs. The guitars are strummed jangly à la "Lola," but with a messy Faces energy. In the video, the singer moved like Rod Stewart.

James White And The Blacks, "(Tropical) Heat Wave" (1979): Pre-rock-pop cleverness given a conga undertow: basically, it's Kid Creole and the Coconuts. Not as powerful as James Chance's '78–'79 Contortions noise, but I like how it gives him a less crooked structure to honk free-jazz skronks in, even if (at least when he lets his chick friend sing) it is just campy bullshit.

Ray Barretto, "El Watusi" (1963): Latin-bugalú missing link between salsa and Sam the Sham. He snorts and laughs a lot, calls you "muchacho" and "caballero," and probably teaches dance steps.

Steve Carlisle, "WKRP In Cincinnati" (1981): Living on the air there, with sultry "Baker Street"/Quarterflash sax. A decade earlier it could've been a moving letter-to-ex-girlfriend singer-songwriter smash (as in "Please Come To Boston" by Dave Loggins).

Little Texas, "Amy's Back In Austin" (1995): More bad sound-quality—some of these tunes have been re-taped so many times they've lost all their treble, and this one seems *slower* than I remember it. But maybe I just remember it wrong. Like the "WKRP" theme, it's sap about a severed relationship and a city. It starts out like John Mellencamp's "Small Town," after which it's a much better Eagles imitation than Little Texas's "You And Forever Me," which I once called the best Eagles imitation ever—the harmonies do it, and the desert wind and La Zona Rosa cafe. But it's not as good an Eagles imitation as "Amie" (if that *is* one) by Pure Prairie League, who lived on the air in Cincinnati.

Seatrain, "13 Questions" (1970): Luc Sante sarcastically compared the Cactus Brothers' awesome "16 Tons" to them in *Why Music Sucks*, so I bought one of their albums at a flea market. I liked their version of Little Feat's trucker anthem "Willin'," and I liked this—which sounds like the Ides of March's greasy 1970 minstrel-funk classic "Vehicle" except for its words, which concern meeting earthmen from outer space, and its weird electric-fiddle-squaredance solo. Which sounds like the Cactus Brothers.

Cuca, "El Son Del Dolor" (1993): Mexicore pachucos who too often slam their funk into Chili Peppers stiffness (and one of whom supposedly designed a big cockroach for the movie *Cronos*) opt for a change to steal riffs from Van Halen's "Jump" instead.

Tapeworm, 1996

SINGLES AGAIN: TANGLED UP IN BLUE

This column (or at least this installment of it) is a mixtape. The songs in it are all hits. Its title sort of comes from a great honky-tonk divorce ditty, by Gary Stewart.

LFO: "GIRL ON TV"

Long ago, and oh so far away, they fell in love with her before the second show: a male groupie anthem from three wicked pissers from Boston and Orlando, wishing on falling stars and (à la the Carpenters) superstars. When main hottie Rich meets his celebrity flygirl from the City of Angels, she's got a green dress on—from Abercrombie & Fitch, one suspects. No idea what the Scooby Snacks (courtesy of Fun Lovin' Criminals) have to do with anything, but God, these guys shooby-doo-wop (their word) sweet: Their acousticized rap flow is Everlast without the macho crap, and in the middle one guy winds his whitebread midrange into R. Kelly territory.

LFO—THE LYTE FUNKY ONES, NOT THE TECHNO ONES.
(PHOTO: DANNY CLINCH)

'NSYNC: "BYE BYE BYE"

Prediction: This is the year teenpop really starts to *kick*. Classical strings at the start, like some early-'80s Jacksons track, then "I'm doing this tonight, you're probably gonna start a fight"—a breakup song, or really, a kick-her-out-the-door song. Sixties garage in spirit—not nice. And though their five-man mesh of (mostly) high harmonies says 'NSync "don't wanna make it tough," over drum machine triplets as funky as Britney's greatest hits they sound tough regardless. Maybe they're saying bye bye to Miss American Pie. Who is sort of their audience, right?

MADONNA: "AMERICAN PIE"

For 28 years we've been on our own, and Kate Moss grows phat in *Rolling Stone*, but that's not the way it used to be. Not as funny as last year's Weird Al *Star Wars* version or Paul Weitz movie version or Rob Sheffield *Roll-*

ing Stone Woodstock version ("as the flames climbed high into the night/ to moonlight the sacrificial rite/I saw Kid Rock laughing with delight"), but not bad: Ms. Ciccone's in Irish brogue mode atop light bright lounge techno, and she can still remember how the music used to make her smile. She excises all the stuff about the Big Bopper and Ritchie Valens and Lennon reading books of Marx and February making her shiver with every paper she'd deliver, not to mention Don McLean's "Stairway To Heaven"- genus soft-to-loud stairway climb. But how come in 28 years I never noticed the weird *lyrical* congruities with Led Zep (via "Book Of Love" and levees breaking), or the blatant "That'll Be The Day" reference, or all the Catholicism motifs (sacred stores, church bells broken, mortal souls saved, faith in God above)? No surprise that the three men Madonna admires most are the Father, Son, and Holy Ghost. But I'm still not convinced she was ever a lonely teenage bronkin' buck.

A3: "WOKE UP THIS MORNING (CHOSEN ONE MIX)"

Good old boys drinking whiskey and rye, or as close to it as British technocrats can come. Now it's a *Sopranos* hit, but in its original album incarnation three years ago it helped kick off an oddly-never-named rootstronica trend that ranges from Lo Fidelity Allstars to Moby. Back-porch picking, barrelhouse piano, and scratchy vinyl effects; then a stoned but electronically embellished lowlife voice imagining the Trenchcoat Mafia: "Woke up this morning, got yourself a gun." In and out of corny gospel born-under-bad-sign/ bad-blue-moon-of-Kentucky-rising/*Omen* imagery, the guy drawls about your head going ding-dong regretting what you did the night before, about how when you woke up everything you had was gone: She'd taken the bed and the chest of drawers, and the boys blamed you for bringing her home. She's crafty; she fucked and ran. Almost immediately you felt sorry. You didn't think this would happen again.

EIFFEL 65: "BLUE (DA BA DEE)"

Riding a boogie-woogie house beat, a white cyborg from Italy literally sings the blues: This is a song about *color*, and in great Thomas Dolby tradition, the most computerized parts are also the most melodic and emotional. He's Mr. Blue, and these are Blue's clues, and everything's blue (not to mention redundant) for "him and himself"; even his little red Corvette is blue. The nonsense syllables in the subtitle make it sound like he's repeatedly chanting, "I'm blue, and indeed I will die." Turn me on, dead man.

MARTINA MCBRIDE: "LOVE'S THE ONLY HOUSE"

The best item on her current *Emotion* is blasphemously entitled "Anything's Better Than Feelin' The Blues," which she pronounces more like "anything's better than feelin' abuse"—and she should know, since her best song ever, "Independence Day," was about an abused woman burning down the house. But in "Love's The Only House," Martina tries to be "American Pie"'s girl-who-sings-the-blues anyway, a Nashville babe in upwardly mobile Sheryl Crow drag like Faith Hill or Shelby Lynne lately. She starts out in a supermarket, so you're hoping that guy she's been chasing all year will forget cranberries too, but instead she's pissed about jerks sneaking 25 items into the express lane. Then she runs into a useless old ex on the street, then she crosses the river into the ghetto where kids wake up with guns, then she remembers that even back in the burbs kids grow up "in a culture of darkness." So she buys poor ladies cartons of milk to assuage her liberal guilt, never realizing that the Stones she's learned harmonica from and the Dylan she's learned talking-blues cadences from represented a culture of darkness themselves—and not just because their words could be as hate-filled as Korn's or Jay-Z's. So maybe, accidentally, this is a song about color, too. On the back cover of McBride's album, everything's red for her and herself: her hair, her hitched-up skirt, her mouth, her bra strap.

SISQÓ: "THONG SONG"

Speaking of underwear: This R&B smash by a weird white-haired Dru Hill associate is right up there with Third Eye Blind saying your little red panties still pass the test, or at least with "Itsy Bitsy Teenie Weenie Yellow Polka Dot Bikini." Jacksons/'NSync-style violin orchestrations at the beginning, goofy spoken intro lying to girls that bathing suits are what boys really talk about, then this strange bumpy vocal rhythm, by way of Timbaland via drum 'n' bass maybe, totally infectious, and mostly I have no idea what Sisqó's saying ("she had dumps like a truck," what?), except when he represents about how her dress was scandalous and "she was livin' la vida loca." Most of the rest might as well be about lisping: "thong th-thong thong thong." I mean, look at the title.

APOLLO FOUR FORTY: "STOP THE ROCK"

Four lads from Liverpool, and like A3 and Eiffel 65, their name starts with a vowel and ends with a number. "Are we a rock band or what?" they ask in the minute-long snippet leading into this song on their album, a challenge on the order of Funkadelic asking why a funk band can't play rock music. Which challenge they live up to: Rockabillish riff, "96 Tears" keyboard fills, ba-ba-ba sung horn lines, frat attitude pushing too hard in a robot-muzik context. "Shake my paranoia," they insist; it runs too deep. They're "dancing like Madonna, into the groovy," except Madonna didn't do "Into The Groovy"—Ciccone Youth did. Finally Apollo give a shout out to their fellow Greek deity Aphrodite, tastefully never mentioning that she was born of the foam of Uranus. Still, very mythological. "You can't stop the rock": Like, they're pushing it up a hill.

STATIC X: "PUSH IT"

At 2:36, possibly the most concise covertly scatological metal gutpunch ever to score on AOR, not to mention one of the most futuristic-sounding: The guitars all feel like synthesizers, if not static. Which is one way out of rock's rut, and the old title from Salt-n-Pepa and the old high-top fade from Kid 'n Play are two more. Ooh, baby baby.

Village Voice, 2 March 2000

SINGLES AGAIN: PARANOIA JUMPS DEEP

Does the proliferation of great singles this year have anything to do with how Napster dishes out songs one at a time, so downloading 14-year-old boys across the nation can compete to see who gets the most hits? Don't be surprised if the album-as-artwork means even less five years from now.

DESTINY'S CHILD: "JUMPIN', JUMPIN'"

11:30 and the club is jumpin', jumpin', and it sounds even better in a car at 11:30 than "3 A.M." by Matchbox 20 sounded in a car at 3 a.m. As with most hits about jumpin'—Kris Kross, House of Pain, Aretha Franklin, Pointer Sisters, Van Halen—it really does jump. Sociologists should note that there may be no bigger band in the country right now among preteen girls—'NSync and Backstreet not excluded. Which, given She'kspere's jazzishly unbalanced syncopations and sophistications, is a surprise. The subject matter's adult, too: all about leaving your man at home because "the club is full of ballers and their pockets full of gold." Who's down with

O.P.P.? Every last lady! (Is that gold in your pocket or are you just happy to see me?) Though given the histrionic dame monotoning "ballers ballers" and "ladies ladies" behind her, no wonder Beyoncé Knowles has started leaving her girls at home as well.

SENSATIONAL: "BEAT, RHYMES & STYLES"

His first Matador single, "Party Jumpin'," jumped less than Mystikal's "Jump" or even Aaron Carter's "Jump Jump"—it was just too *normal*, basically. So factor in his weird-assed WordSound albums, and maybe this addled former Jungle Brother knows what he's doing—passing his scraps off on indie whiteboys who'll eat anything by anyone they think isn't playing with a full deck. The colorful sleeves on Matador's monthly hip-hop installments do stir fond memories of earlier artsy indie Celluloid exploring exotic avant-rap terrain back in '82, though. Plus, Sensational could be Tone Lōc flying to Kool Keith's planet just to spout a million words about it—very few of them individually quotable, but his unpremeditated tone suggests they at least mean a lot to *him*. And the more wasted he seems—the more cotton his mouth twists his tongue through, the more freaky-deaky clanks and birdlike horn-beats acid-wash his background, the more he babbles *about* cheeba—the funnier he is. The most coherent he gets is "Cheech & Chong can get it on/How I get it on without a bong?" And he definitely has a more inventive sense of rhythm than Wesley Willis, Daniel Johnston, even Syd Barrett. Though maybe not Roky Erickson. Or Michael Jackson.

FOREIGN LEGION: "NOWHERE TO HIDE"

As on Non Phixion's Matador "Black Helicopters"/"They Got . . . ," the verses are lunatic-fringe indie-rap conspiracy paranoia, this time singling out 40-ounces, gangsta gangstas, and "crack laced with evil thoughts" as government plots, and linking all manner of horrors to unnamed white men in black suits: Waco, Heaven's Gate, Desert Storm, the Titanic, Vietnam, the grassy knoll, the Oklahoma bombing, Roswell, Prozac, cameras hidden in fire hydrants, pyramids on the moon, the deaths of Biggie and Tupac and JFK and Marvin Gaye and Abe Lincoln and Versace, the cancellation of *Joanie Loves Chachi*, and Hitler changing his name to Liberace. The hook is a single syllable, repeated ad infinitum, that goes "so . . . ," so you can hear the ellipses every time. Hold your cigarette over your mouth so the Illuminati can't see you moving your lips, then give a shout out to "my man Noam Chomsky."

DJ GODFATHER: "WHATCHULOOKINAT??"

Planet-rocking paranoia of a considerably less articulate sort: a mean crack-head voice declaims, "Whatchulookinat bitch??" a couple hundred times, over space-invader dinks sculpted into instrumental changes recalling Robert Ashley as much as Luther Campbell. This clown prince of ghetto-tech's "Via Satellite From Detroit" single is randomized outer-space repetition with plenty of funk in its clank; his megamixes have some dreamscape Eurodisco nightflighting, some delectably buttered electropopcorning, some frat-party booty-snatching on Ecstasy. But this goofy gangsta-techno rant is a composition you can sink your molars into.

DJ ASSAULT: "TECHNOFREAK"/"U CAN'T SEE ME"/ "MY CADDY"/"WE GOT IT ALL"

The other clown prince of ghetto-tech's got two different 12-inches out that say *Belle Isle Tech* on the cover (meaning the Belle Isle in Detroit, not Newfoundland or Virginia). This is the green one. The red one's got screwed-up, stretched-out recastings of "Pusherman" by Curtis Mayfield and possibly "Kyle's Mom's A Bitch" by Joe C (R.I.P.), but the green one's got open space almost as ominous as Phuture or Strafe back when they were inventing acid house. And Assault's eerie atmosphere is more compelling, if less distinctive, than his funny funk; his latest album squeezes 83 cuts into 57 minutes, but this EP's got genuine songs (or, okay, chants: "every freakin' day, every freakin' day") oozing out of the vagueness, then wobbling and percolating and eventually falling into deep wormholes of dub. Or *golf* holes, maybe—though I suppose "My Caddy" is really about a car.

THE WHITE STRIPES: "JOLENE"

A Detroit big-brother/little-sister duo (*white* signifying both their last name and their pigmentation) with an auto-industry ode called "The Big Three Killed My Baby" on another 45, they cover "John The Revelator" live. But at their best, they're entirely deferential: "You could have your choice of men, but I could never love again, he's the only one for me Jolene." The drum gets knocked every 20 seconds or so, then enters a half-minute Zep thump-and-thud midway through; the voice is a high lonesome squeal, the guitar an intense Tom Verlaine/Richard Thompson tapestry. The overall genre, though, is leaden elephant-stomp punk blues, making this male-sung Dolly Parton remake a de facto answer to their Midwestern predecessors Killdozer's cloddish take on Jessi Colter's "I'm Not Lisa." Except it's more sincere, and the gender switcheroo means more, since "Jolene" has always been a rip-her-to-shreds catfight.

Village Voice, 5 December 2000

SINGLES JUKEBOX REVIEWS

MICHAEL FRANTI & SPEARHEAD: "SAY HEY (I LOVE YOU)"

Man, back when I was making Disposable Heroes of Hysterectomy and Disposable Heroes of Hippopotami jokes on my 1992 Pazz & Jop ballot, I sure didn't expect Michael Franti would be blowing up Top 40 radio with a Wyclef-doing-"Don't Worry Be Happy" move 17 years later—not even one featuring junkies in the corner alley right out of "The Message." Suppose this makes Spearhead the most archetypal "political band with one pop hit" since the glory days of Chumbawamba. And if anybody knows whether my wife's Beatnigs LP is worth money now, I'll pass the word on to her. [5]

GIL SCOTT-HERON: "ME AND THE DEVIL"

Production is big and dubby and trips its hop moderately deep but, uh, Gil used to be a pretty great songwriter once, and after 16 years (actually, more like 26 since he did anything anybody much cared about—"Re-Ron" was '84), not to mention a few notable wars and presidents he's yet to sink his teeth into, you'd think he might come back with something more thought-provoking and devastating than a Robert Johnson cover. What happened, did he just read *Mystery Train*? Also, sorry, but changing Johnson's "beat my woman til I get satisfied" to "seed my woman . . ." feels like a whitewash. [6]

BUSY SIGNAL: "DA STYLE DEH"

One of the very few dancehall reggae songs I've unconditionally loved since, like, '80s Wayne Smith "Under Me Sleng Teng" days, which probably means I haven't paid attention to dancehall enough. I first came across it on an otherwise pretty decent Greensleeves comp called *The Biggest Ragga Dancehall Anthems 2009*, and every time, it leaped way out from the Mavados and Chinos and Vybz Kartels. I want to say it sounds somehow

"African" (the drums, the chants), but I'm even less an expert on recent African music than Jamaican, so I can't get more specific than that. What it really sounds like to me, though, is a reincarnation of the Chips' non-charting doo-wop novelty "Rubber Biscuit" from 1955, covered by the Blues Brothers into a Top 40 hit in 1979 after showing up in *Mean Streets*. Which I assume is mere coincidence, unless it isn't. [9]

DORROUGH: "ICE CREAM PAINT JOB"

Dorrough's from Dallas, I live in Austin, and a couple months ago this came on the radio every time I got in my car. Though my car, unfortunately, is not clean on the outside, cream on the inside. Nor are its rims big. But it do ride good. Anyway, what's been clear from first hearing is that, more than almost anybody else on R&B/hip-hop stations this year, Dorrough actually sounds like he's enjoying himself—rap hits this goofy and good-natured are forever an endangered species. Just wish he said what flavor the ice cream is. I hope Neapolitan. [8]

DRAKE: "BEST I EVER HAD"

First time I saw this song listed in *Billboard*, before I read that Drake is the future of rap music, I was really hoping it would be an R&B version of Gary Allan's 2005 hit country version of Vertical Horizon's 2001 rock hit. Now that I hear it, I realize he's just another blasé rapper biting Kanye's phrasing over rattatatats and moody soul samples. "Get it from the back and make ya fuckin' bra strap pop, all up in ya slot 'til the nigga hit the jackpot"—er, no wonder people think the guy's brilliant. Nice that he appreciates girls in sweat pants, though. And knows how the *Andy Griffith* theme goes. Or at least says he does. [5]

THE-DREAM: "SWEAT IT OUT"

Connoisseurs around these parts seem so unanimous in proclaiming him some kind of genius that I'm wondering both whether I'm being willful in "not getting him" and whether, by now, I'd be just as willful if I suddenly did get him. With this particular song, I'll take a wild guess that the attraction is that he's got a spare sound, and some of the specific come-on lines are borderline clever, and he gets intense toward the end, which is supposed to be jarring, as perhaps also are those grunted "hey"s toward the start, maybe? But I'm honestly not sure. I can sort of hear all that, but I doubt I'd notice any of it if others' approval didn't make listening hard for what's good a moral imperative. And none of it makes up for how the song really fucking drags, has no concrete hooks to grab on to, and revolves around a falsetto that never transcends the mediocre into anything especially beautiful or emotive. So, uh, it's "interesting." I guess. [6]

RIHANNA: "WAIT YOUR TURN"

I have to cringe at how people are inevitably going to associate whatever music she makes in the near future with the Chris Brown incident—like decoding Paul-is-dead clues, more or less. I've long been opposed to caring about celebrity personal lives on principle, or at least letting those biographies warp critical judgment, and one shitty thing about the 'oos (a byproduct of hip-hop, probably) is how the phenomenon became more commonplace—or at least, how so many pop stars recorded music that arrogantly *presumes* we keep up with their lives' details. Seems a recent development—most great pop music used to be about *our* lives, not theirs. That said, kudos to Rihanna for showing great strength after everything bad that happened, of course. And I'm not suggesting she's begging the Chris question *here*, though no doubt some folks will interpret the song that way. But oh yeah, did I mention how tuneless it is? Okay, did now. Though maybe the dancehall-accent parts aren't horrible. [3]

MARIAH CAREY: "OBSESSED"

I prefer Mom-and-Pops to corporations, I prefer conversations to press conferences, my Napoleon Complex got me where I am today, Mariah jumped the shark ages before Eminem did, I have no interest in whatever relationship they may have had, and I wish she'd finally ditch the hip-hip attitude horseshit and get back to what she used to be good at. Given all that, I have to admit this is a halfway decent song—she even delivers the line "you're losing your mind" with feeling. I'll make a note of that, and move on. [6]

LADY GAGA: "DANCE IN THE DARK"

Starts out mixing doo-wop Morse code with porn-moaning metal machine music, turns briefly into Grace Jones covering the Normal, then into upbeat downbeat dance-pop that, on a Gaga scale at least, feels kind of generic. Some generic, huh? Then stick a "Vogue"-type rap in there somewhere, and stuff about being a dressed-up vamp tonight. All in a week's work, and her week beats your year. [7]

HEALTH: "DIE SLOW"

The album works as tolerable background clatter largely because these guys get a machine-like rumble going that most pencil-necked indie geeks are too rhythmically inept to even attempt; "Nice Girls," for instance, is built on an oil-can drum ritual Killing Joke might not scoff at. And lots of the rest (including the opening of "Die Slow") pleasantly dumbs down the kind of bombastic *Apocalypse Now* kitsch that Sonic Youth trafficked in back in their Glen Branca protégé days (i.e., when they were more interesting than they've been for the past 20 years.) The problem, surprise surprise, is the singing, so blurry and vague that I have no idea why Health even bothered having any—easy enough to tune out in Muzak mode, but impossible not to get irked by when listening close. I will never understand an aesthetic so deluded to believe that vocals this bloodless could make such noise better, in any conceivable way. In "Die Slow," the vacant nasal-inhaler wheeze atop all but negates any friction from the Sly Foxy factory clank below. [6]

GRIZZLY BEAR: "TWO WEEKS"

What's supposed to make these lethargic twits so otherworldly and awesome again? Must be the harmonies, since as innocuous as they are, they're all I hear, beyond some piddly clinking at the end. And that's enough for a full fucking page in the *NY Times* Sunday Arts section? Which I didn't read? This is hookless, gutless, grooveless, shapeless drivel for college children who still wet Mom's bed. "Doo wop" my ass. [1]

KINGS OF LEON: "RADIOACTIVE"

So is this their "Cannonball" move, their late '80s David Byrne move, or their late '80s U2 move? Or did they do that last one already? Hard for me to separate these hacks' music from all the tonedeafs who think they ever had anything to do with either "Southern rock" or "garage rock," who think they made three (or any) of the best albums of the past decade, who think Caleb "We Don't Want To Go In There And Do Something That Isn't Real And Something That Doesn't Really Move Us" Whatshisface has anything remotely interesting to say to justify any feature that's not a business story about how their promotion and/or management teams have persuaded sheep in high places to take their nondescript tenth-generation post-grunge seriously and helped turn that into a durable career. In the great tradition of the comparably useless Foo Fighters, their interesting-for-five-minutes-in-2003 backstory (they're preacher's kids, y'know!) has clearly proved quite valuable. But at least this track can't be confused with Candlebox, Live, Seven Mary Three, or Blind Melon—I'll give it that. (Also: Pigeon poop!) [4]

TOBY KEITH: "AMERICAN RIDE"

Okay now, here's a song that picks fights and draws lines in the sand—nativist horseshit (tidal wave comin' in from the Mexican border not to mention thugs arrested by Customs with aerosol cans—or maybe that's just anti-graffiti-art?), Christianist horseshit (people getting arrested for singing Christmas carols as if that's ever fucking happened anywhere), sexist horseshit (Mom getting rocks off watching *Desperate Housewives* and spoiled brats learning how to be mean grrrrls from "the youtube" 'cause that's what it takes to get along in the world while Dad works his ass off for the good life), rockist horseshit (beauty queens with plastic surgery becoming pop stars without being able to sing a note), you name it. But also a chorus that seems to accept global warming, at least as a metaphor for the country turning to shit (or "fit," as in "fit's gonna hit the shan.") And Toby's digging the ride anyway—"look ma, no hands!"—so he kicks the thing as hard as just about anything he's done (dude's been covering "Stranglehold" live lately—guess he's getting bored by his mellow period.) He also changes the title from "This American Life," which is what Nashville songster Dave Pahanish named it: Too NPR, maybe? Still, perfect punctuation for a long hot summer of idiot mob uprisings and last-ditch conspiracy lies from old white yokels feeling the earth shifting beneath their feet. When will he learn? [8]

ERIC CHURCH: "SMOKE A LITTLE SMOKE"

Um, perhaps I should preface this review by confessing that I frequently wear a black Eric Church T-shirt, which has his name on the back and "I DON'T LIKE TO FIGHT, BUT I AIN'T SCARED TO BLEED" on the front. Glad they got that comma in there! So okay, that said, in these three minutes the rhythm and echo are Delta blues as electronic dance music, the swing and sway give you what the lyrics promise, the increasing crunch is raging hard rock (add all that up you get: mid '80s ZZ Top?), the quiet-then-loud changes add power in both directions, the "want a little more right, a little less left" makes me wonder why Eric thinks that (especially since he usually tends not to wear his politics on his sleeve) and whether the stuff about his changing definition of "change" is somehow related, the "yeah!" yells are '90s pop grunge (Collective Soul to be exact), the not-planning-for-future stuff hits close to home, the stuff about getting her back sounds like he's deciding whether to take a bath, the rap about pulling out his stash and letting his memory crash makes me wonder if he's a libertarian or just confused. Still, a great track. [8]

LADY ANTEBELLUM: "I RUN TO YOU"

Timely boy and girl harmonize about world spinning faster toward disaster, carefully not specifying how that might happen, updating '80s pop references (title from Bryan Adams, lies becoming truth from "Billie Jean") with just a touch of Rob Thomas gutbust. Bottomless opening Appalachian ozone etherea blooms into propulsive schlock-rock that stands up to months of radio airplay. Internet lyric sites insist they're running from pessimists rather than pestilence. Band opts to retain historically offensive name. [8]

MISSTRESS BARBARA FT. SAM ROBERTS: "I'M RUNNING"

Dueting boy and girl, running away from their pasts and the state of the world and toward each other, with an '80s pop drive—so basically, this is the Great White North version of Lady Antebellum's "I Run To You," right? And I'm sure if Lady Antebellum had grown up listening to New Order records, they'd display the vocal charisma of this afternoon's toenail clippings as well. [7]

THE SWEPTAWAYS AND JENS LEKMAN: "HAPPINESS WILL BE MY REVENGE"

EZ-Listening madrigal choir into clunky kitsch parody of a girl group into some precious Magnetic Fields–style priss blankly crooning cabaret crap about deathbed regrets and Texas snowflakes and, uh, "galaxies of feeling" over a keyboard tuned to the "college ska" setting, then back and forth, then forth and back. I guess it's supposed to be touching. For some people, I don't doubt that it is. Some might even detect a high-minded moral lesson about how it's better to have loved and lost your life than never to have loved at all. But here's the real moral: indie rock still sucks. [2]

Singles Jukebox, 2009–2010

THE YEAR OF TOO MUCH CONSENSUS

Come back, Kevin McFrench. All is forgiven.

Well, OK—Kevin McFrench never existed. He was just a fake daily-paper hack from Ohio with the corniest, rootsiest, stodgiest, most clichéd and clueless white-bread biz-sucking middle-aged middlebrow Midwestern Springsteen-to-Wilco do-gooder dad-rock critical tastes you ever saw. The couple of hilarious Pazz & Jop ballots that early-'00s *Voice* intern Nick Catucci filed in his name didn't even count in the results. And, looking at this year's tally, you get the idea that his tastes are an endangered species.

What would Kevin make of the most whimsically insular prissy-pants indie-rock-centric Top 10 albums list in Pazz & Jop history, I wonder? Heck, even 2007 still had Bruce, plus Robert Plant/Alison Krauss—salt-of-the-earth stuff, right up Kevin's alley. Back in the early '00s, indie nerds were lucky to occupy even three spots. But back then, nobody knew what *Pitchfork* was. (Remember the first time you looked for it and found that farm website?) And damned if eight of this year's Top 10 P&J albums— from Animal Collective, Phoenix, Grizzly Bear, Dirty Projectors, the xx, Raekwon, Flaming Lips, Girls—didn't also make *Pitchfork*'s Top 10. That *doubles*, or comes damn close to doubling, the four or five Top 10 similars apiece in 2008, 2007, 2006, and 2005.

Just as disconcerting, there's this year's Top 10 P&J singles, seven of which come off indie-identified albums that also finished in the Top 10. Unheard of—as a point of comparison, perennial P&J album high-charters Sleater-Kinney never placed a single above #35. In the three decades since singles tabulating started, never before have seven Top 10s emerged from Top 10 albums. The year that came closest was 1987, with six, and it took three verifiable hits by Prince, two by Bruce, and one by R.E.M. to pull it off; Los Lobos's "La Bamba" made the Top 10 that year too, but wasn't actually on their Top 10 charting album. The last time even five singles turned the trick was 2000, and none of those—two OutKasts, two Eminems, one U2—had indie cred.

I apologize for all the math homework right off the bat, but what's going on here? Couldn't be that indie rock is suddenly *better than everything else put together*, could it? Doubtful, even if it's gotten more rhythmic and varied, which people claim, but I can hardly ever get past the inept vocals, so I wouldn't know. Plus, that explanation doesn't explain more encouraging trends further down the P&J results—metal, for one, has never done better. And, to be fair, 21 albums finishing in 2009's P&J Top 40—more than half the list, including a few more indies—didn't place in the *Pitchfork* Top 40 at all.

Anyway, I've got theories. First off: lazy indie voters who turned a fun exercise into a dutiful one by listing random "singles" off albums they also voted for are the new version of lazy AOR voters who used to vote for perfunctory tracks off albums *they* also voted for. Only the genre and technology have changed, and the fact that the AOR squares—back before our newfangled, allegedly singles-oriented, iTunes-through-shitty-speakers era began—almost always got marginalized by radio-imbibing pop and dance and hip-hop fans. Though, hey, at least critics still fell for Lady Gaga this year. (Three Top 13 singles: Who does she think she is—Prince?)

The indie domination at the top of the album list is a harder nut to crack, but a few factors seem worth pondering. For one thing, the poll's electorate has changed—freelance dollars aren't flowing like the old days, and with dailies and weeklies chopping arts positions, newsprint dinosaurs have departed the vocation, voluntarily and involuntarily, in droves. Meanwhile, way younger bloggers and Tweeters who make even less money reviewing music have stepped in. Some vote, and plenty see eye-to-eye with *Pitchfork*.

Also, this is big: Used to be, when you filled out your P&J ballot, you hadn't *seen* very many other Top 10 lists. Now, with websites pretending the year is over well before Thanksgiving and surviving print mags falling in step with their own premature year-end countdowns, it's hard to avoid peering over your neighbor's shoulder. A story snowballs through the year, so by December, critics who don't hear many releases and ones who've heard too many to sort through—enough Pazz & Joppers to pass as a consensus—have had the words "Animal Collective" pounded into their heads so incessantly that boarding the bandwagon seems like a no-brainer.

Probably also didn't hurt that a few critically approved indie albums actually did OK commercially, at least in relation to stuff that did worse—Grizzly Bear's *Veckatimest* and Flaming Lips' *Embryonic* both hit *Billboard*'s Top 10 in slow weeks; Phoenix and Yeah Yeah Yeahs have SoundScanned in the 200,000-unit range. The latter two even wound up listed among the "Top Billboard 200 Albums" of 2009, albeit at a modest #177 and #192, respectively; no other P&J Top Tenner made the list. Especially given the industry's continued double-digit retail nosedive, that's not saying much. It's certainly not Susan Boyle or Taylor Swift. But it's something.

As negligible to horrible as I think most of the bands in the Top 10 are, I'm not second-guessing tastes here. People like what they like, and that apparently goes even for fans of the xx's male singer. I'm also not too cynical about consensus to be happy that my votes for Lady Gaga, Brad Paisley, and K'Naan helped them place in the Top 40. I do wish more Web-bound whippersnappers who claim to enjoy a weird, twisted racket would go out on a limb for, say, the Jono El Grande or Meercaz or Frozen Bears or Okie Dokie records that *Pitchfork* ignored this year. But even though I half-ran it through most of the '00s, Pazz & Jop hasn't coincided with my tastes since the early '80s, and I'm used to it. It's Kevin McFrench I'm concerned about.

Kevin might really dig those Avett Brothers, I bet. But what would he think about Bruce's less-dull-than-usual (and well-regarded, I thought) *Working On A Dream* flopping around way down at #59? And all those other albums that easily would've gone Top 40 in an earlier era: Bob Dylan (#41—did his Christmas record cut into votes?), Allen Toussaint (#43), Rosanne Cash (#46), Levon Helm (#47), Amadou & Mariam (#49), Leonard Cohen (#55).

For the record, no Springsteen voters also voted for the xx or Girls, and only one voted for Animal Collective. Theoretically mainstream old-guard pros like Bill Holdship of Detroit's *Metro Times* and Geoffrey Himes of the *Nashville Scene* both saw only two of their Top 10 albums place in the P&J Top 40; St. Louis stalwart Steve Pick, choosing esoterica like Dave Alvin and the Bottle Rockets and Ian Hunter, got shut out entirely. Back in 1980 in these pages, Robert Christgau divided the Pazz & Jop electorate into "the avant-gardists versus the traditionalists, the radicals versus the conservatives"—you know, Beefheart guys vs. Bruce guys. Me, I like strangeness and skronk, but I also like boogie and beer; still, my basic instincts have always been with the vanguard. But when it's mainly the old farts who seem to have minds of their own, I start to wonder.

Village Voice, 20 January 2010

So I guess the obvious question—maybe it's *always* the obvious question at ends of books, ends of albums, ends of years, ends of decades—is (as Axl Rose once put it, more than two decades ago) "Where do we go now, where do we go?" Is "it" all over?

I dunno. Me, I'm getting old. Right—we *all* are. But I totally fit the cliché. For one thing, I'm having way more fun these days listening to old music (reissues, vinyl picked up for a buck, stuff off my shelves) than new music; that hasn't happened in ages. And it's a warning sign for sure. Nostalgia, by definition, is a retreat into a cocoon, even if the old music teaches you new things. On the other hand, it's sort of healthy—it beats feeling like I *have* to keep up with everything new. As somebody whose sheer volume of listening over the past quarter century can probably can give any other critic on the planet a run for the money (as recently as 2007 and 2008, obsessed with a boom in homemade releases made accessible by web outlets like CDBaby and MySpace, I insanely posted lists of my top 150 albums each year online), I could certainly afford to relax a little.

Also, let's face it: most of my most incisive recent writing—including just about everything I've written for the *Village Voice* in my post-layoff years—has been about *country*: middle-aged white guy music, itself steeped in nostalgia for better days. I'm that grumpy old guy yelling at all those pesky little Grizzly Bear fans to get offa my lawn. Honestly, how much future is there in that? Plus, even if I have yet to see physical copies of my three favorite 2009 albums (Benny's *Amigo Charly Brown: Die Hits Von Gestern Und Auch Heut*, Bigg Robb's *Jerri Curl Muzic*, and Scooter's *Under The Radar Over The Top: The Darkside Edition*, all streamable at rhapsody.com, which I contribute to regularly), my personal listening habits still live mostly in a pre-digital Stone Age. Was obsessed with my personally programmed Pandora station for a while there, but that's long behind me now. I don't Facebook or Twitter, and I still never download MP3s unless an editor holds a loaded deadline to my head. And with most shows starting past my bedtime, I'm not seeing much live music lately, either.

Meanwhile, as has been happening approximately forever, some nincompoops still accuse me of being a "contrarian," implying I've always only "pretended" to like certain music because other critics *don't* like it, and vice versa. Which of course smugly assumes that other critics tend to *agree* on what they like (i.e., usually whatever the person calling me a contrarian likes), and which also conveniently turns a blind eye to all the things I've gone on record as liking that lots of other critics *do* also like (in this book alone, maybe start with the White Stripes, Metallica, Timbaland, Eminem, John Cougar Mellencamp, Michael Jackson, and the Pet Shop Boys), not to mention the thousands of records most other critics dislike that I too have no use for. And it ignores all the critics who've agreed with *me* over the years, and all the ones who disagreed with me until their minds changed. And finally, it ignores almost every word I've ever *written*: space permitting, if I claim that something is good or bad music, I tend to specify *why*. After decades of spelling this out, some days I wonder how much longer I can bear morons with impaired reading comprehension skills calling me a charlatan.

Thing is—and here's where I shoot myself in the foot with my arrogance—I *still* think I'm as up on this music stuff, as a *whole,* and as able to put both that whole and its details into words, as just about anybody out there. The big picture, complete with scope and punchlines and historical context. My writing and thinking about music isn't as dogmatic or hotheaded as it was 25 years ago, but it's smarter. And I'm still somehow making a living at it, long after lots of colleagues, including plenty of great ones, have packed it in. I can't explain that, though it probably helps that I've never *not* been a curmudgeon—sort of like how ZZ Top didn't seem unduly old in the '80s because having beards was always their shtick. I mean, hey, I was a late adopter when it came to CDs, too, and that sure never stopped me. Then again, maybe I've just been in the right place at the right time. As I said back at this book's outset, rock criticism is not a particularly predictive genre, so I won't try.

All I know is, songs and albums and artists worth noting keep coming—week after week, year after year. More than you or I can ever count. My ten-favorite-singles list in 2010 included not just tracks from three country-pop gals (Sunny Sweeney, Mallary Hope, Laura Bell Bundy), but also Nuyorican acid-salsa (Coati Mundi), norteño (Intocable), Southern soul (Sweet Angel), South African house (Pastor Mbhobho), Asian-American dance-pop (Far East Movement), teenage hip-hop (Cali Swag District), and Jamaican dancehall (Vybz Kartel), so who knows where that will lead? One of these days, if global economies of scale are merciful, it might all add up to something exciting again—and, with my luck, it'll most likely emerge from some corner where I haven't been looking. But I plan to keep looking, regardless.

Morgan, Lorrie, 228
Moroder, Giorgio, 260, 288
Mötley Crüe, xii-xiii, 87, 93, 99
Motörhead, 99–103, 137, 306
Mott The Hoople, 306
Mr. Lee, 15–16
Mudhoney, 26
Mullins, Shawn, 281
MX-80 Sound, 42, 50

Nada Surf, 22
Naked Raygun, 44
Necros, 45
New Jack Swing, 164, 269–70, 272, 298
New Kids On The Block, 18–19, 244
Newman, Randy, 23
New Order, 260, 262
New Wave, 25–26
New Wave Of British Heavy Metal,
    122, 137
New York Dolls, 9–10, 278
Nielsen, Ralph & The Chancellors,
    108–9
Nirvana, 7, 26–27, 62–64
Nocera, 252–53
Notorious B.I.G., 155
'NSync, 310
Nugent, Ted, 2, 24, 45, 184–85, 195,
    213, 264
N.W.A., 140, 149

old-school rap, 10–12, 139–40, 144–47,
    173–74
OMC, 76
Opeth, 86
Osbourne, Ozzy, 102, 202
Oslin, K.T., 224–25
O'Sullivan, Gilbert, 288

Paisley, Brad, 240–42
Partridge Family, 288
Pazz & Jop poll, 5–7, 9, 243–45, 322–24
Pere Ubu, 42

Pet Shop Boys, 16, 246, 256–63, 293
Petty, Tom, 295, 302
P-Funk, 165
Phair, Liz, 27, 160–61
Phuture, 16
pigfuck music, 46–47, 52–61
Plant, Robert, 72, 81, 108–16
Poison, 174, 248
Police, 304–5
Poole, Charlie, 167, 287
pop vs. rock, 123, 194, 243–46, 261, 287
Powder River Jack, 219
Powertrip, 90
Prodigy, 155, 278, 302
Pro Set music cards, 255–56
Public Enemy, 143, 173, 210
Public Image Ltd., 91, 114
Puff Daddy, 152, 155–56
punk rock, 26, 35–37, 41–42, 49, 103–4,
    122, 263

Queen, 119
? and the Mysterians, 38

R&B, 140–41, 171–72, 179, 298–300,
    317–18
racial crossover, 163–210
radio, 171–72, 244, 281, 284–85, 287;
    country, 233; in Detroit, 163, 185, 211;
    in 1986, 99, 292–97
Radiohead, 7, 15–16
Rammellzee and K-Rob, 301
Rammstein, 281
Ramones, 32–41
Ratt, 89–90, 99, 308
Raw Power, 97–98
Ray, Johnnie, 114–15
Redd Kross, 93
Reed, Lou, 62, 153
Reid, Vernon, 164–65, 176
Replacements, 43
Rich, John, 213, 215, 233–34
Rihanna, 318

Chuck Eddy is an independent music journalist who has
written for the *Village Voice*, *Creem*, *Rolling Stone*, *Spin*, and
Entertainment Weekly, among others. He is the author of
*Stairway to Hell: The 500 Best Heavy Metal Albums in the
Universe* (1991) and *The Accidental Evolution of Rock'N'Roll:
A Misguided Tour through Popular Music* (1997).

Library of Congress Cataloging-in-Publication Data
Eddy, Chuck.
Rock and roll always forgets : a quarter century of music
criticism / Chuck Eddy ; foreword by Chuck Klosterman.
p. cm.
Includes bibliographical references and index.
ISBN 978-0-8223-4996-9 (cloth : alk. paper)
ISBN 978-0-8223-5010-1 (pbk. : alk. paper)
1. Rock music—1981–1990—History and criticism.
2. Rock music—1991–2000—History and criticism.
3. Rock music—2001–2010—History and criticism.
4. Popular music—1981–1990—History and criticism.
5. Popular music—1991–2000—History and criticism.
6. Popular music—2001–2010—History and criticism.
I. Title.
ML3534.E29 2011
781.64—dc22
2010054504